MORE

ADULT ONLY

JOKES

HB

HINKLER
BOOKS

*Thanks to all those people who emailed jokes,
especially David Field and Thomas Sims,
who can now get back to work.*

 More Adult Only Jokes
First published in 2003 by Hinkler Books Pty. Ltd.
45–55 Fairchild Street
Heatherton Victoria 3202 Australia
www.hinklerbooks.com

ISBN: 978 1 8651 5925 6

Publisher's thanks to Nicolas Brasch for compiling the jokes.
Cover design by Sam Grimmer

Printed and bound in China

CONTENTS

INTRODUCTION

I n this day and age, it's common practice for books to have lengthy introductions in which the author, editor or compiler explain the motivation behind the contents. But this is a joke book for Christ's sake. And whether you've bought, borrowed or pinched this book, you really only want to read the jokes.

So let's get on with it.

A . . . WALKS INTO A BAR

It's easy to see why so many jokes are set in bars.
Bars offer warmth. Bars offer solace. Bars offer companionship.
But more than that, bars offer alcohol.

Three mice are sitting at a bar in a pretty rough neighbourhood late at night, trying to impress each other with how tough they are.

The first mouse sinks a shot of Scotch, slams the glass onto the bar, turns to the second mouse and says, 'When I see a mousetrap, I lie on my back and set it off with my foot. When the bar comes down, I catch it in my teeth, bench press it twenty times to work up an appetite, and then make off with the cheese.'

The second mouse orders up two shots of sour mash, sinks them both, slams each glass onto the bar, turns to the first mouse, and replies, 'Yeah, well when I see rat poison, I collect as much as I can, take it home, grind it up to a powder, and add it to my coffee each morning so I can get a good buzz going for the rest of the day.'

The first mouse and the second mouse then turn to the third mouse.

The third mouse lets out a long sigh and says to the first two, 'I don't have time for this bullshit. I gotta go home and screw the cat.'

A sexy woman in a bar walks up to the counter and motions the bartender over. She starts to run her fingers through his hair and asks to speak to the manager.

The bartender says, 'He isn't here but I can do anything the manger can do for you.'

By this time the woman is running her fingers down his face and into his mouth and is letting him suck on her fingers. She says, 'You're sure he isn't here?'

The bartender says, 'Yes, I'm very sure.'

The woman says, 'Well, I just wanted to tell him there's no toilet paper or soap in the women's toilet.'

The Lone Ranger and Tonto walk into a bar and sit down to drink a beer. After a few minutes, a big tall cowboy walks in and says, 'Who owns the big white horse outside?'

The Lone Ranger stands up, hitches his gun belt, and says, 'I do . . . Why?'

The cowboy looks at the Lone Ranger and says, 'I just thought you'd like to know that your horse is nearly dead!'

The Lone Ranger and Tonto rush outside and sure enough Silver is almost dead from heat exhaustion. The Lone Ranger gets the horse some water and soon Silver starts to feel a little better.

The Lone Ranger turns to Tonto and says, 'Tonto, I want you to run around Silver and see if you can create enough of a breeze to make him feel better.'

Tonto says, 'Sure, Kemosabe' and starts running circles around Silver.

Unable to do anything but wait, the Lone Ranger returns to the bar to finish his drink.

A few minutes later, another cowboy struts into the bar and asks, 'Who owns that big white horse outside?'

The Lone Ranger stands again, and claims, 'I do, what's wrong with him this time?'

The cowboy looks him in the eye and says, 'Nothing, but you left your Injun runnin'.'

A Texan buys a round of drinks for everyone in the bar as he announces that his wife has just produced 'a typical Texas baby boy weighing twenty pounds'. Congratulations shower him from all around, and many exclamations of 'Wow!' are heard. A woman faints due to sympathy pains. Two weeks later, he returns to the bar.

The bartender says, 'Say, you're the father of the typical Texas baby that weighed twenty pounds at birth, aren't ya pardner? How much does he weigh now?'

The proud father answers, 'Fifteen pounds.'

The bartender is puzzled, concerned. 'Why? What happened? He already weighed twenty pounds at birth.'

The Texas father takes a slow swig from his long-neck Lone Star, wipes his lips on his shirtsleeve, leans into the bartender and proudly announces, 'Had him circumcised.'

A man is sitting outside a bar enjoying a quiet drink when a nun starts lecturing him on the evils of alcohol.

'How do you know alcohol is evil?' asks the man. 'Have you ever tasted it?'

'Of course not,' answers the nun.

'Then let me buy you a drink and, afterwards, if you still believe that it's evil, I promise I'll never touch another drop.'

'But I can't possibly be seen to be drinking,' says the nun.

'Right. Well, I'll get the bartender to put it in a teacup for you.'

The man goes inside and asks for a beer and a vodka.

'And would you mind putting the vodka in a teacup?'

'Oh no,' says the bartender. 'It's not that bloody nun again, is it?'

A drunk rolls into a bar, but the bartender refuses to serve him. 'You've had too much to drink,' he says. 'I'm not serving you.'

Five minutes later, the drunk comes in again. The bartender stands firm.

'There's no way I'm serving you more alcohol. You've had more than enough already.'

Five minutes later, the doors open and the drunk lurches in once more.

'Look,' says the bartender, 'I'm not serving you. You're too drunk.'

The drunk nods. 'I guess I must be,' he says. 'This is the third place in a row that's refused to serve me.'

A young stockbroker is unwinding in a bar after a hard week's work. He is in the mood for a bit of fun and so he announces, 'If anyone can drink twenty pints of Guinness, I'll give them $150.'

The bartender lines up the twenty pints on the bar, but there are no immediate takers. Without saying a word, one man gets off his stool, pops out, comes back a few minutes later and declares that he can drink all twenty.

And to everyone's amazement he does. The stockbroker hands over the money and asks the man where he had nipped out to.

'Well,' he says, 'first I had to go to the bar next door to make sure I could do it!'

Two flies walk into a bar, order drinks and sit down for a chat.
First fly: How was your trip down here?
Second fly: It was so cold I rode in a biker's moustache. How was yours?
First fly: I was warm all the way. I rode in a biker chick's pussy. You ought to do it next year.
A year later, the same two flies meet in the same bar.

| First fly: | Did you travel down like I told you? |
| Second fly: | Yes. But somehow I still showed up in a biker's moustache. |

A penguin walks into a bar, walks up to the barman and asks, 'Have you seen my brother?'

'What does he look like?' the barman asks.

A man walks into a bar where there is loud music playing. He goes up to an attractive girl and asks, 'Would you like to dance?'

'I wouldn't dance with you if you were the last man on earth,' she replies.

'I don't think you heard me correctly,' the man says. 'I said you look fat in those pants.'

A man walks into a bar with a dog. He puts the dog on the bar and says to the bartender, 'This is the smartest dog in the world. I bet you $5 that he can answer any question you ask him.'

The bartender agrees and asks the dog, 'What's the cube root of 81?'

'Three,' the dog answers immediately.

'That's amazing,' says the bartender, handing over $5.

At this point, the dog owner has to go to the toilet. He asks the barman to look after the dog, and puts the $5 in the dog's collar.

While the man is in the toilet, the barman says to the dog, 'If you're so smart, go down the road and get me a newspaper.'

So the dog leaves. When the man comes out of the toilet he goes ballistic.

'Where's my dog?' he shouts.

The barman calms the man down and tells him about the newspaper. The man immediately leaves the bar to search for his dog. He eventually finds the dog in an alley, screwing a poodle.

'What are you doing?' the man shouts. 'You've never done this before.'

'I've never had $5 before either.'

A hippopotamus walks into a bar and asks the bartender for a beer.

'That will be $7.50 please,' says the bartender.

So the hippo gives the bartender his money and starts to sip his beer.

'You know we don't have very many hippos in here,' the bartender tells him.

The hippo replies, 'At these prices it's no wonder!'

A bar has a sign up that reads Pianist Wanted. So this guy walks in and tells the owner that he's a great pianist. The owner tells the pianist to play a couple of songs and if he's as good as he claims, then the job is his. So the pianist sits down and plays a song that nearly has the owner in tears.

'What a beautiful song! What's it called?' the owner asks.

'It's called, *The dog's shagging the cat and my wife's doin' my brother.*'

'Um, well, how about playing one more tune.'

So the man plays another tune and this time the manager does break down in tears.

'What do you call that song?' he asks, wiping his eyes.

'*The elephant's taking a shit while the lion's licking his balls.*'

The bar owner tells the pianist that he has the job on one condition. He must not tell the customers the names of the songs he is playing. So the pianist starts playing that night. After every song he gets a standing ovation. After about two hours of solid playing, he announces he is going to have a break. He goes to the toilet to take a piss.

On his way out a man passing says, 'Hey mate, do you know your fly's undone and your cock's hangin' out?'

'Of course I know it. I wrote it!'

A guy is sitting at a bar feeling sorry for himself because his wife just kicked him out. A woman comes up and sits beside him and orders a drink. She looks as depressed as he does.

'Is there something wrong?' the guy asks her.

'My husband just left me. He said I was too kinky.'

The guy says, 'What a coincidence. My wife just kicked me out as well because I was too kinky.'

The woman has an idea. 'Why don't we go back to my place and get kinky together?'

'Sounds perfect,' the guy replies. When they get to her house, she tells him to make himself comfortable while she goes to change. She goes to her room and takes off her clothes. She puts on a leather G-string, a leather bra, black stockings, big, black leather boots and gets out her whip. When she's ready, she goes out to the living room and finds the guy putting his coat and boots back on.

'Where are you going?' she asks. 'I thought we were gonna get kinky together.'

The guy replies, 'I screwed your dog and shat in your purse, how much kinkier can I get?'

A drunk walks into a bar and screams out, 'I'll bet anyone in this bar $100 that I can whistle Dixie out my arsehole.'

The bartender, looking for a good laugh, produces $100 and

lays it on the bar. The drunk matches his money, climbs up on top of the bar, drops his pants, and proceeds to shit all over the place.

The bartender screams, 'What the hell are you doing?'

'Gimme a break pal,' the drunk replies. 'Even Bing Crosby had to clear his throat.'

Aconfident man walks into a bar and takes a seat next to a very attractive woman. He gives her a quick glance, then looks down at his watch for a moment.

The woman notices this and asks, 'Is your date running late?'

'No,' he replies. 'I just bought this state-of-the-art watch and I was testing it.'

'A state-of-the-art watch? What's so special about it?'

'It uses alpha waves to telepathically talk to me,' he explains.

'What's it telling you now?'

'Well, it says you're not wearing any panties . . .'

The woman giggles and replies, 'Well it must be broken then because I am wearing panties!'

The man explains, 'Damn thing must be an hour fast.'

Astruggling bar owner decides that he needs a gimmick to bring more people into his bar. After wracking his brains, he comes up with the idea of holding a competition to find the toughest man in town. He puts up posters around town and advertises in the local newspaper. On the appointed day, his bar is full. The first contestant is a huge man, holding a snapping turtle. The man jumps up on the bar, unzips his pants and whips out his large penis. The man then picks up the snapping turtle and holds it right in front of his dick. With unbelieving eyes, the onlookers gasp as the turtle bites down on the man's penis. The big man let's go of the turtle and starts swaying his body.

The turtle bounces from side to side off the man's hips. After about thirty seconds of this, the man pokes the turtle in the eyes, and the turtle drops to the floor.

'Now,' shouts the big guy. 'Is there another son of a bitch in here that thinks he is tough enough to do that?'

A timid hand at the back of the bar is raised, 'I'll do it, if you promise not to poke me in the eyes.'

A huge muscular man walks into a bar and orders a beer. The bartender hands him the beer and says, 'You know, I'm not gay but I want to compliment you on your physique, it really is phenomenal! I have a question though, why is your head so small?'

The big guy nods slowly. He's obviously fielded this question many times.

'One day,' he begins, 'I was hunting when I got lost in the woods. I heard someone crying for help and finally realised that it was coming from a frog sitting next to a stream. So I picked up the frog and it said, "Kiss me. Kiss me and I will turn into a genie and grant you three wishes." So I looked around to make sure I was alone and gave the frog a kiss. Suddenly, the frog turned into a beautiful, voluptuous, naked woman.

She said, "You now have three wishes."

I looked down at my scrawny body and said, "I want a body like Arnold Schwarzenegger."

She nodded, whispered a spell, and abracadabra there I was, so huge that I burst out of my clothes and was standing there naked.

She then asked, "What will be your second wish?"

I looked hungrily at her beautiful body and replied, "I want to make sensuous love with you here by this stream."

She nodded, lay down, and beckoned to me. We then made love for hours!

Later, as we lay there next to each other, sweating from our glorious lovemaking, she whispered into my ear, "You know, you do have one more wish. What will it be?"

I looked at her and replied, "How about a little head?"'

A man walks up to a bar with an ostrich behind him, and as he sits the bartender comes over and asks for their order.

The man says, 'I'll have a beer,' and turns to the ostrich. 'What's yours?'

'I'll have a beer too,' says the ostrich.

The bartender pours the beer and says, 'That will be $3.40 please.'

The man reaches into his pocket and pulls out the exact change.

The next day, the man and the ostrich come into the bar again, and the man says, 'I'll have a beer.'

And the ostrich says, 'I'll have the same.'

Once again the man reaches into his pocket and pays with exact change. This becomes a routine until late one evening, the two enter again.

'The usual?' asks the bartender.

'Well, it's close to last call, so I'll have a large scotch,' says the man.

'Same for me,' says the ostrich.

'That will be $7.20,' says the bartender. Once again the man pulls the exact change out of his pocket and places it on the bar.

The bartender can't hold back his curiosity any longer. 'Excuse me Sir. How do you manage to come up with the exact change out of your pocket every time?'

'Well,' says the man, 'several years ago I was cleaning the attic and I found an old lamp. When I rubbed it a genie appeared and offered me two wishes. My first wish was that if I ever had to pay for anything, I just put my hand in my pocket, and the right amount of money will always be there.'

'That's brilliant!' says the bartender. 'Most people would wish for a million dollars or something, but you'll always be as rich as you want for as long as you live.'

'That's right! Whether it's a carton of milk or a Rolls Royce, the exact money is always there,' says the man.

The bartender asks, 'One other thing, Sir, what's with the ostrich?'

The man replies, 'My second wish was for a chick with long legs.'

A drunk gets up from the bar and heads for the bathroom. A few minutes later, a loud, blood-curdling scream is heard coming from the bathroom. A few minutes later, another loud scream reverberates throughout the bar. The bartender goes to the bathroom to investigate why the drunk is screaming.

'What's all the screaming about in there?' he says. 'You're scaring my customers!'

'I'm just sitting here on the toilet and every time I flush something comes up and squeezes the hell out of my balls!'

With that, the bartender opens the door, looks in and says, 'You idiot. You're sitting on the mop bucket.'

A grasshopper walks into a bar.
The bartender looks up and says, 'Hey! You're a grasshopper! We have a drink named after you.'

The grasshopper says, 'Really? You have a drink named Kevin?'

A bored guy sits at the bar, looking to strike up a conversation. He turns to the bartender and says, 'What about the government's latest decision to –'

'Stop,' interrupts the bartender. 'I don't allow talk about politics in my bar!'

A few minutes later the guy tries again, 'Did you read where the Pope –'

'No religion talk, either,' the bartender cuts in.

The man tries once more. 'Did you see the game last night?'

'No sports talk. That's how fights start in bars!' the barman says.

'Look, how about sex. Can I talk to you about sex?'

'Sure, that we can talk about,' replies the barkeep.

'Great. Go screw yourself!'

A businessman enters a tavern, sits down at the bar, and orders a double martini on the rocks.

After he finishes the drink, he peeks inside his shirt pocket and orders another double martini. After he finishes that one, he again peeks inside his shirt pocket and orders a double martini.

The bartender says, 'Look, buddy, I'll bring ya martinis all night long. But you gotta tell me why you look inside your shirt pocket before you order a refill.'

The customer replies, 'I'm peeking at a photo of my wife. When she starts to look good, then I know it's time to go home.'

The local bar is so sure that its bartender is the strongest man around that they offer a standing $1000 bet. The bartender squeezes a lemon until all the juice runs into a glass, and hands the lemon to a patron. Anyone who can squeeze one more drop of juice out of it wins the money. Over time many people have tried, but nobody has succeeded.

One day a scrawny little man comes in, wearing thick glasses and a polyester suit, and says in a tiny, squeaky voice, 'I'd like to try the bet.'

After the laughter has died down, the bartender says OK,

grabs a lemon, and squeezes away. He then hands the wrinkled remains of the rind to the little man.

But the crowd's laughter turns to total silence as the man clenches his fist around the lemon and six drops fall into the glass.

As the crowd cheers, the bartender pays the $1000, and asks the little man, 'What do you do for a living? Are you a logger, a weight-lifter, or what?'

The man replies, 'I work for the tax office.'

Joe walks into a bar. With him is a little guy a foot tall. Joe walks up to the bar and the little guy walks over to the piano and starts playing it and singing. The bartender, amazed at the sight of this little guy playing the piano and singing, moves over to Joe and talks to him.

'Hey,' he says, 'that little guy's really good. Where did you find him?'

Joe replies, 'I got him from my genie.'

'You've got a genie?' The bartender asks. 'Do you mind if I borrow him for a little while? I could really use some money.'

'No problem,' Joe says. 'Wish away.'

Whoosh! The genie appears.

'Wow,' gasps the bartender. 'I wish for a thousand bucks!' With a bright flash and a crash of thunder there appears in the bar a thousand ducks.

'Wait a minute,' cries the bartender. 'I asked for a thousand bucks not a thousand ducks!'

'Well,' says Joe, 'do you think I asked for a twelve-inch pianist?'

A good-looking man walks into a singles' bar, gets a drink and takes a seat. During the course of the evening he tries to chat with every single woman who walks into the bar, with no luck. Suddenly a really ugly man walks into the bar. He sits at the bar, and within seconds he is surrounded by women. Very soon he walks out of the bar with two of the most beautiful women.

Disheartened by all this, the good-looking man asks the barman, 'Excuse me, but that really ugly man just came in here and left with those two stunning women. He's as ugly as sin and I'm everything a girl could want but I haven't been able to connect all night. What's going on?'

'Well,' says the barman, 'I don't know how he does it, but he does the same thing every night. He walks in, orders a drink, and just sits there licking his eyebrows.'

Tom, Dick and Harry are in a bar.

Tom says, 'My wife is so stupid, she bought $1000 worth of meat, and we don't even have a freezer.'

'That's nothing,' says Dick. 'My wife is so thick she bought a $20 000 car, and she can't even drive.'

'Pah,' says Harry. 'My wife is so stupid, she booked a trip to Ibiza, and bought 1000 condoms, and she hasn't even got a dick.'

An old Englishman walks into a bar and asks for a bottle of thirty-eight-year-old wine from Lyon, France. The bar tender, not wanting to go to the cellar, gives the Englishman the closest bottle of wine he has.

The Englishman tastes it and says, 'This wine is only two years old and is from Santiago de Chile, almost certainly the west side.'

The bartender is amazed, but at the same time curious, so he gives the Englishman another bottle.

He says, 'This wine is seventeen years old and is from San Diego, California. I'd say from the south-east.'

The bartender is so amazed that he gives the Englishman another bottle.

He tastes it and says, 'This wine is thirty years old and is from Lima, Peru, undoubtedly from the valley.'

Finally the bartender goes to the cellar and gets the right bottle and gives it to the Englishman.

He says, 'Finally, a thirty-eight-year-old wine from Lyon, France.'

An old drunk that has been watching goes up to the Englishman and says, 'Could you please tell me what kind of drink is this?' And he hands the Englishman a cup.

He has a taste and spits it out screaming, 'Yuk. This is piss!'

The drunk replies, 'Yeah I know but could you please tell me from where because I'm so drunk that I don't remember where I live.'

A man walks into a bar with a steak-and-kidney pie on his head. He walks over to the bartender and says, 'Can I have a beer please?'

The bartender gets him his beer but he can't stop staring at the pie on the man's head. Finally the bartender can't bite his tongue any longer.

'Excuse me Sir, but why do you have a steak-and-kidney pie on your head?'

The man replies, 'I always have a steak-and-kidney pie on my head on a Thursday.'

The bartender says, 'But it's Wednesday today.'

'Oh I must look like a right prick then.'

A goldfish walks into a bar, jumps up on a bar stool and looks at the bartender intensely.

'What can I get you?' the bartender asks.

'Water,' the goldfish gasps.

A really drunk woman walks into a bar. She sits down at the bar and yells, 'Heyyyy tenderbar, give me a tinimar, with a pickle on top.'

The bartender gives her a drink, she drinks it down, and then goes, 'Ahhh, heartburn.'

Again, the drunk woman says, 'Heyyyy tenderbar, give me a tinimar, with a pickle on top.'

Again, she drinks the drink and says, 'Ahhh, heartburn.'

This goes on a couple more times when, finally, the bartender gets fed up. The drunk woman tries to order another drink, but the bartender says, 'Look lady, it's not tenderbar, it's bartender; it's not a tinimar, it's a martini; it's not a pickle, it's an olive; and its not heartburn you have, your left tit is hanging in the ashtray!'

A bear walks into a bar. He goes up to the barman and says, 'Can I have a large gin and . . . . tonic please?'

The barman replies, 'Sure, but what's with the big pause?'

'I'm a bear,' says the bear, holding his palms up.

Four men are telling stories in a bar. One man leaves for a bathroom break. Three men are left. The first man says, 'I was worried that my son was gonna be a loser because he started out washing cars for a local dealership. Turns out that he got a break, they made him a salesman, and he sold so many cars that he bought the dealership. In fact, he's so successful that he just gave his best friend a new Mercedes for his birthday.'

The second man says, 'I was worried about my son, too, because he started out raking leaves for a realtor. Turns out he got a break, they made him a commissioned salesman, and he eventually bought the real estate firm. In fact, he's so successful that he just gave his best friend a new house for his birthday.'

The third man says, 'Yeah, I hear you. My son started out

sweeping floors in a brokerage firm. In fact, he's so rich that he just gave his best friend a million in stock for his birthday.'

The fourth man comes back from the toilet. The first three explain that they are telling stories about their kids, so he says, 'Well, I'm embarrassed to admit that my son is a major disappointment. He started out as a hairdresser and is still a hairdresser after fifteen years. In fact, I just found out that he's gay and has several boyfriends. But I try to look at the bright side–his boyfriends just bought him a new Mercedes, a new house, and a million in stock for his birthday.'

Paddy and his two friends are talking at a bar. His first friend says, 'I think my wife is having an affair with the electrician. The other day I came home and found wire-cutters under our bed and they weren't mine.'

His second friend says, 'I think my wife is having an affair with the plumber. The other day I found a wrench under the bed and it wasn't mine.'

Paddy says, 'I think my wife is having an affair with a horse.'

Both his friends look at him with utter disbelief.

'No I'm serious. The other day I came home and found a jockey under our bed.'

A guy walks into a bar with an octopus. He sits the octopus down on a stool and tells everyone in the bar that this is a very talented octopus. He can play any instrument in the world. Everyone in the crowd laughs, so he says he will bet $50 that no-one can bring up an instrument that the octopus can't play.

A guy walks up with a guitar and sets it beside the octopus. The octopus starts playing better than Jimi Hendrix. So the man pays his $50.

Another guy walks up with a trumpet. The octopus plays the

trumpet better than Dizzy Gillespie. So the man pays his $50.

A third guy walks up with bagpipes. He sets them down and the octopus fumbles with them for a minute, then he puts them down with a confused look.

'Ha!' the man says. 'Can't you play it?'

The octopus looks up at the man and says, 'Play it? Sure I can. But first things first. I'm going to screw it as soon as I get its pyjamas off.'

A man is taking his Rottweiler out for a walk. It is a hot day and after a while he decides to go into a bar for a drink. The bartender tells him dogs are not allowed and he must tie it up outside. After a few drinks a woman walks into the bar and asks if someone has a large dog out front.

The man proudly states, 'Yes, it is my Rottweiler, why do you ask?'

She blurts out, 'It's dead.'

Stunned, the man asks, 'Did you hit it with your car'?

She replies, 'No, my dog killed it.'

Knowing how powerful a dog the Rottweiler is, he asks her, 'Pit bull'?

'No, I have a Chihuahua,' she says.

Puzzled, he asks, 'How did your Chihuahua kill my Rottweiler'?

'Well I'm no vet, but I think she got stuck in his throat.'

A man has been in hospital for three weeks. One day, he is so sick and tired of it that he sneaks out of the hospital and down to the nearest pub. He orders a beer and swallows the lot in ten seconds flat. He then orders a second beer and does the same. Then a third and a fourth.

As he orders a fifth beer, he says to the barman, 'I shouldn't be drinking this with what I've got.'

The barman stands back, alarmed, and asks, 'What have you got?'
'About fifty cents,' says the patient.

A $5 note walks into a bar.
Bartender says, 'Get outta here! We don't serve your type.
This is a singles' bar.'

A guy walks into a bar, and there's a horse behind the bar
serving drinks. The guy is staring at the horse, when the
horse says, 'Hey buddy? What are you staring at? Haven't you
ever seen a horse serving drinks before?'
    The guy says, 'No, it's not that. It's just that I never thought
the parrot would sell the place.'

Seventeen blind men walk into a bar.
'Ouch!'
'Ouch!'
'Ouch!'
'Ouch!'
'Ouch!'
'Ouch!'
'Ouch!'
'Ouch!'
'Ouch!'
'Ouch!'
'Ouch!'
'Ouch!'
'Ouch!'
'Ouch!'
'Ouch!'
'Ouch!'

A bartender decides to have some fun with the local drunk. 'Do you want a free drink?' he asks the drunk.

'Sure,' says the drunk. 'What do you want me to do?'

'Well, first I want you to go up to the bouncer on the door and knock him out cold. Then I want you to pull a loose tooth belonging to Saddam, the bulldog in the back room. Finally I want you to have sex with the town tramp who is sitting alone at the end of the bar.'

'No problem,' says the drunk, sliding off his stool.

He staggers over to the bouncer and, taking him by surprise, fells him with a single blow. The bartender is amazed and points to the back room where the bulldog is waiting. The drunk lurches through the door to the back room and the bartender waits to hear the commotion. Any second, he expects to see Saddam amble out of the room, clutching the drunk in his jaw. Instead there is silence. Then after a few minutes the dog starts barking. Five minutes later, the drunk emerges with a satisfied grin.

'Right,' he says. 'Now where's that tramp with the loose tooth?'

A mangy looking guy goes into a bar and orders a drink. The bartender says, 'No way. I don't think you can pay for it.'

The guy says, 'You're right. I don't have any money, but if I show you something you haven't seen before, will you give me a drink?'

The bartender says, 'Only if what you show me ain't risqué.'

'Deal,' says the guy and reaches into his coat pocket and pulls out a hamster. He puts the hamster on the bar and it runs to the end of the bar, down the bar, across the room and up onto the piano, jumps on the keyboard and starts playing Gershwin songs. And the hamster is really good.

The bartender says, 'You're right. I've never seen anything like that before. That hamster is truly good on the piano.' The guy downs the drink and asks the bartender for another.

'Money or another miracle, or else no drink,' says the bartender. The guy reaches into his coat again and pulls out a frog. He puts the frog on the bar, and the frog starts to sing. He has a marvellous voice and great pitch – a fine singer. A stranger from the other end of the bar runs over to the guy and offers him $300 for the frog.

The guy says, 'It's a deal.' He takes the $300 and gives the stranger the frog. The stranger runs out of the bar. The bartender says to the guy, 'Are you some kind of nut? You sold a singing frog for $300? It must have been worth millions. You must be crazy.'

'Not so,' says the guy. 'The hamster is also a ventriloquist.'

A Scottish farmer walks into the neighbourhood pub, and orders a whiskey.

'Ye see that fence over there?' he says to the bartender. 'Ah built it with me own two hands! Dug up the holes with me shovel, chopped doon the trees for the posts by me ownself, laid every last rail! But do they call me "McGregor the Fence-Builder?" No.'

He gulps down the whiskey and orders another. 'Ye see that pier on the loch?' he continues, 'Ah built it me ownself, too. Swam oot into the loch to lay the foondations, laid doon every single board! But do they call me "McGregor the Pier-Builder"? No.'

'But ye screw just one sheep . . .'

A dyslexic walks into a bra . . .

An Irishman walks into a bar and asks for two beers. He then pulls a small green-skinned man out of his pocket and puts him on the counter. As he's drinking one beer and the green man is drinking the other, an Englishman down the bar who has had a few too many says, 'Hey, what's that little green thing down there?'

The green man runs down the bar and gives the Englishman a raspberry right in the face. *Splblblblt!* Then he runs back to the Irishman.

The Englishman mops himself off and says to the Irishman, 'Hey, what is that thing, anyway?'

The Irishman replies, 'Have some respect. He's a leprechaun.'

'Oh, all right,' the Englishman says sullenly. They all go back to drinking beer.

An hour or so later, the Englishman is really plastered.

'Boy, that leprechaun is ugly!' he says.

The leprechaun runs down the bar and gives the Englishman a raspberry again. *Splblblblt!* This time the Englishman is really mad.

'Tell that leprechaun that if he does that again I'll cut his pecker off!' he shouts.

'You can't do that' says the Irishman. 'Leprechauns don't have peckers.'

'How do they pee, then?' asks the Englishman.

'They don't.' says the Irishman. 'They go *Splblblblt!*'

A man walks into a bar and the bartender says, 'I'm sorry, I can't serve you here unless you are wearing a tie.'

The man says, 'OK, I'll be right back,' and goes to his car to find anything he can use for a tie. All he finds is a set of jumper cables, so he ties them around his neck, goes back in and asks, 'How's this?'

The bartender replies, 'Well, OK, but don't start anything.'

A panda walks into a bar, sits down and orders a sandwich. He eats the sandwich, pulls out a gun and shoots the waiter dead. As the panda stands up to go, the bartender shouts, 'Hey! Where are you going? You just shot my waiter and you didn't pay for your sandwich!'

The panda yells back at the bartender, 'Hey man, I'm a panda! Look it up!'

The bartender opens his dictionary and sees the following definition for panda: 'A tree dwelling marsupial of Asian origin, characterised by distinct black and white colouring. Eats shoots and leaves.'

A mouse and a lion walk into a bar, and they're sitting there chugging away at a few ales when a giraffe walks in.

'Get a load of her,' says the mouse. 'I fancy that!'

'Well, why not try your luck?' says the lion.

So the mouse goes over to the giraffe and starts talking to her, and within five minutes they're out the door and gone into the night.

Next day, the lion is in the bar drinking away, and the mouse staggers in. He is absolutely stuffed.

The lion helps his pal up on to a stool, pours a drink down his throat and says, 'What the hell happened to you? I saw you leave with the giraffe, what happened after that? Was she all right?'

The mouse says, 'Yeah, she was really something else – we went out to dinner, had a couple of glasses of wine, and she invited me back to her place to spend the night. And oh, man! I've never had a night like it!'

'But how come you look like you're so exhausted?' asks the lion.

'Well,' says the mouse, 'between the kissing and the screwing, I must have run a thousand miles.'

A man walks into a bar and sits down next to a guy with a dog at his feet. 'Does your dog bite?' he asks.

'No,' the guy replies.

A few minutes later the dog takes a huge chunk out of the man's leg.

'I thought you said your dog doesn't bite,' the man says indignantly.

'That's not my dog.'

A neutron walks into a bar.

'I'd like a beer,' he says.

The bartender promptly serves up a beer.

'How much will that be?' asks the neutron.

'For you,' replies the bartender, 'no charge.'

O n the top of a tall building in a large city, there is a bar. In this bar, a man is drinking heavily. He asks the bartender for a shot of tequila, then walks out to the balcony and jumps off. Minutes later, he appears in the elevator and repeats the whole process. Another guy in the bar watches this happen a number of times until curiosity gets the better of him.

Finally, he goes up to the man and asks, 'Hey, you keep drinking, then jumping off the balcony. And yet, minutes later, you're back again. How do you do it?'

'Well, the shot of tequila provides buoyancy such that when I get near the ground, I slow down and land gently. It's lots of fun. You should try it.'

The guy, who is quite pissed, thinks to himself, Hey, why not? So he goes to the bar, drinks a shot of tequila, then walks out to the balcony and jumps off. *Whooooooooooooooo . . . SPLAT!*

The bartender looks over at the first guy and says, 'Man, you're an arsehole when you're drunk, Superman.'

Asnail crawls up to a bar as it is closing. The snail pounds and pounds on the door until the bartender finally opens it. The bartender looks around and sees nothing until the snail demands a beer.

The bartender looked down and sees him but replies, 'Hey, we're closed now and besides we don't serve snails.'

Then he slams the door. The snail again pounds on the door until the bartender gets so frustrated that he opens the door again and kicks the snail away.

A year later, the bartender is about to close again when he hears a pounding on the door. He opens the door and looks down to see the same snail.

The snail looks up and asks, 'What did you do that for?'

Three men walk into a bar. At the door, a woman stops them and tells them they can only enter if the lengths of their dicks add up to one foot. The first man gets out his dick and it is six inches long. The second man gets his out and it is five inches long. The third man gets his out and it is one inch long, so the woman lets them in.

The first man says, 'Thank God my dick is so long.'

The second man says, 'Thank God my dick is so long.'

The third guy says, 'Thank God I had an erection.'

Aguy walks into a bar, approaches the bartender and says, 'I've been working on a top-secret project on molecular genetics for the past five years and I've just got to talk to someone about it.'

The bartender says, 'Wait a minute. Before we talk about that, just answer a few questions for me . . . When a deer defecates, why does it come out like little pellets?'

The guy doesn't know the answer.

The bartender then asks, 'Why is it that when a dog poops, it lands on the ground and looks like a coiled rope?'

The guy says, 'I don't have any idea.'

The bartender then says, 'You don't know shit . . . and you want to talk about molecular genetics?'

A young man sits down at the bar.

'What can I get you?' the bartender inquires.

'I want six shots of vodka,' says the young man.

'Six shots? Are you celebrating something?'

'Yeah, my first blowjob,' the young man answers.

'Well, in that case, let me give you a seventh on the house.'

'No offence, Sir. But if six shots won't get rid of the taste, nothing will.'

Three women, all with boyfriends named Leroy, are at a bar when one of the women says, 'I'm tired of getting my Leroy mixed up with your Leroy, and her Leroy mixed up with your Leroy. Why don't we all name our Leroys after a soft drink?'

The other two women agree, and the first woman says, 'OK, then, let me go first. I name my Leroy 7-UP.'

The other two women ask her, 'Why 7-UP?'

'Because my Leroy has seven inches and it's always UP!'

All three women holler and hoot and slap each other on the back.

Then the second woman says, 'OK, I'm next, and I name my Leroy Mountain Dew.'

The other two women ask, 'Why Mountain Dew?'

'Because my Leroy can Mount and Dew me anytime.'

All three women holler and hoot and slap each other on the back.

The third woman then stands back and starts thinking and

says, 'You know, those two Leroys were good, but I'm gonna name mine Jack Daniels.'

The other two women shout in unison, 'Jack Daniels? That's not a soft drink – that's a hard liquor!'

The third woman shouts, 'That's my Leroy!'

While a man at a bar savours a double martini, an attractive woman sits down next to him and orders a glass of orange juice.

The man turns to her and says, 'This is a special day. I'm celebrating.'

'I'm celebrating, too,' she replies, clinking glasses with him.

'What are you celebrating?' he asks.

'For years I've been trying to have a child,' she answers. 'Today my gynaecologist told me I'm pregnant!'

'Congratulations,' the man says, lifting his glass. 'As it happens, I'm a chicken farmer, and for years all my hens were infertile. But today they're finally fertile.'

'How did it happen?'

'I switched cocks.'

'What a coincidence,' she says, smiling.

A very shy guy goes into a bar and sees a beautiful woman sitting at the bar.

After an hour of gathering up his courage, he finally goes over to her and asks, tentatively, 'Um, would you mind if I chatted with you for a while?'

She responds by yelling, at the top of her lungs, 'No! I won't sleep with you tonight!'

Everyone in the bar is now staring at them. Naturally, the guy is hopelessly and completely embarrassed and he slinks back to his table.

After a few minutes, the woman walks over to him and apologises.

She smiles at him and says, 'I'm sorry if I embarrassed you. You see, I'm a graduate student in psychology, and I'm studying how people respond to embarrassing situations.'

To which he responds, at the top of his lungs, 'What do you mean $200?'

BLONDES

Why pick on blondes? Because it's fun, that's why!

A bartender is sitting behind the bar on a typical day when the door bursts open and in come four exuberant blondes. They come up to the bar, order five bottles of champagne and ten glasses, take their order and sit down at a large table.

The corks are popped, the glasses are filled and they begin toasting and chanting, 'Fifty-one days, fifty-one days, fifty-one days!'

Soon, three more blondes arrive, take up their drinks and the chanting grows.

'Fifty-one days, fifty-one days, fifty-one days!'

Two more blondes show up and soon their voices are joined in raising the roof.

'Fifty-one days, fifty-one days, fifty-one days!'

Finally, the tenth blonde comes in with a picture under her arm. She walks over to the table, sets the picture in the middle and the table erupts.

Up jump the others, they begin dancing around the table, exchanging high-fives, all the while chanting, 'Fifty-one days, fifty-one days, fifty-one days!'

The bartender can't contain his curiosity any longer, so he walks over to the table. There in the centre is a beautifully framed child's puzzle of the Cookie Monster.

When the frenzy dies down a little bit, the bartender asks one of the blondes, 'What's all the chanting and celebration about?'

The blonde who brought in the picture pipes up, 'Everyone thinks that blondes are dumb and they make fun of us, so, we decided to set the record straight. Ten of us got together, bought that puzzle and put it together. The side of the box said "two to four years", but we put it together in fifty-one days!'

A ventriloquist is touring the clubs and stops to entertain at a bar in a small town. He's going through his usual run of silly blonde jokes when a big blonde woman in the fourth row stands on her chair and says, 'OK jerk, I've heard just about enough of your denigrating blonde jokes. What makes you think you can stereotype women that way? What do a person's physical attributes have to do with their worth as a human being? It's guys like you who keep women like me from being respected at work and in my community, from reaching my full potential as a person, because you and your kind continue to perpetuate discrimination against not only blondes but women at large, all in the name of humour.'

Flustered, the ventriloquist begins to apologise, when the blonde pipes up, 'You stay out of this mister, I'm talking to that little bastard on your knee!'

Why don't blondes like to breastfeed their children? Because it hurts when they boil their nipples.

How do you sink a submarine full of blondes? You knock on the door.

What is dumber than the two brunettes who tried to build a house at the bottom of the ocean?
The two blondes who tried to burn it down.

What's blonde-brunette-blonde-brunette-blonde-brunette-blonde?
A blonde doing cartwheels.

What do you call a blonde with half a brain?
Gifted.

Why does a blonde keep a wire coat hanger in the back seat of her car?
In case she locks her keys in.

What do you call a blonde in a business suit, sitting on a tree, holding a briefcase?
A branch manager

Why did the blonde snort Sweet 'N Low?
She thought it was Diet Coke.

What does a blonde say after two years of university?
Would you like fries with that?

Why did the blonde cross the road?
I don't know, and neither does she.

One cold winter's day, a blonde decides she wants to take up ice fishing. When she gets to the pond, she begins to cut a hole in the ice. As she does, she hears a voice.

'There's no fish there.'

Puzzled, the blonde picks up her stuff and cuts another hole a few metres away. Again, she hears the voice.

'There's no fish there.'

The blonde is confused, but still determined. A few metres away, she begins to cut another ice hole.

'There's no fish there,' she hears.

She immediately turns her head to the sky and says, 'Is that you, God?'

'No! It's the manager of the ice-skating rink. There's no fish in there!'

A blonde decides one day that she is sick and tired of all these blonde jokes and how all blondes are perceived as stupid, so she decides to show her husband that blondes really are smart. While her husband is off at work, she decides that she is going to paint a couple of rooms in the house. The next day, straight after her husband leaves for work, she gets down to the task at hand. Her husband arrives home at 5.30 p.m. and smells the distinctive smell of paint. He walks into the living room and finds his wife lying on the floor in a pool of sweat. He notices that she is wearing a ski jacket and a fur coat at the same time.

'Honey, are you OK?' he asks her.

'Yes,' she replies.

'Then what are you doing?' he asks.

'I wanted to prove to you that not all blonde women are dumb and I wanted to do it by painting the house,' she replies.

'Then why are you wearing a ski jacket over a fur coat?' he asks.

'Well,' she replies, 'I was reading the directions on the paint can and it says: "For best results, put on two coats".'

Did you hear about the blonde who bought an AM radio?
It took her a month to realise that she could play it at night.

Why did the blonde scale the chain-link fence?
To see what was on the other side.

How do you make a blonde laugh on Saturday?
Tell her a joke on Wednesday.

Why has the wave been outlawed at football games?
Because all the blondes used to drown.

What was the last thing a blonde heard before dying of old age?
'Today children, we will learn our ABCs.'

What do you call a blonde with a leather jacket?
A rebel without a clue.

Why did the blonde wear high-heel shoes?
Her mother once told her not to sell herself short.

What goes stop, go, stop, go, stop, go?
A blonde at a flashing red light.

A business man gets on an elevator. When he enters, there's a blonde already inside and she greets him by saying, 'T-G-I-F.'

He smiles at her and replies, 'S-H-I-T.'

She looks at him, puzzled, and again says, 'T-G-I-F.'

He acknowledges her remark again by answering, 'S-H-I-T.'

The blonde is trying to be friendly, so she smiles her biggest smile and says as sweetly as possible, 'T-G-I-F.'

The man smiles back to her and once again replies with a quizzical expression, 'S-H-I-T.'

The blonde finally decides to explain things, and this time she says, 'T-G-I-F, Thank Goodness It's Friday, get it?'

The man answers, 'Sorry, Honey, it's Thursday.'

A young blonde from a Manhattan finishing school is so depressed that she decides to end her life by throwing herself into the ocean.

When she goes down to the docks, a handsome young sailor notices her tears, takes pity on her, and says, 'Look, you've got a lot to live for. I'm off to Europe in the morning, and if you like, I can stow you away on my ship. I'll take good care of you and bring you food every day.' Moving closer, he slips his arm around her shoulder and adds, 'I'll keep you happy and you'll keep me happy.'

The girl nods. What does she have to lose? That night, the sailor smuggles her aboard and hides her in a lifeboat. From then on, every night he brings her three sandwiches and a piece of fruit and they make passionate love until dawn. Three weeks later, during a routine search, she is discovered by the captain.

'What are you doing here?' he asks.

'I have an arrangement with one of the sailors,' she explains. 'He's taking me to Europe, and every night he comes down and screws me.'

'He sure is, lady,' says the captain. 'This is the Staten Island Ferry.'

Why was the blonde's coffin shaped like a triangle?
Because every time her head hit a pillow her legs opened.

What do you call a brunette standing between two blondes?
An interpreter.

How does a blonde get hurt raking leaves?
She falls out of the tree!

Did you hear the one about the blonde with a bumper sticker
that says: 'All blondes aren't dumb?'
   No-one can read it because it's hung upside-down.

Why do blondes like sunroofs?
More leg room.

What do you call five blondes lying on a beach?
A public access.

What happened to the blonde tap dancer?
She fell in the sink.

What's the difference between a smart blonde and
Bigfoot?
Maybe someday we'll find Bigfoot.

How do you confuse a blonde?
Put her in a round room and tell her to sit in a corner.

What is the difference between a blonde and a supermarket
trolley?
Supermarket trolleys have a mind of their own.

Two blondes are out walking when they come across some
tracks.
'Those are deer tracks,' says the first.
'No they're not, those are fox tracks,' says the second.
They're still arguing when the train hits them.

A blonde and a brunette are in an elevator when a really hot
guy gets in. They look at the back of his head, and see that he
has dandruff. He gets off the elevator and the brunette turns to
the blonde and says jokingly, 'That guy needs Head & Shoulders.'
The blonde replies, 'How do you give shoulders?'

Did you hear about the blonde who tried to kill herself?
She jumped out a cellar window.

Why can't blondes pass their driving tests?
Because every time the car stops they jump in the back seat.

Did you hear the one about the blonde fox that got stuck in a
trap?
She chewed off three legs and was still stuck.

Why did the blonde have square boobs?
She forgot to take the tissue out of the box.

What's an intelligent blonde?
A Golden Retriever.

What did they call the blonde that was found dead in the closet?
The 1994 Hide and Seek Champion.

Why was the blonde's brain the size of a pea after exercising?
It swelled up!

How can you tell when a blonde has been baking chocolate-chip cookies?
There are M&M's shells all over the floor.

Did you hear about the blonde who died drinking milk?
The cow fell on her.

A blonde is overweight, so her doctor puts her on a diet.
'I want you to eat regularly for two days, then skip a day, and repeat this procedure for two weeks. The next time I see you, you'll have lost at least two kilos.'

When the blonde returns, she's lost nearly eight kilos.

'Why, that's amazing!' the doctor says. 'Did you follow my instructions?'

The blonde nods. 'I'll tell you, though, I thought I was going to drop dead that third day.'

'From hunger, you mean?' asks the doctor.

'No, from all that skipping.'

A highway patrolman pulls alongside a speeding car on the freeway. Glancing at the car, he is astounded to see that the blonde behind the wheel is knitting! Realising that she was oblivious to his flashing lights and siren, the cop cranks down his window, turns on his bullhorn and yells, 'Pull over!'

'No,' the blonde yells back. 'It's a scarf.'

A Russian, an American, and a blonde are talking one day. The Russian says, 'We were the first in space!'

The American says, 'We were the first on the moon!'

The blonde says, 'So what, we're going to be the first on the sun!'

The Russian and the American look at each other and shake their heads.

'You can't land on the sun, you idiot! You'll burn up!' says the Russian.

The blonde replies, 'We're not stupid, you know. We'll go at night.'

A blonde is playing *Trivial Pursuit* one night. It's her turn. She rolls the dice and she lands on 'Science and Nature'. Her question is: 'If you are in a vacuum and someone calls your name, can you hear it?'

She thinks for a while and then asks, 'Is it on or off?'

A blonde arrives for her university final examination, which consists of questions requiring yes or no answers. She takes her seat in the examination hall and stares hopelessly at the exam paper for five minutes. Then in a fit of inspiration, she takes her purse out, removes a coin and starts tossing the coin and marking the answer sheet 'yes' for heads and 'no' for tails. Within half an hour she is finished, while the rest of the class is still writing madly. During the last few minutes, she is seen desperately throwing the coin, muttering and sweating. The moderator, alarmed, approaches her and asks what is going on.

'I finished the exam in half an hour,' she tells him, 'but I'm rechecking my answers.'

A blonde's house is burning down. She runs next door to call the fire station.

'Hurry, Hurry my house is burning to the ground!'

'How do we get there?' the dispatcher asks.

She replies sarcastically, 'On your fire truck, duh!'

What do a blonde and a turtle have in common?
Once they're on their back, they're screwed.

How does a blonde turn the light on after sex?
She opens the car door.

What's the mating call of a blonde?
'I'm sooooo drunk!'

What's the mating call of a brunette?
'Is that damn blonde gone yet?'

What do a bleach blonde and an aeroplane have in common?
They both have black boxes.

What did the blonde say when her boyfriend blew in her ear?
'Thanks for the refill, honey.'

What do you call a line of blondes standing ear to ear?
A wind tunnel.

What do you call a bunch of blondes standing ear to ear with a hose at the end?
An air compressor.

Why do blondes leave empty milk cartons in the fridge?
In case someone wants black coffee.

What does a blonde say after she knocks over a priceless antique vase and it cracks on the ground?
'It's OK daddy, I'm alright'

What would a blonde say if you asked her the score?
Twenty-four to twenty-eight, a tie.

After months of trying, a young man finally gets a date with a blonde who lives in the same apartment block. To prepare for his big date, the young man goes up on to the roof of his apartment building to sunbake. Not wanting any tan lines to show, he sunbakes in the nude. Unfortunately, the young man falls asleep while on the roof and ends up with a sunburned penis. But he is determined not to miss his date, so he puts some lotion on his penis and wraps it in gauze.

The blonde shows up for the date at the man's apartment and the young man treats her to a home-cooked dinner, after which they go into the living room to watch a movie. During the movie, the young man's sunburn starts acting up. He excuses himself, goes into the kitchen and pours a tall, cool glass of milk. He then places his sunburned penis in the milk and experiences immediate relief. The blonde, wondering what he is doing, wanders into the kitchen to see him with his penis immersed in a glass of milk.

Upon seeing this, she exclaims, 'So that's how you guys load those things!'

A university lecturer in an anatomy class asks his students to sketch a naked man. As the lecturer walks around the class checking the sketches he notices that a sexy, young, blonde student has sketched the man with an erect penis.

The lecturer comments, 'Oh, no, I wanted it the other way.'

She replies, 'What other way?'

One day, a blonde and a brunette are sitting together for lunch. The brunette sets a thermos on the table, and the blonde asks what it is.

'It's a thermos,' says the brunette. 'It keeps hot things hot and cold things cold.'

The blonde stares in awe as the brunette pours steaming hot coffee out to show her. The next day, the blonde is showing off her 'new' thermos to another blonde.

'See this?' she asks.

'What is it?' the other blonde asks.

'It's a thermos, and it keeps hot things hot, and cold things cold!'

'Oh, what do you have in it?' the new blonde asks.

'Two cups of coffee and an ice block.'

What do you call a blonde in an institute for higher learning?
A visitor.

What do you call an eternity?
Four blondes in four cars at a four-way stop.

Why do blondes have TGIF written on their shoes?
Toes Go In First.

What do smart blondes and UFOs have in common?
You always hear about them but never see them.

What did the blonde say when she opened the box of Cheezels?
'Oh look, Daddy. Doughnut seeds!'

Why did the blonde stare at the can of frozen orange juice?
Because it said concentrate.

Why do blondes always smile during lightning storms?
They think their picture is being taken.

How can you tell when a blonde sends you a fax?
It has a stamp on it.

What do you do if a blonde throws a pin at you?
Run, she's got a grenade in her mouth!

How can you tell if a blonde has been using your computer?
There is white-out all over the monitor.

Three seventeen-year-old girls – a blonde, a brunette and a redhead – are drinking in a bar. Suddenly, a cop walks in and the three run outside. He notices and follows them into an alley where there are three garbage bags but no sign of the girls. The police officer walks over to the first garbage bag and gives it a small kick.

The brunette, hiding inside, says, 'Meow.'

The officer says, 'Oh it's just a bunch of cats.'

He then kicks the next bag where the redhead is hiding.

She says, 'Woof, woof.'

The officer says, 'It's only a bunch of dogs.'

Finally, he kicks the last bag where the blonde is hiding.

She says, 'Potatoes, potatoes.'

A blonde goes to work one morning crying her eyes out.
Her boss asks sympathetically, 'What's the matter?'

The blonde replies, 'Early this morning I got a phone call saying that my mother had passed away.'

The boss, feeling very sorry, says to the young woman, 'Why don't you take the day off to relax and rest?'

'No, I'm better off staying at work. I need to keep my mind off it and I have the best chance of doing that here.'

The boss agrees and allows the blonde to work as usual.

'If you need anything, just let me know,' he says.

After a few hours, the boss decides to check on the blonde. He looks out of his office and sees the blonde crying hysterically. He rushes up to her, asking, 'What's so bad now? Are you gonna be OK?'

'No!' exclaims the blonde. 'I just got a call from my sister. She told me that her mum died too!'

What did the dumb blonde say when she found out she was pregnant?

'Gee, I hope it's mine.'

Why did the blonde throw bread into the toilet?
To feed her toilet duck

What do blondes and beer bottles have in common?
They're empty from the neck up.

What is the first thing a blonde does in the morning?
Goes home.

Why did the blonde cross the road?
Never mind that, what the hell was she doing out of the kitchen?

A brunette and a blonde are walking along in a park. The brunette says suddenly, 'Awww, look at the dead birdie.'

The blonde stops, looks up, and says, 'Where?'

A blonde is walking down the street with her blouse open and her right breast hanging out.

A policeman approaches her and says, 'Ma'am, are you aware that I could cite you for indecent exposure?'

She says, 'Why, officer?'

'Because your breast is hanging out.'

She looks down and says, 'Oh my God! I left the baby on the bus again!'

A blonde is driving down an old country road when she spots another blonde in a wheat field rowing a boat. She pulls over to the side of the road and stops the car. Staring in disbelief she stands at the side of the road to watch the woman for a while.

When she can't stand it any more she calls out to the blonde in the field, 'Why are you rowing a boat in the middle of the field?'

The blonde in the field stops rowing and responds, 'Because it's an ocean of wheat.'

The blonde standing on the side of the road is furious.

She yells at the blonde in the field, 'It's blondes like you that give the rest of us a bad name.'

The blonde in the field just shrugs her shoulders and begins rowing again.

The blonde on the side of the road is beside herself and shakes her fist at the blonde in the field, then yells, 'If I could swim I would come out there and kick your arse.'

A blonde, a redhead and a brunette are competing in the English Channel Breast Stroke Competition. The redhead wins and the brunette comes second. However, there is no sign of the final contestant. Hours and hours go by, causing grave concern and worry. Just as everyone is losing hope, the blonde finally arrives. The crowd is extremely happy and relieved to see her. They embrace the young woman as she comes ashore.

After all of the excitement dies down, the blonde leans over to the judge and whispers, 'I hate to be a bad loser, but I think those other girls used their arms.'

Two tourists are driving through Louisiana. As they approach Natchitoches, they start arguing about the pronunciation of the town. They argue back and forth until they stop for lunch.

As they stand at the counter, one tourist asks the blonde employee, 'Before we order, could you please settle an argument for us? Would you pronounce the name of this place . . . very slowly?'

The blonde girl leans over the counter and says, 'Burrrrrrrr, gerrrrrrr, Kiiiiing.'

John gets a call from his very blonde girlfriend Buffy.
'I've got a problem,' says Buffy.

'What's the matter?' asks John.

'Well, I bought this jigsaw puzzle, but it's too hard. None of the pieces fit together and I can't find any edges.'

'What's the picture of?' asks John.

'It's of a big rooster,' replies Buffy.

'All right,' says John. 'I'll come over and have a look.'

So he goes over to Buffy's house and she greets him by saying, 'Thanks for coming over.' Buffy leads John into her kitchen and shows him the jigsaw puzzle on the kitchen table.

John looks at the puzzle and then turns to her and says, 'For heaven's sake, Buffy, put the corn flakes back in the box.'

Did you hear about the blonde who put lipstick on her forehead so she could make up her mind?

Did you hear about the blonde who threw away her weight-loss video because she noticed that the people on the video were not losing weight either?

Why can't you tell blondes knock-knock jokes?
Because they go answer the door.

Why can't a blonde have more than a ten-minute lunchbreak?
Because otherwise you have to retrain her.

If a blonde and a brunette jumped off a building at the same time, who would land first?
 The brunette – the blonde would need to stop for directions.

How do you put a sparkle in a blonde's eye?
Shine a torch in her ear.

What do a blonde and a postage stamp have in common?
Lick 'em, stick 'em, send 'em

What does a blonde owl say?
'What? What?'

Why don't blondes eat pickles?
They keep getting their heads stuck in the jar.

Why do blondes wear panties?
To keep their ankles warm.

And then there was the blonde who named her pet zebra
Spot . . .

A blonde gets a dent in her car and takes it to the repair shop.
The panel-beater, noticing that the woman is blonde, decides
to have a wee bit of fun. So he tells her all she has to do is take
her car home and blow in the exhaust pipe until the dent pops
itself out.

So the blonde goes home and gives it a try. After fifteen
minutes of this the blonde's friend, who is also blonde, comes
over and asks what she is doing.

'I'm trying to pop out this dent, but it's not really working.'

'Duh. You have to roll up the windows first!'

A blonde has a sharp pain in her side.
The doctor examines her and says, 'You have acute
appendicitis.'

The blonde yells at the doctor, 'I came here to get medical
help, not a stupid compliment!'

A blonde says to a brunette, 'Every time I sip my coffee, I get a pain in my eye.'

The brunette says, 'Well maybe you should take the spoon out of the cup.'

A blonde goes for a job interview in an office. The interviewer starts with the basics.

'So, Miss, can you tell us your age, please?'

The blonde counts carefully on her fingers for half a minute before replying, 'Ehhhh . . . twenty-two!'

The interviewer tries another straightforward one to break the ice.

'And can you tell us your height, please?'

The young woman stands up and produces a measuring tape from her handbag. She then traps one end under her foot and extends the tape to the top of her head.

She checks the measurement and announces 'Five foot two!'

This isn't looking good so the interviewer goes for the real basics; something the interviewee won't have to count, measure, or lookup.

'Just to confirm for our records, your name please?'

The blonde bobs her head from side to side for about ten seconds, mouthing something silently to herself, before replying, 'Mandy!'

The interviewer is completely baffled at this stage, so he asks, 'What in the world were you doing when I asked you your name?'

'Ohhhh, that!' replies the blonde. 'I was just running through that song, "Happy birthday to you, happy birthday to you, happy birthday dear . . ."'

A blonde sits down in a bar next to a redhead. Both of them are having a good time when the news comes on the TV.

The woman reporter shouts out, 'This just in! A man is at the edge of a cliff attempting to jump.'

The redhead leans over to the blonde and whispers, 'I bet you $50 that the man's gonna jump.'

The blonde responds, 'You're on.'

So, both of the women stare at the news waiting to find out what happens next. Finally, the man jumps. The blonde turns to the redhead and hands her the $50.

The redhead, feeling guilty, says, 'I can't take that money. I saw the news earlier this morning. I knew he was going to jump off the cliff.'

The blonde says, 'Well, I saw it too. But I never would have thought that he'd do it again.'

Passing an office building late one night, a blonde sees a sign that says Press Bell for Night Watchman.

She does so, and after several minutes she hears the watchman clomping down the stairs.

The uniformed man unlocks first one gate, then another, shuts down the alarm system, and finally makes his way through the revolving door.

'Well,' he snarls at the blonde. 'What do you want?'

'I just want to know why you can't ring the bell for yourself.'

What do you call a couple of blondes in the front seat of a car?

Air bags.

Did you hear about the blonde who bought a pair of water-skis? She's still looking for a lake with a slope.

What's the difference between a blonde guy and a blonde girl? The blonde girl's sperm count is higher.

How do blondes' brain cells die? Alone.

A blonde is visiting interstate for the first time. She wants to see the art gallery but doesn't know how to get there. Fortunately, a police officer walks past.

'Excuse me, officer,' asks the blonde. 'How do I get to the art gallery?'

The officer replies, 'Wait at this bus stop for the No. 54 bus. It'll take you straight there.'

She thanks the officer and he walks off. Three hours later the police officer returns to the same area and, sure enough, the blonde is still waiting at the same bus stop.

The officer says, 'Excuse me, but to get to the art gallery, I said to wait here for the No. 54 bus and that was three hours ago! Why are you still waiting?'

The blonde replies, 'Don't worry, officer, it won't be long now. The forty-fifth bus just went by!'

A blonde keeps having the same weird dream every day, so she goes to her doctor.

Doctor: What is your dream about?

Blonde: I am being chased by a vampire!

Doctor *(giggling quietly)*: So, what is the scenery like?

Blonde: I am running in a hallway.

Doctor: Then what happens?

Blonde: Well that's the weird thing. In every single dream, the same thing happens. I always come to this door, but I

can't open it. I keep pushing the door and pushing the
door, but it wouldn't budge!

Doctor: Does the door have any letters on it?

Blonde: Yes.

Doctor: And what do the letters spell?

Blonde: Pull.

How do you make a one-armed blonde fall out of a tree?
Wave to her.

What do you call blondes in a freezer?
Frosted Flakes.

Why did the blonde turn into the ditch?
She left her blinker on.

How do you know when a blonde's been sending email?
You see a bunch of envelopes stuffed into the disk drive.

Why did the blonde jump off the cliff?
Because she thought her maxi-pad had wings.

What do blondes and cow pies have in common?
The older they get, the easier they are to pick up.

Why are blonde jokes so stupid?
So brunettes can get them.

SHE WAS SO BLONDE . . .

. . . she got stabbed in a shoot-out.

. . . she told me to meet her at the corner of 'Walk' and 'Don't Walk'.

. . . she tried to drown a fish.

. . . she got locked in a grocery store and starved to death.

. . . they had to burn the school down to get her out of third grade.

. . . she asked for a price check at the $2 Shop.

. . . she thought Boyz II Men was a day-care centre.

. . . when she saw a sign that said Under 17 Not Admitted, she went home and got sixteen friends.

. . . when she heard that 90% of all crimes occur around the home, she moved.

...when she missed the No. 44 bus, she took the No. 22 bus twice instead.

BATTLE OF THE SEXES

As someone much wiser than me once said, 'Men are from Earth. Women are from Earth. Deal with it.'

When a woman says, 'C'mon, This place is a mess! You and I need to clean. Your pants are on the floor and you'll have no clothes if we don't do laundry now!'

A man hears, 'C'mon . . . blah, blah, blah . . . You and I . . . blah, blah, blah, blah, blah . . . on the floor . . . blah, blah, blah . . . no clothes . . . blah, blah, blah, blah . . . now!'

WOMEN'S ENGLISH

Yes. = No.

No. = Yes.

Maybe. = No.

I'm sorry. = You'll be sorry.

We need. = I want.

It's your decision. = The correct decision should be obvious by now.

Do what you want. = You'll pay for this later.

We need to talk. = I need to complain.

Sure . . . go ahead. = I don't want you to.

I'm not upset. = Of course I'm upset, you moron!

You're certainly attentive tonight. = Is sex all you ever think about?

This kitchen is so inconvenient. = I want a new house.

I want new curtains. = and carpeting, and furniture, and wallpaper . . .

Hang the picture there. = No, I mean hang it there!

I heard a noise. = I noticed you were almost asleep.

Do you love me? = I'm going to ask for something expensive.

How much do you love me? = I did something today you're really not going to like.

I'll be ready in a minute. = Kick off your shoes and find a good game on TV.

Is my bum fat? = Tell me I'm beautiful.

You have to learn to communicate. = Just agree with me.

Are you listening to me? = Too late, you're dead.

Was that the baby? = Why don't you get out of bed and walk him until he goes to sleep.

I'm not yelling! = Yes I am yelling because I think this is important.

MEN'S ENGLISH

I'm hungry. = I'm hungry.

I'm sleepy. = I'm sleepy.

I'm tired. = I'm tired.

Do you want to go to a movie? = I'd eventually like to have sex with you.

Can I take you out to dinner? = I'd eventually like to have sex with you.

Can I call you sometime? = I'd eventually like to have sex with you.

May I have this dance? = I'd eventually like to have sex with you.

Nice dress! = Nice cleavage!

You look tense; let me give you a massage. = I want to fondle you.

What's wrong? = I don't see why you are making such a big deal out of this.

What's wrong? = What meaningless, self-inflicted, psychological trauma are you going through now?

What's wrong? = I guess sex tonight is out of the question.

I'm bored. = Do you want to have sex?

I love you. = Let's have sex now.

I love you, too. = OK, I said it . . . we'd better have sex now!

Yes, I like the way you cut your hair. = I liked it better before.

Yes, I like the way you cut your hair. = $50 and it doesn't look that much different!

Let's talk. = I am trying to impress you by showing that I am a deep person, so that you'd like to have sex with me.

Will you marry me? = I want to make it illegal for you to have sex with other guys.

Can I help with dinner? = Why isn't it already on the table?

It's a guy thing. = There is no rational thought pattern connected with it, and you have no chance at all of making it logical.

It would take too long to explain. = I have no idea how it works.

We're going to be late. = Now I have a legitimate excuse to drive like a maniac.

Take a break, honey, you're working too hard. = I can't hear the game over the vacuum cleaner.

That's interesting, dear. = Are you still talking?

It's a really good movie. = It's got guns, knives, fast cars, and beautiful women.

That's women's work. = It's difficult, dirty, and thankless.

You know how bad my memory is. = I remember the theme song to *F Troop*, the address of the first girl I ever kissed and the Vehicle Identification Numbers of every car I've ever owned, but I forgot your birthday.

I was just thinking about you, and got you these roses. = The girl selling them on the corner was a real babe.

Oh, don't fuss. I just cut myself, it's no big deal. = I have actually severed a limb, but will bleed to death before I admit I'm hurt.

Hey, I've got my reasons for what I'm doing. = And I sure hope I think of some pretty soon.

I can't find it. = It didn't fall right into my outstretched hands, so I'm completely clueless.

What did I do this time? = What did you catch me at?

I heard you. = I haven't the foggiest clue what you just said, and am hoping desperately that I can fake it well enough so that you don't spend the next three days yelling at me.

You know I could never love anyone else. = I am used to the way you yell at me, and realise it could be worse.

You look terrific. = Oh, God, please don't try on one more outfit. I'm starving.

I'm not lost. I know exactly where we are. = No-one will ever see us alive again.

We share the housework. = I make the messes, she cleans them up.

Uh huh; Sure, honey *or* Yes, dear. = Absolutely nothing. It's a conditioned response.

HOW TO SATISFY A WOMAN EVERY TIME

Caress, praise, pamper, relish, savour, massage, make plans, fix, empathise, serenade, compliment, support, feed, tantalise, bathe, humour, placate, stimulate, stroke, console, purr, hug, coddle, excite, pacify, protect, phone, correspond, anticipate, nuzzle, smooch, toast, minister to, forgive, sacrifice for, ply, accessorise, leave, return, beseech, sublimate, entertain, charm, lug, drag, crawl, treat equally, spackle, oblige, fascinate, attend, implore, bawl, shower, shave, trust, grovel, ignore, defend, coax, clothe, brag about, acquiesce, fuse, fizz, rationalise, detoxify, sanctify, help, acknowledge, polish, upgrade, spoil, embrace, accept, butter-up, hear, understand, jitterbug, locomote, beg, plead, borrow, steal, climb, swim, nurse, resuscitate, repair, patch, super-glue, respect, entertain, calm, allay, kill for, die for, dream of, promise, deliver, tease, flirt, commit, enlist, pine, cajole, murmur, snuggle, snoozle, snurfle, elevate, enervate, alleviate, spot-weld, serve, rub, rib, salve, bite, taste, nibble, gratify, take her places, scuttle like a crab on the ocean floor of her existence, diddle, doodle, hokey-pokey, hanky-panky, crystal blue persuade, flip, flop, fly, don't care if I die, swing, slip, slide, slather, mollycoddle, squeeze, moisturise, humidify, lather, tingle, slam-dunk, keep on rockin' in the free world, wet, slicken, undulate, gelatinise, brush, tingle, dribble, drip, dry, knead, fluff, fold, ingratiate, indulge, wow, dazzle, amaze, flabbergast, enchant, idolise and worship, and then go back, Jack, and do it again.

HOW TO SATISFY A MAN EVERY TIME

Show up naked . . . with beer.

Nobody will ever win the battle of the sexes. There's too much fraternizing with the enemy.

How does a man show he's planning for the future? He buys two cases of beer instead of one.

Why do men become smarter during sex? Because they are plugged into a genius.

Why don't women blink during foreplay? They don't have time.

Why does it take one million sperm to fertilise one egg? They won't stop for directions.

Why did God put men on earth? Because a vibrator can't mow the lawn.

Why don't women have men's brains?
Because they don't have penises to put them in.

What do electric trains and breasts have in common?
They're intended for children, but it's the men who usually end up playing with them.

Why do men masturbate?
It's sex with someone they love.

Why were men given larger brains than dogs?
So they won't hump women's legs at cocktail parties.

Why did God make men before women?
You need a rough draft before you make the final copy.

Why is a man's pee yellow and his sperm white?
So he can tell if he is coming or going.

What is the thinnest book in the world?
What men know about women.

How many men does it take to screw in a light bulb?
One. Men will screw anything.

How does a man take a bubble bath?
He eats beans for dinner.

What's a man's idea of foreplay?
A half hour of begging.

How can you tell if a man is sexually aroused?
He's breathing.

What's the difference between men and government bonds?
Government bonds mature.

How do you save a man from drowning?
Take your foot off of his head.

How can you tell if a man is happy?
Who cares?

How many men does it take to change a roll of toilet paper?
Nobody knows. It's never happened.

How are men like parking spots?
The good ones are always taken and the only ones left are disabled.

What is a man's idea of helping out with housework?
Lifting his leg so you can vacuum.

THE BENEFITS OF BEING A WOMAN

- We got off the *Titanic* first.

- We get to flirt with systems support men who always return our calls, and are nice to us when we blow up our computers.

- Our boyfriends' clothes make us look elfin and gorgeous. Guys look like complete idiots in ours.

- We can be groupies. Male groupies are stalkers.

- We can cry and get off speeding fines.

- We've never lusted after a cartoon character or the central figure in a computer game.

- Taxis stop for us.

- Men die earlier, so we get to cash in on the life insurance.

- We don't look like a frog in a blender when dancing.

- Free drinks, free dinners.

- We can hug our friends without wondering if they're gay.

- We can hug our friends without wondering if *we're* gay.

- New lipstick gives us a whole new lease on life.

- If we're not making enough money we can blame the glass ceiling.

- It's possible to live our whole lives without ever taking a group shower.

- No fashion faux pas we make could ever rival The Speedo.

- We don't have to fart to amuse ourselves.

- If we forget to shave, no-one has to know.

- We can congratulate our team-mate without ever touching her bum.

- If we have a zit, we know how to conceal it.

- We don't have to reach down every so often to make sure our privates are still there.

- If we're dumb, some people will find it cute.

- We don't have to memorise *Caddyshack* or *Fletch* to fit in.

- We have the ability to dress ourselves.

- We can talk to people of the opposite sex without having to picture them naked.

- If we marry someone twenty years younger, we're aware that we look like an idiot.

- We know that there are times when chocolate really can solve all your problems.

- We'll never regret piercing our ears.

- We can fully assess a person just by looking at their shoes.

- We'll never discover we've been duped by a Wonderbra.

- We know which glass was ours by the lipstick mark.

MEN ARE LIKE . . .

. . . bananas – they older they get, the less firm they are.

. . . bank accounts – without a lot of money, they don't generate much interest.

. . . bike helmets – handy in an emergency, but otherwise they just look silly.

. . . blenders – you need one, but you're not quite sure why.

. . . coffee – the best ones are rich, warm, full-bodied, and can keep you up all night long.

. . . coolers – load them with beer and you can take them anywhere.

. . . copiers – you need them for reproduction, but that's about it.

. . . chocolate bars – sweet, smooth and they usually head right for your hips.

. . . curling irons – they are always hot, and they are always in your hair.

. . . high heels – they're easy to walk on once you get the hang of it.

. . . horoscopes – they always tell you what to do and are usually wrong.

. . . lava lamps – fun to look at, but not all that bright.

. . . laxatives – they irritate the crap out of you.

. . . mascara – they run at the first sign of emotion.

. . . mini skirts – if you are not careful they'll creep up your legs.

. . . noodles – they lack taste and they're always in hot water.

. . . placemats – they only show up when there's food on the table.

. . . plungers – they spend most of their lives in a hardware store or the bathroom.

. . . popcorn – they satisfy you, but only for a little while.

. . . used cars – they're easy to get, cheap and often prove to be unreliable.

. . . weather – nothing can be done to change them.

A man is talking to God and asks, 'God, why did you make women so beautiful?'
'So that you would find them attractive,' God replies.
Then the man asks, 'But why did you have to make them so dumb?'
'So that they would find you attractive!'

A man is driving up a steep, narrow mountain road. A woman is driving down the same road. As they pass each other, the woman leans out of the window and yells, 'Pig!'

The man immediately leans out of his window and replies, 'Bitch!'

They each continue on their way, and as the man rounds the next corner, he crashes into a pig in the middle of the road.

A passenger plane runs into a terrible storm. The plane gets pounded by rain, hail, wind, and lightening. The passengers are screaming. They are sure the plane is going to crash and they are all going to die.

At the height of the storm, a young woman jumps up and exclaims, 'I can't take this anymore! I can't just sit here and die like an animal, strapped into a chair. If I am going to die, let me die feeling like a woman. Is there anyone here man enough to make me feel like a woman?'

She sees a raised hand in the back and a muscular man starts to walk up to her seat. As he approaches her, he takes off his shirt. She can see the man's muscles even in the poor lighting of the plane.

He stands in front of her, shirt in hand and says to her, 'I can make you feel like a woman before you die. Are you interested?'

She nods her head yes.

The man hands her his shirt and says, 'Here. Iron this.'

H ow many men does it take to open a beer? None. It should be opened by the time she brings it.

Why is a laundromat a really bad place to pick up women?
Because a woman who can't even afford a washing machine will never be able to support you.

Why do women have smaller feet then men?
So they can stand closer to the kitchen sink.

How do you fix a woman's watch?
You don't. There's a clock on the oven.

Why do men pass more gas than women do?
Because women don't shut up long enough to build up pressure.

If your dog is barking at the back door and your wife is yelling at the front door, which do you let in first?
The dog of course. At least he'll shut up after you let him in.

What's worse than a male chauvinist pig?
A woman who won't do what she's told.

What do you call a woman with two brain cells?
Pregnant.

What do you call a woman who has lost 95% of her intelligence?
Divorced.

A woman walks into a supermarket and loads up her trolley with the following items:

- 1 bar of soap
- 1 toothbrush
- 1 tube of toothpaste
- 1 loaf of bread
- 1 pint of milk
- 1 single serving of cereal
- 1 single-serve frozen dinner
- 1 can of Soup For One
- 1 can of light beer

The guy at the check-out looks at her and says, 'Single, are you?'

The woman smiles sweetly and replies, 'How did you guess?'

'Because you're ugly.'

T hree guys are having a relaxing day fishing. Out of the blue, they catch a mermaid who begs to be set free, in return for granting each of them a wish.

One of the guys just doesn't believe it, and says, 'OK, if you can really grant wishes, then double my IQ.'

The mermaid says, 'Done!'

Suddenly, the guy starts reciting Shakespeare flawlessly and analysing it with extreme insight.

The second guy is so amazed he says to the mermaid, 'Triple my IQ.'

The mermaid says, 'Done!'

The guy starts to spout out all the mathematical solutions to problems that have been stumping scientists and mathematicians for years.

The last guy is so enthralled with the changes in his friends that he says to the mermaid, 'Quintuple my IQ.'

The mermaid looks at him and says, 'You know, I normally

don't try to change people's minds when they make a wish, but I really wish you'd reconsider.'

The guy says, 'Nope, I want you to increase my IQ times five, and if you don't do it, I won't set you free.'

'Please,' says the mermaid, 'You don't know what you're asking. It'll change your entire view on the universe, won't you ask for something else? A million dollars, anything?'

But no matter what the mermaid says, the guy insists on having his IQ increased by five times its usual power.

So the mermaid sighs and says, 'Done.'

And he becomes a woman.

A woman and a man are involved in a car accident; it's a bad one. Both of their cars are totally demolished but amazingly neither of them is hurt.

After they crawl out of their cars, the woman says, 'Wow, just look at our cars! There's nothing left, but fortunately we are unhurt. This must be a sign from God that we should meet and be friends and live together in peace for the rest of our days.'

The man replies, 'I agree with you completely. This must be a sign from God!'

The woman continues, 'And look at this, here's another miracle. My car is completely demolished but this bottle of wine didn't break. Surely God wants us to drink this wine and celebrate our good fortune.'

Then she hands the bottle to the man. The man nods his head in agreement, opens it, drinks half the bottle, and extends it back to the woman. Politely, the woman refuses to accept the bottle.

The man asks, 'Aren't you having any?'

The woman replies, 'No. I think I'll just wait for the police . . .'

THE FIVE SECRETS TO A GREAT RELATIONSHIP (FEMALE VERSION)

1. It is important to find a man who works around the house, occasionally cooks and cleans and who has a job.
2. It is important to find a man who makes you laugh.
3. It is important to find a man who is dependable, respectful and doesn't lie.
4. It is important to find a man who's good in bed and who loves to have sex with you.
5. It is important that these four men never meet.

THE FIVE SECRETS TO A GREAT RELATIONSHIP (MALE VERSION)

1. It is important to find a woman who cooks and cleans.
2. It is important to find a woman who makes good money.
3. It is important to find a woman who likes to have sex.
4. It is important that these three women never meet.

REJECTED DR SEUSS BOOKS

Are You My Proctologist?

Aunts in My Pants!

Fox in Detox!

Herbert the Pervert Likes Sherbet!

Horton Fakes an Orgasm!

Horton Hires a Ho!

My Pocket Rocket Needs a Socket!

Oh, the Places You'll Scratch and Sniff!

One Bitch, Two Bitch, Dead Bitch, Blue Bitch!

The Cat in the Blender!

The Flesh-Eating Lorax!

The Grinch's Ten Inches!

Who Shat in the Hat?

Yentl the Lentil!

Your Colon Can Moo – Can You?

Zippy the Rabid Gerbil!

THE SANCTITY OF MARRIAGE

There's no institution more worthy, more satisfying or more important than marriage – so my wife tells me!

John brings his new colleague, Peter, home for dinner. As they arrive at the door, his wife rushes up, throws her arms around John and kisses him passionately.

'My goodness,' says Peter, 'and how long have you been married?'

'Twenty-two years,' replies John.

'You must have a fantastic marriage if your wife greets you like that after all those years.'

'Don't be fooled! She only does it to make the dog jealous.'

A man in his backyard is trying to fly a kite. He throws the kite up in the air, the wind catches it for a few seconds, and then it comes crashing back down. He tries this a few more times, while his wife watches from the kitchen window.

Muttering to herself that men need to be told how to do everything, she opens the window and yells to her husband, 'You need more tail.'

The man turns with a confused look on his face and says, 'Make up your mind. Last night you told me to go fly a kite!'

A man is sure that his wife is losing her hearing but the wife refuses to see a hearing specialist. The man goes to the specialist to ask his advice. The specialist tells him to go home and start talking to his wife from various distances to check just how close he has to be for her to hear him.

He comes in the front door and calls, 'What's for dinner?'

No reply. He proceeds to the lounge room and calls again, 'What's for dinner?'

No reply. He goes right into the kitchen and stands behind his wife and shouts, 'What's for dinner!'

The wife glares at him and shouts back, 'For the third time, lamb chops!'

A man spends six hours in a bar before rolling home to his wife blind drunk.

'Where have you been?' she demands.

'I've been to this amazing bar,' he slurs, rocking on his feet. 'It's called the Golden Saloon and everything there is golden. At the front there are two huge golden doors, the floors are golden and even the urinals are golden.'

'What rubbish,' snaps the wife. 'I don't believe a word of it.'

'Here,' said the husband, rummaging in his pocket for a piece of paper. 'Ring this number if you don't believe me.'

So the following day she phones the number on the slip of paper.

'Is this the Golden Saloon?' she asks.

'It is,' replies the bartender.

'Tell me,' says the wife, 'do you have two huge golden doors at the front of the building?'

'Sure do,' says the bartender.

'And do you have golden floors?'

'Yup.'

'What about golden urinals?'

There's a long pause and then the wife hears the bartender yell, 'Hey, Duke, I think I got a lead on the guy that pissed in your saxophone last night.'

A guy goes out drinking every night of the week before rolling home drunk, at midnight, to a frosty welcome from his long-suffering wife. She tells a friend how unbearable the atmosphere is becoming between herself and her husband. The friend suggests she try a different tack – instead of haranguing him when he gets in, she should treat him with compassion. That night, the husband staggers in late as usual, but this time he is greeted with a friendly kiss. His wife sits him in his favourite chair, brings him his slippers and makes him a nice cup of tea. He can hardly believe it. Where are the insults and accusations?

After a while she says, 'It's getting late now, dear. I think we'd better go upstairs to bed.'

'We might as well,' slurs the husband. 'I'll be in trouble when I get home anyway.'

A couple return from their honeymoon and it's obvious to everyone that they are not talking to each other. The groom's best man takes him aside and asks what is wrong.

'Well,' replies the man, 'when we had finished making love on the first night, as I got up to go to the bathroom I put a $50 note on the pillow without thinking.'

'Oh, you shouldn't worry about that too much,' says his friend. 'I'm sure your wife will get over it soon enough. She can't expect you to have been saving yourself all these years!'

The groom nods gently and says, 'I don't know if I can get over it though. While I was in the bathroom she gave me $20 change!'

A fireman is getting increasingly frustrated about the lack of sex he is getting at home so he decides to take some action.

When he gets home after work, he sits his wife down and tells her, 'At work, we are trained to respond to bells. I want the same thing to happen at home. When I ring this bell once, I want you to take all of your clothes off. When I ring this bell twice, I want you to rush upstairs and into the bedroom. And when I ring the bell three times, I want you to jump onto the bed so that we can make love.'

To his amazement, his wife agrees. The next day, after the fireman and his wife have had dinner, he rings the bell once. His wife immediately strips. Next, he rings the bell twice. His wife runs upstairs and into the bedroom. He follows her and when they are both in the bedroom he rings the bell three times. Within a minute, they are at it on the bed. Just as he is reaching the height of passion, his wife reaches for the bell and rings it four times.

The fireman stops what he is doing and asks, 'What are you doing?'

'That's four bells,' his wife replies. 'Four bells mean I need more hose. You're nowhere near the fire.'

A rich man and a poor man are Christmas shopping for their wives. The poor man asks the rich man what he is getting for his wife.

'I'm getting her a mink coat and a Porsche. I reckon if she doesn't like the mink coat, she'll like the Porsche. What about you?'

The poor man replies, 'I'm getting her a pair of slippers and a dildo. I reckon if she doesn't like the slippers she can go screw herself.'

A man and a woman are married. One day the husband, thinking he's being funny, grabs his wife's boobs as she's getting into the shower and says to her, 'You know, if these were firm, you wouldn't need a bra!'

His wife is really angry; it was a rude thing to say. The next day, as she's getting out of the shower, he grabs her arse and says, 'You know, if this was firm, you wouldn't need a girdle!'

Now the wife is really pissed off and she's plotting her revenge. So the next day, as her husband is getting out of the shower, she grabs his dick and says, 'You know, if this was firm I wouldn't need your brother!'

Bill visits his parents the day after his wedding. His father takes him aside and asks, 'How did it go last night, son?'

Bill winks and elbows his dad. 'Great. You know, the way she was acting, I think I could have screwed her.'

A guy is discussing his upcoming wedding with his friend. 'I'm not sure if my future bride is a virgin or not,' he says.

His mate replies, 'Oh, there's an easy test for that. All you need is some red paint, some green paint and a shovel.'

'What for?' asks the guy, confused.

'You paint one ball red and one ball green. On your honeymoon, if she laughs and says, "Those are the funniest balls I've ever seen!" you hit her with the shovel.'

Following an especially angry argument, Mr and Mrs Smith go to bed without speaking to each other. Needing to arise early the following morning, Mr Smith leaves a note on his wife's bedside table that says: 'Wake me at six.'

Mr Smith awakes at ten the following morning and rolls out of bed to see a note on his bedside table: 'It's six, you bum! Get out of bed!'

A married couple are in a terrible accident and the woman's face is severely burned. The doctor tells the husband that they can't graft any skin from her body because she is so skinny. So the husband decides to donate some of his own skin for the operation. However, the doctor finds that the only suitable place to take the skin is from his buttocks. The husband requests that no-one be told of this, because, after all, it is a very delicate matter.

After the surgery is complete, everyone is astounded at the woman's new face. She looks more beautiful than she did before! All her friends and relatives rant and rave at her youthful looks. She is alone with her husband one day and she wants to thank him for what he did.

She says, 'Dear, I just want to thank you for everything you did for me! There is no way I could ever repay you.'

He replies, 'Oh don't worry, Honey, I get thanks enough every time your mother comes over and kisses you on your cheek.'

A newly-married couple move into a house and the wife notices a mirror hanging on the wall.

She goes up to it and says, 'Mirror Mirror on the wall, what part of my body does my husband like most of all?'

And the mirror replies, 'Your tits.'

She then says, 'Mirror Mirror on the wall, give me size forty-four.'

And hey presto, she gets really big tits. Excitedly she rushes downstairs to show her husband, who is amazed upon seeing her. He asks her what happened and she tells him about the mirror.

The husband rushes upstairs to the mirror and says, 'Mirror Mirror on the wall, what part of my body does my wife like most of all?'

'Your dick.'

'Mirror Mirror on the wall, make my dick touch the floor.'
So his legs fall off.

A wife wakes in the middle of the night to find her husband missing from bed. She gets out of bed and checks around the house. She hears sobbing from the cellar. After turning on the light and descending the stairs, she finds her husband curled up into a little ball, sobbing.

'Honey, what's wrong?' she asks, worried about what could hurt him so much.

'Remember, twenty years ago, I got you pregnant? And your father said I had to marry you or go to jail?'

'Yes, of course,' she replies.

'Well, today I would have been a free man.'

A man is complaining to a friend, 'I had it all – money, a beautiful house, a big car, the love of a beautiful woman. Then *pow!* It was all gone.'

'What happened?' asks the friend.

'My wife found out.'

A businessman is on an overnight train trip with his secretary. They both retire to their respective rooms but a while later the secretary comes into the man's room and says, 'Excuse me Mr Johnston, but could you please pass me a blanket?'

Mr Johnston asks, 'Do you want to be Mrs Johnston for the night?'

The secretary thinks for a moment then says, 'That would be nice.'

To this Mr Johnston says, 'Good. Get your own bloody blanket.'

After just a few years of marriage, filled with constant arguments, a young man and his wife decide the only way to save their marriage is to try counselling. When they arrive, the counsellor opens the floor for discussion.

'What seems to be the problem?'

The husband holds his long face down without anything to say. Meanwhile, his wife begins talking at 100km an hour describing all the wrongs within their marriage.

After fifteen minutes of listening to the wife, the counsellor goes over to her, picks her up by her shoulders, kisses her passionately for several minutes, and sits her back down. The wife is speechless.

The counsellor looks over at the husband who is staring in disbelief and says, 'Your wife needs that at least twice a week!'

The husband scratches his head and replies, 'I can have her here on Tuesdays and Thursdays.'

Congratulations my boy!' says the groom's uncle. 'I'm sure you'll look back and remember today as the happiest day of your life.'

'But I'm not getting married until tomorrow,' protests his nephew.

'I know,' replies the uncle. 'That's exactly what I mean.'

A man has six children and is very proud of his achievement. He is so proud of himself that he starts calling his wife Mother of Six, in spite of her objections.

One night they go to a party. The man decides that it's time to go home, and wants to find out if his wife is ready to leave as well. He shouts at the top of his voice, 'Shall we go home Mother of Six?'

His wife, irritated by her husband's lack of discretion shouts back, 'Anytime you're ready, Father of Four!'

A man is drunk and in no shape to drive, so he wisely leaves his car parked and walks home. As he is walking unsteadily along, he is stopped by a policeman.

'What are you doing out here at 2 a.m.?' asks the officer.

'I'm going to a lecture,' the man says.

'And who is going to give a lecture at this hour?' the cop asks.

'My wife,' says the man.

This man is sitting quietly reading his paper one morning, peacefully enjoying himself, when his wife sneaks up behind him and whacks him on the back of his head with a huge black frying pan.

'What was that for?' asks the man

'What was that piece of paper in your pants pocket with the name Marylou written on it?'

'Oh honey. Don't you remember two weeks ago when I went to the horse races? Marylou was the name of one of the horses I bet on.'

The wife seems satisfied and goes off to work, feeling a bit sheepish.

Three days later the man is once again sitting in his chair reading and his wife repeats the frying-pan swatting.

'What's that for this time?' he asks.

'Your horse rang,' says his wife.

A husband is sent out by his wife to buy some fruit and vegetables. But they have to be organic. He goes to the market and has a good look around but can't find any.

So he grabs an old, tired-looking employee and says, 'These vegetables are for my wife. Have they been sprayed with any poisonous chemicals?'

The produce guy looks at him and says, 'No. You'll have to do that yourself.'

A man goes to the police station wanting to speak to the burglar who broke into his house the night before.

'You'll get your chance in court,' says the desk sergeant.

'No, no, no!' says the man. 'I want to know how he got into the house without waking my wife. I've been trying to do that for years!'

A woman goes into a store to buy her husband a pet for his birthday. After looking around, she finds that all the pets are very expensive. She tells the clerk she wants to buy a pet, but she doesn't want to spend a fortune.

'Well,' says the clerk. 'I have a very large bullfrog. They say it's been trained to give blowjobs.'

'Blowjobs!'

'It hasn't been proven, but we've sold thirty of them this month,' he says.

The woman thinks it will make a great gag gift, and what if it's true . . . no more blowjobs for her. So she buys the frog and gives it to her husband. When she explains froggy's ability to him, he is extremely sceptical and laughs it off.

The woman goes to bed happy, thinking she may never need to perform this less than riveting act again. In the middle of the night, she is awakened by the noise of pots and pans flying everywhere. She runs downstairs to the kitchen, only to find her husband and the frog reading cookbooks.

'What are you two doing at this hour?' she asks.

The husband replies, 'If I can teach this frog to cook, you're out of here.'

A young couple, just married, are in the honeymoon suite on their wedding night. As they undress for bed, the husband, who is a big burly man, tosses his pants to his bride and says, 'Here put these on.'

She puts them on and the waist is twice the size of her body.

'I can't wear your pants,' she says.

'That's right,' says the husband, 'and don't you forget it. I'm the one who wears the pants in this family!'

With that she flips him her panties and says, 'Try these on.'

He tries them on and finds he can only get them on as far as his kneecap.

He says, 'I can't get into your panties.'

She says, 'That's right, and that's the way it's going to be until your attitude changes.'

Did you hear about the new edition of Playboy for married men?

It has the same centrefold every month.

DATING VS MARRIAGE

When you are dating . . . Farting is never an issue.
When you are married . . . You make sure there's nothing flammable near your husband at all times.

When you are dating . . . He takes you out to have a good time.
When you are married . . . He brings home a six pack and says, 'What are you going to drink?'

When you are dating . . . He holds your hand in public.
When you are married . . . He flicks your ear in public.

When you are dating . . . A single bed for two isn't *that* bad.
When you are married . . . A king-size bed feels like an army cot.

When you are dating . . . You are turned on at the sight of him naked.
When you are married . . . You think to yourself, 'Was he *always* this hairy?'

When you are dating . . . You enjoy foreplay.
When you are married . . . You tell him, 'If we have sex, will you leave me alone?'

When you are dating . . . He hugs you when he walks by for no particular reason.
When you are married . . . He grabs your boobs any chance he gets.

When you are dating . . . You picture the two of you together, growing old together.
When you are married . . . You wonder who will die first.

When you are dating . . . Just looking at him makes you feel all mushy.
When you are married . . . When you look at him, you want to claw his eyes out.

When you are dating . . . He knows what the clothes hamper is.
When you are married . . . The floor will suffice as a dirty clothes storage area.

When you are dating . . . He understands if you aren't in the mood.
When you are married . . . He says, 'It's your job.'

When you are dating . . . He understands that you have male friends.
When you are married . . . He thinks they are all out to steal you away.

When you are dating . . . He likes to discuss things.
When you are married . . . He develops a blank stare.

When you are dating . . . He calls you by name.
When you are married . . . He calls you 'Hey' and refers to you when speaking to others as 'She'.

CULTURAL DIVERSITY

Cultural diversity is the politically correct term for taking the piss out of people from particular backgrounds. Hey, it might not be the right thing to do, but it's fun, isn't it?

A Japanese man walks into a currency exchange in America with ¥2000 and walks out with $72. The next week he walks in with ¥2000, but only gets $66. He asks the lady why he got less money this week than last week.

The lady says, 'Fluctuations.'

The man says, 'Fluck you clazy Amelicans too!'

An Italian man, a Frenchman and a Jewish man are talking about having sex with their wives.

The Italian says, 'Last night was absolutely fantastic. First, I smeared olive oil all over my wife's body. Then I rubbed it in. We slid against each other while we were making love and she moaned and screamed for forty minutes.'

'Wow,' says the Frenchman. 'That sounds good. But I can do better than that. Last night, I smeared *crème brûlée* all over my wife's body. While we were making love, I licked the *crème brûlée* off her and she moaned and screamed for over an hour.'

'That's very impressive,' says the Jewish man, 'but I can better that. Last night, I rubbed chicken liver all over my wife's body and kept rubbing it in while we made love. She yelled and screamed for six hours.'

'Six hours!' the other men exclaim. 'That's amazing. You must be an incredible lover.'

'Not at all,' says the Jewish man. 'After we had finished, I wiped my hands on our new curtains.'

An Englishman, a Frenchman, and Elle Macpherson are sitting together in a train travelling through Switzerland when the train enters a tunnel and the car goes completely dark. There's a kissing noise, and then the sound of a really large slap. When the train comes out of the tunnel, Elle Macpherson and the Englishman are sitting as if nothing has happened, and the Frenchman is holding his slapped face.

The Frenchman is thinking, 'That English chap must have kissed Elle Macpherson and she swung at him, missed, and slapped me.'

Elle Macpherson is thinking, 'That French guy must have tried to kiss me, accidentally kissed the Englishman, and got slapped for it.'

And the Englishman is thinking, 'This is great. The next time the train goes through a tunnel, I'll make another kissing noise and slap that French guy again!'

A Swiss guy, looking for directions, pulls up at a bus stop where two Englishmen are waiting.

'*Entschuldigung, koennen Sie Deutsch sprechen?*' he says.

The two Englishmen just stare at him.

'*Excusez-moi, parlez vous Français?*'

The two continue to stare.

'*Parlare Italiano?*'

No response, '*¿Hablan ustedes Espanol?*'

Still nothing. The Swiss guy drives off, extremely disgusted. The first Englishman turns to the second and says, 'Y'know, maybe we should learn a foreign language.'

'Why?' asks the other, 'That bloke knew four languages, and it didn't do him any good.'

Two Swedes, Sven and Ole, work together and are laid off together. They go to the unemployment office. Asked his occupation, Ole says, 'Panty stitcher. I sew the elastic onto cotton panties.'

The clerk looks up panty stitcher. Finding it classed as unskilled labour, she gives him $300 per week unemployment pay. Sven is then asked his occupation.

'Diesel fitter,' he replies.

Since diesel fitter is a skilled job, the clerk gives Sven $600 per week. When Ole finds out he is furious. He storms back to the office to find out why his friend and co-worker is collecting double his pay.

The clerk explains, 'Panty stitchers are unskilled and diesel fitters are skilled labourers.'

'What skill?' yells Ole. 'I sew the elastic on the panties, Sven pulls them down on his head and says, "Yah, diesel fitter."'

Three guys are on a trip to Saudi Arabia. One day, they stumble into a harem tent filled with over 100 beautiful women. They start getting friendly with all the women, when suddenly the sheik comes in.

'I am the master of all these women. No-one else can touch them except me. You three men must pay for what you have done today. You will be punished in a way corresponding to your profession.'

The sheik turns to the first man and asks him what he does for a living.

'I'm a cop,' says the first man.

'Then we will shoot your penis off,' says the sheik. He then turns to the second man and asks him what he does for a living.

'I'm a fireman,' says the second man.

'Then we will burn your penis off,' says the sheik.

Finally, he asks the last man, 'And you, what do you do for a living?'

The third man answers, with a sly grin, 'I'm a lollipop salesman!'

A n Englishman, a Frenchman and a Russian are viewing a painting of Adam and Eve frolicking in the Garden of Eden.

'Look at their reserve, their calm,' muses the Englishman. 'They must be English.'

'Nonsense,' the Frenchman disagrees. 'They're naked, and so beautiful. Clearly, they are French.'

'No clothes, no shelter,' the Russian points out, 'they have only an apple to eat, and they're being told this is paradise. They must be Russian.'

T he Indians ask their chief in autumn if the winter is going to be cold or not. Not really knowing an answer, the chief replies that the winter is going to be cold and that the members of the village should collect wood to prepare themselves.

Being a good leader, he then phones the National Weather Service and asks, 'Is this winter going to be cold?'

The man on the phone responds, 'This winter is going to be quite cold indeed.'

So the chief goes back to his people and tells them to collect even more wood.

A week later he calls the National Weather Service again and asks, 'Is it going to be a very cold winter?'

Yes,' the man replies, 'it's going to be a very cold winter.'

So the chief goes back to his people and orders them to find every scrap of wood they can.

Two weeks later he calls the National Weather Service again and asks, 'Are you sure that this winter is going to be very cold?'

'Absolutely,' the man replies, 'the Indians are collecting wood like crazy!'

An Englishman, an Irishman and a Scotsman have been working as jackaroos out west for many months, and are feeling the need of a woman. They therefore get together and acquire, by mail order from Canberra, an inflatable sex doll. They draw lots, and the Englishman gets the first shot. Half an hour or so later, he comes out of the spare room with a smile on his face.

'Bloody great is that! Better than the wife any day!'

Encouraged, the Scotsman goes in, and emerges after a few minutes with a grin. 'Yer nae bloody wrong, Jimmy. It was worth the cost o' a pint.'

The Irishman takes his turn, and emerges after only a short while with a puzzled and frustrated frown. 'Oi don't know what youse was raving on about. It's bloody useless! All oi did was give her a little love bite, and she lets out a bloody great fart and flies out the window.'

A Scottish man moves to America and attends his first baseball game. When the first player hits the ball everyone stands up around him yelling 'Run! Run!'

So the Scot stands up and yells, 'Run ya bastard, run!'

When the next man hits the ball the Scot stands up with the crowd and yells, 'Run ya bastard, run!'

The next man is at the plate. The pitcher throws four foul balls so the batter starts walking. The Scot, not knowing the rules, stands up and yells, 'Run ya bastard, run!'

Everyone around starts laughing so a kind man leans over and quietly says, 'He doesn't have to run, he's got four balls.'

In reply to this news the Scot stands up again and yells to the player, 'Walk with pride man!'

A cowboy is caught by some Indians and is about to be executed when they ask him if he has a last request. The cowboy says yes, walks over to his horse and whispers something in its ear. The horse takes off like a mad thing over the hills and returns after a short while with a beautiful, naked blonde on its back. The cowboy takes the blonde to a teepee and has sex with her. Then he comes back out and requests another talk with his horse. The Indians, amazed, agree. So the cowboy walks over to the horse and whispers in his ear again. The horse takes off and return with a beautiful, naked redhead. The cowboy takes her into another teepee and has sex with her. He comes out and once more asks to talk to his horse. The Indians once more agree. So he walks over to the horse and whispers something else into its ear. The horse takes off and returns with a beautiful, naked brunette on its back. The cowboy takes the brunette to a teepee and has sex with her. Then he comes back out and requests another talk with his horse. The Indians, totally amazed by this point, agree again.

So the cowboy walks over to his horse and says, 'I'm only going to do this once more, now read my lips, "posse".'

A Texan lands in Sydney, and is picked up by a taxi. After requesting a tour of the city, he starts into a tirade about the small-town airport and how in Texas they have larger runways on their ranches.

They are soon crossing the Sydney Harbour Bridge, and the Texan is further unimpressed, 'I have a duck pond bigger than that harbour, and an ornamental bridge to span it that makes this look like a toy.'

The Sydney-Newcastle Expressway also gets his scorn.

'Is this a road, or a track?' he shouts with contempt.

So when a kangaroo jumps out in front of the cab, causing

the sudden and severe application of the brakes, the driver can't help himself.

'Bloody grasshoppers!' he says.

Paddy is sitting at a bar when a very well-dressed gentleman comes and sits down next to him. After a while they start a conversation. Paddy asks the gentleman what he does for a living.

The gentleman replies, 'I'm Professor of Logic at Dublin University.'

'Oh,' says Paddy, 'What's this here logic?'

'Well,' says the Professor, 'logic is when things or events follow each other. To give you a demonstration, I've noticed that you have very rough hands. This tells me that you are a manual labourer.'

'Dat's roight,' says Paddy, 'Oi works digging trenches.'

'And to carry this one point further, being a manual worker, you would have a big garden shed,' says the Professor.

'Dat's roight,' says Paddy, 'Oi has a big garden shed.'

'Well there you are,' says the Professor. 'Logic . . . one thing follows another in a logical sequence. And to take it one step further, if you have a big garden shed, then you would have a big garden.'

'Yes, Oi have half an acre at home, vegies for all the family,' says Paddy.

'See . . . logical progression. One thing follows another. And, to take it one step further, if you have a big garden, you would have a big family,' says the Professor.

'Ah, yes, dere is nine in the family,' says Paddy.

'There, logical progression,' says the Professor. 'And, to take it even one step further, if you have a big family, you would be having sex regularly.'

'Certainly,' Paddy emphasises. 'Six nights a week and twice on Sunday.'

'Ah, and if you were having sex that regularly, you would not have to masturbate,' says the Professor.

'Oh, never, never, not for many, many years,' says Paddy.

'Well,' says the Professor. 'There you are, logical progression. One thing follows another.'

With that the Professor bids farewell to Paddy and leaves the pub.

Patrick, sitting at the bar, then sidles up to Paddy and asks, 'Who was that, Paddy?'

'Oh,' says Paddy, 'That was a very educated gentleman. He's a Professor of Logic at Dublin University.'

'Logic?' says Patrick, 'What's logic?'

'I'll tell you all about it,' says Paddy. 'Tell me, Patrick, have you got a big garden shed?'

'Why no,' says Patrick.

'Well,' says Paddy, 'I always thought you were a wanker!'

Nelson Mandela is sitting at home watching the telly when he hears a knock at the door. When he opens it, he is confronted by a little Chinese man, clutching a clipboard and yelling, 'You sign! You sign!'

Behind him is an enormous truck full of car exhausts. Nelson is standing there in complete amazement when the Chinese man starts to yell louder, 'You sign! You sign!'

Nelson says to him, 'Look mate, you've obviously got the wrong bloke. Now go away.'

And he shuts the door in his face. The next day he hears a knock at the door again. When he opens it, the Chinese man is back, with a huge truck full of brake pads.

He thrusts his clipboard under Nelson's nose, yelling, 'You sign! You sign!'

Nelson is getting a bit pissed off by now, so he shoves the Chinese man back, shouting, 'Look, you've got the wrong bloke I don't want them!'

He slams the door in his face again. The following day Nelson is resting, and late in the afternoon, he hears a knock on the door again.

Upon opening the door, the Chinese man thrusts the same clipboard under his nose, shouting, 'You sign! You sign!'

Behind him are two large trucks full of car windscreens. Nelson loses his temper completely, picks the little man up by his shirt front and yells at him, 'Look, I don't want these. Do you understand? You must have the wrong name. Who do you want to give these to?'

The Chinese man looks at him a bit puzzled, consults his clipboard, and says, 'You not Nissan Main-dealer?'

An American tourist gets the shock of his life when a Mexican with a six-shooter jumps out from behind a cactus.

'Take my money, my car but don't kill me,' says the tourist.

'I no kill you if you do what I say,' says the Mexican. 'Just unzip your pants and start masturbating.'

Although shocked the tourist does what he is told.

'Right, now do it again,' says the Mexican.

The Yank protests, but with the gun against his nose, he manages again.

'And yet again, Gringo, or I shoot you dead.'

With sweat running down his brow, the Yank manages a final effort and falls to the ground, exhausted.

'Good,' says the Mexican. 'Now, you give my sister a ride to the next village.'

A Scotsman and a Jew go to a restaurant. After a hearty meal, the waitress comes by with the inevitable bill. To the amazement of all, the Scot is heard to say, 'I'll pay it.'

And he actually does. The next morning's newspaper carries a news item headed: 'Jewish Ventriloquist Found Murdered in Alley.'

A man stumbles up to the only other patron in a bar and asks if he can buy him a drink.

'Why of course,' comes the reply.

The first man then asks, 'Where are you from?'

'I'm from Ireland,' replies the second man.

'You don't say, I'm from Ireland too! Let's have another round to Ireland.'

'Of course,' replies the second man.

Curious, the first man then asks, 'Where in Ireland are you from?'

'Dublin.'

'I can't believe it,' says the first man. 'I'm from Dublin too! Let's have another drink to Dublin.'

'Of course,' replies the second man.

Curiosity again strikes and the first man asks, 'What school did you go to?'

'Saint Mary's,' replies the second man. 'I graduated in '62.'

'This is unbelievable. I went to Saint Mary's and I graduated in '62, too.'

About this time, one of the regulars comes in and sits down at the bar.

'What's been going on?' he asks the bartender.

'Nothing much,' replies the bartender. 'The O'Malley twins are drunk again.'

A salesman is driving toward home in Northern Arizona when he sees a Navajo man hitchhiking. Because the trip has been long and quiet, he stops the car and the Navajo man climbs in. During their small talk, the Navajo man glances surreptitiously at a brown bag on the front seat between them.

'If you're wondering what's in the bag,' offers the salesman, 'it's a bottle of wine. I got it for my wife.'

The Navajo man is silent for awhile, nods several times and says, 'Good trade.'

An attractive woman from New York is driving through a remote part of Arizona when her car breaks down. An Indian on horseback comes along and offers her a ride to a nearby town. She climbs up behind him on the horse and they ride off. The ride is uneventful except that every few minutes the Indian lets out a *Whoo!* It's so loud that it echoes from the surrounding hills. When they arrive in town, he lets her off at the local service station, and yells one final *Yahoo!* Then he rides off.

'What did you do to get that Indian so excited?' asks the service station attendant.

'Nothing. I merely sat behind him on the horse, put my arms around his waist, and held onto his saddle horn so I wouldn't fall off.'

'Lady,' the attendant says, 'Indians ride bareback.'

Two cannibals capture an explorer. Both are hungry and they decide to share him. The first cannibal starts at the feet and the second starts on his head. After about five minutes of gnawing away, the first cannibal asks, 'How are you doing?'

The other cannibal replies, 'I'm having a ball!'

The first cannibal screams, 'Slow down. You're going too fast.'

A guy has spent five years travelling all around the world making a documentary on native dances. At the end of this time, he has every single native dance of every indigenous culture in the world on film. He winds up in Australia, in Alice

Springs, so he pops into a pub for a well-earned beer. He gets talking to one of the local Aborigines and tells him about his project.

The Aborigine asks the guy what he thought of the Butcher Dance.

The guy's a bit confused and says, 'Butcher Dance? What's that?'

'What? You haven't seen the Butcher Dance?'

'No, I've never heard of it.'

'Oh mate. You are crazy. How can you say you filmed every native dance if you haven't seen the Butcher Dance?'

'Umm. I got a corroboree on film just the other week. Is that what you mean?'

'No no, not corroboree. Butcher Dance is much more important than corroboree.'

'Oh, well how can I see this Butcher Dance then?'

'Mate, Butcher Dance is right out bush. It takes many days of travel to go see Butcher Dance.'

'Look, I've been everywhere from the forests of the Amazon, to deepest darkest Africa, to the frozen wastes of the Arctic filming these dances. Nothing will prevent me from recording this one last dance.'

'OK, mate. You drive north along Stuart Highway towards Darwin. After you drive 250km, you'll see a dirt track off to the left. Follow the dirt track for 150km until you see a huge, dead gum tree – biggest tree you ever seen. Here you gotta leave the car, because it's much too rough for driving. You strike out due west into the setting sun. You walk three days 'til you hit a creek. You follow this creek to northwest. After two days you reach a place where the creek flows out of rocky mountains. It's much too difficult to cross the mountains here though. You now head south for a half day 'til you see a pass through the mountains. The pass is very difficult and very dangerous. Takes two, maybe three days to get through the rocky pass. When you're through, head northwest for four days 'til you reach a big, huge rock – 15m high and shaped like a man's head. From the rock, walk due west for two days and you reach a village. Here you'll see the Butcher Dance.'

So the guy grabs his camera crew and equipment and heads out. After a couple of hours he finds the dirt track. The track is in a shocking state and he's forced to crawl along at a snail's pace and so he doesn't reach the tree until dusk and he's forced to set up camp for the night.

He sets out bright and early the following morning. His spirits are high and he's excited about the prospect of capturing on film this mysterious dance which he has never heard mentioned before. True to the directions he has been given, he reaches the creek after three days and follows it for another two until he reaches the rocky mountains. The merciless sun is starting to take its toll by this time and his spirits are starting to flag, but wearily he trudges on until he finds the pass through the hills – nothing will prevent him from completing his life's dream.

The mountains prove to be every bit as treacherous as his guide said and at times he almost despairs of getting his bulky equipment through. But after three and a half days of back breaking effort he finally forces his way clear and continues his long trek. When he reaches the huge rock, four days later, his water is running low and his feet are covered with blisters. Yet he steels himself and heads out on the last leg of his journey. Two days later he virtually staggers into the village where the Aborigines feed him and give him fresh water. He begins to feel like a new man. Once he's recovered enough, the guy goes before the village Elder and tells him that he has come to film their Butcher Dance.

'Oh mate. It's very bad you come today. Butcher Dance last night. You're too late. You missed the dance.'

'Well, when do you hold the next dance?'

'Not 'til next year.'

'Well, I've come all this way. Couldn't you just hold an extra dance for me, tonight?'

'No, no, no. Butcher Dance is very sacred. Only held once a year. If we hold more, the spirits get very angry. You want to see Butcher Dance you come back next year.'

The guy is devastated, but he has no other option but to head back to civilization and back home.

The following year, he heads back to Australia and, determined not to miss out again, sets out a week earlier than last time. He is quite willing to spend a week with the Aboriginal people before the dance is performed in order to ensure he is present to witness it. However, right from the start things go wrong.

Heavy rains that year have turned the dirt track to mud and the car gets bogged every few kilometres, finally forcing him to abandon his vehicle and slog through the mud on foot almost half the distance to the tree. He reaches the creek and the mountains without any further hitch, but halfway through the ascent of the mountain he is struck by a fierce storm which rages for several days, during which he is forced to cling forlornly to the mountainside until it subsides. It would be suicide to attempt to scale the treacherous paths in the face of such savage elements. Then, before he has travelled a kilometre out from the mountains, he sprains his ankle badly which slows down the rest of his journey to the rock enormously. Eventually, having lost all sense of how long he has been travelling, he staggers into the community at about 12 noon.

'The Butcher Dance!' gasps the guy. 'Please don't tell me I'm too late.'

The Elder recognises him and says, 'No, whitefella. Butcher Dance performed tonight. You arrived just in time.'

Relieved beyond measure, he spends the rest of the afternoon setting up his equipment - preparing to capture the night's ritual on celluloid. As dusk falls, the Aborigines start to cover their bodies in white paint and adorn themselves in birds' feathers and animal skins. Once darkness has settled fully over the land, the dancers form a circle around a huge roaring fire.

A deathly hush descends over the performers and spectators alike as a wizened old figure with elaborate swirling designs covering his entire body enters the circle and begins to chant. Some sort of witch doctor or medicine man, thinks the guy, and he whispers to the Elder, 'What's he doing?'

'Hush,' whispers the Elder. 'You're the first whitefella to ever see the most sacred of our rituals. You must remain silent. This holy man, he asks that the spirits of the Dreaming watch as we demonstrate our devotion to them through our dance and, if they like our dancing, will they be so gracious as to watch over us and protect us for another year.'

The chanting of the holy man reaches a stunning crescendo before he moves himself from the circle. From somewhere the rhythmic pounding of clapsticks reverberate out across the land and the dancers begin to sway to the stirring rhythm. The guy is becoming caught up in the fervour of the moment himself. This is it. He now realises beyond all doubt that his wait has not been in vain. He is about to witness the ultimate performance of rhythm and movement ever conceived by humanity.

The Elder strides to his position in the circle and, in a big booming voice, starts to sing, 'You butch yer right arm in. You butch yer right arm out. You butch yer right arm in and you shake it all about . . .'

♪

An Englishman, a Scotsman, and an Irishman walk into a pub. They each buy a pint of Guinness. Just as they are about to enjoy their creamy beverages, three flies land in each of their pints and become stuck in the thick heads.

The Englishman pushes his beer away from him in disgust. The Scot fishes the offending fly out of his beer and continues drinking it as if nothing has happened. The Irishman too, picks the fly out of his drink, holds it out over the beer and then starts yelling, 'Spit it out, spit it out, you bastard.'

An Indian boy goes to his mother one day with a puzzled look on his face.

'Say, mum, why is my bigger brother named Mighty Storm?'

She tells him, 'Because he was conceived during a mighty storm.'

Then he asks, 'Why is my sister named Cornflower?'

His mother replies, 'Well, your father and I were in a cornfield when we made her.'

'And why is my other sister called Moonchild?'

The mother says, 'We were watching the moon landing while she was conceived.' She pauses and asks her son, 'Tell me, Torn Rubber, why are you so curious?'

The National Transportation Safety Board recently divulged that they had funded a project with American car-makers over the past five years. In the covert project, car-makers installed black boxes in 4WD pickup trucks in an effort to determine, in fatal accidents, the circumstances in the last fifteen seconds before the crash.

They were surprised to find in forty-nine of the fifty states the last words of drivers in 61.2% of fatal crashes were, 'Oh, Shit!'

Only the state of Texas was different. There, 89.3% of the final words were, 'Hey Y'all, hold my beer and watch this!'

Three third-graders – a Jew, an Italian, and an African American – are on the playground at recess. The Jewish kid suggests that they play a new game.

'Let's see who has the largest dick,' he says.

'OK,' they all agree.

The Jewish kid pulls down his zipper and whips it out.

'That's nothing,' says the Italian kid.

He whips his out. His is a couple of inches longer. Not to be outdone, the African American whips his out. It is by far the biggest, dwarfing the other two in both length and width. The Jewish and Italian kids are stunned and amazed.

'Wow, that thing is huge,' they exclaim.

That night, eating dinner at home, the African American's mother asks him what he did at school today.

'Oh, we worked on a science project, had a maths test and read out loud from a new book . . . and during recess, my friends and I played "Let's see who has the largest dick."'

'What kind of game is that, honey?' asks his mother.

'Well, me, Sidney and Anthony each pulled out our penises, and I had the biggest! The other kids say it's because I'm black. Is that true, Mum?'

His mum replies, 'No, honey. It's because you're twenty-three.'

ONLY IN THE WESTERN WORLD . . .

. . . can a pizza get to your house faster than an ambulance.

. . . are there disabled parking places in front of a skating rink.

. . . do people order double cheeseburgers, large fries, and a diet coke.

. . . do banks leave both doors open and then chain the pens to the counters.

. . . do people leave cars worth thousands of dollars in the driveway and put useless junk in the garage.

. . . do people use answering machines to screen calls, and then use call waiting to make sure they don't miss a call from someone they didn't want to talk to in the first place.

. . . do people buy hot dogs in packs of ten and buns in packs of eight.

. . . do people use the word 'politics' to describe the process so well: *poli* in Latin meaning 'many' and *tics* meaning 'bloodsucking creatures'.

A black woman is filling out forms at the welfare office. Under 'Number of Children' she writes '10' and where it says 'List Names of Children' she writes 'Leroy'.

When she hands in the form, the woman behind the desk points out, 'Now here where it says "List Names of Children" you're supposed to write the names of each one of your children.'

'Dey all named Leroy,' says the black woman.

'That's very unusual. When you call them, how do they know which one you want?' asks the welfare worker.

'Oh, den I uses the last names.'

An Englishman is walking down the street when he sees an Irishman with a very long pole and a yardstick. He's standing the pole on its end and trying to reach the top of it with his yardstick. Seeing the Irishman's ignorance, the Englishman wrenches the pole out of his hand, lays it on the sidewalk, measures it with the yardstick, and says, 'There! Three yards long.'

The Irishman grabs the yardstick and shouts, 'You idiot Englishman. I don't care how long it is. I want to know how high it is.'

Two Polish guys rent a boat and go fishing in a lake. They are amazed at the number of fish that they catch that day, so one says to the other, 'We'll have to come back here tomorrow.'

The other asks, 'But how will we remember where this spot is?'

The first guy then takes a can of spray paint, paints an X on the bottom of the boat, and says, 'We'll just look for this X tomorrow.'

The other guy says, 'You idiot! How do you know we'll get the same boat?'

Mrs Cohen, Mrs Levy, and Mrs Lefkovitz are discussing their sons.

Mrs Cohen says, 'Now my Sheldon, what a man! A world-famous lawyer, he is, with big shot clients, a mansion in Beverly Hills, a summer home in Hawaii. He has a beautiful wife, and everything a man could want in the world.'

Mrs Levy says, 'That's nice. Lemmie tell you about my son Jonathan. He is a doctor, a world-famous researcher. He travels across the world on conferences, talks, lectures. He was nominated for a Nobel Prize in Medicine. What a man!'

Mrs Lefkowitz says, 'My Hershel, he's an engineer. Now, he makes maybe $35 000 a year, and he's not famous. But his penis is so long, you can line up ten pigeons in a row on it.'

The ladies sip their tea for a while.

Then, Mrs Cohen says, 'Actually, I got a confession to make. Sheldon's an up-and-coming lawyer in Los Angeles, but he doesn't have a mansion or a summer home. He's a bright young man with a good future.'

Mrs Levy says, 'Well, I got a confession too. Jonathan is a good doctor, and he got his share of scholarships, but a Nobel prize-winner, he isn't.'

They all look expectantly at Mrs Lefkowitz.

'Well, all right, I'll tell the truth too. The last bird gotta stand on one leg.'

WHITE ONE LINERS

What's white and fourteen inches long?
Absolutely nothing!

What do you call 500 000 white guys jumping out of a plane?
Snow.

What do you call a bunch of white guys in a circle?
A dope ring!

What do you call 300 white men chasing a black man?
The PGA tour.

Why do so many white people get lost skiing?
It's hard to find them in the snow.

What did the white guy do before his blood test?
He studied.

What's the difference between a white man and a snake?
One is an evil, cold-blooded, venomous, slimy creature of Satan, and the other is a snake.

What's the flattest surface to iron your jeans on?
A white girl's arse.

What did the black guy do with his M&M's?
Ate them.

What did the white guy try to do with his?
Put them in alphabetical order.

What did the white guy see when he looked at his family tree?
A straight line.

George goes on a vacation to Jerusalem with his family, including his mother-in-law. During their vacation in Jerusalem, George's mother-in-law dies. With the death certificate in his hand, George goes to the American Consulate Office to make arrangements to send the body back to the United States for a proper burial. The Consul tells George that it will be very, very expensive to send the body back to the United States for burial. It could cost him as much as $5000. The Consul tells him that, in most cases, the person responsible for the remains decides to bury the body in Jerusalem. This would only cost him $150.

George thinks for some time and answers, 'I don't care how much it will cost to send the body back, that's what I want to do.'

The Consul says, 'You must have loved your mother-in-law very much considering the difference in price.'

'No, it's not that,' says George. 'You see, I know of a case, many years ago, of a man who was buried here in Jerusalem. On the third day he arose from the dead. I just can't take that chance.'

During the Olympic men's figure skating, the Russian competitor skates around to some classical music in a slightly dull costume and performs some excellent leaps, but without any great artistic feel for the music.

The Judges' scores read: Britain 5.8; Russia 5.9; United States 5.5; Ireland 6.0.

Next comes the American competitor in a sparkling stars and stripes costume, skating to some rock 'n' roll music. He gets the crowd clapping, but is not technically as good as the Russian. He slightly misses landing a triple Salchow and loses the centre during a spin. But, artistically, it is a more satisfying performance.

The Judges' scores read: Britain 5.8; Russia 5.5; United States 5.9; Ireland 6.0.

Finally out comes the Irish competitor wearing a tatty old donkey jacket, with his skates tied over his wellies. He trips straight away and bangs his nose, which starts bleeding. He tries to get up, staggers a few paces then slips again. He spends his entire 'routine' getting up then falling over again. Finally he crawls off the ice a tattered and bleeding mess.

The Judges' scores read: Britain 0.0; Russia 0.0; United States 0.0; Ireland 6.0.

The other three judges turn to the Irish judge and demand in unison, 'How the hell can you give that mess 6.0?'

The Irish judge replies, 'You've gotta remember, it's damn slippery out there.'

An Irish guy wins a brand new sports car in a contest. He drives around for days waving at a bunch of bikers. One day the bikers stop him, draw a circle in the dirt and say, 'If you step out of that circle, we will kick your arse.'

They pick up hammers and start busting up his new car. They look back and the Irish man is smiling. They hit the car some more and he is laughing. They walk over to him and the leader pulls out a gun and shoots all the tyres. The Irish guy's face is turning red from laughing so hard.

The leader turns around and asks, 'Why are you laughing, we just busted up your car.'

The Irish guy says, 'I know, but I stepped out of the circle nine times.'

An Irish guy is walking down the street carrying a brown paper bag. He runs into one of his friends, who asks, 'What do you have in the bag?'

The man tells his friend that he has some fish in the bag.

His friend says, 'Well, I'll make you a bet. If I can guess how many fish you have in the bag, you have to give me one.'

The man says, 'I'll tell you what. If you can guess how many fish I have, you can have them both.'

An Irish guy is hired to paint the lines on the road. On the first day he paints 10km, and his employers are amazed. But, the second day he paints just five, and on the third day, he paints only 1km of the road. Disappointed, his boss asks what the problem is.

The Irish guy replies, 'Well Sir, every day I have to walk farther and farther to get back to the paint bucket.'

An Irish guy wants to buy a saw to cut down some trees in his backyard. He goes to a chainsaw shop and asks about various chainsaws.

The dealer tells him, 'Look, I have a lot of models, but why don't you save yourself a lot of time and aggravation and get the top-of-the-line model. This chainsaw will cut a hundred cords of wood for you in one day.'

So the Irish guy takes the chainsaw home and begins cutting down the trees. After cutting for several hours and only cutting two cords, he decides to quit. He thinks there is something wrong with the chainsaw.

'How can I cut for hours and only cut two cords?' the Irish guy asks himself. 'I will begin first thing in the morning and cut all day.'

So, the next morning the Irish guy gets up at 4 a.m. and cuts and cuts and cuts till nightfall, and he only manages to cut five cords. He is convinced that his saw is at fault.

'The dealer told me it would cut one hundred cords of wood in a day, no problem. I will take this saw back to the dealer,' he says to himself.

The very next day he brings the saw back to the dealer and explains the problem. The dealer, baffled by the Irish guy's claim, removes the chainsaw from the case.

The dealer says, 'Huh, it looks fine.'

Then the dealer starts the chainsaw with no problems.

The Irishman says, 'Hey. What's that noise?'

A twelve-year-old boy goes up to his Irish neighbour and says, 'I was looking in your bedroom window last night and I saw your wife giving you a blow job. Nyah, nyah, nyah.'

The Irish guy laughs and answers, 'The joke's on you, Johnny. Nyah, nyah, nyah – I wasn't even home last night.'

An Irish guy is travelling on a plane when the pilot makes an announcement.

'Folks, we just had one engine go out, but don't worry, this plane can fly just fine on two engines. All it means is that we'll be about an hour late.'

An hour later, the pilot gets on the intercom again.

'Folks, don't get alarmed, but a second engine just went out, but please don't worry. This plane is designed to fly safely on one engine. However, it's likely that we'll now be about two hours late.'

After that announcement, the Irish guy turns to the person sitting next to him and says, 'Well, I sure hope that third engine doesn't go out. We'll be up here all night.'

SIGNS COLLECTED BY A FLIGHT ATTENDANT ALONG HER TRAVELS

The sign in a Norwegian lounge reads:
LADIES ARE REQUESTED NOT TO HAVE CHILDREN IN THE BAR

Tacked on the door of a Moscow hotel room:
IF THIS IS YOUR FIRST VISIT TO THE U.S.S.R., YOU ARE WELCOME TO IT

An airline ticket office in Copenhagen reminds you:
WE TAKE YOUR BAGS AND SEND THEM IN ALL DIRECTIONS

In a certain African hotel you may choose between:
A ROOM WITH A VIEW OF THE SEA OR THE BACKSIDE OF THE COUNTRY

A sign on a clothing store in Brussels read:
COME INSIDE AND HAVE A FIT

A hotel notice in Madrid informs:
IF YOU WISH DISINFECTION ENACTED IN YOUR
PRESENCE, PLEASE CRY OUT FOR THE CHAMBERMAID

This notice was posted on a Rumanian hotel elevator:
THE LIFT IS BEING FIXED FOR THE NEXT DAYS. DURING
THAT TIME WE REGRET THAT YOU WILL BE UNBEARABLE.

In the window of a Swedish furrier the message reads:
FUR COATS MADE FOR LADIES FROM THEIR OWN SKIN

The room service in a Lisbon hotel tells you:
IF YOU WISH FOR BREAKFAST, LIFT THE TELEPHONE AND
ASK FOR ROOM SERVICE. THIS WILL BE ENOUGH FOR YOU TO
BRING YOUR FOOD UP

This sign was posted in a Scottish harbour:
FOR SALE BOAT SINGLE OWNER GREEN IN COLOUR

A sign at Budapest's zoo requests:
PLEASE DO NOT FEED THE ANIMALS. IF YOU HAVE ANY
SUITABLE FOOD GIVE IT TO THE GUARD ON DUTY.

A Polish hotel informs prospective visitors in a flyer:
AS FOR THE TROUT SERVED YOU AT THE HOTEL
MONOPOL, YOU WILL BE SINGING ITS PRAISE TO YOUR
GRANDCHILDREN AS YOU LIE ON YOUR DEATHBED

A Seville tailor makes clear how he will handle commissions:
ORDER NOW YOUR SUMMER SUIT, BECAUSE IS BIG RUSH WE WILL EXECUTE CUSTOMERS IN STRICT ROTATION

A dentist's doorway in Istanbul proclaims:
AMERICAN DENTIST, 2TH FLOOR. TEETH EXTRACTED BY LATEST METHODISTS.

The concierge in a Sorrento hotel lets guests know he's on the job:
CONTACT THE CONCIERGE IMMEDIATELY FOR INFORMATIONS. PLEASE DON'T WAIT LAST MINUTES THEN IT WILL BE TOO LATE TO ARRANGE ANY INCONVENIENCES.

Some German hospitals now display the sign:
NO CHILDREN ALLOWED IN THE MATERNITY WARDS

A Roman doctor proclaims himself a:
SPECIALIST IN WOMEN AND OTHER DISEASES

The sign at the concierge's desk in an Athens hotel reads:
IF YOU CONSIDER OUR HELP IMPOLITE, YOU SHOULD SEE THE MANAGER

A sign in a Kowloon hotel warns:
IS FORBIDDEN TO STEAL HOTEL TOWELS. PLEASE IF YOU ARE NOT PERSON TO DO SUCH IS PLEASE NOT TO READ NOTICE.

Visitors in a Czechoslovakian tourist agency are invited to:
TAKE ONE OF OUR HORSE-DRIVEN CITY TOURS – WE GUARANTEE NO MISCARRIAGES

A Rome laundry suggests:
LADIES, LEAVE YOUR CLOTHES HERE AND SPEND THE AFTERNOON HAVING A GOOD TIME

A sign posted in Germany's Black Forest reads:
IT IS STRICTLY FORBIDDEN ON OUR BLACK FOREST CAMPING SITE THAT PEOPLE OF DIFFERENT SEX, FOR INSTANCE, MEN AND WOMEN, LIVE TOGETHER IN ONE TENT UNLESS THEY ARE MARRIED WITH EACH OTHER FOR THAT PURPOSE

A London restaurant advertised for help this way:
WANTED: MAN TO WASH DISHES AND TWO WAITRESSES

A notice in a Vienna hotel urges:
IN CASE OF FIRE DO YOUR UTMOST TO ALARM THE HALL PORTER

On a Leipzig (Germany) elevator:
DO NOT ENTER THE LIFT BACKWARDS, AND ONLY WHEN LIT UP

On a Belgrade (Yugoslavia) elevator:
TO MOVE THE CABIN, PUSH BUTTON FOR WISHING

FLOOR. IF THE CABIN SHOULD ENTER MORE PERSONS, EACH
ONE SHOULD PRESS A NUMBER OF WISHING FLOOR.
DRIVING IS THEN GOING ALPHABETICALLY BY NATIONAL
ORDER.

On a Paris hotel elevator:
PLEASE LEAVE YOUR VALUES AT THE FRONT DESK

In an Athens Hotel:
VISITORS ARE EXPECTED TO COMPLAIN AT THE OFFICE
BETWEEN 9 A.M. AND 11 A.M. DAILY

In a Yugoslav Hotel:
THE FLATTENING OF UNDERWEAR WITH PLEASURE IS THE
JOB OF THE CHAMBERMAID

In a Japanese Hotel:
YOU ARE INVITED TO TAKE ADVANTAGE OF THE
CHAMBERMAID

In a Moscow Hotel:
YOU ARE WELCOME TO VISIT THE CEMETERY
WHERE FAMOUS RUSSIAN AND SOVIET COMPOSERS, ARTISTS
AND WRITERS ARE BURIED DAILY EXCEPT THURSDAY

On a Swiss menu:
OUR WINES LEAVE YOU NOTHING TO HOPE FOR

At an Austrian ski lodge:
NOT TO PERAMBULATE THE CORRIDORS IN THE HOURS
OF REPOSE IN THE BOOTS OF ASCENSION

On a Polish menu:
SALAD A FIRM'S OWN MAKE; LIMPID RED BEET SOUP
WITH CHEESY DUMPLINGS IN THE FORM OF A FINGER
ROASTED DUCK LET LOOSE; BEEF RASHERS BEATEN UP IN
THE COUNTRY PEOPLE'S FASHION.

In a Hong Kong tailor shop:
LADIES MAY HAVE A FIT UPSTAIRS

In a Bangkok dry cleaners:
DROP YOUR TROUSERS HERE FOR BEST RESULTS

In a Paris dress shop:
DRESSES FOR STREET WALKING

In a Soviet newspaper:
THERE WILL BE A MOSCOW EXHIBITION OF ART BY 16 000
SOVIET REPUBLIC PAINTERS AND SCULPTORS. THESE WERE
EXECUTED OVER THE PAST TWO YEARS.

At a Swiss mountain inn:
SPECIAL TODAY – NO ICE CREAM

At an Acapulco hotel:
THE MANAGER HAS PERSONALLY PASSED ALL THE WATER SERVED HERE

In a Tokyo shop:
OUR NYLONS COST MORE THAN COMMON, BUT YOU'LL FIND THEY ARE BEST IN THE LONG RUN

In a Japanese hotel:
COOLES AND HEATES: IF YOU WANT JUST CONDITION OF WARM IN YOUR ROOM, PLEASE CONTROL YOURSELF

At a Tokyo car rental firm:
WHEN PASSENGER OF FOOT HAVE IN SIGHT, TOOTLE THE HORN. TRUMPET HIM MELODIOUSLY AT FIRST, BUT IF HE STILL OBSTACLES YOUR PASSAGE THEN TOOTLE HIM WITH VIGOUR.

In a Majorcan shop:
ENGLISH WELL TALKING. HERE SPEECHING AMERICAN.

A PLANK SHORT

*This is a section about all those people who are a
kangaroo loose in the top paddock, two rungs short of a ladder,
one brick shy of a load, a few feathers short of
a whole duck . . . You get the picture!*

In a small community in the deep south of America, Ephraim
Chuckbucket marries Ellie-May Wilson. On his wedding night,
Ephraim rushes home to his parents' shack, and bangs furiously
on the door. Pa Chuckbucket comes out in his vest and long
johns, and is amazed to see his son standing there on the
doorstep on his wedding night.

'Why bust ma breeches, boy – what y'all doin' down home on
this night of all nights?'

'Pa, she's a virgin.'

'Well I'll be goldarned! You done right, son. You just come on
in here. If she ain't good enough fur her own family, she sure as
hell ain't good enough fur ours.'

Two hillbilly kids, Buckwheat and Darla are in school, and the
teacher asks Darla, 'How do you spell "dumb"?'

Darla says, 'd-u-m-b, dumb.'

The teacher says, 'Very good, now use it in a sentence.'

She says, 'Buckwheat is dumb.'

'Now spell "stupid".'

Darla says, 's-t-u-p-i-d, stupid.'

The teacher says, 'Very good, now use it in a sentence.'

Darla says, 'Buckwheat is stupid.'

Then the teacher calls on Buckwheat and says, 'Buckwheat, spell "dictate".'

Buckwheat stands and says, 'd-i-c-t-a-t-e, dictate.'

The teacher says, 'Very good, now use it in a sentence.'

'I may be dumb, and I may be stupid, but Darla says my dictate good!'

Two college basketball players are taking an important final exam. If they fail, they will be on academic probation and they won't be allowed to play in the big game next week. The exam is fill-in-the-blank.

The last question reads, 'Old MacDonald had a _____'

Bubba is stumped. He has no idea what to answer. But he knows he needs to get this one right to be sure he passes.

Making sure the examiner isn't watching, he taps Tiny on the shoulder.

'Pssst. Tiny. What's the answer to the last question?'

Tiny laughs. He looks around to make sure the examiner hasn't noticed, then he turns to Bubba.

'Bubba, you're so stupid. Everyone knows Old MacDonald had a farm.'

'Oh yeah,' says Bubba. 'I remember now.'

He picks up his No. 2 pencil and starts to write the answer in the blank. He stops. Tapping Tiny's shoulder again, he whispers, 'Tiny, how do you spell farm?'

'You are really dumb, Bubba. That's so easy. Farm is spelled e-i-e-i-o.'

Two guys of limited intelligence are on a ship that sinks in the middle of the ocean. They manage to inflate a rubber life-raft and grab a box of provisions before their ship slips below the surface. After floating under blazing heat for six days they run out of food and water. On the tenth day, bleary eyed and half dead from heat, thirst and starvation, they spot a small object floating toward them in the water. As it draws near, they can see that it is an oil lamp. They grab the lamp and rub it. *Woosh!*

Out pops a tired old genie who says, 'OK. So you freed me from this stupid lamp, yadda, yadda, yadda. But hey, I've been doing this three wishes stuff for a long time now and quite frankly, I'm burned out. You guys get only one wish and then I'm outta here. Make it a good one.'

The first guy, without hesitation or thought blurts out, 'Give us all the beer we can drink for the rest of our lives.'

'Fine,' says the genie, and he instantly turns the entire ocean into beer.

'Great move Einstein!' says the second guy, slapping the first guy in the head. 'Now we're gonna have to piss in the *boat.*'

Three guys are trying to sneak into the Olympic village to scoop souvenirs and autographs. The first says, 'Let's watch the registration table to see if there's a crack in the security system that we can use to scam our way in.'

Immediately, a burly athlete walks up to the table and states, 'Angus MacPherson. Scotland. Shot-put.' He opens his gym bag to display a shot-put to the registration attendant.

The attendant says, 'Very good, Mr MacPherson. Here is your packet of registration materials, complete with hotel keys, passes to all Olympic events, meal tickets, and other information.'

The first guy gets inspired and grabs a small tree sapling, strips off the limbs and roots, walks up to the registration table and states, 'Chuck Wagon. Canada. Javelin.'

The attendant says, 'Very good, Mr Wagon. Here is your packet of registration materials, hotel keys, passes, meal tickets, and so forth. Good luck!'

The second guy grabs a small manhole cover, walks up to the registration table and states, 'Dusty Rhodes. Australia. Discus.'

The attendant says, 'Terrific, Mr Rhodes. Here is your packet of registration materials, hotel keys, a full set of passes, and meal tickets. Enjoy yourself.'

They scamper in, but suddenly realise the third guy is missing. They groan, because he's a bit of a simpleton. They forgot to make sure he doesn't do something stupid and blow their cover stories.

Just then he walks proudly up to the table with a roll of barbed wire under his arm and states, 'Foster Bean. Hardwick, Vermont. Fencing.'

Emily Sue passes away and Billy-Bob calls the emergency number. The operator tells Billy-Bob that she will send someone out right away.

'Where do you live?' she asks.

Billy-Bob replies, 'At the end of Eucalyptus Drive.'

The operator asks, 'Can you spell that for me?'

There is a long pause and finally Billy-Bob says, 'How 'bout if I drag her over to Oak Street and you pick her up there?'

BUSINESS IS BUSINESS

*Given that so many jokes are told around the water
cooler in the workplace, it's only right that we feature
a section with jokes about those very people who spend their
valuable working time telling them.*

A man is in a VIP airport lounge en route to Seattle. He is meeting with a very important client who is also flying to Seattle but she is running a bit late. While waiting, he notices Bill Gates sitting in a chair enjoying a cognac. Being a forward type of guy, the man approaches Bill Gates and introduces himself. He explains to Gates that he is conducting some very important business and that he would really appreciate it if Gates could throw a quick 'Hello Paul' at the man while he is with his client. Gates agrees. Ten minutes later, while the man is conversing with his client, he feels a tap on his shoulder. It is Gates. The man turns around and looks up at him.

Bill Gates says, 'Hi Paul, what's happening?'

The man replies, 'Piss off, Bill, I'm in a meeting.'

MARKETING 101

You see a gorgeous girl at a party. You go up to her and say, 'I'm fantastic in bed.'

That's direct marketing.

You're at a party with a bunch of friends and see a gorgeous girl. One of your friends goes up to her, points at you, and says, 'He's fantastic in bed.'

That's advertising.

You're at a party and see a gorgeous girl. You get up and straighten your tie, walk up to her and pour her a drink. You open the door for her, pick up her bag after she drops it, offer her a ride, and then say, 'By the way, I'm fantastic in bed.'

That's public relations.

You're at a party and see a gorgeous girl. She walks up to you and says, 'I hear you're fantastic in bed.'

That's brand recognition.

Three businessmen, all chairmen of multinational companies, are taking a morning stroll on the beach before they give a presentation at a major convention. As they walk, they come across a fisherman lazing on the warm sand between two large fishes. They stop to chat with him.

'What are you doing on the beach?' the first businessman asks.

'I'm waiting for customers to come to the beach later in the day so I can sell my fish. If I sell both fish, I will make $20.'

'Why don't you go out and catch more fish before the customers arrive?' asks the second businessman.

'What would I do with more fish?'

'You would get more money if you sold more fish,' says the businessman.

The fisherman asks, 'What would I do with more money?'

The third businessman explains, 'You could buy a small boat, go out to sea and catch more fish.'

'What would I do with even more fish?'

'You could eventually buy a trawler and get other people to catch the fish,' says the third businessman. 'You could then become wealthy on the back of other people, relax on the beach and enjoy the sun and the sand.'

'Exactly,' says the fisherman, lying on the beach.

A small business owner has two employees, Jack and Jill. Business is bad and the business owner has to lay one of them off but is having a hard time deciding which one to let go. He decides that the first one to leave for lunch is the one that he'll lay off.

But both of them stay and eat at their desks.

Then he decides that the first one to leave work at the end of the day will be the one he fires. They both get up and leave at the same time.

He has to let one of them go. Which one? He decides on Jill.

The owner walks out to Jill's car as she is about to get in and says, 'Jill, I am trying to decide whether to lay you or Jack off. What do you think?'

Jill says, 'You'd better just jack off. I'm already late for an appointment.'

S mith goes to see his supervisor in the front office. 'Boss,' he says, 'we're doing some heavy house-cleaning at home tomorrow and my wife needs me to help with the attic and the garage, moving and hauling stuff.'

'We're short-handed, Smith' the boss replies. 'I can't give you the day off.'

'Thanks, boss,' says Smith 'I knew I could count on you!'

T hree contractors are visiting a tourist park – one is from New York, another from Texas, and the third from Florida.

At the end of the tour, the guard asks them what they do for a living. When they all reply that they are contractors, the guard says, 'Hey, we need one of the rear fences redone. Why don't you guys take a look at it and give me a bid?'

So, to the back fence they all go to check it out. First to step up is the Florida contractor. He takes out his tape measure and pencil, does some measuring and says, 'Well I reckon the job will run to about $900. That's $400 for materials, $400 for my crew, and $100 profit for me.'

Next is the Texas contractor. He also takes out his tape measure and pencil, does some quick calculating and says, 'Looks like I can do this job for $700. That's $300 for materials, $300 for my crew, and $100 profit for me.'

Without so much as moving, the New York contractor says, '$2700.'

The guard, incredulous, looks at him and says, 'You didn't even measure like the other guys! How did you come up with such a high figure?'

'Easy,' says the New Yorker. 'That's $1000 for me, $1000 for you and we hire the guy from Texas.'

Four people are in the final stages of interviewing for a prestigious job. The managing director decides to call them in, one by one, and ask them a question. The first applicant is called in.

The managing director poses the question, 'What is the fastest thing in the world?'

The applicant thinks for a moment, then replies, 'That would have to be a thought.'

'Why do you say that?' asks the managing director.

'Well, a thought takes no time at all . . . it is in your mind in an instant, then gone again.'

'Ahh, very good. Thank you,' replies the director.

Next the same question is posed to the second applicant. 'What is the fastest thing in the world?'

She pauses and replies, 'That would have to be a blink.'

'Why?' asks the managing director.

'Because you don't even think about a blink, it's just a reflex. You do it in an instant.'

The managing director thanks her and calls in the next person. The third applicant is asked what the fastest thing in the world is, and after hesitating for a brief moment, he replies, 'I would have to say electricity.'

'Why?'

'Because a man can flip a switch, and immediately, 10km away a light will go on.'

'I see, very good,' replies the managing director.

Then, the final applicant is called in. He, too, is asked, 'What is the fastest thing in the world?'

'That's easy,' he replies. 'That would have to be diarrhoea!'

Rather stunned, the managing director asks, 'Why do you say that?'

'Well, last night after dinner, I was lying in my bed and I got the worst stomach cramps, and before I could think, blink or turn on the lights . . .'

A marketing manager gets married to a woman who has previously been married eight times. On his wedding night, his wife informs him that she is still a virgin.

She explains, 'My first husband was a sales representative who spent our entire marriage telling me, in grandiose terms, "It's gonna be great!"

My second husband was from software services; he was never quite sure how it was supposed to function, but he said he would send me the documentation.

My third husband was an accountant. His comment was that he knew how, but he just wasn't sure whether or not it was his job.

My fourth husband was a teacher, and he simply said, "Those who can, do; those who can't, teach."

My fifth husband was an engineer. He told me that he understood the basic process but needed three years to research, implement, and design a new state-of-the-art method.

My sixth husband was a psychiatrist and all he ever wanted to do was talk about it.

My seventh husband was a help-desk coordinator and he kept teaching me how to do it myself.

My eighth husband was in technical support, and he kept saying, "Don't worry, it'll be up any minute now."'

The wife says sweetly to her new husband, 'Now I am married to you, a man of marketing.'

The husband looks at his wife and simply says, 'I know I have the product, I'm just not sure how to position it.'

GRADUATES

A graduate with a science degree asks, 'Why does it work?'

A graduate with an engineering degree asks, 'How does it work?'

A graduate with an accounting degree asks, 'How much will it cost?'

A graduate with a law degree asks, 'Who gave it permission to work?'

A graduate with an arts degree asks, 'Would you like fries with that?'

OLD HANDS

Old accountants never die, they just lose their balance.

Old actuaries never die, they just get broken down by age and sex.

Old chemists never die, they just fail to react.

Old chemists never die, they just reach equilibrium.

Old cosmologists never die, they just go to another world.

Old doctors never die, they just loose their patience.

Old dynamicists never die, they just lose their attraction.

Old electricians never die, they just lose contact.

Old geologists never die, they just recrystallise.

Old laser physicists never die, they just become incoherent.

Old lawyers never die, they just threaten their doctor with malpractice.

Old lawyers never die, they just lose their appeal.

Old mathematicians never die, they just tend to zero.

Old mathematicians never die, they just lose some of their functions.

Old professors never die, they just lose their faculties.

Old programmers never die, they just gosub without return.

Old programmers never die, they just branch to a new address.

Old publishers never die, they just go out of print.

Old statisticians never die, they just become non-significant.

Old thermodynamicists never die, they just achieve their state of maximum entropy.

Old soldiers never die. Young ones do.

PROFESSIONALS

An accountant is someone who knows the cost of everything and the value of nothing.

An actuary is someone who brings a fake bomb on a plane, because that decreases the chances that there will be another bomb on the plane.

An archaeologist is a person whose career lies in ruins.

An architect is someone who makes beautiful models, but unaffordable realities.

An auditor is someone who arrives after the battle and bayonets all the wounded.

A banker is someone who lends you his umbrella when the sun is shining and wants it back the minute it begins to rain.

A chemical engineer is someone who is doing for a profit what an organic chemist only does for fun.

A consultant is someone who takes the watch off your wrist and tells you the time.

A diplomat is someone who can tell you to go to hell in such a way that you will look forward to the trip.

An economist is an expert who will know tomorrow why the things he predicted yesterday didn't happen today.

An editor is a person employed on a newspaper whose business it is to separate the wheat from the chaff, and to see that the chaff is printed.

A journalist is someone who spends 50% of the time not saying what he knows and 50% of the time talking about things he doesn't know.

A lawyer is a person who writes a 10 000 word document and calls it a brief.

A mathematician is a blind man in a dark room looking for a black cat that isn't there.

A modern artist is someone who throws paint on canvas, wipes it off with a cloth and sells the cloth.

A philosopher is a person who doesn't have a job but at least understands why.

A lecturer is someone who talks in someone else's sleep.

A programmer is someone who solves a problem you didn't know you had in a way you don't understand.

A psychologist is someone who charges a lot of money to ask you questions that your wife asks for free.

A schoolteacher is a disillusioned woman who used to like children.

A sociologist is someone who, when a beautiful woman enters the room, is watching everybody else.

A statistician is someone who is good with numbers but lacks the personality to be an accountant.

A topologist is a man who doesn't know the difference between a coffee cup and a doughnut.

ONE PARACHUTE

You are one of three people on a malfunctioning aeroplane with only one parachute. How would you react?

Pessimist:	you refuse the parachute because you might die on the jump anyway.
Optimist:	you refuse the parachute because people have survived crashes just like this before.
Procrastinator:	you play a game of Monopoly for the parachute.
Bureaucrat:	you order a feasibility study on parachute use in multi-engine aircraft under code red conditions.
Computer scientist:	you design a machine capable of operating a parachute as well as a human being could.
Mathematician:	you refuse to accept the parachute without proof that it will work in all cases.
Engineer:	you make another parachute out of aisle curtains and dental floss.

Psychoanalyst:	you ask the other people what the shape of a parachute reminds them of.
Doctor:	you say you need to run more tests, then take the parachute in order to make your next appointment.
Lawyer:	you charge one parachute for helping sue the airline.
Judge:	after reminding the others of their constitutional right to have a parachute, you take it and jump out.
Economist:	your only rational and moral choice is to take the parachute, as the free market will take care of the other people.
Statistician:	you plot a demand curve by asking the others, at regular intervals, how much they would pay for a parachute.
Tax auditor:	you confiscate the parachute along with the other people's luggage, wallets, and gold fillings.
Manager:	as you jump out with the parachute, you tell the others to work hard and not expect handouts.
Consultant:	you tell the others not to worry, since it won't take you long to learn how to fix a plane.
Salesperson:	you sell the others the parachute at top retail rates and get the names of their friends and relatives who might like one too.
Advertiser:	you strip-tease while singing that what the other people need is a neon parachute with a computer altimeter for only $39.99.
Philosopher:	you ask how the others know the parachute actually exists.
Teacher:	you give the others the parachute and ask them to send you a report on how well it worked.
English major:	you explicate simile and metaphor in the parachute instructions.

Language major:	you read the parachute instructions in all four languages.
Dramatist:	you tie the others down so they can watch you develop the character of a person stuck on a falling plane without a parachute.
Modern Painter:	you hang the parachute on the wall and sign it.
Auto mechanic:	as long as you are looking at the plane engine, it works fine.

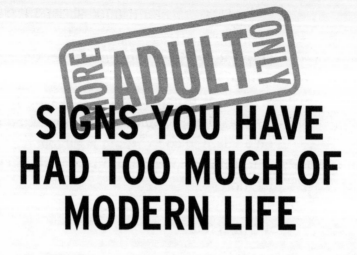

SIGNS YOU HAVE HAD TOO MUCH OF MODERN LIFE

- Cleaning up the dining area means getting the fast food bags out of the back seat of your car.

- Every commercial on television has a website address at the bottom of the screen.

- You buy a computer and a week later it is out of date . . . and now sells for half the price you paid.

- You exchange emails several times a day with a stranger from South Africa, but you haven't spoken to your next door neighbour yet this year.

- You consider second-day air delivery painfully slow.

- You have a list of fifteen phone numbers to reach your family of three.

- You haven't played solitaire with a real deck of cards in years.

- You hear most of your jokes via email instead of in person.

- You try to enter your password on the microwave.

- Your daughter just bought a CD of all the records your uni flatmates used to play that you most despised.

- Your idea of being organised is multicoloured post-it notes.

- Your reason for not staying in touch with family is that they do not have email addresses.

BELIEVE IT OR NOT

This is the transcript of a radio conversation between a US naval ship and Canadian authorities off the coast of Newfoundland. You decide whether it is real or made up.

Canadians: Please divert your course fifteen degrees to the south to avoid a collision.

Americans: Recommend you divert your course fifteen degrees to the north to avoid a collision.

Canadians: Negative. You will have to divert your course fifteen degrees south to avoid a collision.

Americans: This is the Captain of a US Navy ship. I say again, divert *your* course.

Canadians: No. I say again, you divert *your* course.

Americans: This is the aircraft carrier *U.S.S. Lincoln*, the second-largest ship in the United States' Atlantic fleet. We are accompanied by three destroyers, three cruisers and numerous support vessels. I *demand* that you change your course fifteen degrees north. I say again, that's one five degrees north, or counter-measures will be undertaken to ensure the safety of this ship!

Canadians: This is a lighthouse. You decide.

The following question was supposedly given on a chemistry exam, 'Is hell exothermic (gives off heat) or endothermic (absorbs heat)? Support your answer with proof.'

Most of the students wrote proofs of their beliefs using Boyle's Law (gas cools off when it expands and heats up when it is compressed) or some variant.

One student, however, wrote the following:

'First, we need to know how the mass of hell is changing in time. So, we need to know the rate that souls are moving into hell and the rate they are leaving. I think that we can safely assume that once a soul gets to hell, it will not leave. Therefore, no souls are leaving.

'As for how many souls are entering hell, let's look at the different religions that exist in the world today. Some of these religions state that if you are not a member of their religion, you will go to hell. Since there are more than one of these religions and since people do not belong to more than one religion, we can project that all people and all souls go to hell.

'With birth and death rates as they are, we can expect the number of souls in hell to increase exponentially. Now, we look at the rate of change of the volume in hell because Boyle's Law states that in order for temperature and the pressure in hell to stay the same, the volume of hell has to expand as souls are added. This gives two possibilities:

1. If hell is expanding at a slower rate than the rate at which souls enter hell, then the temperature and pressure in hell will increase until all hell breaks loose.

2. Of course, if hell is expanding at a rate faster than the increase of souls in hell, then the temperature and pressure will drop until hell freezes over.

'So which is it?

'If we accept the postulate given to me by Ms Therese Banyan during my Freshman year, that "it will be a cold night in hell before I sleep with you", and take into account the fact that I still have not succeeded in that area, then (2) cannot be true, and so hell is exothermic.'

This student got the only A.

Journalist Barbara Walters filed a report on gender roles in Kuwait a few years prior to the first Gulf War. She noted then that, in traditional Islamic fashion, women customarily walked about a few paces behind their husbands. Recently, Walters returned to Kuwait and observed that the *men* now walked a few paces behind their wives. She approached one of the Kuwaiti women for an explanation.

'This is marvellous,' Barbara said. 'What enabled women here to achieve this reversal of roles?'

The Kuwaiti woman replied, 'Land mines.'

This is supposedly true. Do you believe it?
On 20 July 1969, as commander of the Apollo 11 Lunar Module, Neil Armstrong was the first person to set foot on the moon. His first words after stepping on the moon, 'That's one small step for a man, one giant leap for mankind,' were televised to earth and heard by millions.

But just before he re-entered the lander, he made the enigmatic remark, 'Good luck, Mr Gorsky.'

Many people at NASA thought it was a casual remark concerning some rival Soviet Cosmonaut. However, upon checking, there was no Gorsky in either the Russian or American space programs. Over the years many people questioned Armstrong as to what the 'Good luck Mr Gorsky' statement meant, but Armstrong always just smiled. On 5 July 1995, in Tampa Bay, Florida, while answering questions following a speech, a reporter brought up the twenty-six-year-old question to Armstrong. This time he finally responded. Mr Gorsky had died and so Neil Armstrong felt he could answer the question. In 1938 when he was a kid in a small Midwest town, he was playing baseball with a friend in the backyard. His friend hit a fly ball, which landed in his neighbour's yard by the bedroom windows. His neighbours were Mr and Mrs Gorsky. As he leaned down to pick up the ball, young Armstrong heard Mrs Gorsky shouting at Mr Gorsky.

'A blow job! You want a blow job? You'll get a blow job when the kid next door walks on the moon!'

HISTORY AS SEEN BY YOUNG PEOPLE

This is a compilation of answers by American history students.

1. Ancient Egypt was inhabited by mummies and they all wrote in hydraulics. They lived in the Sarah Dessert and travelled by Camelot. The climate of the Sarah is such that the inhabitants have to live elsewhere.

2. The bible is full of interesting caricatures. In the first book of the bible, Guinessis, Adam and Eve were created from an apple tree. One of their children, Cain, asked, 'Am I my brother's son?'

3. Moses led the Hebrew slaves to the Red Sea, where they made unleavened bread which is bread made without any ingredients. Moses went up on Mount Cyanide to get the Ten Commandments. He died before he ever reached Canada.

4. Solomon had three hundred wives and seven hundred porcupines.

5. The Greeks were a highly sculptured people, and without them we wouldn't have history. The Greeks also had myths. A myth is a female moth.

6. Actually, Homer was not written by Homer but by another man of that name.

7. Socrates was a famous Greek teacher who went around giving people advice. They killed him. Socrates died from an overdose of wedlock. After his death, his career suffered a dramatic decline.

8. In the Olympic Games, Greeks ran races, jumped, hurled the biscuits, and threw the Java.

9. Eventually, the Romans conquered the Greeks. History calls people Romans because they never stayed in one place for very long.

10. Julius Caesar extinguished himself on the battlefields of Gaul. The Ides of March murdered him because they thought he was going to be made king. Dying, he gasped out, 'Tee hee, Brutus.'

11. Nero was a cruel tyranny who would torture his subjects by playing the fiddle to them.

12. Joan of Arc was burnt to a steak and was canonised by Bernard Shaw. Finally Magna Carta provided that no man should be hanged twice for the same offence.

13. In midevil times most people were alliterate. The greatest writer of the futile ages was Chaucer, who wrote many poems and verses and also wrote literature.

14. Another story was William Tell, who shot an arrow through an apple while standing on his son's head.

15. Queen Elizabeth was the Virgin Queen. As a queen she was a success. When she exposed herself before her troops they all shouted 'hurrah'.

16. It was an age of great inventions and discoveries. Gutenberg invented removable type and the bible. Another important invention was the circulation of blood. Sir Walter Raleigh is a historical figure because he invented cigarettes and started smoking. And Sir Francis Drake circumcised the world with a 100-foot clipper.

17. The greatest writer of the Renaissance was William Shakespeare. He was born in the year 1564, supposedly on his birthday. He never made much money and is famous only because of his plays. He wrote tragedies, comedies, and hysterectomies, all in Islamic pentameter. Romeo and Juliet are an example of a heroic couplet.

18. Writing at the same time as Shakespeare was Miguel Cervantes. He wrote Donkey Hote. The next great author was John Milton. Milton wrote Paradise Lost. Then his wife died and he wrote Paradise Regained.

19. During the Renaissance America began. Christopher Columbus was a great navigator who discovered America while cursing about the Atlantic. His ships were called the Nina, the Pinta, and the Santa Fe.

20. The Pilgrims crossed the ocean, and this was called Pilgrim's Progress. The winter of 1620 was a hard one for the settlers. Many people died and many babies were born. Captain John Smith was responsible for all this.

21. One of the causes of the Revolutionary War was the English put tacks in their tea. Also, the colonists would send their parcels through the post without stamps. Finally the colonists won the War and no longer had to pay for taxis. Delegates from the original thirteen states formed the Contented Congress. Thomas Jefferson, a Virgin, and Benjamin Franklin were two singers of the Declaration of Independence. Franklin discovered electricity by rubbing two cats backwards and declared, 'A horse divided against itself cannot stand.' Franklin died in 1790 and is still dead.

22. The Constitution of the United States was adopted to secure domestic hostility. Under the constitution the people enjoyed the right to keep bare arms.

23. Abraham Lincoln became America's greatest Precedent. Lincoln's mother died in infancy, and he was born in a log cabin which he built with his own hands. Abraham Lincoln freed the slaves by signing the Emasculation Proclamation. On the night of 14 April 1865, Lincoln went to the theatre and got shot in his seat by one of the actors in a moving picture show. The believed assassinator was John Wilkes Booth, a supposedly insane actor. This ruined Booth's career.

24. Meanwhile in Europe, the enlightenment was a reasonable time. Voltaire invented electricity and also wrote a book called Candy.

25. Gravity was invented by Issac Walton. It is chiefly noticeable in the autumn when the apples are falling off the trees.

26. Johann Bach wrote a great many musical compositions and had a large number of children. In between he practised on

an old spinster which he kept up in his attic. Bach died from 1750 to the present. Bach was the most famous composer in the world and so was Handel. Handel was half German half Italian and half English. He was very large.

27. Beethoven wrote music even though he was deaf. He was so deaf he wrote loud music. He took long walks in the forest even when everyone was calling for him. Beethoven expired in 1827 and later died for this.

28. The French Revolution was accomplished before it happened and catapulted into Napoleon. Napoleon wanted an heir to inherit his power, but since Josephine was a baroness, she couldn't have any children.

29. The sun never set on the British Empire because the British Empire's in the East and the sun sets in the West.

30. Queen Victoria was the longest queen. She sat on a thorn for sixty-three years. She was a moral woman who practised virtue. Her death was the final event which ended her reign.

31. The nineteenth century was a time of a great many thought inventions. People stopped reproducing by hand and started reproducing by machine. The invention of the steamboat caused a network of rivers to spring up. Cyrus McCormick invented the McCormick raper, which did the work of a hundred men.

32. Louis Pasteur discovered a cure for rabbis. Charles Darwin was a naturalist who wrote the Organ of the Species. Madman Curie discovered radio. And Karl Marx became one of the Marx brothers.

33. The First World War, caused by the assignation of the Arch-
Duck by an anarchist, ushered in a new error in the anals of
human history.

Excerpt from an article about a bank robbery which
supposedly appeared in the *Dublin Times* in
May 1999:

'Once inside the bank shortly after midnight, their efforts at
disabling the internal security system got underway immediately.
The robbers, who expected to find one or two large safes filled
with cash and valuables, were surprised to see hundreds of
smaller safes scattered throughout the bank. The robbers
cracked the first safe's combination, and inside they found only
a bowl of vanilla pudding. As recorded on the bank's audio-tape
system, one said, 'At least we'll get a bit to eat.'

The robbers opened up a second safe, and it also contained
nothing but vanilla pudding. The process continued until all the
safes were opened. They found not one pound sterling, a
diamond, or an ounce of gold. Instead, all the safes contained
covered bowls of pudding. Disappointed, the robbers made a
quiet exit, each leaving with nothing more than a queasy,
uncomfortably full stomach.

The newspaper headline read:

'Ireland's Largest Sperm Bank Robbed Early This Morning'

EMPLOYEE OF THE MONTH

These individual quotes were reportedly taken from actual
employee performance evaluations in a large US Corporation.

• 'Since my last report, this employee has reached rock bottom
. . . and has started to dig.'

- 'His men would follow him anywhere . . . but only out of morbid curiosity.'

- 'I would not allow this employee to breed.'

- 'This employee is really not so much of a "has-been", but more of a definite "won't be".'

- 'Works well when under constant supervision and cornered like a rat in a trap.'

- 'When she opens her mouth, it seems that it is only to change feet.'

- 'He would be out of his depth in a parking-lot puddle.'

- 'This young lady has delusions of adequacy.'

- 'He sets low personal standards and then consistently fails to achieve them.'

- 'This employee is depriving a village somewhere of an idiot.'

- 'This employee should go far . . . and the sooner, the better.'

- 'He's got a full six-pack, but lacks the plastic thing to hold it all together.'

- 'A gross ignoramus – 144 times worse than an ordinary ignoramus.'

- 'He certainly takes a long time to make his pointless.'

- 'He doesn't have ulcers, but he's a carrier.'

- 'I would like to go hunting with him sometime.'

- 'He's been working with glue too much.'

- 'He would argue with a signpost.'

- 'He has a knack for making strangers immediately.'

- 'He brings a lot of joy whenever he leaves the room.'

- 'When his IQ reaches fifty, he should sell.'

- 'If you see two people talking and one looks bored . . . he's the other one.'

- 'She has a photographic memory, but with the lens cover glued on.'

- 'A prime candidate for natural de-selection.'

- 'Donated his brain to science before he was done using it.'

- 'Gates are down, the lights are flashing, but the train isn't coming.'

- 'He has two brains: one is lost and the other is out looking for it.'

- 'If he were any more stupid, he'd have to be watered twice a week.'

- 'If you gave him a penny for his thoughts, you'd get change.'

- 'If you stand close enough to him, you can hear the ocean.'

- 'It's hard to believe that he beat one million other sperms to the egg.'

- 'One neuron short of a synapse.'

- 'Some drink from the fountain of knowledge; he only gargled.'

- 'Takes him two hours to watch *60 minutes*.'

- 'The wheel is turning, but the hamster is dead.'

TRANSLATION IN ADVERTISEMENTS

The Dairy Association's huge success with the campaign 'Got Milk?' prompted them to expand advertising to Mexico. It was soon brought to their attention that the Spanish translation read 'Are you lactating?'

Coors put its slogan, 'Turn It Loose,' into Spanish, where it was read as 'Suffer from Diarrhoea'.

Scandinavian vacuum manufacturer Electrolux used the following in an American campaign, 'Nothing sucks like an Electrolux'.

Clairol introduced the 'Mist Stick', a curling iron, into Germany only to find out that mist is slang for manure. Not too many people had use for the 'Manure Stick'.

When Gerber started selling baby food in Africa, they used the same packaging as in the US, with the smiling baby on the label. Later they learned that in Africa, companies routinely put pictures on the label of what's inside, since many people can't read.

Colgate introduced a toothpaste in France called Cue, the name of a notorious porno magazine.

An American T-shirt maker in Miami printed shirts for the Spanish market which promoted the Pope's visit. Instead of 'I Saw the Pope' *(el Papa)*, the shirts read 'I Saw the Potato' *(la papa)*.

Pepsi's 'Come Alive with the Pepsi Generation' translated into 'Pepsi Brings Your Ancestors Back from the Grave' in Chinese.

Frank Perdue's chicken slogan, 'It takes a strong man to make a tender chicken' was translated into Spanish as 'It takes an aroused man to make a chicken affectionate.'

When American Airlines wanted to advertise its new leather first class seats in the Mexican market, it translated its 'Fly in Leather' campaign literally, which meant 'Fly Naked' *(vuela en cuero)* in Spanish.

Hunt-Wesson introduced Big John products in French Canada as Gros Jos. Later they found out that in slang this means 'big breasts'.

Bank Caixa Econômica Federal in Brazil offered 'Hot Money' in an advertisement in English, obviously unaware of the fact that hot money means stolen money in normal slang.

The Coca-Cola name in China was first read as *Kekoukela*, meaning 'Bite the Wax Tadpole' or 'Female Horse Stuffed with Wax', depending on the dialect. Coke then researched 40 000 characters to find a phonetic equivalent *kokou kole*, translating into 'happiness in the mouth.'

When Parker Pen marketed a ball-point pen in Mexico, its ads were supposed to have read, 'It won't leak in your pocket and embarrass you.' The company thought that the word *embarazar* (to impregnate) meant to embarrass, so the ad read, 'It won't leak in your pocket and make you pregnant'.

DESERTED ISLANDS

These deserted islands sure have a lot of passing traffic.

A man a dog and a sheep are stranded on an island with no food or water, nothing. Months have passed and there is no hope of them ever getting off this island; they are pretty much going to die there. One night, as they all go to sleep, the man quietly gets up and moves close to the sheep and puts his arm round it. He then carefully flips the sheep onto its stomach, pulls his pants down, and flopps his dick out. Suddenly, the dog gets up and starts barking at the man and scares him away from the sheep. The days and nights pass and the more the man tries to have sex with the sheep, the more the dog scares him off. One morning they all go for a walk along the beach looking for ships and boats. Suddenly, the man hears screaming coming from the sea. He looks over at the water and sees a woman drowning a few metres from shore, so he rushes down, dives in and saves the helpless women, and brings her back to the beach. The man looks at the woman and realises that she is very, very hot. She has big boobs, a hot arse and sexy legs.

The woman says to the man, 'You saved my life, anything you want I'll do, anything.'

The man thinks for a while and finally says, 'You couldn't take the dog for a walk, could you?'

A man and his wife have been stranded on a deserted island for many years. One day another man washes up on shore. The new man and the wife are very attracted to each other right away, but realise certain protocols must be observed. The husband, however, is very glad to see the second man.

'Now we will be able to have three people doing eight hour shifts in the watchtower, rather than two people doing twelve-hour shifts.'

The new man is only too happy to help and volunteers to do the first shift. He climbs up the tower and is soon standing watch. Soon the husband and wife start placing stones in a circle to make a fire to cook supper. The second man yells down, 'Hey, no screwing!'

They yell back, 'We're not screwing!'

A few minutes later they start to put driftwood into the stone circle. Again the second man yells down, 'Hey, no screwing!'

Again they yell back, 'We're not screwing!'

Later they are putting palm leaves on the roof of their shack to patch leaks. Once again the second man yells down, 'Hey, I said no screwing!'

They yell back, 'We're not screwing!'

Finally the shift is over so the second man climbs down from the tower and the husband starts to climb up. He's not even halfway up before the wife and the second man are screwing each other's brains out.

The husband looks out from the tower and says, 'Son-of-a-gun. From up here it *does* look like they're screwing.'

A hurricane comes unexpectedly. The ship goes down and is lost. A man finds himself swept up on the shore of an island with no other people, no supplies, nothing. Only bananas and coconuts. Used to five-star hotels, this guy has no idea what to do, so for the next four months he eats bananas, drinks coconut juice and longs for his old life. He fixes his gaze on the sea, hoping to spot a rescue ship.

One day, as he is lying on the beach, he spots a movement

out of the corner of his eye. It's a rowboat, and in it is the most gorgeous woman he has ever seen. She rows up to him.

In disbelief, he asks her, 'Where did you come from? How did you get here?'

'I rowed from the other side of the island,' she says. 'I landed here when my cruise ship sank.'

'Amazing,' he says. 'I didn't know anyone else had survived. How many are there? You were lucky to have a rowboat wash up with you.'

'It's only me,' she says, 'and the rowboat didn't wash up; nothing did.'

He is confused. 'Then how did you get the rowboat?'

'Oh, simple,' replies the woman. 'I made the rowboat out of materials that I found on the island. I whittled the oars from gum-tree branches. I wove the bottom from palm branches and the sides and stern came from a coconut tree.'

'B-b-but that's impossible,' stutters the man. 'You had no tools or hardware. How did you manage?'

'Oh, that was no problem,' replies the woman. 'On the other side of the island there is a very unusual stratum of alluvial rock exposed. I found that if I fired it to a certain temperature in my kiln, it melted into forgeable ductile iron. I used that for tools, and used the tools to make the hardware. But enough of that,' she says. 'Where do you live?'

Sheepishly, he confesses that he has been sleeping on the beach the whole time.

'Well, let's row over to my place, then,' she says.

After a few minutes of rowing she docks the boat at a small wharf. As the man looks to the shore he nearly falls out of the boat. Before him is a stone walk leading to an exquisite bungalow painted in blue and white. While the woman ties up the rowboat with an expertly woven hemp rope, the man can only stare ahead, dumbstruck.

As they walk into the house, she says casually, 'It's not

much, but I call it home. Sit down, please; would you like a drink?'

'No, no thank you,' he says, still dazed. 'I can't take any more coconut juice.'

'It's not coconut juice,' the woman replies. 'I have a still. How about a pina colada?'

Trying to hide his amazement, the man accepts, and they sit down on her couch to talk.

After they have exchanged their stories, the woman announces, 'I'm going to slip into something comfortable. Would you like to take a shower and shave? There is a razor upstairs in the cabinet in the bathroom.'

No longer questioning anything, the man goes into the bathroom. There in the cabinet is a razor made from a bone handle. Two shells honed to a hollow ground edge are fastened onto its end inside a swivel mechanism.

'This woman is amazing,' he muses. 'What next?'

When he returns, she greets him wearing nothing but vines – strategically positioned – and smelling faintly of gardenias. She beckons him over to sit down next to her.

'Tell me,' she begins, suggestively, slithering closer to him, 'we've been out here for a very long time. You've been lonely. There's something I'm sure you really feel like doing right now, something you've been longing for all these months. You know . . .'

She stares into his eyes. He can't believe what he is hearing.

'You mean?' he replies, '. . . I can check my email from here?'

GOVERNMENT

*Whether it's the taxation department, local government
or the highest office in the land, there are plenty of
laughs to be had in government. Unfortunately,
the laughs are usually unintended.*

A little boy wants $100 badly and prays for two weeks but nothing happens. Then he decides to write a letter to God requesting the $100. When the postal authorities receive the letter addressed to God, Australia, they decide to send it to the prime minister. The prime minister is so impressed, touched, and amused that he instructs his secretary to send the little boy a $5 note. He thinks this will appear to be a lot of money to a little boy. The little boy is delighted with the $5 and sits down to write a thank you note to God which reads:

'Dear God,

Thank you very much for the money that you sent. However I noticed that for some reason you sent it through Canberra and as usual they deducted $95.'

A new tax inspector is eager to make a name for himself. So he decides to review the tax returns of the local synagogue. He interrogates the rabbi, asking him what the synagogue does with the wax drippings from the Shabbat, Havdallah and Chanukah candles. The rabbi, pleased to show the inspector that nothing goes to waste, responds that the used wax is collected and sent to a candle factory, which in turn sends the temple new candles.

'What about the crumbs from the matzo you eat at Passover?' asks the inspector.

'Simple,' the rabbi responds. 'We collect all the crumbs, send them to the matzo bakery and they send us matzo meal.'

'All right,' says the inspector, refusing to give up. 'I know that you're a mohel as well as a rabbi. What do you do with the leftovers from the circumcisions?'

'Easy,' says the rabbi. 'We send them to the tax office and they send us little pricks like you.'

President George W. Bush is visiting an elementary school and spends time in one of the classrooms. The children are in the middle of a discussion related to words and their meanings. The teacher asks the president if he would like to lead the class in the discussion of the word, 'tragedy'. So the illustrious leader asks the class for an example of a tragedy.

One little boy stands up and offers, 'If my best friend, who lives next door, is playing in the street and a car comes along and runs him over, that would be a tragedy.'

'No,' says Bush, 'that would be an accident.'

A little girl raises her hand, 'If a school bus carrying fifty children drove off a cliff, killing everyone involved, that would be a tragedy.'

'I'm afraid not,' explains Mr President. 'That's what we would call a great loss.'

The room goes silent. No other children volunteer. President Bush searches the room.

'Isn't there someone here who can give me an example of a tragedy?'

Finally, in the back of the room, a small boy raises his hand. In a quiet voice he says, 'If Air Force One, carrying Mr and Mrs Bush, was struck by a missile and blown up to smithereens, by a terrorist like Osama bin Laden, that would be a tragedy.'

'Fantastic,' exclaims Bush, 'that's right. And can you tell me why that would be a tragedy?'

'Well,' says the boy, 'because it wouldn't be an accident, and it certainly wouldn't be a great loss.'

The Queen of England and George W. Bush are riding in the royal carriage down Pall Mall chatting politely when one of the horses breaks wind. The smell is terrible and both the Queen and President Bush are too embarrassed to say anything until the Queen has to break the awkward silence.

'Mr President, I'm so terribly sorry. As you now realise, there are some things over which even the Queen of England has no control.'

Very graciously, President Bush replies, 'Think nothing of it Your Majesty. If you had not said anything, I would have thought it was the horse.'

George W. Bush and Dick Cheney go out to dinner. The waitress asks them what they would like to order. After looking at the menu, Cheney says he would like a piece of prime rib with all the trimmings, and Bush says he would like a quickie. At that, the waitress storms off, shouting over her shoulder how she thought all that horrible behaviour and language was over, now that Bush was president.

So, Bush sits there, looking confused, and Cheney leans over and says, 'Uh, Mr President, that's pronounced "quiche".'

A man comes home from the Social Security Office.
'Honey,' he says to his wife, 'I finally convinced them that I'm old enough to collect Social Security.'

'How?' his wife asks, knowing that the department of records in the small town in which he was born was flooded, and he couldn't get a copy of his birth certificate.

'I just unbuttoned my shirt and showed them all the grey hairs on my chest,' replies the man. 'That convinced them that I'm old enough.'

His wife retorts, 'Then while you were at it, why didn't you whip out your dick and get disability, too?'

A man is required to report to the taxation department. He asks his accountant for advice on what to wear.

'Wear your shabbiest clothing. Let them think you are a pauper,' says the accountant.

Then he asks his lawyer the same question, but gets the opposite advice.

'Do not let them intimidate you. Wear your most elegant suit and tie,' says his lawyer.

Confused, the man goes to his priest, tells him of the conflicting advice, and requests some resolution of the dilemma.

'Let me tell you a story,' replies the priest. 'A woman, about to be married, asks her mother what to wear on her wedding night.

"Wear a heavy, long, flannel nightgown that goes right up to your neck," she says.

But when she asks her best friend, she gets conflicting advice,

"Wear your most sexy negligee, with a V neck right down to your navel."'

The man protests, 'What does all this have to do with my problem with the taxation department?'

'No matter what you wear,' replies the priest. 'You're going to get screwed.'

Three boys are talking in the schoolyard. Each is bragging about how great their fathers are.

The first one says, 'Well, my father runs the fastest. He can fire an arrow, and start to run at the same time. I tell you, he gets there before the arrow!'

The second one says, 'Ha! You think that's fast! My father is a hunter. He can shoot his gun and be there before the bullet!'

The third boy listens to the other two boys and shakes his head. He then says, 'You two know nothing about fast. My father is a public servant. He stops working at 4.30 p.m. and he's home by 3.45!'

Sleeping Beauty, Tom Thumb and Don Juan are having a terrible fight.

'I am the most beautiful person in the world,' proclaims Sleeping Beauty.

'No, you're not,' answer Don Juan and Tom Thumb.

'I am the smallest person in the world,' shouts Tom Thumb.

'No, you're not,' say Sleeping Beauty and Don Juan.

'I've had more lovers than any person in the world,' announces Don Juan.

'No, you haven't,' reply Tom Thumb and Sleeping Beauty.

They decide that if the three of them are to get along, they need a mediator, and decide that Merlin, clearly the smartest person in the world, is the ideal choice. Merlin agrees, and summons them all to his palace, where he announces he will meet with them one at a time.

Sleeping Beauty goes in first and not a minute later comes out beaming.

'I am the most beautiful person in the world, Merlin said so.'

In goes Tom Thumb and out he comes as quickly as Sleeping Beauty:

'I am the smallest person in the world, Merlin agrees.'

In goes Don Juan and in he stays, a half hour, an hour, an hour and a half later.

Finally he emerges, distraught, muttering, 'Who the hell is Bill Clinton?'

A farmer discovers one day that one of his hens is laying square eggs. Deciding to exploit this phenomenon, he calls the Department of Agriculture which is very interested and takes the hen in return for very generous compensation.

But, once installed in the Department of Agriculture, the hen returns to laying oval eggs. Summoned to investigate, the farmer comes to see the chicken and asks her what the problem is.

The chicken responds, 'You think I'm going to keep on busting my arse now that I'm a government employee?'

A businessman on his deathbed calls his friend and says, 'Bill, I want you to promise me that when I die, you will have my remains cremated.'

'And what,' his friend asks, 'do you want me to do with your ashes?'

The businessman says, 'Just put them in an envelope and mail them to the Tax Office. Write on the envelope, "Now, you have everything."'

The Los Angeles Police Department (LAPD), the FBI, and the CIA are all trying to prove that they are the best at apprehending criminals. The President decides to give them a test. He releases a rabbit into a forest and each of them has to catch it.

The CIA goes in first. They place animal informants throughout the forest. They question all plant and mineral witnesses. After three months of extensive investigations they conclude that rabbits do not exist.

The FBI goes in. After two weeks with no leads they burn the forest, killing everything in it, including the rabbit, and they make no apologies. The rabbit had it coming.

The LAPD goes in. They come out two hours later with a badly beaten bear. The bear is yelling, 'OK! OK! I'm a rabbit! I'm a rabbit!'

RELIGION

*The world of humour would be much the poorer
without priests, rabbis and other religious figures.
And if you ever get the chance to see God perform,
don't miss it. I hear he does a terrific stand-up routine.*

A preacher tells his congregation that anything they can think
of, old or new, is discussed somewhere in the bible and, in
fact, that the entirety of the human experience can be found in
the bible.

After the service, he is approached by a woman who says,
'Preacher, I don't believe the bible mentions PMS.'

The preacher replies that he is sure it must in be there
somewhere and that he will look for it. The following week after
the service, the preacher calls the woman aside and shows her a
passage which reads, 'And Mary rode Joseph's ass all the way to
Bethlehem.'

One day in the synagogue, the rabbi is conducting prayers
when he hears an argument going on at the back. Yossi and
Jacob are involved in a heated discussion.

'Jacob I tell you, black is a colour.'

'No Yossi, black is no colour.'

'Yes, black is a colour!'

The rabbi steps in. 'What is this? We are conducting prayers
here and you two are waking the dead. Have a little respect,
no?'

'We are sorry Rabbi,' says Yossi, 'but it is a most important question. Dear Rabbi, we know you are a man of great education. You are a teacher of our community. Can you tell us please, is black a colour?'

So the rabbi stops to consider this. 'Well brothers, I can't give you the number or name of the appropriate scripture just now, but yes, I am sure that we Jews believe that black is a colour. Now, may I get back to the prayers?'

And he returns to reading the prayers. Soon he hears another argument from the back of the synagogue.

'White is a colour.'

'No, White is no colour!'

Again, the rabbi steps in. 'Jacob, Yossi, what are you doing? We are in a synagogue trying to pray to our God, the saviour, and you two are still arguing! My friends, please! Stop this.'

'We are sorry Rabbi, truly sorry,' says Yossi again. 'But we have an extremely important question and we must seek your advice. Please Rabbi, can you tell us, is white a colour?'

So the rabbi, trying to maintain his patience with these two, looks for an answer.

'God help me. Yes,' he says, 'white is a colour too. God has also given us white as a colour. Now gentlemen, please, I beg you. May I continue with the prayers?'

He begins again when he hears Yossi say to Jacob, 'You see Jacob? No question, you can trust me. I sold you a colour TV.'

THE BIBLE IN FIFTY WORDS

The official abridged version

God made. Adam bit. Noah arked. Abraham split. Joseph ruled. Jacob fooled. Bush talked. Moses balked. Pharaoh plagued. People walked. Sea divided. Tablets guided. Promise landed. Saul freaked. David peeked. Prophets warned. Jesus born. God

walked. Love talked. Anger crucified. Hope died. Love rose. Spirit
flamed. Word spread. God remained.

Father Ignatius is required to take an urgent trip to the
Vatican, leaving young Father Bernard in charge of the parish.
Father Bernard's only concern is the correct penance for each
sin disclosed during confession. Father Ignatius reassures him.

'Don't worry, my son. There are days when I forget, but I
simply ask one of the choirboys. You know how retentive the
memories of pubescent boys are.'

Father Ignatius duly departs, and on the second day, Father
Bernard is completely thrown by a confession from one of his
flock who tells him that he has recently received a blow job.
Remembering the advice he was given, he rushes into the
vestry, where the choirboys are robing for Vespers.

He sidles up to one of the older boys, and enquires, 'What's
the going rate for a blow job?'

'Thirty bucks and a Mars Bar.'

A Catholic priest and a rabbi live across the road from each
other in one of the better suburbs of Adelaide. Over the
years, the one-upmanship between them has become intense,
and it comes to a head when the priest buys a brand-new BMW
and parks it ostentatiously on his drive. Within an hour, the rabbi
has a brand new Mercedes parked on his drive. The same
afternoon, the priest washes his car and polishes it lovingly. The
rabbi follows suit. The priest then comes down his drive with a
bottle of holy water and sprinkles it over the bonnet of his new
pride and joy. With a triumphant smile, the rabbi comes out of
his house with a hacksaw, and saws half an inch off the end
of his exhaust pipe.

A nun is sitting at a window in her convent when she is handed a letter from home. She opens it and a $10 note drops out. She is most pleased at receiving the gift from home, but as she reads the letter her attention is distracted by the actions of a shabbily dressed stranger who is leaning against a post in front of the convent. She can't get him off her mind and, thinking that he might be in financial difficulties, she takes the $10 note and puts it in an envelope. On the envelope she writes, 'Don't despair, Sister Eulalia'. And she throws it out the window to him. He picks it up, reads it, looks at her with a puzzled expression, tips his hat and goes off down the street.

The next day she is in her cell saying her prayers when she is told that a man is at the door and he insists on seeing her. She goes down and finds the same stranger waiting for her. Without saying a word he hands her a roll of bills. When she asks what all the money is for, he replies, 'It's your winnings. Don't Despair came in at five to one.'

A priest gets sick and tired of all the people in his parish who keep confessing adultery.

One Sunday, in the pulpit, he says, 'If I hear one more person confess to adultery, I'll quit!'

Well, everyone likes him, so they come up with a code word. People who commit adultery will say they 'have fallen'. This seems to satisfy the old priest and things go well, until the priest dies at a ripe old age. About a week after the new priest arrives, he visits the mayor of the town and seems very concerned.

The priest says, 'You have to do something about the footpaths in town. When people come into the confessional, they keep talking about having fallen.'

The Mayor starts to laugh, realising that no-one has told the new priest about the code word.

But the priest shakes an accusing finger at the mayor and says, 'I don't know what you're laughing about. Your wife fell three times this week.'

A man's car breaks down near a monastery. He goes to the monastery, knocks on the door, and says, 'My car broke down. Do you think I could stay the night?'

The monks graciously accept him, feed him dinner, and even fix his car. As the man tries to fall asleep, he hears a strange sound. The next morning, he asks the monks what the sound was, but they say, 'We can't tell you. You're not a monk.'

The man is disappointed but thanks them anyway and goes on his merry way. Some years later, the same man breaks down in front of the same monastery. Once again, the monks accept him, feed him, and even fix his car. That night, he hears the same strange noise that he heard years earlier. The next morning, he asks what it is, but the monks reply, 'We can't tell you. You're not a monk.'

The man says, 'All right, all right. I'm dying to know what that strange sound is. If the only way I can find out is to become a monk, how do I become a monk?'

The monks reply, 'You must travel the earth and tell us how many blades of grass there are and the exact number of grains of sand. When you find this out, you will be a monk.'

The man sets about his task. Forty-five years later, he returns and knocks on the door of the monastery.

He says, 'I have travelled the earth and have found out what you asked. There are 121 845 333 29 101 blades of grass and 673 231 812 456 732 129 999 grains of sand on the earth.'

The monks reply, 'Congratulations. You are now a monk. We shall now show you the way to the sound.'

The monks lead the man to a wooden door, where the head monk says, 'The sound is right behind that door.'

The man reaches for the knob, but the door is locked.

He says, ' May I have the key?'

The monks give him the key, and he opens the door. Behind the wooden door is another door made of stone. The man demands the key to the stone door. The monks give him the key, and he opens it, only to find a door made of ruby. He demands another key from the monks, who provide it. Behind that door is another door, this one made of sapphire. So it goes until the man has gone through doors of emerald, silver, topaz and amethyst.

Finally, the monks say, 'This is the last key to the last door.'

The man is relieved. He unlocks the door, turns the knob, and behind that door he is amazed to find the source of that strange sound.

But, I can't tell you what it is, because you're not a monk.

A priest is walking past a pub when he sees a small boy drinking beer and smoking a Cuban cigar. The priest is shocked to the core.

'Why aren't you in school?' he asks the boy.

''Cause I'm only four.'

A man is driving down a deserted stretch of highway when he notices a sign out of the corner of his eye.

It reads: 'Sisters of Mercy House of Prostitution – 10km.'

He thinks it is just a figment of his imagination and drives on without a second thought. Soon, he sees another sign which says: 'Sisters of Mercy House of Prostitution – 5km.'

He realises that these signs are for real. Then he drives past a third sign saying: 'Sisters of Mercy House of Prostitution – Next Right.'

His curiosity gets the best of him and he pulls into the drive.

On the far side of the parking lot is a sombre stone building with a small sign next to the door reading: 'Sisters of Mercy'.

He climbs the steps and rings the bell. The door is answered by a nun in a long black habit who asks, 'What may we do for you, my son?'

He answers, 'I saw your signs along the highway, and was interested in possibly doing business.'

'Very well, my son. Please follow me.'

He is led through many winding passages and is soon quite disoriented. The nun stops at a closed door, and tells the man, 'Please knock on this door.'

He does as he is told and the door is answered by another nun in a long habit, holding a tin cup. This nun instructs, 'Please place $50 in the cup, then go through the large wooden door at the end of this hallway.'

He gets $50 out of his wallet and places it in the second nun's cup. He trots eagerly down the hall and slips through the door, pulling it shut behind him. As the door locks behind him, he finds himself back in the parking lot, facing another small sign: 'Go in Peace, You Have Just Been Screwed by the Sisters of Mercy.'

Before they can be ordained, three young men have to undergo an ordeal which will test the chastity of their thoughts. Ordered by a priest to strip, the trio have rubber bands fastened to their private parts and are ushered into a bedroom where a beautiful girl lies naked on the bed.

After a few moments there is a loud *boing!* The first seminarian is told to go to the showers to cool his ardour.

A moment later there is a second loud *boing!* The owner of that rigid member is also sent to the showers.

Minutes pass, and when nothing happened to the third aspiring clergyman, he is congratulated by the priest.

'Well done, my son,' he enthuses. 'Now go and join the others in the shower.'

Boing!

A n elderly doctor and a Baptist minister are seated next to each other on a plane. The plane is delayed on the ground due to some technical problems. Just after taking off, the pilot offers his apologies to the passengers and announces that a round of free drinks will be served.

When the charming flight attendant comes round with her trolley, the doctor orders a gin and tonic for himself. The flight attendant then asks the minister whether he wants anything.

He replies, 'Oh No! Thank you. I would rather commit adultery than drink alcohol.'

The elderly doctor promptly hands his gin and tonic back to the flight attendant and says, 'Madam, I did not know there was a choice.'

I n a small town in Ireland, the Catholic priest and the Protestant minister rarely spend any time together, not out of hatred, mostly out of time spent with their respective herds. The only time they see each other on a regular basis is on Monday mornings, as they pass each other exercising on their bicycles. One Monday morning the priest is peddling along when he sees his fellow servant of god walking toward him.

He stops and asks, 'Reverend, what has happened to you? Your bike is missing.'

'Father,' the minister replies, 'I'm afraid to say that one of my parishioners has sinned against God, and stolen me bike.'

'Reverend, reverend, reverend, I understand your dilemma. Once, early in my career, I had one of my flock steel a bottle of wine from the church. The next Sunday, I gave a hell-fire sermon on the ten commandments – stressing 'thou shalt not steal'. The next morning I woke up to find a bottle of wine on my doorstep with a note saying 'forgive me, Father'. It helped me and I am sure it will help you.'

'Thank you, Father. We will see how it works next Monday'

One week later, the priest gets on his bike and hits the road, looking for the minister. Within minutes he sees the minister peddling toward him. They stop next to one another and shake hands.

'I am so pleased things worked out for you, Reverend.'

'Well, you see, Father. It didn't work out in quite the way we thought it might. You see, I prepared the sermon you suggested and I stressed 'though shalt not steal', but then, when I got to the part about 'thou shalt not commit adultery', I remembered I had left me bike at Mrs O'Brien's house.'

A Christian woman has to do a lot of travelling for her business, so she does a lot of flying. But flying makes her nervous so she always takes her bible along with her to read, as it helps her to relax. One day she is sitting next to a man. When he sees her pull out her bible he gives a little chuckle and goes back to what he is doing.

After a while he turns to her and asks, 'You don't really believe all that stuff in there do you?'

The woman replies, 'Of course I do. It is the bible.'

He says, 'Well what about that guy that was swallowed by that whale?'

She replies, 'Oh, Jonah. Yes I believe that, it is in the bible.'

He asks, 'Well, how do you suppose he survived all that time inside the whale?'

The woman says 'Well. I don't really know. I guess when I get to heaven I will ask him.'

'What if he isn't in heaven?' the man asks sarcastically.

'Then *you* can ask him,' replies the woman.

An irregular church goer is leaving church one day when the priest grabs his arm and pulls him aside.

The priest says to him, 'You need to join the Army of the Lord!'

'I'm already in the Army of the Lord, Father,' the man says.

The priest questions, 'Then how come I don't see you at church except at Christmas and Easter?'

He whispers back, 'I'm in the secret service.'

One balmy evening in Rome the Pope decides to take a walk. He slips out the rear door of the Vatican and is walking through the back alleys of Rome when he sees a ten-year-old boy smoking a cigarette. The Pope gently says to him, 'Young man, you're much too young to smoke!'

The kid looks up at the Pope and says, 'Screw you!'

The Pope is completely taken aback. 'What?' he says. 'You say that to me, the Pontiff, the Vicar of Christ, the head of the entire Roman Catholic Church? I am the spiritual leader for millions of people, young man, the representative of God, and you dare say that to me? No, no, no, kid. Screw you!'

One morning the Pope awakes in his bed chamber in the Vatican. To his surprise, he notices that he has woken up with a massive erection. Perplexed, he calls on his personal physician.

'Doctor, this should not be possible,' he says, 'I'm the Pope, and I'm celibate! I haven't had one of these for thirty years!'

The doctor replies, 'Well, father, this is a natural phenomenon for all men, and it will happen even to you from time to time.'

The Pope exclaims, 'But you must do something about this. I have Mass in an hour, and this thing isn't going away.'

The doctor replies, 'You have two options. Either I can administer an injection to your penis to make the problem go away, which will hurt and make you feel ill, or you can make love to a woman.'

The Pope says, 'No, I do not want the injection, so get me a nun. But there are three considerations. First, she must be blind so she cannot see who does this thing to her. Second, she must be deaf so she cannot hear who does this thing to her. Third, she's gotta have really big tits.'

A farmer goes to confession for the first time in twenty years and tells the priest he's been having sexual intercourse with a pig ever since his wife died.

The priest asks him if he intends to continue doing it and whether the pig is a male or female.

'No! I'm not doing it anymore!' says the farmer. 'And the pig is a female, of course. What the hell do you think I am? A goddam queer?'

Three nuns have been behaving very well, so the mother superior says to them, 'Look sisters you have all behaved really well lately and just for that I want you three to go out and do something bad for a change.'

The first nun comes back and says, 'I robbed a bank.'

The mother superior says, 'That's alright dear, just take a sip from the holy water now.'

The second nun comes back and says, 'I stole a car.'

The mother superior says, 'That's alright dear, just take a sip from the holy water now.'

The third nun comes back and says, 'I pissed in the holy water.'

The Pope finally dies, as all of us must, and goes to heaven to meet the Lord. God welcomes him in, telling him he was one of His most loyal servants on earth, and that he is free to do whatever he pleases in heaven. So the Pope decides to spend his time fulfilling his dream: to learn the original Hebrew language and then to translate the bible for himself. He goes to the great library, and spends years poring over the books, learning Hebrew, while even the angels are amazed at his dedication to religion and his perseverance. Finally, the Pope judges himself ready to begin the translation of the original bible. So there he is, reading, translating and writing; reading, translating and writing; reading, translating and writing; until the angels outside one day hear yelling and screaming from within.

The next instant the Pope bursts forth, red in the face, eyes popping, yelling hoarsely, 'Shit, crap, Godammit! I can't bloody believe it!' he bellows. 'Celebrate . . . the bloody order was celebrate!'

A four-year-old pre-schooler goes to Mass with his mum. The little boy tugs on his mum's sleeve and says, 'Mum, how does he know all that stuff?'

She replies, 'Well, honey, he goes to priest school.'

The little boy responds, 'I go to pre-school too and I didn't learn all *that* stuff!'

Two nuns are riding their rickety old bikes down the bumpy back streets of Rome late one summer afternoon. It starts getting quite dark and the two nuns are a little nervous.

The younger nun steers her bicycle closer to the older nun and says, 'You know, I've never come this way before.'

The older nun nods her head knowingly and says, 'It's the cobblestones.'

Four Catholic women are having coffee. The first Catholic woman tells her friends, 'My son is a priest. When he walks into a room, everyone calls him "Father".'

The second Catholic woman chirps, 'My son is a bishop. Whenever he walks into a room, people call him "Your Grace".'

The third Catholic crone says, 'My son is a cardinal. Whenever he walks into a room, he's called "Your Eminence"'.

Since the fourth Catholic woman sips her coffee in silence, the first three women give her a subtle 'Well . . .?'

So she replies, 'My son is six foot two, has plenty of money, broad square shoulders, is terribly handsome, dresses very well, has a tight muscular body, tight hard buns and a very nice bulge. And whenever he walks into a room women gasp, "Oh, my Lord!"'

A drunken man staggers in to a Catholic church and sits down in a confession box and says nothing. The bewildered priest coughs to attract his attention, but still the man says nothing. The priest then knocks on the wall three times in a final attempt to get the man to speak.

Finally, the drunk says, 'No use knockin' mate, there's no paper in this one either.'

A priest and a rabbi are in a bar having a drink when the priest says, 'Your religion is a unique one in that you do not eat pork. In all the years that you have been a rabbi, have you not at least once eaten pork?'

'Well, I must confess,' replies the rabbi, 'I did once give in to weakness while at a barbecue. They were roasting a pig and the smell got to me and I tried the pork and I must say it was wonderful.'

After a pause the rabbi continues, 'Now I must say your religion is quite unique in that priests do not have sex. Are you prepared to tell me that you have never experienced sex in your whole life?'

The priest replies, 'Yes I must confess that once when I was young, I did have sex.'

The rabbi says, 'It was a hell of lot a better than pork, wasn't it?'

An Amish woman and her daughter are riding in an open buggy one cold, blustery January day.

The daughter says to the mother, 'My hands are freezing cold.'

The mother replies, 'Put your hands between your legs. The body heat will warm them up.'

So the daughter does, and her hands warm up. The next day, the daughter is riding in the buggy with her boyfriend.

The boyfriend says, 'My hands are freezing cold.'

The daughter says, 'Put them between my legs, the body heat will warm them up.'

The next day, the boyfriend is driving in the buggy with the daughter.

He says, 'My nose is freezing cold.'

The daughter says, 'Put it between my legs. It will warm up.'

He does, and his nose warms up. The next day, the boyfriend is driving again with the daughter and he says, 'My penis is frozen solid.'

The daughter says, 'Put it between my legs, the body heat will warm it up.'

The next day, the daughter is driving in the buggy with her mother, and she says to her mother, 'Have you ever heard of a penis?'

The slightly concerned mother says, 'Sure, why do you ask?'

The daughter says, 'Well, they make one hell of a mess when they thaw out.'

A crook decides to rob a church. He breaks in and starts collecting valuable items when he notices the priest. The crook wants to kill the priest, as he is the only witness. So he pulls out his gun, and fires.

The crook misses and curses, 'Damn, I missed.'

The priest, with courage, says to the crook, 'If you swear in the house of God again, you will be struck by lightning.'

The crook shoots again, misses, and again says, 'Damn, I missed.'

Suddenly, the heavens open up and a bolt of lightening thunders down and hits the priest.

Then a voice from above cries out, 'Damn, I missed.'

A young preacher is contacted by the local funeral director to hold a graveside committal service at a small local cemetery for someone with no family or friends. The preacher starts out early but quickly gets lost, making several wrong turns. He arrives half an hour late, the hearse is nowhere in sight, and the workmen are eating lunch. The pastor goes to the open grave and finds the vault lid already in place. Taking out his book, he reads the service.

As he is returning to his car, he overhears one of the workmen say, 'Do you think we should tell him that's the septic tank?'

SCHOOLDAYS

Were our schooldays really this amusing?
I don't remember them this way. But then,
I was too busy studying.

Little Tommy is doing very badly in maths. His parents try everything – tutors, flash cards, special learning centres, in short, everything they can think of. Finally, in a last ditch effort, they take Tommy down and enrol him in the local Catholic school. After the first day, little Tommy comes home with a very serious look on his face. He doesn't kiss his mother hello. Instead, he goes straight to his room and starts studying. Books and papers are spread out all over the room and little Tommy is hard at work. His mother is amazed. She calls him down to dinner and to her shock, the minute he is finished he marches back to his room and in no time he is back hitting the books as hard as before. This goes on for some time, day after day, while the mother tries to understand what made all the difference. Finally, little Tommy brings home his report card. He quietly lays it on the table and goes up to his room to study. With great trepidation, his mum looks at it and to her surprise, little Tommy got an A in maths. She can no longer hold her curiosity.

She goes to his room and says, 'Son, what was it? Was it the nuns?'

Little Tommy looks at her and shakes his head.

'Was it the books, the discipline, the structure, the uniforms?'

Little Tommy looks at her and says, 'Well, on the first day of school, when I saw that guy nailed to the plus sign, I knew they weren't fooling around.'

THE MORE ADULT ONLY JOKE BOOK

A school boy is assigned a paper on childbirth and asks his parents, 'How was I born?'

'Well honey . . .' says his slightly prudish mother, 'the stork brought you to us.'

'Oh,' says the boy. 'Well, how did you and daddy get born?' he asks.

'Oh, the stork brought us too.'

'Well how were grandpa and grandma born?' he persists.

'Well darling, the stork brought them too!' says his mother, by now starting to squirm a little.

Several days later, the boy hands in his paper to the teacher.

It begins, 'This report has been very difficult to write because there hasn't been a natural childbirth in my family for three generations.'

One day the teacher asks the children in class to give examples of what is not good to put in one's mouth.

Little Johnny says, 'It is not good to put a lit light bulb in one's mouth.'

The teacher replies, 'That is correct, but why?'

Little Johnny answers, 'I don't know, but my mum always tells my dad "Turn off the light before you put it in my mouth!"'

A young female teacher is giving an assignment to her sixth-grade class one day. It is a large assignment so she starts writing high up on the chalkboard. Suddenly, there is a giggle from one of the boys in the class.

She quickly turns and asks, 'What's so funny, Patrick?'

'Well teacher, I just saw one of your garters.'

'Get out of my classroom,' she yells. 'I don't want to see you for three days.'

The teacher turns back to the chalkboard. Realising she has

178 • THE MORE ADULT ONLY JOKE BOOK

forgotten to title the assignment, she reaches to the very top of the chalkboard. Suddenly there is an even louder giggle from another male student.

She quickly turns and asks, 'What's so funny Billy?'

'Well miss, I just saw both of your garters.'

Again she yells, 'Get out of my classroom! This time the punishment is more severe. I don't want to see you for three weeks.'

Embarrassed and frustrated, she drops the eraser when she turns around again. So she bends over to pick it up. This time there is an enormous burst of laughter from another male student. She quickly turns to see Little Johnny leaving the classroom.

'Where do you think you're going, Little Johnny?' she asks.

'Well teacher, from what I just saw, my school days are over!'

For weeks a six-year-old lad keeps telling his first-grade teacher about the baby brother or sister that is expected at his house. One day his mother allows the boy to feel the movements of the unborn child in her belly. The six-year-old is obviously impressed, but makes no comment. Furthermore, he stops telling his teacher about the impending event.

The teacher finally sits the boy down and says, 'Tommy, whatever has become of that baby brother or sister you were expecting at home?'

Tommy bursts into tears and confesses, 'I think Mummy ate it!'

The first-grade teacher is starting a new lesson on multi-syllable words. She thinks it will be a good idea to ask a few of the children for examples of words with more than one syllable.

'Jane, do you know any multi-syllable words?'

After some thought Jane proudly replies, 'Monday.'

'Great Jane. That has two syllables, Mon . . . day. Does anyone know another word?'

'I do! I do!' replies Johnny.

Knowing Johnny's more mature sense of humour she picks Mike instead. 'OK Mike, what is your word.'

'Saturday,' says Mike.

'Great, that has three syllables.'

Not wanting to be outdone, Johnny says, 'I know a four-syllable word. Pick me! Pick me!'

Not thinking he can do any harm with a word that large the teacher reluctantly says, 'OK. Johnny what is your four-syllable word?'

Johnny proudly says, 'Mas . . . tur . . . ba . . . tion.'

Shocked, the teacher, trying to retain her composure says, 'Wow, Johnny. Four syllables! That's certainly is a mouthful.'

'No Ma'am, you're thinking of "blowjob", and that's only two syllables.'

Johnny is always saying that he is too smart for the first grade. He thinks he should at least be in the third grade. One day, his teacher has had enough. She takes Johnny to the principal's office and explains Johnny's request, while Johnny waits in the outer office. The principal tells Johnny's teacher that he will give the boy a test and if Johnny fails to answer any of the special questions he is to go back to the first grade and behave. The teacher agrees. Johnny is brought into the room. The principal tells Johnny his terms and Johnny agrees.

'What is three times three?' asks the principal.

'Nine,' replies Johnny.

'What's six times six?'

'Thirty-six.'

'What's nine times nine?'

'Eighty-one.'

And so it goes with every question the principal thinks a third-grader should know. Johnny appears to have a strong case.

The principal tells the teacher, 'I think Johnny can go on to the third grade.'

The teacher, knowing Little Johnny's tendency toward sexual wisecracks, says to the principal, 'Let me ask him some questions before we make that decision?'

The principal and Johnny both agree, Johnny with a sly look on his face.

The teacher begins by asking, 'What does a cow have four of that I have only two of?'

'Legs,' Johnny answers.

'What is in your pants that you have but I don't have?' asks the teacher.

The principal's eyes open wide! Before he can stop Johnny's expected answer, he says, 'Pockets.'

The principal breathes a sigh of relief and tells the teacher, 'I think we should put Johnny in the fifth grade. I missed the last two questions myself!'

Johnny asks his teacher if he can go to the bathroom and she says yes. When he goes to wipe his arse, he finds that there is no toilet paper, so he uses his hand.

When he gets back to class, his teacher asks, 'What do you have in your hand?'

Johnny thinks quickly, 'A little leprechaun and if I open my hand he'll get scared away.'

He is then sent to the principal's office and the principal asks him, 'What do you have in your hand?'

Johnny tells him, 'A little leprechaun and if I open my hand he'll get scared away.'

He is sent home and his mum asks him, 'What do you have in your hand?'

Johnny says, 'A little leprechaun and if I open my hands he'll get scared away.'

He is then sent to his room and told to stay there till his dad comes home. His dad comes home, goes upstairs and says to Johnny, 'What do you have in your hand?'

So again Johnny says, 'A little leprechaun and if I open my hand he'll get scared away.'

Then his dad gets really mad and yells, 'Open your hand!'

Johnny opens his hand and says, 'Look Dad you scared the shit out of him!'

A pre-school teacher says to her class, 'Who can use the word "definitely" in a sentence?'

First a little girl says, 'The sky is definitely blue.'

The teacher says, 'Sorry, Amy, but the sky can also be grey or orange.'

Then a little boy says, 'Trees are definitely green.'

'Sorry, but in the autumn the trees are brown.'

Johnny from the back of the class stands up and asks, 'Does a fart have lumps?'

The teacher looks horrified and says, 'Johnny! Of course not!'

'OK. Then I have *definitely* shit my pants.'

A Teacher asks the children to discuss what their dads do for a living.

Mary says, 'My dad is a lawyer. He puts the bad guys in jail.'

Jack says, 'My dad is a doctor. He makes all the sick people better.'

All the kids in the class have their turn except Stevie.

Teacher says, 'Stevie, what does your dad do?'

Stevie says, 'My dad is dead.'

'I'm sorry to hear that, but what did he do before he died?'
'He turned blue and shat on the carpet.'

The third-grade teacher decides to test her students' ability to recognise objects from a description.

She says to the class, 'I am holding an object behind my back that is round, red and you can eat it.'

Suzie says, 'Miss, that's an apple.'

'Very good Suzie, that shows you are thinking,' replies the teacher. 'Now I am holding something that is yellow and long and can be eaten.'

David says, 'That's a banana miss.'

'Very good David, that shows you are thinking,' the teacher says.

Johnny puts his hand up and asks for a turn and the teacher lets him have a go.

'I am holding something under my desk something that is thin, an inch long and has a red head.'

The teacher is aghast. 'That's disgusting Johnny.'

Johnny replies, 'No Miss, it's a match, but it shows you're thinking.'

A teacher cautiously approaches the subject of sex education with her fourth-grade class because she realises Johnny's propensity for sexual innuendo. But Johnny remains attentive throughout the entire lecture. Finally, towards the end of the lesson, the teacher asks for examples of sex education from the class.

One little boy raises his hand, 'I saw a bird in her nest with some eggs.'

'Very good, William,' coos the teacher.

'My mummy had a baby,' says little Esther.

'Oh, that's nice,' replies the teacher.

Johnny raises his hand. With much fear and trepidation, the teacher calls on him.

'I was watchin' TV yesterday, and I saw the Lone Ranger. He was surrounded by hundreds and hundreds of Indians. And they all attacked at one time. And he killed every one of them with his two guns.'

The teacher is relieved but puzzled, 'And what does that have to do with sex education, Johnny?'

'It'll teach those Indians not to screw with the Lone Ranger.'

Johnny walks into the classroom, and the teacher says, 'Johnny, have you done your homework?'

He replies, 'No Miss.'

She says, 'If you don't have it done by tomorrow then I'm going to make a call to your parents.'

As Johnny is walking home from school he sees two greyhounds racing. One gets so far ahead of the other that it just stops and the other one rams its head right up its arse.

Johnny takes out a piece of paper and writes it all down, saying to himself, 'This is going to be my homework.'

The next day at school the teacher says, 'Johnny, have you done your homework?'

He says, 'Sure have.'

He goes up to the front of the class and starts telling them what he saw. 'Yesterday I was walking home from school when I saw these two greyhounds racing, and one rammed its head right up the other's arse.'

The teacher says, 'Johnny, we don't use the word arse in the classroom, it's rectum.'

Johnny says, 'Rectum? Hell, it damn near killed 'em.'

TEN SIMPLE RULES FOR DATING MY DAUGHTER

RULE ONE

If you pull into my driveway and honk you'd better be delivering a package, because you're sure not picking anything up.

RULE TWO

You do not touch my daughter in front of me. You may glance at her, so long as you do not peer at anything below her neck. If you cannot keep your eyes or hands off my daughter's body, I will remove them.

RULE THREE

I am aware that it is considered fashionable for boys of your age to wear their trousers so loosely that they appear to be falling off their hips. Please don't take this as an insult, but you and all of your friends are complete idiots. Still, I want to be fair and open minded about this issue, so I propose this compromise: You may come to the door with your underwear showing and your pants ten sizes too big, and I will not object. However, in order to ensure that your clothes do not, in fact, come off during the course of your date with my daughter, I will take my electric nail gun and fasten your trousers securely in place to your waist.

RULE FOUR

I'm sure you've been told that in today's world, sex, without using a 'barrier method' of some kind, can kill you. Let me elaborate, when it comes to sex, I am the barrier, and I will kill you.

RULE FIVE

It is usually understood that in order for us to get to know each other, we should talk about sports, politics, and other issues of the day. Please do not do this. The only information I require from you is an indication of when you expect to have my daughter safely back at my house, and the only word I need from you on this subject is 'early'.

RULE SIX

I have no doubt you are a popular fellow, with many opportunities to date other girls. This is fine with me as long as it is OK with my daughter. Otherwise, once you have gone out with my little girl, you will continue to date no-one but her until she is finished with you. If you make her cry, I will make you cry.

RULE SEVEN

As you stand in my front hallway, waiting for my daughter to appear, and more than an hour goes by, do not sigh and fidget. If you want to be on time for the movie, you should not be dating. My daughter is putting on her makeup, a process that can take longer than painting the Golden Gate Bridge. Instead of just standing there, why don't you do something useful, like changing the oil in my car?

RULE EIGHT

The following places are not appropriate for a date with my daughter: Places where there are beds, sofas, or anything softer than a wooden stool. Places where there are no parents, policemen, or nuns within eyesight. Places where there is darkness. Places where there is dancing, holding hands, or happiness. Places where the ambient temperature is warm enough to induce my daughter to wear shorts, tank tops, midriff T-shirts, or anything other than overalls, a sweater, and a goose down parka – zipped up to her throat. Movies with a strong romantic or sexual theme are to be avoided; movies that feature chainsaws are OK. Hockey games are OK. Old folks' homes are better.

RULE NINE

Do not lie to me. I may appear to be a pot-bellied, balding, middle-aged, dim-witted has-been. But on issues relating to my daughter, I am the all-knowing, merciless god of your universe. If I ask you where you are going and with whom, you have one chance to tell me the truth, the whole truth and nothing but the truth. I have a shotgun, a shovel, and five acres behind the house. Do not trifle with me.

RULE TEN

Be afraid. Be very afraid. It takes very little for me to mistake the sound of your car in the driveway for a chopper coming in over a rice paddy near Hanoi. When my Agent Orange starts acting up, the voices in my head frequently tell me to clean the guns as I wait for you to bring my daughter home. As soon as you pull into the driveway you should exit your car with both hands in plain sight. Speak the perimeter password, announce in a clear voice that you have brought my daughter home safely and early, then return to your car – there is no need for you to come inside. The camouflaged face at the window is mine.

X

Slightly risqué.

The Smiths have no children and decide to use a proxy father to start their family. On the day the proxy father is to arrive, Mr Smith kisses his wife and says, 'I'm off. The man should be here soon.'

Half an hour later, just by chance, a door-to-door baby photographer rings the doorbell, hoping to make a sale.

'Good morning madam. You don't know me but I've come to –'

'Oh, no need to explain. I've been expecting you,' Mrs Smith cuts in.

'Really?' the photographer asks. 'Well, good! I've made a specialty of babies.'

'That's what my husband and I had hoped. Please come in and have a seat. Just where do we start?' asks Mrs Smith, blushing.

'Leave everything to me. I usually try two in the bathtub, one on the couch and perhaps a couple on the bed. Sometimes the living room floor is fun too; you can really spread out.'

'Bathtub, living room floor? No wonder it didn't work for Harry and me.'

'Well madam, none of us can guarantee a good one every time. But if we try several different positions and I shoot from six or seven angles, I'm sure you'll be pleased with the results.'

'I hope we can get this over with quickly,' gasps Mrs Smith.

'Madam, in my line of work, a man must take his time. I'd love to be in and out in five minutes, but you'd be disappointed with that, I'm sure.'

'Don't I know it!' Mrs Smith exclaims.

The photographer opens his briefcase and pulls out a portfolio of his baby pictures. 'This was done on the top of a bus in the middle of London.'

'Oh my god!' Mrs Smith exclaims, tugging at her handkerchief.

'And these twins turned out exceptionally well, when you consider their mother was so difficult to work with.' The photographer hands Mrs Smith the picture.

'She was difficult?' asks Mrs Smith.

'Yes, I'm afraid so. I finally had to take her to Hyde Park to get the job done right. People were crowding around four and five deep, pushing to get a good look.'

'Four and five deep?' asks Mrs Smith, eyes wide in amazement.

'Yes,' the photographer says. 'And for more than three hours too. The mother was constantly squealing and yelling. I could hardly concentrate. Then darkness approached and I began to rush my shots. Finally, when the squirrels began nibbling on my equipment I just packed it all in.'

Mrs Smith leans forward. 'You mean they actually chewed on your, er . . . um . . . ah . . . equipment?'

'That's right. Well madam, if you're ready, I'll set up my tripod so that we can get to work.'

'Tripod?' Mrs Smith looks extremely worried now.

'Oh yes, I have to use a tripod to rest my Canon on. It's much too big for me to hold while I'm getting ready for action. Madam? Madam? . . . Good Lord, she's fainted!'

A professor is sent to darkest Africa to live with a primitive tribe. He spends years with them, teaching them reading, writing, maths and science. One day the wife of the tribe's chief gives birth to a white child.

The members of the tribe are shocked, and the chief pulls the professor aside and says, 'Look here! You're the only white man we've ever seen and this woman gave birth to a white child. It doesn't take a genius to work out what happened!'

The professor thinks quickly, 'No, Chief. You're mistaken. What you have here is a natural occurrence . . . what we in the civilised world call an albino! Look at that field over there. All of the sheep are white except for one black one. Nature does this on occasion.'

The chief is silent for a moment, then says, 'Tell you what. You don't say anything more about the sheep and I won't say anything more about the baby.'

Boy meets girl in a nightclub. The customary rituals are observed, but before too long it is bodice-ripping time back at his place. The girl enters the bedroom with half her clothes already back in the entrance hall. She is somewhat taken aback to see rows and rows of cuddly teddy bears of different shapes and sizes arranged on a large dresser along one wall of the bedroom. She says nothing, partly because her mouth is occupied, and partly because the air is thick with the sound of clothes being hastily discarded. The usual carnal exchange occurs, and the couple sink back exhausted onto the pillows.

The girl is crass enough to ask, 'How was it?'

The bloke replies, 'Pick any toy from the bottom shelf.'

Joe and Jim are sitting in a bar having a chat. Joe mentions that he is going on holiday to a place called Ocean View.

'Ocean View!' exclaims Jim, 'They've got a great pub there. I'm not sure of its name but the first time you go there, you don't have to pay for your drinks. It's all free.'

'Wow,' replies Joe, 'I can't wait.'

'And that's not all,' says Jim. 'When you've had enough to drink, they take you to a room out the back and you engage in as much free sex as you want.'

'I don't believe it,' says Joe.

'It's true,' Jim reassures him.

'Have you been there?' Joe asks.

'No. But my sister told me about it.'

A construction worker on the third floor of a building needs a handsaw. He sees one of the labourers on the first floor and yells down to him, but the man indicates that he cannot hear. So, the guy on the third floor tries to use signals. He points to his eye meaning 'I' then at his knee meaning 'need' then he moves his hand back and forth meaning 'handsaw'.

The man on the first floor nods, then drops his pants and begins to masturbate. The man on the third floor freaks out and runs down to the first floor yelling, 'What the hell is wrong with you! Are you stupid or something? I was saying that I needed a handsaw!'

The labourer looks at the construction worker and says, 'I knew that, I was just trying to tell you that I was coming.'

A big Texan ambles into a Dallas men's room and does a double-take at the little guy standing at the next urinal. He's holding his dick with two hands and smiling.

The Texan asks, 'How long is that snake fella?'

'Fourteen inches.'

'Is that fourteen inches soft?'

'Yes.'

'Well how long is it when it's hard?'

The little guy answers proudly, 'I don't know. It takes so much blood, I faint!'

A youth takes his father to the doctor. The doctor gives them the bad news that the father is dying of cancer. The father tells his son that he has had a good life and wants to stop at the bar on the way home to celebrate it. While at the bar, the father sees several of his friends. He tells them that he is dying of AIDS.

When the friends leave the son asks, 'Dad, you are dying of cancer. Why did you tell them that you are dying of AIDS?'

The father replies, 'I don't want them screwing your mother after I'm gone!'

A man joins the crew of a ship. After a few days he gets restless and asks, 'What does one do about sex around here?'

The others direct him to a large gun barrel with a hole in it. At first he does not like the idea much but, when he tries it, he finds it surprisingly enjoyable. He has another go the next day, and again the day after.

Then he asks, 'Can I do this every day?'

'Yes, every day, except Wednesday.'

'Why not on Wednesday?'

'Wednesday is *your* turn inside the barrel.'

A guy is sitting in a bar alone one night when he notices an attractive woman, also alone. He asks her to join him for a drink and to his surprise, she agrees. After a couple of drinks, she asks him if he'd like to come back to her place. The pair jump into a taxi and as soon as they get back to her flat they dive onto the bed and spend the night hard at it. Finally, the spent young bloke rolls over, pulls out a cigarette from his jeans and searches for his lighter. Unable to find it, he asks the girl if she has one on hand.

'There might be some matches in the top drawer,' she replies.

Opening the drawer of the bedside table, he finds a box of matches sitting neatly on top of a framed picture of another man. Naturally, the bloke begins to worry.

'Is this your husband?' he inquires nervously.

'No, silly,' she replies, snuggling up to him.

'Your boyfriend then?'

'No, don't be daft,' she says, nibbling away at his ear.

'Well, who is he then?' demands the bewildered bloke.

Calmly, the girl takes a match, strikes it across the side of her face and replies, 'That's me before the operation.'

A fter a few years of married life, a guy finds that he is unable to perform anymore. He goes to his doctor, and his doctor tries a few things but nothing works.

Finally the doctor says to him, 'This is all in your mind,' and refers him to a psychiatrist.

After a few visits to the shrink, the shrink confesses, 'I am at a loss as to how you can possibly be cured.' Finally the psychiatrist refers him to a witch doctor.

The witch doctor says, 'I can cure this,' and throws some powder on a flame. There is a flash with billowing blue smoke.

The witch doctor says, 'This is powerful healing but you can only use it once a year! All you have to do is say "one, two, three" and it shall rise for as long as you wish!'

The guy then asks the witch doctor, 'What happens when it's over?'

The witch doctor says, 'All you or your partner has to say is "one, two, three, four" and it will go down. But be warned it will not work again for a year.'

The guy goes home and that night he is ready to surprise his wife with the good news.

So he is lying in bed with her and says, 'One, two, three.'

Suddenly he gets an erection.

His wife turns over and says, 'What did you say "one, two, three" for?'

One day a little boy walks by a house. On the front porch of the house is an old man.

The man says to the boy, 'Where are you going with that chicken wire?'

The boy says, 'To catch chickens.'

The man says, 'You can't catch chickens with chicken wire.'

After a couple of hours the boy returns with a dozen chickens on the wire. The man is amazed and asks the boy for his secret. But he doesn't reveal it. The next day, the same boy walks by the same man, but now he has some duct tape.

'Where you going with duct tape, boy?'

'To catch ducks.'

'You can't catch ducks with duct tape.'

'Watch!' says the boy.

A few hours later, he returns with four ducks lined along the tape. Again the old man is amazed and really wants the secret, but the boy will not reveal it. The next day, the boy walks by again.

The old man says, 'Where you going with that stick?'

The boy says, 'This ain't no stick, this here is a pussy willow.'

The old man says, 'Wait here so I can grab my hat and I'll be right with ya!'

A man is walking through a hotel lobby when he accidentally bumps into a woman beside him. As he does, his elbow goes into her breast. They are both quite startled. The man turns to her and says, 'Ma'am, if your heart is as soft as your breast, I know you'll forgive me.'

She replies, 'If your penis is as hard as your elbow, I'm in room 1221.'

A representative for a condom company is on her way to an international condom convention. While rushing through the airport, she drops the briefcase carrying her samples, scattering condoms across the floor. She notices a passer-by looking at her as she tries to get the condoms back into her briefcase.

'It's OK,' she says. 'I'm going to a convention.'

A beautiful woman loves growing tomatoes, but can't seem to get her tomatoes to turn red. One day while taking a stroll she comes upon a male neighbour who has the most beautiful garden full of huge red tomatoes.

The woman asks the man, 'What do you do to get your tomatoes so red?'

The man responds, 'Well, twice a day I stand in front of my tomato garden and expose myself, and my tomatoes turn red from blushing so much.'

Well, the woman is so impressed, she decides to try doing the same thing to her tomato garden to see if it works. So twice a day for two weeks she exposes herself to her garden hoping for the best.

One day the man is passing by and asks the woman, 'By the way, How did you make out? Did your tomatoes turn red?'

'No' she replies, 'but my cucumbers are enormous.'

A married man gets home early from work and hears strange noises coming from the bedroom. He rushes upstairs to find his wife naked on the bed, sweating and panting.

'What's up?' he asks.

'I'm having a heart attack,' cries the woman.

He rushes downstairs to grab the phone, but just as he's dialling, his four-year-old son comes up and says, 'Daddy! Daddy! Uncle Ted's hiding in your closet and he's got no clothes on!'

The guy slams the phone down and storms upstairs into the bedroom, past his screaming wife, and rips open the wardrobe door. Sure enough, there is his brother, totally naked, cowering on the closet floor.

'You bastard!' says the husband. 'My wife's having a heart attack and all you can do is run around the house naked scaring the kids?'

Two cosmonauts (male and female) are sent to Uranus to begin cultural bonding with the aliens of that planet. Eventually, talk gets around to reproduction, and the Uranians offer to demonstrate how they do it. Uranian One stands in front of Uranian Two, places his hand over a special metal plate and vibrates for thirty seconds. Immediately afterwards, a small Uranian pops out of a special hatch in Uranian Two's crotch. The Uranians then ask the Earthlings to demonstrate how they do it, and they duly oblige. The Uranians then ask where the Earthling baby is. They are told that it takes nine months.

Uranian One asks, 'Then why all the rush at the end?'

Little Jimmy's parents are trying to potty train him. When he goes to the bathroom, though, he hits everything but the toilet. Mum then has to go in and clean up after him. After two weeks, she has had enough, and takes Jimmy to the doctor.

After the examination, the doctor says, 'Well, his unit is too small. An old wives' tale says to give him two slices of toast each morning and his unit will grow. He will then be able to hold it and aim straight.'

Next morning, Jimmy jumps out of bed and runs down to the kitchen. On the table are twelve slices of toast.

'Mum,' Jimmy yells. 'The doc said I only had to eat two slices.'

'I know,' his mum says and smiles 'The other ten are for your father.'

While in the playground with his friend, Alex notices that Jimmy is wearing a brand new, shiny watch.

'Did you get that for your birthday?' asks Alex.

'Nope,' replies Jimmy.

'Well, did you get it for Christmas then?'

Again Jimmy says, 'Nope.'

'You didn't steal it, did you?' asks Alex.

'No,' says Jimmy. 'I went into mum and dad's bedroom the other night when they were "doing the nasty". Dad gave me his watch to get rid of me.'

Alex is extremely impressed with this idea, and extremely jealous of Jimmy's new watch. He vows to get one for himself. That night, he waits outside his parents' bedroom until he hears the unmistakable noises of lovemaking. Just then, he swings the door wide open and boldly strides into the bedroom.

His father, caught in mid-stroke, turns and says angrily, 'What do you want now?'

'I wanna watch,' Alex replies.

Without missing a stroke, his father says, 'Fine. Stand in the corner and watch, but keep quiet.'

A young couple is invited to a swanky masked Halloween party. The wife comes down with a terrible headache and tells her husband to go to the party without her and have a good time. Being the devoted husband, he protests, but she argues and says she is going to take some aspirin and go to bed.

She tells him there is no need for him to miss the fun. So he takes his costume and away he goes.

The wife, after sleeping soundly for about an hour, awakens without pain, and as it is still early she decides to go to the party. Because hubby doesn't know what her costume is, she thinks she will have some kicks watching her husband to see how he acts when she's not around. She joins the party and soon spots her husband cavorting around on the dance floor. He's dancing with every nice chick he can and copping a feel here, and taking a little kiss there. His wife sidles up to him and, being a rather seductive babe herself, he leaves his partner high and dry and devotes his time to the new action. She lets him go as far as he wishes; naturally, since he is her husband. Finally he whispers a little proposition in her ear and she agrees, so off they go to one of the cars and have a little bang. Just before the unmasking at midnight, she slips out, goes home, puts the costume away and gets into bed, wondering what kind of excuse he will have for his nocturnal behaviour.

She is sitting up reading when he comes in, and she asks him how the party went.

He says, 'Oh, the same old thing. You know I never have a good time when you're not there.'

Then she asks, 'Did you dance much?'

He replies, 'I'll tell you, I never even danced one dance. When I got to the party I met Pete, Bill and some other guys, so we went into the den and played poker all evening. But I'll tell you . . . the guy that I loaned my costume to sure had one hell of a time!'

A mother and father take their young son to the circus. When the elephants appear, the son is intrigued by them.

He turns to his mother and says, 'Mum, what's that hanging between the elephant's legs?'

The mother is very embarrassed, and says, 'Oh, it's nothing son.'
So the son turns to his father and asks the same question.
The father replies, 'It's the elephant's penis, son.'
So the son says, 'Why did mum say it was nothing?'
The father draws himself up, and says proudly, 'Because I've spoiled that woman, son.'

A guy goes into a chemist to buy condoms.
The clerk says, 'What size?'
The guy says, 'Gee, I don't know.'
The clerk says, 'Go see Jill in aisle six.'
He goes over to see Jill, who grabs him by the crotch and yells, 'Medium!'
The guy is mortified. He hurries over to pay and gets out of the store. Another guy comes in to buy condoms. The clerk asks the size and again sends him over to Jill in aisle six.
Jill grabs him and yells, 'Large!'
The guy struts over to the register, pays, and leaves. A high school kid comes in to buy condoms.
The clerk says, 'What size?'
The kid, very embarrassed, says, 'I've never done this before. I don't know what size.'
The clerk sends him over to Jill in aisle six, who grabs him and yells, 'Clean-up in aisle six!'

Three guys go to a striptease joint. The young woman on stage, wearing only a thong and a smile, comes up to the first guy and performs her dance for him. He takes out $100 and slaps it on her right cheek. It sticks.
Then she proceeds to the second guy and does the same dance. The second guy takes out $100 and slaps it on her left cheek. It sticks.

She then goes to the third guy and performs her dance. The third guy pulls out his wallet, only to realise that he does not have any cash. So he takes out his credit card, swipes it between her cheeks and takes the $200.

A man and his young son are in the chemist when the son comes across the condoms and asks his father what they are.

The dad replies, 'Well son, those are condoms and they're for protection when you're having sex.'

The son then picks up one of the packs and asks why it has three condoms in it.

The dad replies, 'Those are for high-school boys. One for Friday, one for Saturday, and one for Sunday.'

The son then picks up one with six condoms and asks, 'Why six?'

The dad replies, 'Well son, those are for uni students. Two for Friday, two for Saturday and two for Sunday.'

The son then notices the twelve-pack of condoms and asks the same question.

The dad replies, 'Son, those are for married men. One for January, one for February, one for March . . .'

A couple have been married for fifteen years. One afternoon they are working in the garden together.

As the wife is bending over pulling weeds, the husband says, 'Hey honey, you are getting fat. Your bum is getting huge. I bet it's as big as the gas grill now.'

The husband, feeling he needs to prove his point, gets a measuring tape, measures the grill and then measures his wife's bum.

'Yep,' he says, 'Just what I thought, they're about the same size.'

The wife gets very angry and decides to let him do the gardening alone. She goes inside and doesn't speak to her husband for the rest of the day.

That evening when they go to bed, the husband cuddles up to his wife and says, 'How about it, Hon? How about a little lovemaking?'

The wife rolls over and turns her back to him, giving him the cold shoulder.

'What's the matter?' he asks.

She replies, 'You don't think I'm going to fire up this big gas grill for one little weenie, do you?'

A fellow is talking to his buddy, and he says, 'I don't know what to get my wife for her birthday. She has everything, and besides, she can afford to buy anything she wants, so I'm stumped.'

His buddy says, 'I have an idea. Why don't you make up a certificate that says she can have two hours of great sex, any way she wants it. She'll probably be thrilled!'

So the first guy does just that.

The next day his buddy asks, 'Well, did you take my suggestion? How'd it turn out?'

'She loved it. She jumped up, thanked me, kissed me on the mouth, and ran out the door yelling, "I'll see you in two hours!"'

John takes his blind date to the carnival.

'What would you like to do first, Kim?' he asks.

'I want to get weighed,' says the girl. They amble over to the weight guesser. The man guesses 55kg. Kim gets on the scale and it reads 53kg and she wins a prize.

Next the couple go on the Ferris wheel. When the ride is over, John again asks Kim what she would like to do.

'I want to get weighed,' she says. Back to the weight guesser they go. Since they have been there before, the man guesses Kim's correct weight, and John loses his dollar. The couple walk around the carnival and again John asks where to next.

'I want to get weighed,' Kim responds.

By this time, John thinks she is really weird and takes her home early, dropping her off with a handshake.

Kim's roommate, Laura, asks, 'How'd it go?'

Kim responds, 'Oh, Waura, it was wousy.'

H oward is feeling guilty. No matter how he tries to forget about it, he can't. The guilt and sense of betrayal are overwhelming.

Every once in a while he hears a soothing voice trying to reassure him, 'Howard, don't worry about it. You aren't the first doctor to sleep with one of his patients and you won't be the last.'

But invariably the other voice brings him back to reality, 'Howard, you're a veterinarian.'

A woman is having a passionate affair with an inspector from a pest-control company. One afternoon they are carrying on in the bedroom together when her husband arrives home unexpectedly.

'Quick,' says the woman to her lover, 'into the closet.'

She bundles him in the closet stark naked. The husband, however, becomes suspicious and, after a search of the bedroom, discovers the man in the closet.

'Who are you?' he asks.

'I'm an inspector from Bugs-B-Gone,' says the exterminator.

'What are you doing in there?' the husband asks.

'I'm investigating a complaint about an infestation of moths,' the man replies.

'And where are your clothes?' asks the husband.

The man looked down at himself and says, 'Those little bastards.'

A guy approaches the ticket window of a movie theatre with a chicken under his arm, and asks for two tickets. The girl at the counter wants to know who he's taking in with him.

He replies, 'Well, my pet chicken, of course.'

The girl tells him that he can't take a chicken into the theatre, so he goes around the corner, stuffs the chicken into his trousers, and returns. He buys his ticket and goes in.

Inside the theatre, the chicken starts to get hot and begins to squirm. The man unzips his fly so the chicken can stick its head out, get some air and watch the movie. Sitting next to him is Agnes.

She elbows Myrtle and whispers, 'Myrtle, this man over here has just unzipped his pants.'

Myrtle whispers back, 'Oh, don't worry about it. You've seen one, you've seen them all.'

Agnes says, 'I know. But this one's eating my popcorn.'

A young couple have been married for a couple of weeks, and the man is always after his wife to quit smoking.

One afternoon, she lights up after some lovemaking, and he says, 'You really ought to quit.'

She is getting tired of his nagging and says, 'I really enjoy a good cigarette after sex.'

He replies, 'But they stunt your growth.'

'Have you ever smoked?' she asks.

'No.'

Smiling and dropping her gaze to his groin, she says, 'So, what's your excuse?'

Two lovers are really into spiritualism and reincarnation. They vow that if either dies, the one remaining will try to contact the partner in the other world exactly thirty days after the death. Unfortunately, a few weeks later, the young man dies in a car crash. True to her word, his sweetheart tries to contact him in the spirit world exactly thirty days later.

At the séance, she calls out, 'John, John, this is Martha. Do you hear me?'

A ghostly voice answers her, 'Yes Martha, this is John. I can hear you.'

Martha tearfully asks, 'Oh John, what is it like where you are?'

'It's great. There are azure skies, a soft breeze, sunshine most of the time, the grass is green and the cows have beautiful eyes.'

'What do you do all day?' asks Martha.

'Well, Martha, we get up before sunrise, eat a good breakfast, and then there's nothing but making love until noon. After lunch, we nap until two and then make love again until about five. After dinner, we go at it again until we fall asleep about 11 p.m.'

Martha is somewhat taken aback. 'Is that what heaven really is like?'

'Heaven? I'm not in heaven, Martha.'

'Well, then, where are you?'

'I'm a bull on a stud farm.'

A man is going door-to-door doing a sexual survey in Jeff's neighbourhood.

'How many times a week do you sleep with your wife?' asks the man.

'Three times,' Jeff says without hesitation.

'That is once more often than your neighbour,' the man says, writing.

'That makes sense,' Jeff says, 'after all, she's *my* wife.'

XX

Risqué.

Simon Pureheart has three daughters, and prides himself on the fact that they have been brought up innocent and unsullied. One day, he decides to test his hypothesis, and calls his eldest daughter April, aged twenty, into his study.

He flops his dick out onto the desk, and enquires, 'What's this?'

'That's a prick.'

Mortified, he banishes her from the family home with ringing words that include 'ingratitude', 'slut' and 'brazen harlot'. He then calls in his middle daughter May (aged eighteen), with precisely the same result. She is also sent packing with a stern warning about hellfire and eternal damnation. Finally, it is the turn of little June, aged fifteen.

'Surely,' thinks Simon, 'this one will still be pure.'

He slaps his old man onto the desk, and demands, 'What's this?'

'That, father, is a penis,' replies June.

'Praise be to God,' responds Simon. 'Do you know that both your older sisters called that a prick?'

'You don't call that a prick, do you?'

Marie decides to do something wild that she hasn't done before, so she decides to rent her first X-rated adult video. She goes to the video store and, after looking around for a while, selects a title that sounds very stimulating. She drives home, lights some candles, slips into something comfortable, and puts the tape in the VCR. To her disappointment, there's nothing but static on the screen, so she calls the video store to complain.

'I just rented an adult movie from you and there's nothing on the tape but static.'

'Sorry about that. We've had problems with some of those tapes. Which title did you rent?'

'It's called *Head Cleaner*.'

Mark and Bubba, two army buddies, are on leave and decide to go to Bubba's house and get drunk. Lo and behold they run out of beer so Bubba says that he will go for more. As he is leaving he tells his wife Linda-Lou to show Mark her best Southern hospitality, which she agrees to do. Bubba comes back with the beer and finds Mark and Linda-Lou screwing right on the kitchen floor.

Bubba yells, 'What are you doing Linda-Lou?'

She replies, 'You told me to show Mark my best Southern hospitality.'

Bubba then says, 'Gee whiz girl, arch your back, poor Mark's balls are on the cold kitchen floor.'

A wife is in bed with her lover when she hears her husband's key in the door.

'Stay where you are,' she says. 'He's so drunk he won't even notice you're in bed with me.'

Sure enough, the husband slumps into bed, none the wiser. But a few minutes later, through a drunken haze, he sees six feet sticking out at the end of the bed.

He turns to his wife. 'Hey, there are six feet in this bed. There should only be four. What's going on?'

'Nonsense,' says the wife. 'You're so drunk you've miscounted. Get out of bed and try again. You can see better from over there.'

The husband climbs out of bed and counts. 'One, two, three, four. You're right, you know.'

A young man is showing off his new sports car to his girlfriend. She is thrilled at the speed.

'If I do 250kph, will you take off your clothes?' he smirks.

'OK,' says his adventurous girlfriend.

As he gets up to 250kph, she peels off all her clothes. Unable to keep his eyes on the road, the car skids on some gravel and flips over. The naked girl is thrown clear, but the boyfriend is jammed beneath the steering wheel.

'Go and get help!' he cries.

'But I can't! I'm naked and my clothes are gone!'

'Take my shoe,' he says, 'and cover yourself.'

Holding the shoe over her privates, the girl runs down the road and finds a service station. Still holding the shoe between her legs, she pleads to the service station proprietor for help.

'Please help me! My boyfriend's stuck!'

The proprietor looks at the shoe and says, 'There's nothing I can do. He's in too far.'

A husband and wife decide they need to use code to indicate that they want to have sex without letting their children in on it. They decide on the word 'typewriter'.

One day the husband tells his five-year-old daughter, 'Go tell your mummy that daddy needs to type a letter.'

The child tells her mother what her dad said, and her mum responds, 'Tell your daddy that he can't type a letter right now 'cause there is a red ribbon in the typewriter.'

The child goes back to tell her father what mummy said.

A few days later the mum tells the daughter, 'Tell daddy that he can type that letter now.'

The child tells her father, returns to her mother and announces, 'Daddy said never mind about the typewriter, he already wrote the letter by hand.'

A guy stumbles from a bar with his keys in his hand. A cop sees him and asks, 'Can I help you Sir?'

'Yesshh. Ssshhomebody shtole my carr.'

The cop asks him, 'Well, where did you last see it?'

The guy thinks for a while, 'At the end of dissh key.'

The cop looks at him and notices that his tool is hanging down from his pants.

'Sir, are you aware that you are exposing yourself to the whole world to see?'

The guy looks down woefully and says, 'Oh my goddd. Thheey got my girlfriend too.'

Two women are at their local shopping mall, when one happens to see her husband emerging from a florist shop carrying a large bunch of roses.

'Oh no,' she says 'Looks like I'll have to spread the legs tonight.'

"Why?' asks the other. 'Don't you own a vase?'

A guy goes to a pharmacist and says, 'Listen, I've got these twin girls coming over this weekend, and they are hot, very hot. Would you have something to keep me going all night? It's going to be a wild weekend.'

The pharmacist goes into the back room, comes back with an old dusty bottle and says, 'This stuff is potent. Drink only one teaspoon of it, and I guarantee that you will be going all weekend. You'll tire them out. Let me know how it goes.'

The weekend goes by and on Monday morning, the

pharmacist goes to work and finds the same guy waiting for him on the door-step.

The pharmacist says, 'What are you doing here so early? How was your weekend?'

The guy replies, 'Quick, I need some muscle lotion.'

The pharmacist, knowing what the guy has been doing all weekend, says, 'Are you crazy, you can't put that on your penis. The skin is way too sensitive.'

The guy says, 'No, no, it's not for that, it's for my arm.'

'What? What happened?' asks the pharmacist.

'Well . . . I drank the whole bottle of your potion.'

'Oh my god, and then what?'

'The girls never showed up!'

A married woman is having an affair. Whenever her lover comes over, she puts her nine-year-old son in the closet. One day the woman hears a car in the driveway and, thinking it's her husband, puts her lover in the closet, as well.

Inside the closet, the little boy says, 'It's dark in here, isn't it?'

'Yes it is,' the man replies.

'You wanna buy a baseball?' the little boy asks.

'No thanks,' the man replies.

'I think you do want to buy a baseball,' the little extortionist continues.

'OK. How much?' the man replies after considering the position he is in.

'Twenty-five dollars,' the little boy replies.

'Twenty-five dollars?' the man repeats but complies to protect his hidden position.

The following week, the lover is visiting the woman again when she hears a car in the driveway and again places her lover in the closet with her little boy.

'It's dark in here, isn't it?' the boy starts off.

'Yes it is,' replies the man.

'Wanna buy a baseball glove?' the little boy asks.

'OK. How much?' the hiding lover responds, acknowledging his disadvantage.

'Fifty dollars,' the boy replies and the transaction is completed.

The next weekend, the little boy's father says, 'Hey, son. Go get your ball and glove and we'll play some catch.'

'I can't. I sold them,' replies the little boy.

'How much did you get for them?' asks the father, expecting to hear the profit in terms of lizards and candy.

'Seventy-five dollars,' the little boy says.

'Seventy-five dollars? That's thievery! I'm taking you to church right now. You must confess your sin and ask for forgiveness,' the father explains as he hauls the child away.

At the church, the little boy goes into the confessional, draws the curtain, sits down, and says, 'It's dark in here, isn't it?'

'Don't you start that shit in here,' the priest says.

A pianist is hired to play background music for a movie. When it is completed he asks when and where he can see the film. The producer sheepishly confesses that it is actually a porno film and it is due out in a month. A month later, the musician goes to a porno theatre to see it. With his collar up and dark glasses on, he takes a seat in the back row, next to a couple who also seem to be in disguise.

The movie is even raunchier than he had feared, featuring group sex, S&M and even a dog. After a while, the embarrassed pianist turns to the couple and says, 'I'm only here to listen to the music.'

'Yeah?' replies the man. 'We're only here to see our dog.'

Pingi the penguin is a long-haul truck driver. One day, while driving across a desert, his truck starts to play up. Spotting a garage in the distance, he coaxes his
vehicle to it, and asks the mechanic to have a look at it. Finding the heat of the sun unbearable, as penguins are wont to do, Pingi retreats into the cafe and has a couple of cooling drinks. Still hot, he then has some ice-cream, but as penguins are not built to handle ice-cream (flippers being most unsuitable), most of the ice-cream ends up all over him.

Covered with ice-cream, he wanders back to where the mechanic is finishing up.

'How are things going?' asks Pingi.

'It looks like you've blown a seal,' says the mechanic.

'No,' replies Pingi, 'it's ice-cream.'

A man takes good care of his body. He lifts weights and jogs 10km every day. One morning he looks into the mirror admiring his body and notices that he is sun-tanned all over, with the exception of his penis. So he decides to do something about that.

He goes to the beach, completely undresses, and buries himself in the sand, except for his penis, which he leaves sticking out of the sand.

A bit later, two little old ladies come strolling along the beach, one using a cane to help her get along. Upon seeing the thing sticking out of the sand, the lady with the cane begins to poke the penis with her cane.

Remarking to the other little old lady, she says, 'There really is no justice in the world.'

The other little old lady asks, 'What do you mean by that'?

The first little old lady replies, 'Look at that. When I was twenty, I was curious about it. When I was thirty, I enjoyed it. When I was forty, I asked for it. When I was fifty, I paid for it.

When I was sixty, I prayed for it. When I was seventy, I forgot about it. Now that I'm eighty, the damned things are growing wild, and I'm too old to squat.'

A man with a twenty-five-inch penis goes to his doctor to complain that he is unable to get any women to have sex with him. They all tell him that his penis is too long.

'Doctor,' he asks, in total frustration, 'is there any way you can shorten it?'

The doctor replies, 'Medically son, there is nothing I can do. But, I do know this witch who may be able to help you.'

So the doctor gives him directions to the witch. The man calls upon the witch and relays his story.

'Witch, my penis is twenty-five inches long and I can't get any women to have sex with me. Can you help me shorten it?'

The witch stares in amazement, scratches her head, and then replies, 'I think I have a solution to your problem. What you have to do is go to this pond deep in the forest. In the pond, you will see a frog sitting on a log who can help solve your dilemma. First you must ask the frog, will you marry me? Each time the frog declines your proposal, your penis will be five inches shorter.'

The man's face lights up and he dashes off into the forest.

Finding the frog, he says, 'Will you marry me?'

The frog looks at him dejectedly and replies, 'No.'

The man looks down and suddenly his penis is five inches shorter.

'Wow,' he screams out loud. 'This is great. But it's still too long at twenty inches, so I'll ask the frog to marry me again.'

'Frog, will you marry me?' the guy shouts.

The frog rolls its eyes back in its head and screams back, 'No!'

The man feels another twitch in his penis, looks down, and it is another five inches shorter.

The man laughs, 'This is fantastic.' He looks down at his penis again, fifteen inches long, and reflects for a moment. Fifteen inches is still a monster, just a little less would be ideal.

Grinning, he looks across the pond and yells out, 'Frog will you marry me?'

The frog looks back across the pond shaking its head, 'How many damn times do I have to tell you? No, no and for the last time, no!'

A guy buys a second-hand Harley Davidson which is almost in mint condition. Before riding off, he asks the owner how he managed to keep it in such good shape.

'Well,' says the owner, 'it's pretty simple. Just make sure that if the bike is outside and it's going to rain, rub Vaseline on the chrome. It protects it from the rain.'

The next night, the guy goes over to his girlfriend's house for dinner. It's the first time he's been there and she meets him on the doorstep.

'Honey,' she says, 'I gotta tell you something about my parents before you go in. When we eat dinner, we don't talk. In fact, the person who says anything during dinner has to do the dishes.'

'No problem,' he says. And in they go.

The boyfriend is astounded. Right smack in the middle of the living room is a huge stack of dirty dishes. In the family room, another huge stack of dishes. Piled up the stairs, dirty dishes. In fact, everywhere he looks, dirty dishes. They sit down to dinner and, sure enough, no-one says a word. As dinner progresses, the boyfriend decides to take advantage of the situation. So he leans over and kisses his girlfriend. No-one says a word. So he decides to reach over and fondle her breasts. He looks at her parents, but still they keep quiet. So he stands up, grabs his girlfriend, strips her naked, and they make love right on the dinner table. Still, no-one says a word.

'Her mum's kinda cute,' he thinks. So he grabs his girlfriend's mum and has his way with her right there on the dinner table. Again, total silence. Then, a few raindrops hit the window and the boyfriend realises it's starting to rain. He thinks he'd better take care of the motorcycle, so he pulls the Vaseline from his pocket. Suddenly the father stands up and shouts, 'All right, all right! I'll do the damn dishes.'

Time after time, night after night Tom just can't last long while having sex with his wife. He feels horrible, he feels like he is disappointing her.

She constantly reassures him saying, 'Honey, don't worry about it. It's alright.'

But he decides that he is going to do whatever he can to remedy the problem. After a day or two of thought, Tom decides to ask his doctor.

The doctor looks at him and says, 'Believe it or not, it's not an uncommon problem. Have you ever tried masturbating before you have sex with your wife?'

Tom replies, 'No.'

'Well,' the doctor continues, 'if you do, it will take you longer to come when you're having sex with your wife.'

Tom smiles and says, 'Thanks doc, I'll give it a try.'

The next day while Tom is at work, he receives a call from his wife. She warns him that she is extremely horny and that she is going to attack him the moment he walks through the door.

This gets him excited, but then he realises that if she attacks him when he walks through the door, he won't be able to try out the doctor's suggestion.

Tom tries to think of somewhere he can go to try his new technique. He can't do it at his desk. The mail room is too risky. So is the toilet. He decides he will just pull over on his way home, get under his truck and act like he's working on it, nobody will know.

Tom leaves work and gets about halfway home before he decides he's found just as good a place as any to do what he must do. He pulls over, gets under his truck and starts masturbating, eyes closed imaging that it's his wife giving him a hand job. After a few minutes he feels someone hit him on the leg.

Startled, Tom yells out, 'What? Who's there?'

A reply comes sharply, ' I'm the sheriff, mind if I ask what you're doin'?'

Tom has to think fast, 'It appears I have an oil leak or something, I'm just checking it out.'

The sheriff replies, 'Oh, OK. But you might also want to check your parking brake while you're down there, your truck rolled down the hill five minutes ago.'

A man and a woman have been dating for about a year and their relationship is taking a turn towards the serious. The man proposes and the woman accepts, however she tells him that she wants him to know that her chest is as flat as a baby's chest.

He says that he loves her and that her measurements don't matter to him.

'Anyway,' he continues. 'My penis is the size of a baby.'

She says that she loves him for who he is and that size doesn't matter at all.

On the day of the wedding all goes well. That night the happy couple check into the honeymoon suite at a resort hotel. The blushing bride is in the bathroom putting on a sexy nightie. Her husband is in the bed waiting. As she enters the bedroom, she reminds him of her confession about her chest being like a baby's.

'Don't worry honey,' he says.

She takes off her night gown and her breasts are the smallest he has ever seen. He says that he is going to get undressed and reminds her of his confession about his penis being like a baby.

As he takes off his pants, the new bride says, 'Good God Almighty. I thought you said your penis was like a baby!'

'It is,' he says, 'Nine pounds and twenty-one inches long.'

A husband suspects his wife is having an affair. He needs to go on a business trip for several days, so he decides to set a trap for her. He puts a bowl of milk under the bed. From the bed springs, he suspends a spoon. He has it calibrated so that her weight on the bed will not drop the spoon into the milk. But, if there is any more weight than that, the spoon will drop into the milk and he will detect it upon his return home.

He comes home several days later. The first thing he does is reach under the bed and retrieve the bowl. It's full of butter.

Bordering on the obscene.

A convicted murderer escapes from prison after spending twenty-five years inside. While on the run, he breaks into a house and ties up a young couple who have been sleeping in the bedroom. He ties the man to a chair on one side of the room and ties the woman to the bed. He gets on the bed right over the woman, and appears to be kissing her neck. Suddenly he gets up and leaves the room, though not the house.

As soon as possible the husband makes his way across the room to his bride, his chair in tow, and whispers, 'Honey, this guy hasn't seen a woman in years. I saw him kissing your neck. Just cooperate and do anything he wants. If he wants to have sex with you, just go along with it and pretend you like it. Whatever you do don't fight him or make him mad. Our lives depend on it! Be strong and I love you.'

After spitting out the gag in her mouth, the half-naked wife says, 'Darling, I'm so relieved you feel that way. You're right, he hasn't seen a woman in years, but he wasn't kissing my neck. He was whispering in my ear. He said he thinks you're really cute and asked if we kept the Vaseline in the bathroom. Be strong and I love you, too.'

It is George the mailman's last day on the job after thirty-five years of carrying the mail through all kinds of weather to the same neighbourhood. When he arrives at the first house on his route he is greeted by the whole family there, who roundly and soundly congratulate him and send him on his way with a tidy gift envelope. At the second house they present him with a box of fine cigars. The folks at the third house hand him a selection of terrific fishing lures.

At the fourth house, a strikingly beautiful woman in a revealing negligee meets him at the door. She takes him by the hand, gently leads him through the door (which she closes behind him), and leads him up the stairs to the bedroom where she blows his mind with the most passionate love he has ever experienced. When he has had enough they go downstairs, where she fixes him a giant breakfast: eggs, potatoes, ham, sausage, blueberry waffles, and freshly squeezed orange juice. When he is truly satisfied she pours him a cup of steaming coffee. As she is pouring, he notices a dollar bill sticking out from under the cup's bottom edge.

'All this was just too wonderful for words,' he says, 'but what's the dollar for?'

'Well,' she says, 'last night, I told my husband that today would be your last day, and that we should do something special for you. I asked him what to give you. He said, "Screw him. Give him a dollar." The breakfast was my idea.'

A retired sea dog visits a prostitute.

After a minute or two on the job, he enquires, 'How am I doing, m'dear?'

'In naval language, you're steaming ahead at three knots.'

'How d'ye mean?' demands the old salt.

'You're not in, you're not hard, and you're not getting your money back.'

A man and a woman start to have sex in the middle of a dark forest.

After fifteen minutes of this, the man finally gets up and says, 'Damn, I wish I had a torch.'

The woman says, 'So do I. You've been eating grass for the last ten minutes!'

A man is walking along the street when he sees a ladder going into the clouds. As any of us would do, he climbed the ladder. He reaches a cloud, upon which sits a rather plump and very ugly woman.

'Screw me or climb the ladder to success,' she says.

No contest, thought the man, so he climbs the ladder to the next cloud. On this cloud is a slightly thinner woman, who is slightly easier on the eye.

'Screw me hard or climb the ladder to success,' she says.

'Well,' thinks the man, 'might as well carry on.'

On the next cloud is another woman who, this time, is quite attractive.

'Screw me now or climb the ladder to success,' she utters. As he turns her down and goes on up the ladder, the man thinks to himself that this is getting better the further he goes. On the next cloud is an absolute beauty. Slim, attractive, the lot.

'Screw me here and now or climb the ladder to success,' she flirts.

Unable to imagine what could be waiting, and being a gambling man, he decides to climb again. When he reaches the next cloud, there is a huge, ugly man.

'Hello,' says the ugly, fat man, 'I'm Cess!'

A middle-aged man and woman meet, fall in love, and decide to get married. On their wedding night they settle into the bridal suite at their hotel and the bride says to her new groom, 'Please promise to be gentle . . . I am still a virgin.'

The startled groom asks, 'How can that be? You've been married three times before.'

The bride responds, 'Well you see it was this way: My first husband was a psychiatrist and all he ever wanted to do was talk about it. My second husband was a gynaecologist and all he ever wanted to do was look at it. My third husband was a stamp collector and all he ever wanted to do was . . . God I miss him.'

Three prostitutes are living together: a mother, a daughter and a grandmother. One night the daughter comes home looking very down.

'How did you do tonight, dear?' asks her mother.

'Not too good.' replies the daughter, 'I only got $20 for a blow job.'

'Wow!' says the mother, 'In my day, we were glad to get $5 for a blow job!'

'Good God!' says the grandmother. 'In my day, we were glad just to get something warm in our stomachs!'

A couple are having a quickie in the back of a car in a dark lane.

The man says to the woman, 'This is fantastic, but why are your ankles banging against my ears?'

'I've still got my tights on.'

Bill Bodgy is a travelling toy salesman who is going through a period of low sales. He arrives one morning at the door of a large mansion, and is met by a nine-year-old boy. He enquires if either of the boy's parents are home, and receives a negative reply. He tells the boy that he is selling the latest thing in trail bikes, and will come back later in order to speak to the boy's parents. The boy tells him not to bother, since he is too advanced for that sort of thing. The salesman tries to push his product, and then foolishly agrees that if he can do everything the boy can do, the boy will ask for a bike for Christmas. If not, then Bill must give him a bike. First of all, the boy jumps onto the roof of a nearby shed, balances along the ridge, and jumps off with a somersault. Thanking his lucky stars he has kept fit, Bill copies him. Next the boy does five handstands on the lawn, with the same response from Bill. The boy then takes Bill into the house, and into a rear bedroom, in which a stunning twenty-five-year-old girl is lying in bed.

'My cousin Jackie,' explains the boy. 'She's a flight attendant with Qantas, and has just come off an international flight and taken a couple of sleeping pills. Nothing will wake her. Is this deal still on?'

Somewhat apprehensive, but desperate for a sale, Bill agrees. The boy pulls down the bedclothes to reveal a skimpy bikini nightie. He then replaces the bedclothes, and invites Bill to copy his actions. Sweat breaking from his brow, Bill does as invited. The boy then pulls down the bedclothes a second time, and slides the nightie top up to reveal the most immaculate pair of tits. Bill does the same, now trembling. The boy then slides down the bottom half of the nightie, to reveal all. Shaking like a leaf, Bill follows suit.

The boy then takes out his dick, folds it in half, and announces, 'I'll have a red one with racing handles.'

An upper-class Englishman is holidaying in far north Queensland, Australia. His car breaks down and he starts walking to the nearest town, 20km away. While he is walking, he gets caught in a flash tropical storm. By the time he gets to the town, he is wet through. He walks into the pub and orders a scotch. It tastes terrible but it's better than nothing. He looks around the pub for the toilet but all he can see is a pub full of outback Aussies, drinking, cursing and spitting. He asks the barman where the toilet is and the barman gestures to a door at the back of the pub.

The Englishman trudges outside into the rain. All he can see through the rain is two big piles of shit, one much bigger than the other. He walks over to the smaller pile, relieved that someone had the sense to start a new pile since the larger one was clearly unmanageable. He has his pants around his ankles and is in the process of relieving himself when a gunshot rings out and a bullet smacks into the heap just beside him. He turns around, in a somewhat vulnerable position, and sees this huge Aussie guy standing at the door of the pub with a smoking gun in his hand.

'What's going on?' stammers the Englishman in fear.

The Aussie bellows back, 'Get the hell out of the Ladies you dirty bastard.'

A guy goes to a tattoo parlour and offers the tattoo artist $1000 to tattoo a $100 note on his cock. The artist agrees, but is curious and asks the man why he wants to do this.

The man replies, 'I have my reasons but I would rather not tell you right now.'

The artist goes ahead and does the job. But, all the while he is anxious with curiosity over why this man wants a $100 note on his penis. So, he tells the man that he really needs to know the reason why and says that the man can keep the $1000 if he tells him the reason for putting a $100 note on his cock.

'OK,' says the man. 'First, I like to play with my money. Second, I like to watch my money grow. And third, and most importantly, the next time my wife wants to blow $100, she can stay home to do it.'

Three sisters decide to get married on the same day to save their parents the expense of separate weddings. As a further step to reduce the price tag, the three sisters resolve to spend their honeymoon night at home. Later that night, their mother can't sleep, so she goes to the kitchen for a cup of tea. On her way, she tiptoes by her oldest daughter's bedroom and hears her screaming.

The mother thinks to herself, 'That's normal, especially on her wedding night.'

She sneaks by her second-oldest daughter's room and hears her laughing.

'That's normal too,' she says, smiling to herself.

Finally, she slips by her youngest daughter's room where she doesn't hear a peep, but she thinks nothing of it. The next morning in the kitchen, after the husbands have gone out, the woman asks her eldest daughter about last night's noises.

'Well Mum,' she replies, 'you always said if it hurt I should scream.'

'You're absolutely right sweetheart,' the mother assures her, and turns to her middle daughter.

'Now why were you laughing?' she asks.

'You always said if it tickled, I could laugh,' she answers.

'True enough, honey.' The mother smiles, remembering her newlywed days.

'Now it's your turn, baby,' she says, turning to her youngest daughter. 'Why was it so quiet in your room last night?'

'Mum, don't you remember? You always told me never to talk with my mouth full.'

A couple are going through some tough times, so they agree that the woman will walk the streets for a night and see if she can make a bit of money. The guy drops her off on a corner in a rough area of town and drives off. The next morning he picks her up and finds her with her hair a mess, make-up smudged and obviously needing a lot of rest.

She climbs in the car and excitedly says, 'Look honey, I made $40.50.'

'Which of the buggers gave you fifty cents?' he asks.

'All of them!' she says.

A hippie gets onto a bus and sits next to a nun in the front seat. The hippie looks over and asks the nun if she will have sex with him. The nun, surprised by the question, politely declines and gets off at the next stop.

When the bus starts on its way the driver says to the hippie, 'I can tell you how you can get that nun to have sex with you.'

The hippie says that he'd love to know, so the bus driver tells him that every Tuesday evening at midnight the nun goes to the cemetery and prays to God. 'If you went dressed in a robe and glow in the dark paint mask she would think you are God and you could command her to have sex with you.'

The hippie decides this is a great idea, so the next Tuesday he goes to the cemetery and waits for the nun to show up. At midnight, sure enough, the nun shows up and begins praying. The hippie jumps out from hiding and says, 'I am God! I have heard your prayers and I will answer them, but . . . first you must have sex with me.'

The nun agrees but asks for anal sex so she might keep her virginity, because she is married to the church. The hippie agrees to this and has his way with the nun.

After the hippie finishes he stands up and rips off the mask and shouts, 'Ha! Ha! Ha! I'm the hippie!'

Then the nun jumps up and shouts, 'Ha! Ha! Ha! I'm the bus driver!'

One morning, a golfer approaches the first tee, only to find another guy approaching from the other side. They begin talking and decide to play nine holes together. After teeing off, they set off down the fairway, continuing their chat.

'What do you do?' the first man asks.

'I'm a salesman. What about you?'

'I'm a hit man for the mob.'

The hit man notices that the first guy starts getting a little nervous and continues, 'Yeah. I'm the highest-paid guy in the business. I'm the best.'

He stops, sets down his bag of clubs, and pulls out a fancy, high-powered rifle that is loaded with all types of scopes and sights. He then asks the man where he lives.

Still nervous, the man replies, 'In a subdivision just west of here.'

The hit man places the gun against his shoulder, faces west, peers into a scope and asks, 'What colour roof ya' got?'

'Grey.'

Then he asks 'What colour siding?'

'Yellow.'

'You got a silver Toyota?'

'Yeah,' replies the first man who is now completely amazed by the accuracy of the hit man's equipment. 'That's my wife's car.'

'That your red pickup next to it?'

Looking baffled the man asks if he can look through the scope.

When he looks through the sights, he says, 'Hell. That's my buddy Jeff's truck. What the hell is he doing there if I'm . . . ?'

The hit man looks through the scope once more.

'Your wife a blonde?'

'Yeah.'

'Your buddy got black hair?'

'Yeah!'

'Well, I don't know how to tell you, but I think you've got a problem. They're going at it like a couple of teenagers in there,' says the hit man.

'Problem? They've got the problem. I want you to shoot both of them, right now.'

The hit man pauses and says, 'Sure. But it'll cost you. Like I said, I'm the best. I get paid $5000 per shot.'

'I don't care. Just do it. I want you to shoot her right in the head, then shoot him right in the balls.'

The hit man agrees, turns, and takes up a firing position. He stares into the sights, taking careful aim.

He then says, 'You know what buddy? This is your lucky day. I think I can save you $5000!'

Mother is in the kitchen making supper for her family when her youngest daughter walks in.

'Mother, where do babies come from?'

'Well dear . . . a mummy and a daddy fall in love and get married. One night they go into their room and they kiss and hug and have sex. That means the daddy puts his penis in the mummy's vagina. That's how you get a baby, honey.'

'Oh I see, but the other night when I came into your room you had daddy's penis in your mouth. What do you get when you do that?'

'Jewellery, dear.'

Blondie is sitting on a beach in Florida, attempting to strike up a conversation with the attractive gentleman reading on the blanket beside hers.

'Hello, Sir,' she says, 'Do you like movies?'

'Yes, I do,' he responds, then returns to his book.

Blondie persists, 'Do you like gardening?'

The man again looks up from his book. 'Yes, I do,' he says politely before returning to his reading.

Undaunted, Blondie asks, 'Do you like pussycats?'

With that, the man drops his book and pounces on Blondie, ravishing her as she's never been ravished before.

As the cloud of sand begins to settle, Blondie drags herself to a sitting position and pants, 'How did you know that was what I wanted?'

The man thinks for a moment and replies, 'How did you know my name was Katz?'

Two buddies are sharing drinks while discussing their wives. 'Does your wife ever . . . well, you know . . . does she . . . well, let you do it doggie style?' asks one of the two.

'Not exactly,' his friend replies. 'She's more into the trick dog aspect of it.'

'Oh, I see. Kinky stuff, huh?'

'No. Whenever I make a move, she's most likely to roll over and play dead.'

XXXX

Yuk!

Nigel Nofriends has a very strange fetish, which one day proves very costly. He persuades a 'sexual services consultant' in his local brothel to let him insert his big toe into a place normally reserved for eager members of a higher order. A few days later, the toe in question erupts into all sorts of strange blotches, scabs and other unusual blemishes. He takes it straight round to the doctor, who shakes his head in amazement.

'Well I certainly know what you've got, although God knows how you got it. Believe it or not, you've got syphilis of the big toe. Funny thing, actually – half an hour ago, I had a very attractive young woman in here with athlete's fanny.'

A guy goes to his doctor.
'Doctor,' he says, 'I have an embarrassing problem.'

'I'm sure it's nothing I haven't seen before,' the doctor tells him.

'Well,' says the man. 'Look at this.'

And he pulls his pants down. His dick is bright orange. The doctor agrees that he has never seen anything like it before. The doctor consults all his medical books, rings around his doctor friends and does some research on the Internet. But he cannot find anything about orange dicks.

Finally, the doctor says to the man, 'Maybe there's a clue in your daily routine. Tell me what you do.'

'Nothing out of the ordinary,' says the man. 'In the morning

I go to work. From nine to five, I work in an office. Then I go home. I have dinner at about six-thirty. Then I watch the seven o'clock news on TV. And from seven-thirty until bed time I watch porno movies and eat Cheezels.'

Jack is a shift worker. Every morning on his way home from work, just as the sun is coming up, he passes by Joe's farm. Joe is the town drunk. Now, one morning, Jack is walking past Joe's farm when he hears a huge commotion coming from the barn. Jack walks over to see what is happening, just in time to see Joe, drunk as a skunk, humping all the cows.

'Listen Joe,' Jack warns, 'if you don't stop getting drunk and staying up all night humping farm animals you're gonna have a heart attack and die one day.'

Joe promptly waves him off and staggers over to the horse for some more fun. The next morning, Jack again walks by Joe's farm and hears the pigs squeekin' and squealin' for their lives. Jack walks over and sees Joe, drunk as a skunk, screwing the pigs.

'Listen Joe,' Jack warns again, 'if you don't stop getting drunk and staying up all night humping farm animals you're gonna have a heart attack and die one day.'

Again, Joe shrugs off the warning and grabs the donkey. The next morning, as Jack walks by Joe's farm, he can't hear anything. So he walks around to the back of the barn to see Joe lying in the middle of the field motionless.

'Poor Joe,' Jack says to himself, 'stayed up all night screwin' farm animals and now he's died from a heart attack.'

Just then Joe looks up, points to the sky and says, 'Shhh, buzzards!'

Jim phones his office in the morning and says to his boss, 'Boss, I'm not coming in today, I'm sick.'

His boss says, 'Exactly how sick are ya?'
Jim replies, 'Well, I'm in bed with my sister!'

A king and a queen rule a large kingdom. The king is short in vital parts and the queen has to seek solace with every Tom, Dick and Harry. After some time, the king grows suspicious of the queen's escapades and wants to punish the subjects willing to risk their lives for a fling with her.

He seeks the services of his court magician to help identify the culprits. The magician builds an invisible contraption that is attached to the queen's waist. The mechanism is simple, it slices any elongated object that ventures anywhere within an inch of the queen's waist.

Having set his trap the king sets off on a hunting trip and returns to his palace, after spending a sleepless week, burning with curiosity. Immediately after his arrival he summons the queen's private bodyguards to his foyer and dispatches all his attendants. He orders them to undress. All of them have lost their penises! He next summons the palace guards and the result is the same. By mid-afternoon he realises that there is not a single male soul in the vicinity who had not made a valiant attempt only to be left without a penis.

The only man left is his minister and, to his surprise, the king finds him to be the only man who has a penis left.

Pleased with his minister's loyalty, he asks him what punishment would befit all the others. In reply, he receives only a blubbering sound from the minister's mouth.

TEN THINGS NOT TO SAY TO YOUR NEW GIRLFRIEND'S PARENTS

1. My parole officer thinks Sara has a calming effect on me.

2. Did you see that saucer that flew over town yesterday?

3. Which one of you taught Sara to give such great head?

4. Can you believe it! Those shitheads at the corner market won't cash my welfare cheque!

5. We're going to keep our relationship quiet for now. My wife can be rather vindictive at times.

6. Those home pregnancy kits aren't very reliable, in my opinion.

7. Sara is so pretty I've decided to give up being bisexual just for her.

8. Nice place you got here. That painting looks expensive. I bet a nice home like this came with a safe already built in, didn't it?

9. There ain't nothing that beats that great feeling of knowing your HIV test results are negative! I bet Sara's will be OK too.

10. Can I pull my car in your garage? I'm not sure how long that cop car will stay lost.

VIAGRA

The invention of Viagra has brought a smile to many faces . . . through a range of new jokes, of course.

A man finally gets his prescription for Viagra. Anxious to try it out, he takes one as soon as he gets home, and waits for his wife to come home from work. However, in his excitement he leaves the package open on the table and his pet parrot eats all of the pills. Seeing what happened and panicking, the man grabs the bird and stuffs him into the freezer to cool off.

Unfortunately, the man's own Viagra kicks in just as his wife comes home and it is hours before he remembers the parrot. He runs and looks in the freezer expecting the worst, only to find the bird breathing heavily, drained with sweat and totally exhausted.

'What happened?' the man asks, 'you were in there for hours and yet you're not only alive but you're sweating like crazy?'

The parrot pants, 'Man, have you ever tried to pry apart the legs on a frozen chicken?'

A n elderly gentleman goes to the local chemist and asks the pharmacist for Viagra.

The pharmacist replies, 'That's no problem. How many do you want?'

The man answers, 'Just a few, maybe four, but cut each one into four pieces.'

The pharmacist says, 'That won't do you any good.'

'That's all right. I don't need them for sex anymore as I am over eighty years old. I just want it to stick out far enough so I don't pee on my shoes.'

A woman walks into a pharmacy and asks, 'Do you have Viagra?'

'Yes, I do,' the pharmacist replies.

'Does it really work?' she asks.

He chuckles and says, 'It certainly does.'

'Can you get it over the counter?' she asks.

'If I take two of them,' he answers.

G retchen asks her husband, 'Would you like some breakfast? Bacon, eggs, perhaps a slice of toast? Maybe some pancakes with maple syrup? Grapefruit and coffee to follow?'

He declines. 'It's this Viagra,' he says, 'it's really taken the edge off my appetite.'

At lunch time, she asks, 'Would you like something? A bowl of home made soup, perhaps, with a grilled cheese sandwich? Perhaps a plate of snacks and a glass of milk?'

He declines. 'It's this Viagra,' he says, 'It's really taken the edge off my appetite.'

Come dinner time, she asks, 'Do you want anything to eat? I'll go to the cafe and buy you a burger supper. Maybe a fat juicy steak? Maybe you'd like a pizza delivered? Or a tasty stir-fry that would only take a couple of minutes?'

He declines. 'It's this Viagra,' he says, 'it's really taken the edge off my appetite.'

'Well,' she says. 'Would you mind getting off me? I'm bloody starving!'

A man goes to a doctor and says, 'Doctor, I have a sexual performance problem. Can you help me?'

'Oh, that's not a problem anymore!' announces the proud physician. 'They just came out with this new wonder drug, Viagra, that does the trick. You take some pills and your problems are history.'

So, the doctor gives the man a prescription and sends him on his merry way. A couple of months later, the doctor runs into his patient on the street.

'Doctor, Doctor!' exclaims the man excitedly, 'I've got to thank you! This drug is a miracle! It's wonderful!'

'Well, I'm glad to hear that,' says the pleased physician. 'What does your wife think about it?'

'Wife?' asks the man. 'I haven't been home yet.'

THE INNOCENCE
OF KIDS

*Those innocent little comments that kids come
out with are so amusing. The frightening
thing is, they're usually the truth.*

A small boy is awoken in the middle of the night by strange
noises from his parents' room, and he decided to investigate.
As he enters their bedroom, he is shocked to see his mum and
dad shagging for all they are worth.

'Dad!' he shouts. 'What are you doing?'

'It's OK,' his father replies. 'Your mother wants a baby, that's all.'

The small boy, excited at the prospect of a new baby brother,
is pleased and goes back to bed with a smile on his face. Several
weeks later, the little boy is walking past the bathroom and is
shocked to discover his mother giving oral gratification to his
father.

'Dad!' he shouts. 'What are you doing now?'

'Son, there's been a change of plan,' his father replies. 'Your
mother did want a baby, but now she wants a BMW.'

One evening, during a violent thunderstorm, a mother is
tucking her young son into bed.

She is about to turn off the light when he asks with a tremor in
his voice, 'Mummy, will you sleep with me tonight?'

His mother smiles and gives him a reassuring hug. 'I can't
dear,' she says, 'I have to sleep with Daddy.'

A long silence is broken at last by a shaken little voice saying, 'The big sissy.'

A father asks his ten-year-old son, Johnny, if he knows about the birds and the bees.

'I don't want to know,' Johnny says, bursting into tears.

Confused, the father asks Johnny what is wrong.

'Oh Daddy,' Johnny sobs. 'At age six I got the "there's no Santa" speech. At age seven I got the "there's no Easter bunny" speech. Then at age eight you hit me with the "there's no tooth fairy" speech! If you're going to tell me now that grown-ups don't really screw, I've got nothing left to live for.'

A couple have two little boys, ages eight and ten, who are excessively mischievous. The two are always getting into trouble and their parents are sure that if any mischief occurs in their town, their two young sons are in some way involved. The parents are at their wits' end as to what to do about their sons' behaviour. The mother has heard that a clergyman in town has been successful in disciplining children in the past, so she asks her husband if he thinks they should send the boys to speak with the clergyman.

The husband says, 'We might as well. We need to do something before I really lose my temper.'

The clergyman agrees to speak with the boys, but asks to see them individually. The eight-year-old goes to meet with him first.

The clergyman sits the boy down and asks him sternly, 'Where is God?'

The boy makes no response, so the clergyman repeats the question in an even sterner tone, 'Where is God?'

Again the boy makes no attempt to answer, so the clergyman

raises his voice even more and shakes his finger in the boy's face, 'Where is God!'

At that the boy bolts from the room and runs directly home slamming himself in his closet.

His older brother follows him into the closet and says, 'What happened?'

The younger brother replies, 'We are in *big* trouble this time. God is missing. And they think we did it!'

A man, who is sentenced to life imprisonment, decides to dig a tunnel to escape. He works for many months on this tunnel, and finally finishes it. He decides to break out during the day, figuring that the guards will not suspect this. As he breaks through the ground to the surface, he finds himself in a pre-school playground.

He is surprised, but he rejoices anyway, shouting, 'I'm free, I'm free!'

At this a little girl approaches him, puts her hand on her hip, and says, 'Big deal! I'm four!'

A small boy is lost, so he goes up to a policeman and says, 'I've lost my dad!'

The cop asks, 'What's he like?'

The little boy replies, 'Beer and women!'

Little girl in church:	Why is the bride dressed in white?
Mummy:	White is the colour of joy, and today is the most joyful day of her life.
Little girl:	Then why is the groom wearing black?

Little Joe sees his daddy's car pass the playground and go into the woods. Curious, he follows the car and sees Daddy and Aunt Susie in a passionate embrace.

Joe finds this exciting and can barely contain himself as he runs home and starts to tell his mother, 'Mummy, Mummy, I was at the playground and Daddy and –'

Mummy tells him to slow down. She wants to hear the story.

So Joe tells her, 'I was at the playground and I saw Daddy go into the woods with Aunt Susie. I went back to look and he was giving Aunt Susie a big kiss, then he helped her take off her shirt, then Aunt Susie helped Daddy take his pants off, then Aunt Susie laid down on the seat, then Daddy –'

At this point, Mummy cut him off and said, 'Joe, this is such an interesting story, suppose you save the rest of it for supper time. I want to see the look on Daddy's face when you tell it tonight.'

At the dinner table, Mummy asks Joe to tell his story. Joe starts his story, describing the car going into the woods, the undressing, laying down on the seat, and '. . . then Daddy and Aunt Susie did that same thing that Mummy and Uncle Bill used to do when Daddy was in the navy.'

Little Pete is passing his parents' bedroom in the middle of the night, in search of a glass of water. Hearing a lot of moaning and thumping, he peeks in and catches his folks going for it.

Before dad can even react, Pete exclaims, 'Oh, boy! Horsey ride! Daddy, can I ride on your back?'

Daddy, relieved that Pete's not asking more uncomfortable questions, and seeing the opportunity not to break his stride, agrees. Pete hops on and daddy starts going to town. Pretty soon mummy starts moaning and gasping.

Pete cries out, 'Hang on tight, daddy! This is the part where me and the milkman usually get bucked off.'

Mikey and Jane are only ten years old, but they just know that they are in love. One day they decide that they want to get married, so Mikey goes to Jane's father to ask him for her hand. Mikey bravely walks up to him and says, 'Mr Smith, me and Jane are in love and I want to ask you for her hand in marriage.'

Thinking that this is the cutest thing, Mr Smith replies, 'Well Mikey, you are only ten. Where will you two live?'

Without even taking a moment to think about it, Mikey replies, 'In Jane's room. It's bigger than mine and we can both fit there nicely.'

Still thinking this is just adorable, Mr Smith says with a huge grin, 'OK then how will you live? You're not old enough to get a job. You'll need to support Jane.'

Again, Mikey instantly replies. 'Our allowance. Jane makes $5 a week and I make $10 a week. That's about $60 a month, and that'll do us just fine.'

By this time Mr Smith is a little shocked that Mikey has put so much thought into this. So, he thinks for a moment, trying to come up with something that Mikey won't have an answer for.

After a second, Mr Smith says, 'Well Mikey, it seems like you have got everything worked out. I just have one more question for you. What will you do if the two of you should have little ones of your own?'

Mikey just shrugs his shoulders and says, 'Well, we've been lucky so far.'

A boy wakes up in the middle of the night and goes to the bathroom. On the way back to bed, he passes his parents room. When he looks in, he notices the covers bouncing.

He calls to his dad, 'Hey Dad, what are you doing?'

Dad answers, 'Playing cards.'

The boy asks, 'Who's your partner?'

Dad answers, 'Your mum.'

The boy then passes by his older sister's room. Again, he notices the covers bouncing.

He calls to his sister, 'Hey Sis, what are you doing?'

The sister answers, 'Playing cards.'

The boy asks, 'Who's your partner?'

She answers, 'My boyfriend.'

A little later, dad gets up and goes to the bathroom. As he passes the boy's room, he notices the covers bouncing.

He calls to his son, 'What are you doing?'

The boy answers, 'Playing cards.'

Dad asks, 'Really? Who's your partner?'

The boy answers, 'You don't need a partner if you have a good hand.'

A few months after his parents divorce, Little Johnny passes by his mum's bedroom and sees her rubbing her body and moaning, 'I need a man, I need a man!'

Over the next couple of months, he sees her doing this several times. One day, he comes home from school and hears her moaning. When he peeks into her bedroom, he sees a man on top of her.

Little Johnny runs into his room, takes off his clothes, throws himself on his bed, starts stroking himself, and moans, 'Ohh, I need a bike! I need a bike!'

Little Johnny comes home from Catholic school with a black eye.

His father sees it and says, 'Johnny, how many times do I have to tell you not to fight with the other boys?'

'But Dad, it wasn't my fault. We were all in church saying our prayers. We all stood up and my teacher in front of me had her dress in the crack of her bum. I reached over and pulled it out. That's when she hit me.'

'Johnny,' the father says, 'you don't do those kinds of things to women.'

Sure enough, the very next day Johnny comes home with the other eye black and blue. Johnny's father says, 'Johnny, I thought we had a talk.'

'But Dad,' Johnny says, 'It wasn't my fault. There we were in church saying our prayers. We all stood up and my teacher in front of us had her dress in the crack of her bum. Then Louie, who was sitting next to me, saw it and he reached over and pulled it out. Now I know she doesn't like this, so I pushed it back in.'

Little Johnny comes home from school to see his pet rooster dead in the front yard. Rigor mortis has set in and it is flat on its back with its legs in the air.

When his Dad comes home Johnny says, 'Dad our rooster's dead and his legs are sticking in the air. Why are his legs sticking in the air?'

His father, thinking quickly, says, 'Son, that's so God can reach down from the clouds and lift the rooster straight up to heaven.'

'Gee Dad that's great,' says little Johnny.

A few days later, when Dad comes home from work, Johnny rushes out to meet him yelling, 'Dad, Dad we almost lost Mum today.'

'What do you mean?' asks Dad.

'I got home from school early today and went up to your bedroom and there was Mum flat on her back with her legs in the air screaming, "Jesus I'm coming, I'm coming." If it hadn't of been for Uncle George holding her down we'd have lost her for sure.'

Little Johnny, on a particularly reckless day, is playing in the backyard. Soon, some honeybees start swirling around, annoying little Johnny. He stomps on them in his temper.

His father catches him trampling the honeybees and, after a brief moment of thought, he says, 'That's it! No honey for you for one month!'

Later that afternoon, Johnny ponders some butterflies, and soon starts catching them and crushing them under his feet.

His father again catches him and, after a brief moment of thought, says, 'No butter for you for one month!'

Early that evening, Johnny's mother is cooking dinner, and gets jumpy when cockroaches start scurrying around the kitchen floor. She begins stomping on them one by one until all the cockroaches are dead. Johnny's mother looks up to find Johnny and his father watching her.

Johnny says, 'Are you going to tell her, Daddy, or should I?'

One day, Grandma sends her grandson, Peter, down to the water hole to fetch some water for cooking the dinner. As he is dipping the bucket in, he sees two big eyes looking back at him. He drops the bucket and hightails it for Grandma's kitchen.

'Now, where's my bucket and my water?' Grandma asks him.

'I can't get any water from that water hole, Grandma,' cries Peter. 'There's a huge ol' alligator down there.'

Now don't you mind that ol' alligator, Peter. He's been there for a few years now, and he's never hurt no-one. Why, he's probably as scared of you as you are of him.'

'Well, Grandma,' replies Peter, 'If he's as scared of me as I am of him, then that water ain't fit to drink.'

One day a sweet little girl becomes puzzled about her origin. 'How did I get here, mummy?' she asks.

Her mother replies, using a well-worn phrase, 'Why God sent you, honey.'

'And did God send you too, mummy?'

'Yes, sweetheart, he did.'

'And daddy and grandma and grandpa and their mums and dads, too?'

'Yes, honey, all of them, too.'

The child shakes her head in disbelief.

'Then you're telling me there's been no sex in this family for over 200 years? No wonder everyone is so grouchy.'

Two little boys go into a grocery store. One is nine, one is four. The nine-year-old grabs a box of tampons from the shelf and carries it to the register.

The cashier asks, 'Oh, these must be for your mum, huh?'

The nine-year-old replies, 'Nope, not for my mum.'

Without thinking, the cashier responds, 'Well, they must be for your sister then?'

The nine-year-old quips, 'Nope, not for my sister either.'

The cashier has now become curious. 'Oh. Not for your mum and not for your sister, who are they for?'

The nine-year-old says, 'They're for my four-year-old little brother.'

The cashier is surprised. 'Your four-year-old little brother?'

The nine-year-old explains, 'Well yeah, they say on TV if you wear one of these you can swim or ride a bike and my little brother can't do either of them!'

THINGS NOT TO SAY OR DO AT A JOB INTERVIEW

- After detailing your greatest achievement, qualify with, 'Of course I was totally hammered at the time.'

- Although parking is free, insist that they validate something or you're not leaving.

- Ask if it's OK for you to sit on the floor.

- Ask if there is only one emergency exit, then grin and say, 'Boy! I bet this floor would be in trouble if someone barricaded it.'

- Ask the secretary if she'll sit on your lap during the interview.

- Claim you wouldn't even need a sit-in job if Al Einstein hadn't stolen your secret patent for '2000 Flushes'.

- Constantly fidget with your underwear waistband, then blurt, 'The strawberry ones are the stickiest, don't ya' think?'

- Inquire about the office policy on friends staying over.

- Mention your resume would have been stronger but you didn't feel like making anything else up.

- Over-emphasise your ability to use a copier.

- See a photo of the interviewer's family on desk, point, and start laughing uncontrollably.

- Sniff two of your fingers, then hold them out toward interviewer and say, 'Smell these, these smell funny to you?'

- Upon walking in to the office for the first time, ask the receptionist to hold all your calls.

- Walk into the interviewer's office with a tape measure, measure the office from a few angles, put it away, and declare, '*Now* we can begin.'

- When making small talk and the Simpson trial comes up, shout, 'You mean Homer and Marge are in some kind of trouble?'

LAWYERS

This section is included despite the fact that lawyers may decide to sue for defamation. But then they've got to prove that the jokes about them are not true. And they couldn't do that, could they?

A man walks into a bar with his alligator and asks the bartender, 'Do you serve lawyers here?'

'Sure do,' replies the bartender.

'Good,' says the man. 'Give me a beer, and I'll have a lawyer for my 'gator.'

A housewife, an accountant and a lawyer are asked, 'How much is two plus two?'

'Four,' says the housewife.

'I think it's either three or four,' says the accountant. 'Let me run those figures through my spreadsheet one more time.'

The lawyer pulls the drapes, dims the lights and asks in a hushed voice, 'How much do you want it to be?'

A primary-school teacher is asking students what their parents do for a living.

'Tim, you go first,' she says. 'What does your mother do all day?'

Tim stands up proudly and says, 'She's a doctor.'

'That's wonderful. How about you, Amy?'

Amy shyly stands up, scuffs her feet and says, 'My father is a mailman.'

'Thank you, Amy,' says the teacher. 'What about your father, Billy?'

Billy proudly stands up and announces, 'My daddy plays piano in a whorehouse.'

The teacher is aghast and promptly changes the subject to geography. Later that day she goes to Billy's house and rings the bell. Billy's father answers the door. The teacher explains what his son has said and demands an explanation.

Billy's father says, 'I'm actually a lawyer. How can I explain a thing like that to a seven-year-old?'

What is the difference between a tick and a lawyer? A tick falls off you when you die.

Why does the law society prohibit sex between lawyers and their clients?

To prevent clients from being billed twice for essentially the same service.

What do you call a lawyer who doesn't chase ambulances? Retired.

What do you call a smiling, sober, courteous person at a bar association convention?

The caterer.

Why are lawyers like nuclear weapons? If one side has one, the other side has to get one. Once launched, they cannot be recalled. When they land, they screw up everything forever.

What do lawyers use for birth control?
Their personalities.

What can a goose do that a duck can't, and a lawyer should?
Stick his bill up his arse.

Four surgeons are taking a coffee break and are discussing their work.

The first says, 'I think accountants are the easiest to operate on. You open them up and everything inside is numbered.'

The second says, 'I think librarians are the easiest to operate on. You open them up and everything inside is in alphabetical order.'

The third says, 'I like to operate on electricians. You open them up and everything inside is colour-coded.'

The fourth one says, 'I like to operate on lawyers. They're heartless, spineless, gutless, and their heads and their arse are interchangeable.'

A lawyer and a blonde are sitting next to each other on a long flight. The lawyer leans over to her and asks if she would like to play a fun game. The blonde just wants to take a nap, so she politely declines and rolls over to the window to catch a few winks. The lawyer persists and explains that the game is really easy and a lot of fun.

He explains, 'I ask you a question, and if you don't know the answer, you pay me $5, and vice-versa.'

Again, she politely declines and tries to get some sleep. The lawyer, now somewhat agitated, says, 'OK, if you don't know the answer you pay me $5, and if I don't know the answer, I will pay you $500.' He reckons that since she is a blonde that he will easily win the match. This offer catches the blonde's attention and, realising that there will probably be no end to this torment unless she plays, agrees to the game.

The lawyer asks the first question. 'What's the distance from the earth to the moon?'

The blonde doesn't say a word, reaches in to her purse, pulls out a $5 note and hands it to the lawyer. Now, it's the blonde's turn.

She asks the lawyer, 'What goes up a hill with three legs, and comes down with four?'

The lawyer looks at her with a puzzled look. He takes out his laptop computer and searches all his references. He taps into the air-phone with his modem and searches the Net and the Library of Congress. Frustrated, he sends emails to all his co-workers and friends he knows. All to no avail. After over an hour, he wakes the blonde and hands her $500. The blonde politely takes the $500 and turns away to get back to sleep.

The lawyer, who is more than a little miffed, wakes the blonde and asks, 'Well, so what *is* the answer?'

Without a word, the blonde reaches into her purse, hands the lawyer $5, and goes back to sleep.

A loser can't get a date. He goes to a bar and asks a guy there how to get a date.

The guy says, 'It's simple. I just say, I'm a lawyer.'

So the guy goes up to a pretty woman and asks her out. After she says no, he tells her that it was probably a good thing because he has a case early in the morning.

She says, 'Oh. You're a lawyer?'

He says, 'Why yes I am.'

So they go to his place and when they are in bed, screwing, he starts to laugh to himself.

When she asks what is so funny, he answers, 'Well, I've only been a lawyer for fifteen minutes, and I'm already screwing someone!'

What's the difference between a lawyer and a rooster?
When a rooster wakes up in the morning, its primal urge is to cluck defiance.

Have you heard about the lawyer's word processor?
No matter what font you select, everything comes out in fine print.

Did you hear about the new microwave lawyer?
You spend eight minutes in his office and get billed as if you'd been there eight hours.

Did you hear about the group of terrorists who hijacked a plane full of lawyers?
They called down to ground control with their list of demands, threatening that if their demands weren't met, they would release one lawyer every hour.

How can you tell when a lawyer is lying?
His lips are moving.

If you see a lawyer on a bicycle, why should you swerve to avoid hitting him?
That might be your bicycle.

How many lawyers does it take to roof a house?
Depends on how thin you slice them.

How do you get a group of lawyers to smile for a picture?
Just say 'Fees!'

Why are lawyers so good at racketball?
Because they stoop so low.

How does an attorney sleep?
First he lies on one side, and then on the other.

What would happen if you locked a zombie in a room full of lawyers?
He would starve to death.

What do you call a lawyer with an IQ of fifty?
Senator.

What do you call a lawyer gone bad?
Your honour.

What does it mean when a lawyer tells his clients he has a sliding fee schedule?
It means that after you pay his bill, it's financially hard to get back on your feet.

What do you call 5000 dead lawyers at the bottom of the ocean?

A good start!

Why do they bury lawyers twelve feet deep?
Because deep down, they are really good guys.

Why won't sharks attack lawyers?
Professional courtesy.

What do you have when a lawyer is buried up to his neck in sand?

A shortage of sand.

One day, a teacher, a garbage collector, and a lawyer all die and go to heaven. St Peter is there but is having a bad day since heaven is getting crowded. When they get to the gate, St Peter informs them that there will be a test to get into heaven – they each have to answer a single question.

To the teacher, he says, 'What was the name of the ship that crashed into the iceberg and sank with all its passengers?'

The teacher thinks for a second and then replies, 'That would be the *Titanic*, right?'

St Peter lets him through the gate. Then he turns to the garbage man, and, thinking that heaven doesn't really need all the stink that this guy would bring into it, decides to make the question a little harder, 'How many people died on the ship?'

The garbage man guesses, '1228.'

'That happens to be right; go ahead.'

St Peter turns to the lawyer, 'Name them.'

A wealthy lawyer has a summer house in the country, to which he retreats for several weeks of the year. Each summer, the lawyer invites a friend to spend some time at his place.

On one occasion, he invites a Czechoslovakian friend to stay with him. The friend, eager to get a freebie from a lawyer, agrees. They have a splendid time in the country – rising early and enjoying the great outdoors. Early one morning, the lawyer and his Czechoslovakian companion go out to pick berries for their morning breakfast. As they go around the berry patch, gathering blueberries and raspberries in tremendous quantities, along come two huge bears – a male and a female. Well, the lawyer, seeing the two bears, immediately dashes for cover. His friend, though, isn't so lucky, and the male bear reaches him and swallows him whole. The lawyer runs back to his Mercedes, tears into town as fast has he can, and gets the local backwoods sheriff. The sheriff grabs his shotgun and dashes back to the berry patch with the lawyer. Sure enough, the two bears are still there.

'He's in that one!' cries the lawyer, pointing to the male, while visions of lawsuits from his friend's family dance in his head. The sheriff looks at the bears and, without batting an eye, levels his gun, takes careful aim, and shoots the female.

'What'd ya do that for!' exclaims the lawyer, 'I said he was in the other!'

'Exactly,' replies the sheriff, 'but would *you* believe a lawyer who told you that the Czech was in the male?'

A group of professional men have finished a day's hunt and are relaxing around the fire. Their hunting dogs occupy a clearing nearby. One of the men observes that it is remarkable how the dogs have acquired the traits of their owners. The musician's dog is softly howling strains of the *Moonlight Sonata*. The engineer's dog is using his paw to perform calculations in the dust. The lawyer's dog is screwing the others.

A defending attorney is cross-examining a coroner.
'Before you signed the death certificate had you taken the man's pulse?'

'No, Sir.'

'And did you listen for a heartbeat?'

'No, I didn't.'

'So when you signed the death certificate you had not taken any steps to make sure the man was actually dead, had you?'

The coroner, tired of the browbeating, says, 'Well, let me put it this way. The man's brain was sitting in a jar on my desk, but for all I know he could be out there, practising law somewhere!'

Two lawyers are stranded on a deserted island, nothing around them for miles and miles but water. They've been stranded here for quite some time, so they've gotten quite bored with one another. One day, as they are sitting around not talking to each other, they see the body of a naked woman, floating face-up, heading towards them. Within a few minutes, the body washes up on shore. They race towards her and, though she is unconscious, she is very much alive.

One lawyer says to the other, 'Well, you know it's been a long time . . . do you think we should, you know, screw her?'

The other lawyer responds, 'Out of what?'

A local charity office realises that it has never received a donation from the town's most successful lawyer.

A local volunteer calls to solicit a donation, saying, 'Our research shows that even though your annual income is over a million dollars, you do not give one penny to charity. Wouldn't you like to give back to your community by donating some money to our worthy cause?'

The lawyer thinks for a moment and says, 'First, did your

research show that my mother is dying after a long, painful illness and has huge medical bills far beyond her ability to pay?'

Embarrassed, the volunteer mumbles, 'Uh, no.'

'Secondly, that my brother, a disabled veteran, is blind and confined to a wheelchair and is unable to support his wife and six children?'

The stricken volunteer rep begins to stammer an apology but is cut off.

'Thirdly, that my sister's husband died in a dreadful traffic accident,' the lawyers voice rises in indignation, 'leaving her penniless with a mortgage and three children?'

The humiliated volunteer, completely beaten, says simply, 'I had no idea.'

The lawyer then says '. . . and if I don't give any money to *them*, why should I give any to you?'

An old man is on his death bed. He wants badly to take all his money with him. He calls his priest, his doctor and his lawyer to his bedside.

'Here's $30 000 cash to be held by each of you. I trust you to put this in my coffin when I die so I can take all my money with me.'

At the funeral, each man put an envelope in the coffin. Riding away in a limousine, the priest suddenly breaks into tears and confesses that he only put $20 000 into the envelope because he needs $10 000 for a new baptistery.

'Well, since we're confiding in each other,' says the doctor, 'I only put $10 000 in the envelope because we need a new machine at the hospital which costs $20 000.'

The lawyer is aghast. 'I'm ashamed of both of you,' he exclaims. 'I want it known that when I put my envelope in that coffin, it held my personal cheque for the full $30 000.'

Two tigers are stalking through a jungle in Asia. Suddenly, the one to the rear reaches out with his tongue, and licks the posterior of the tiger in front of him.

The startled front tiger turns and says, 'Cut it out.'

The rear tiger apologises, and they continue onward.

About five minutes later, it happens again.

The front tiger turns, growling, 'I said stop it.'

The rear tiger again apologises, and they continue. Another five minutes pass, and again the front tiger feels the unwanted tongue.

The front tiger turns, giving the rear tiger a ferocious glare, and angrily hisses, 'What is it with you?'

The rear tiger replies, 'I'm sorry. I really didn't mean to offend you. But I just ate a lawyer and I'm trying to get the taste out of my mouth!'

Defence attorney:	What is your age?
Little old woman:	I am eighty-six years old.
Defence attorney:	Will you tell us, in your own words, what happened to you?
Little old woman:	There I was, sitting in my swing on my front porch on a warm spring evening, when a young man comes creeping up on the porch and sits down beside me.
Defence attorney:	Did you know him?
Little old woman:	No, but he sure was friendly.
Defence attorney:	What happened after he sat down beside you?
Little old woman:	He started to rub my thigh.
Defence attorney:	Did you stop him?
Little old woman:	No, I didn't stop him.
Defence attorney:	Why not?

Little old woman:	It felt good. Nobody has done that since my Abner passed away some thirty years ago.
Defence attorney:	What happened next?
Little old woman:	He began to rub my breasts.
Defence attorney:	Did you stop him then?
Little old woman:	Hell no, I didn't stop him.
Defence attorney:	Why not?
Little old woman:	Why, Your Honour, his rubbing made me feel all alive and excited. I haven't felt that good in years!
Defence attorney:	What happened next?
Little old woman:	Well, I was feeling so spicy that I just spread my old legs and said to him, 'Take me, young man, take me!'
Defence attorney:	Did he take you?
Little old woman:	Hell, no. That's when he yelled, 'April Fool!' And that's when I shot the son of a bitch!

A man dies and is taken to his place of eternal torment by the devil. As he passes sulphurous pits and shrieking sinners, he sees a man he recognises as a lawyer, making love to a beautiful woman.

'That's not fair,' he complains. 'I face torment for all eternity, and that lawyer gets to spend it making love to a beautiful woman.'

'Shut up!' barks the devil, jabbing the man with his pitchfork. 'Who are you to question her punishment?'

A trial has been scheduled in a small town, but the court clerk has forgotten to call in a jury panel. Rather than adjourning what he thinks is an exceptionally simple case, the judge orders his bailiff to go through the courthouse and round up enough people to form a jury. The bailiff returns with a group of lawyers.

The prosecutor feels that it will be an interesting experiment to try a case before a jury of lawyers, and the defence counsel has no objection, so the jury is empanelled. The trial goes very quickly – after only an hour of testimony, and very short closing arguments, both sides rest. The jury is then instructed by the judge, and sent back to the jury room to deliberate.

After nearly six hours, the trial court is concerned that the jury has not returned with a verdict. The case has in fact turned out to be every bit as simple as he had expected, and it seems to him that they should have been back in minutes. He sends the bailiff to the jury room, to see if they need anything.

The bailiff returns, and the judge asks, 'Are they close to reaching a verdict?'

The bailiff shakes his head, and replies, 'Your Honour, they're still doing nomination speeches for the position of foreman.'

How do you get a lawyer out of a tree?
Cut the rope.

Do you know how to save a drowning lawyer?
No? Good!

What is the definition of a shame?
A busload of lawyers going off a cliff.
What is the definition of a crying shame?
An empty seat on the bus.

Where can you find a good lawyer?
In the cemetery.

What's the difference between a lawyer and a boxing referee?
A boxing referee doesn't get paid extra for a longer fight.

What's the difference between a lawyer and a leech?
When you die, a leech will stop sucking your blood and drop off.

Chicago sends its police chief, fire chief, and city attorney to a municipal management conference in Indiana. While driving through a rural area, their car breaks down, and they seek assistance at a nearby farmhouse. The farmer tells them that the local garage is closed, and that they are welcome to spend the night, but that he only has one spare bed. He tells them that somebody can sleep on his couch, but that one of them would have to spend the night in his barn.

The police chief announces that he will volunteer to sleep in the barn. A short time later there is a knock at the door. It's the police chief, complaining that he can't sleep. There are pigs in the barn, and they remind him of insults that have been yelled at him, and he is too disturbed to sleep.

The fire chief says that he will trade with the police chief, and goes out to the barn. A short time later, there is another rapping at the door. It's the fire chief, who complains that the cows in the barn remind him of Mrs O'Leary's cow, which started the great Chicago fire. He has tried to sleep, but keeps having nightmares where they are kicking over lanterns and setting the barn ablaze.

The city attorney declares, 'You two are such babies. I will go sleep in the barn.'

Everything seems fine, until a few minutes later, there's another knock at the door. When the occupants answer it, they find the very indignant cows and pigs.

'Y ou are a cheat!' shouts the attorney to his opponent.
'And you're a liar!' bellows the opposition.
Banging his gavel loudly, the judge interjects, 'Now that both attorneys have been identified for the record, let's get on with the case.'

T wo lawyers go into a café and order two drinks. Then they produce sandwiches from their briefcases and start to eat.
The waiter becomes quite concerned and marches over and tells them, 'You can't eat your own sandwiches in here.'
The lawyers look at each other, shrug their shoulders and exchange sandwiches.

A junior partner in a firm is sent to a far-away state to represent a long-term client accused of robbery. After days of trial, the case is won, the client acquitted and released. Excited about his success, the attorney telegraphs the firm, 'Justice prevailed'.
The senior partner replies in haste, 'Appeal immediately'.

A young associate is romantically ambushed in a darkened room of his law firm. After months of the social isolation that comes from eighty-hour work weeks, the associate is happy to reciprocate. However, when asked by a friend to identify the lover, he is puzzled.
'All I know for sure is that it was a partner – I had to do all the work.'

What's the difference between a lawyer and an angry rhinoceros?
The lawyer charges more.

What's the difference between a lawyer and a trampoline?
You take off your shoes to jump on a trampoline.

What's the difference between a lawyer and a catfish?
One is a scum-sucking bottom feeder, and the other is a catfish.

What's the difference between a dead skunk in the road and a dead lawyer in the road?
There are skid marks in front of the skunk.

What's the difference between a hooker and a lawyer?
A hooker will stop screwing you after you are dead.

What's the difference between a lawyer and a gigolo?
A gigolo only screws one person at a time.

What's the difference between a lawyer and a vampire?
A vampire only sucks blood at night.

What's the difference between a good lawyer and a bad lawyer?
A bad lawyer can let a case drag out for several years.
A good lawyer can make it last even longer.

LAW ENFORCEMENT

*Laws are in place for one reason only. To turn the
general population against those who enforce the law.*

A man is driving a car when another driver passes by and
tosses a lit cigarette out the window and straight into the
window of his car. The cigarette lands on the driver's lap. He
grabs it and tries to toss it back out of his window.
Unfortunately, it gets caught in the folds of his shirt and sets fire
to his arm. He is in agony but he keeps driving, as smoke starts
to billow out of the window. After travelling a couple of
kilometres, he hears a siren behind him.

'Great,' he thinks, 'it's a fire engine coming to help.'

He pulls over and is amazed to see two police officers
approaching. One of the officers reaches into his pocket and
pulls out a book of tickets. The officer writes on the top ticket,
hands it to the driver and walks away. The driver reads the
ticket. He had been charged with being in possession of a
firearm.

Two policemen knock on a guy's door.
He answers, 'Yes?'

'Good evening Mr Smith. I'm afraid that we have some
terrible news, and some great news about your missing wife,'
says one of the cops.

'What's the terrible news?' asks Mr Smith.

'Scuba divers found your wife's body at the bottom of the bay
this morning,' replies the officer, solemnly.

THE MORE ADULT ONLY JOKE BOOK

'This is terrible,' sobs Mr Smith. 'What could possibly be good news after that?'

'Well,' answers one of the cops, 'when they pulled her up, the divers found three 10kg lobsters and a dozen blue crabs still hanging on to her body.'

'You people are sick,' replies Mr Smith, disgustedly, 'where is the body? I still need to identify it.'

'I'm afraid you can't see the body yet,' says the cop, 'they won't be bringing her back up again until later this afternoon.'

A guy comes out of a shop and sees a parking officer writing a ticket. The guy walks up to the parking officer and says, 'Come on mate, how about giving a guy a break?'

The officer ignores the guy and continues to write the ticket. Then, the guy calls the officer a pencil-necked geek. The officer glares at him and starts writing another ticket for having bald tyres. The officer finishes the second ticket and puts it on the car with the first.

The guy then says, 'How about a donut, tubby?'

The officer starts writing a third ticket. This goes on for about twenty minutes. The more the guy abuses the officer, the more tickets the officer writes. When the car has ten tickets pasted on the windscreen, the guy walks away. His car is parked around the corner.

A ndy is sentenced to prison. During his stay, he gets along well with the guards and all his fellow inmates. The warden sees that deep down, Andy is a good person and makes arrangements for Andy to learn a trade while doing his time. After three years, Andy is recognised as one of the best carpenters in the local area. Often he is given a weekend pass to do odd jobs for the citizens of the community and he always reports back to prison

264 • THE MORE ADULT ONLY JOKE BOOK

before the end of Sunday night. The warden is thinking of remodelling his kitchen and in fact has done much of the work himself. But he lacks the skills to build a set of kitchen cupboards and the large counter top which he has promised his wife. So he calls Andy into his office and asks him to complete the job for him. But, alas, Andy refuses.

He tells the warden, 'Gosh, I'd really like to help you, but counter fitting is what got me into prison in the first place.'

An old country sheriff always says, 'It could have been worse.' No matter what happens, the old sheriff always has the same answer, 'It could have been worse.'

One day, two deputies in the sheriff's office answer an emergency call at a farmhouse. When they walk in, they find the nude bodies of a man and a woman in the bedroom. They have been shot to death. When they go to the living room, they find the body of a man with a gun at his side.

'No doubt about it,' one deputy says to the other. 'This was a double murder and suicide. This guy came home and found his wife in bed with somebody else and shot them both. Then he shot himself.'

'You're right,' the other deputy replies. 'Double murder and suicide. But I'll bet you when the sheriff gets here he's going to say "It could have been worse."'

'No way. How could it be worse? There are three people in the house, and all of them have been shot to death. It couldn't be worse. You're on.'

About that time, the old sheriff arrives at the scene. He walks into the bedroom and sees the two nude bodies. He then walks into the living room and sees the man on the floor with the gun by his side.

'No doubt about it,' the sheriff says, shaking his head. 'It was a double murder and suicide. This guy came home and found his wife in bed with somebody else and shot them both. Then he shot himself.' After hesitating for a moment, the old sheriff looks his deputies squarely in the eyes. 'But, you know,' he says, 'it could have been worse.'

The deputy who has lost the bet jumps up and shouts, 'Sheriff, how could it have been worse? There are three people in this farmhouse, and all three of them are dead. It couldn't have been worse.'

'Yes it could,' the sheriff retorts. 'You see that guy there on the floor? If he had come home yesterday, that would be me dead in that bed.'

The stockbroker is nervous about being in prison because his cellmate looks like a real thug.

'Don't worry,' the gruff-looking fellow says, 'I'm in here for a white-collar crime too.'

'Well, that's a relief,' sighs the stockbroker. 'I was sent to prison for fraud and insider trading.'

'Oh nothing fancy like that for me,' grins the convict. 'I just murdered a couple of priests.'

'Hello, is this the drug squad?'

'Yes. What do you want?'

'I'm calling to report about my neighbour Jimmy Smith. He is hiding marijuana inside his firewood.'

'Thank you very much for the call, Sir.'

The next day, members of the drug squad descend on Jimmy's house. They search the shed where the firewood is kept. Using axes, they bust open every piece of wood, but find no marijuana. They apologise to Jimmy and leave.

The phone rings at Jimmy's house.

'Hey, Jimmy, did the drug squad come?'

'Yeah!'

'Did they chop your firewood?'

'Yep.'

'Happy Birthday Jimmy!'

Jim and Joe are driving down the road drinking a couple of bottles of beer when they spot a police roadblock. Jim starts panicking.

'We're gonna get busted for drinking these beers.'

'Don't worry, Jim,' Joe says. 'We'll just pull over and finish drinking these beers, peel off the label and stick it on our foreheads, and throw the bottles under the seat.'

'What for?' asks Jim.

'Just let me do the talking, OK?' says Joe.

They finish their beers, throw the empty bottles under the seat, and each put a label on their forehead. When they reach the roadblock, the police officer says, 'You boys been drinking?'

'No, Sir,' says Joe, 'we're on the patch.'

A young officer is working late at the Pentagon one evening. As he comes out of his office about 8 p.m. he sees a general standing by the classified document shredder in the hallway, a piece of paper in his hand.

'Do you know how to work this thing?' the general asks. 'My secretary's gone home and I don't know how to run it.'

'Yes, Sir,' says the young officer, who turns on the machine, takes the paper from the general, and feeds it in.

'Now,' says the general, 'I just need one copy.'

A truck driver is driving through a small town. His load is a truck full of bowling balls. In this town there are two cops who hate truck drivers with a passion. The truck driver sees the two of them and turns off at the next exit. There, he sees a little black boy on a bike, trying to hitch a ride.

The driver picks the little boy up but tells him, 'You can't ride up here but you can ride in the back if you like.'

So he puts the boy and his bike in the back and gets back on the highway. The two cops see him and pull him over. They start giving him hell and are just looking for something to charge him with. They can't find anything so they are about to let him go when one says to the other, 'We forgot to check the back.'

So one goes to the back, opens the doors, slams them back and quickly comes up to the truck driver. He is whiter than a ghost and scared as hell, yet manages to spurt out, 'Get the hell out of my town, get the hell out of my county, get the hell out of my state and don't ever come back.'

So the truck driver leaves.

When they get back into the car, the other cop turns to his colleague and says, 'What the hell did you see back there?'

The cop replies, 'That guy was carrying a truck load of black babies and one had already hatched and stolen a bike.'

A woman is driving her old beat up car on the highway with her seven-year-old son. She tries to keep up with the traffic but the other cars are flying by her. After getting caught in a large group of cars racing down the road, she looks at her speedometer to see she is doing 30km over the speed limit. Slowing down, she moves over to the side and gets out of the clump that soon leaves her behind. She looks up and sees the flashing lights of a police car. Pulling over, she waits for the officer to come up to her car.

He says, 'Ma'am do you know why I pulled you over?'

Her son pipes up from the back seat, 'I do . . . because you couldn't catch the other cars!'

A police officer in a small town stops a motorist speeding down High Street.

'But officer,' the man says, 'I can explain.'

'Just be quiet,' snaps the officer. 'I'm going to let you cool your heels in jail until the chief gets back.'

'But, officer, I just wanted to say –'

'I said to keep quiet! You're going to jail!'

A few hours later the officer looks in on his prisoner and says, 'Lucky for you the chief's at his daughter's wedding. He'll be in a good mood when he gets back.'

'Don't count on it,' answers the fellow in the cell. 'I'm the groom.'

A policeman is patrolling a local parking lot overlooking a golf course. He drives by a car and sees a couple inside with the dome light on. There's a young man in the driver's seat reading a computer magazine and a young woman in the back seat knitting. He stops to investigate. He walks up to the driver's window and knocks.

The young man looks up, cranks the window down, and says, 'Yes Officer?'

'What are you doing?' the policeman asks.

'What does it look like?' answers the young man. 'I'm reading this magazine.'

Pointing towards the young woman in the back seat, the officer asks, 'And what is she doing?'

The young man looks over his shoulder and replies, 'What does it look like? She's knitting.'

'And how old are you?' the officer asks the young man.

'I'm nineteen,' he replies.

'And how old is she?' asks the officer.

The young man looks at his watch and says, 'Well, in about twelve minutes she'll be sixteen.'

A speeding motorist is caught by radar from a police helicopter in the sky. An officer pulls him over and begins to issue a traffic ticket.

'How did you know I was speeding?' the frustrated driver asks.

The police officer points sombrely toward the sky.

'You mean,' asks the motorist, 'that even He is against me?'

A man is driving down the road with twenty penguins in the back seat. The police stop him and say that he can't drive around with the penguins in the car and he should take them to the zoo. The man agrees and drives off. The next day the same man is driving down the road with twenty penguins in the back again.

He is stopped by the same police officer who says, 'Hey! I thought I told you to take those penguins to the zoo.'

The man replies, 'I did. Today I'm taking them to the movies.'

THINGS YOU SHOULD NEVER SAY TO A COP

- Aren't you that guy from the Village People?

- Bad cop! No donut!

- Do you know why you pulled me over? OK, just so one of us does.

- Excuse me . . . is 'stick up' hyphenated?

- Gee, Officer . . . that's terrific . . . the last officer only gave me a warning too!

- Gee, that gut sure doesn't inspire confidence.

- Hey, can you give me another one of those full cavity searches?

- Hey, is that a 9mm? That's nothing compared to this .44 Magnum.

- Hey, you must have been doin' at least 180kph to keep up with me . . . Good job!

- I almost became a cop, but I decided to finish high school instead.

- I can't reach my licence unless you hold my beer.

- I pay your salary!

- I thought you had to be in relatively good physical condition to be a cop.

- I was trying to keep up with traffic. Yes, I know there are no other cars around – that's how far ahead of me they are.

- Is it true that people become cops because they're too dumb to work at McDonald's?

- So, uh, you on the take, or what?

- Sorry, Officer, I didn't realise my radar detector wasn't plugged in.

- Well, when I reached down to pick up my bag of crack, my gun fell off my lap and got lodged between the brake pedal and the gas pedal, forcing me to speed out of control.

- What do you mean, 'Have I been drinking?' You're the trained specialist.

- Wow, you look just like the guy in the picture on my girlfriend's nightstand.

- You're not gonna check the trunk, are you?

COURTROOM CAPERS

*There are millions of jokes about judges, lawyers
and other people in the legal profession.
Some of them are even set in a courtroom.*

Dan marries one of a pair of identical twins. Less than a year later, he is in court filing for a divorce.

'OK,' the judge says. 'Tell the court why you want a divorce.'

'Well, Your Honour,' Dan says. 'Every once in a while my sister-in-law comes over for a visit, and because she and my wife are so identical looking, every once in a while I end up making love to her by mistake.'

'Surely there must be some difference between the two women,' the judge says.

'There sure is Your Honour. That's why I want the divorce,' he replies.

An English anthropologist is doing research in an isolated African village, and the tribal chief asks if he would like to attend a trial his people are conducting that afternoon.

'You'll be surprised,' says the chief, 'at how well we've copied your country's legal procedures. You see, we have read accounts of many English trials in your newspapers, and incorporated them into our judicial system.'

When the Englishman arrives at the wooden courthouse, he is truly amazed to see how closely the African court officials resemble those in England. The counsels are suitably attired in long black robes and the traditional white powdered wigs. Each argues his case with eloquence and in proper judicial language. But he can't help being puzzled by the occasional appearance of a bare-breasted native woman running through the crowd waving her arms frantically.

After the trial, the anthropologist congratulates his host on what he has seen and then asks, 'What was the purpose of having a semi-nude woman run through the courtroom during the trial?'

'I really don't know,' confesses the chief, 'but in all the accounts we read in your papers about British trials, there was invariably something about "an excited titter running through the gallery."'

Two young guys are picked up by the cops for smoking dope and appear in court before the judge.

The judge says, 'You seem like nice young men, and I'd like to give you a second chance rather than jail time. I want you to go out this weekend and try to show others the evils of drug use and get them to give up drugs forever. I'll see you back in court Monday.'

On Monday, the two guys are back in court, and the judge says to the first one, 'How did you do over the weekend?'

'Well, Your Honour, I persuaded seventeen people to give up drugs forever.'

'Seventeen people? That's wonderful. What did you tell them?'

'I used a diagram, Your Honour. I drew two circles like this and told them this big circle is your brain before drugs and this small circle is your brain after drugs.'

'That's admirable. And you, how did you do?' the judge asks the second boy.

'Well, Your Honour, I persuaded 150 people to give up drugs forever.'

'One hundred and fifty people! That's amazing! How did you manage to do that?'

'Well, I used a similar approach. I said, This small circle is your arsehole before prison . . .'

A husband and wife are divorcing and are in the process of arguing in front of a judge over custody of the children. The mother is asked to give her side of the story and explains that since she has brought the children into this world, she should retain custody of them. The judge nods his head in agreement, then turns to the man for his side of the story.

The man thinks for a few moments, then stands and says, 'Judge, when I put a quarter in a candy machine and a candy bar comes out, does it belong to me or the machine?'

Three frogs are arrested and brought into the courtroom for sentencing.

The judge asks the first frog, 'What's your name?'

'Frog.'

'What were you arrested for?'

'Blowing bubbles in the water.'

Then he asks the second frog, 'What's your name?'

'Frog.'

'What were you arrested for?'

'Blowing bubbles in the water.'

Then he asks the third frog, 'What's your name?'

'Bubbles.'

At the height of a political corruption trial, the prosecuting attorney attacks a witness.

'Isn't it true,' he bellows, 'that you accepted $5000 to compromise this case?'

The witness stares out the window, as though he hasn't heard the question.

The prosecutor again blares, 'Isn't it true that you accepted $5000 to compromise this case?'

The witness still doesn't respond. Finally, the judge leans over and says, 'Sir, please answer the question.'

'Oh,' the startled witness says, 'I thought he was talking to you.'

At the start of an important trial, a small town attorney calls his first witness to the stand. She seems like a sweet, elderly woman.

He approaches her and asks, 'Mrs Jones, do you know me?'

She responds, 'Why, yes, I do know you Mr Williams. I've known you since you were a young boy. You've become a huge disappointment to me. You lie, you cheat on your wife, and you manipulate people and talk about them behind their backs. You think you're a hot shot lawyer, when you haven't the brains to realise you never will amount to anything more than a two-bit paper pusher. Yes, I know you.'

The lawyer is stunned. Not knowing what else to do he points across the room and asks, 'Mrs Jones, do you know the defence attorney?'

She replies, 'Why, of course I do. I've known Mr Bradley since he was a youngster, too. I used to baby-sit him for his parents. And he, also, is a real disappointment. He's lazy, bigoted, never has a nice word to say about anybody, and he drinks like a fish. He's been divorced five times, and everybody knows that his law practice is one of the shoddiest in the entire state. Yes, I know him.'

The judge raps his gavel, to quiet the tittering among the

spectators in the courtroom. Once the room is silent, he calls both attorneys to his bench.

In a quiet, menacing voice, he warns, 'If either of you asks her if she knows me, you'll be jailed for contempt!'

A young woman, several months pregnant, boards a bus and sits opposite a young man. He smiles and, feeling embarrassed, she changes her seat. But it is to no avail, for the young man smiles even more broadly when she sits down. Again she moves to another seat and he grins again. After the fourth move, the young man just rolls up and roars with laughter. The woman complains and duly summons him.

'Well, young man,' says the judge. 'Have you anything to say in your defence against this charge?'

'Your Honour, when the young woman got on the bus, her condition was obvious. However, that did not prompt my smile, but she sat under an advertisement that read "Coming Shortly – The Gold Rush Twins". The woman seemed indignant when I smiled and she got up and took another seat beneath a shaving stick advertisement, which read "William's Stick Did the Trick." She moved a third time and sat beneath a poster that read "Sloane's Liniments Will Remove Swelling". It was after she had moved her seat for the fourth time that I lost control of my merriment for above her was the slogan "Dunlop Rubber Goods Would Have Prevented this Accident".'

MAKING MUSIC

I thought musicians worked together in cooperation and harmony. That was, until I started reading these jokes. They hate each other!

St Peter is screening some new arrivals.
He asks a man, 'What did you do on earth?'
The man says, 'I was a doctor.'
St Peter says, 'OK, go right through those pearly gates. Next! What did you do on earth?'
'I was a school teacher.'
'Go right through those pearly gates. Next! And what did you do on earth?'
'I was a musician.'
'Go around the side, up the freight elevator, through the kitchen.'

How many musicians does it take to change a light bulb?
Five. One to change the light bulb and four to stand around and say, 'Man, if I'd had his studio time, I could have done that.'

How many country and western singers does it take to change a light bulb?
Three. One to change the bulb and two to sing about the old one.

How many sound men does it take to change a light bulb?
'One, two, one, two . . .'

How many punk-rock musicians does it take to change a light bulb?
   Two. One to screw in the bulb and the other to smash the old one on his forehead.

How many jazz musicians does it take to change a light bulb?
Don't worry about the changes. We'll fake it!

What happens if you play blues music backwards?
Your wife returns to you, your dog comes back to life, and you get out of prison.

What do you get when you play New Age music backwards?
New Age music.

What does it say on a blues singer's tombstone?
'I didn't wake up this morning . . .'

What's the difference between a puppy and a country music singer-songwriter?
   Eventually the puppy stops whining.

How do you make a million dollars singing jazz?
Start with two million.

Michael Caine goes up to Milton Berle during a party and asks, 'What kind of cigar are you smoking there?'

'It's a Lawrence Welk,' says Milton.

'What's a Lawrence Welk?' Michael asks.

Milton says, 'It's a piece of crap with a band wrapped around it.'

The guitarist B.B. King has been on a six month world tour. The day he comes home also happens to be his birthday. So his girlfriend thinks she'll give him a very special present to show how much she loves him. She gets the letter B tattooed on both cheeks of her bum. When B.B. King comes home there she is, dressed in her sexiest clothing.

'Welcome home honey,' she says. 'Sit down. I've got a very special present for you, baby.'

She pulls her panties down, turns around, and wiggles her arse in his face.

'What the hell!' he shouts. 'Who the hell is Bob?'

The symphony orchestra is performing Beethoven's *Ninth*. In the piece, there's a long passage, about twenty minutes, during which the bass violinists have nothing to do.

Rather than sit around that whole time looking stupid, some bassists decide to sneak offstage and go to the tavern next door for a quick one.

After slamming several beers in quick succession, one of them looks at his watch and says, 'Hey! We need to get back!'

'No need to panic,' says a fellow bassist. 'I thought we might need some extra time, so I tied the last few pages of the conductor's score together with string. It'll take him a few minutes to get it untangled.'

A few moments later they stagger back to the concert hall

and take their places in the orchestra. About this time, a member of the audience notices the conductor seems a bit edgy and says as much to her companion.

'Well, of course,' says her companion. 'Don't you see? It's the bottom of the *Ninth*, the score is tied, and the bassists are loaded.'

Angus is asked why there are drones on the bagpipe when they make such a distressing sound.

He answers, 'Without the drones, I might as well be playing the piano.'

What's the first thing a musician says at work?
'Would you like fries with that?'

What do you call a musician without a significant other?
Homeless.

Why do musicians have to be awake by six o'clock?
Because most shops close by six thirty.

What would a musician do if he won a million dollars?
Continue to play gigs until the money ran out.

THE STAGES OF A MUSICIAN'S LIFE:

Who is [name]?
Get me [name].
Get me someone who sounds like [name].

Get me a young [name].
Who is [name]?

There are two people walking down the street. One is a musician. The other doesn't have any money either.

What's the definition of an optimist?
A folk musician with a mortgage.

Donald MacDonald from the Isle of Skye is admitted to Oxford University, and is now living in his first year of residence there. His clan is very excited that one of their own has made it into the upper class of education, but they are concerned how he'll do in 'that strange land'. After the first month, his mother comes to visit, with reinforcements of whiskey and oatmeal.

'And how do you find the English students, Donald?'
she asks.

'Oh, Mother,' he replies, shaking his head sadly, 'they're such terrible, noisy people. The one on that side keeps banging his head against the wall, and won't stop, and the one on the other side screams and screams and screams away into the night.'

'But Donald! How do you manage with those dreadful noisy English neighbours?'

'Well, mother, I just ignore 'em. I just stay here and play my bagpipes.'

What's the definition of a gentleman?
Someone who can play the bagpipes, but doesn't.

Musician: Did you hear my last recital?
Friend: I hope so.

'Do you love music?'
'Yes, but never mind, go ahead and play.'

An efficiency consultant gives his critique of Schubert's
Unfinished Symphony:

'All twelve violins played the same notes. This is unnecessary duplication. Their number should be cut. For a considerable period the oboe players had nothing to do. Their number should be reduced and their work spread evenly among other staff. No useful purpose is served by repeating with horns the passage that was already handled by the strings. If such redundancies were eliminated, the concert could be cut by twenty minutes. The symphony has two movements. Mr Schubert should have been able to achieve his musical goals in one.

In conclusion: If Mr Schubert had paid attention to these matters, he would have had time to finish the symphony.'

Richard Wagner is walking down the street in Berlin one day and comes across an organ-grinder who is grinding out the overture to *Tannhäuser*.

Wagner stops and says, 'As a matter of fact, you are playing it too fast.'

The organ-grinder at once recognises Wagner, tips his hat, and says, 'Oh thank you, Herr Wagner! Thank you, Herr Wagner!'

The next day Wagner returns to the same spot and finds the organ-grinder grinding out the overture at the correct tempo. Behind him is a big sign: 'Pupil of Richard Wagner.'

What's the difference between a moose and a blues band?
The moose has the horns up front and the arsehole behind.

St Peter is checking IDs at the pearly gates, and he comes to a
Texan.

'Tell me, what have you done in life?' asks St Peter.

The Texan says, 'Well, I struck oil, so I became rich, but I
didn't sit back on my laurels. I divided all my money among my
entire family in my will, so our descendants are all set for about
three generations.'

St Peter says, 'That's quite something. Come on in. Next!'

The second guy in line has been listening, so he says,
'I struck it big in the stock market, but I didn't selfishly just
provide for my own like that Texan guy. I donated five million to
Save the Children.'

'Wonderful!' says St Peter. 'Come in. Who's next?'

The third guy has been listening, and says timidly with a
downcast look, 'Well, I only made $5000 in my entire lifetime.'

'Heavens!' says St Peter. 'What instrument did you play?'

A guy walks into the doctor's office and says, 'Doc, I haven't had
a bowel movement in a week.'

The doctor gives him a prescription for a mild laxative and
tells him, 'If it doesn't work, let me know.'

A week later the guy is back, 'Doc, still no movement.'

The doctor says, 'Hmm, guess you need something stronger.'

So he prescribes a powerful laxative. Another week later the
poor guy is back, 'Doc, *still* nothing!'

The doctor, worried, says, 'We'd better get some more
information about you to try to work out what's going on. What
do you do for a living?'

'I'm a musician.'

The doctor looks up and says, 'Well, that's it! Here's $10. Go get something to eat!'

'**A** music critic is like a eunuch, he knows exactly how it ought to be done.'

Beethoven had an ear for music . . .

Why did the Philharmonic disband? Excessive sax and violins.

Two musicians are driving down a road. All of a sudden they notice the Grim Reaper in the back seat. Death informs them that they had an accident and they are both dead. But, before he takes them into eternity, he is able to grant each musician one last request to remind them of their past life on earth. The first musician says he was a country and western singer and would like to hear eight choruses of *Achy-Breaky Heart* as a last hoorah!

The second musician says, 'I was a jazz musician. Kill me now!'

A man walks up to a pianist in a bar. The man has a wad of bills in his hand and asks if the pianist can play a jazz chord. The pianist does as requested.

'No, no,' the man says. 'A jazz chord.'

The pianists does a bit of improvising but the man doesn't like that either.

'No, no, no! A jazz chord. You know, a jazz chord, to say, ah love you.'

Son: Mother, I want to grow up and be a rock 'n' roll musician.

Mother: Now son, you have to pick one or the other. You can't do both.

What is the difference between the men's final at Wimbledon and a high-school musical?

The tennis final has more men.

How does a young man get a part in the high-school musical?
On the first day of school he turns into the wrong classroom.

What is the difference between a world war and a high-school musical?

The musical causes more suffering.

Why do high-school choruses travel so often?
It keeps assassins guessing.

What is the difference between a high-school musical director and a chimpanzee?

It's scientifically proven that chimpanzees are able to communicate with humans.

THE STRING SECTION

'Haven't I seen your face before?' a judge demands, looking down at the defendant.

'You have, Your Honour,' the man answers hopefully.
'I gave your son violin lessons last winter.'
   'Ah, yes,' recalls the judge. 'Twenty years!'

A first violinist, a second violinist, a virtuoso violist, and a bass player are at the four corners of a football field. At the signal, someone drops a $100 note in the middle of the field and they run to grab it. Who gets it?
   The second violinist, because:
   No first violinist is going anywhere for only $100;
   there's no such thing as a virtuoso violist;
   the bass player hasn't worked out what it's all about.

M aestro (to horns):   Give us the F in tune!
   Violist (to Maestro):   Please can we have the F-in' tune too?

A couple is having marital difficulties and they decide to consult a marriage counsellor. After meeting with them, the counsellor tells them that their problems could all be traced to a lack of communication.
   'You two need to talk,' he says. 'So, I recommend that you go to a jazz club. Just wait until it's time for the bass player to solo. Then you'll be talking just like everyone else.'

A viola player is returning from a gig, and, feeling tired, decides to stop at a roadside cafe for a rest and a cup of coffee. Halfway through the cup he remembers he's left his viola on the passenger's seat of the car. He rushes outside, but it's too late. Someone has broken the window and put two more violas on the rear seat.

What does a viola player do so as not to look ridiculous?
He puts his viola into a violin box.

Three violin manufactures have all done business for years on the same block in the small town of Cremona, Italy. After years of peaceful co-existence, the Amati shop decides to put a sign in the window saying, 'We make the best violins in Italy.'

The Guarneri shop soon follows suit, and puts a sign in their window proclaiming, 'We make the best violins in the world.'

Finally, the Stradivarius family puts a sign on their shop saying, 'We make the best violins on the block.'

What's the difference between a violin and a viola?
There is no difference. The violin just looks smaller because the violinist's head is so much bigger.

What's the difference between a violin and a fiddle?
A fiddle is fun to listen to.

Why are viola jokes so short?
So violinists can understand them.

How do you tell the difference between a violinist and a dog?
The dog knows when to stop scratching.

How many second violinists does it take to change a light bulb?
None. They can't get up that high!

String players' motto: It's better to be sharp than out of tune.

Why is a violinist like a SCUD missile?
Both are offensive and inaccurate.

Why don't viola players suffer from haemorrhoids?
Because all the arseholes are in the first violin section.

What's the difference between a fiddle and a violin?
No-one minds if you spill beer on a fiddle.

Why do violinists put a cloth between their chin and their instrument?
Violins don't have spit valves.

Why should you never drive a roof nail with a violin?
You might bend the nail.

A violinist says to his wife, 'Oh, baby, I can play you just like my violin.'
His wife replies, 'I'd rather have you play me like a harmonica!'

Jacques Thibault, the violinist, was once handed an autograph book by a fan while in the greenroom after a concert.
'There's not much room on this page,' he says. 'What shall I write?'

Another violinist, standing by, offered the following helpful hint, 'Write your repertoire.'

How do you make a cello sound beautiful?
Sell it and buy a violin.

Did you hear about the bassist who was so out of tune his section noticed?

How do you make a double bass sound in tune?
Chop it up and make it into a xylophone.

A double bass player arrives a few minutes late for the first rehearsal of the local choral society's annual performance of Handel's *Messiah*.

He picks up his instrument and bow, and turns his attention to the conductor. The conductor asks, 'Would you like a moment to tune?'

The bass player replies with some surprise, 'Why? Isn't it the same as last year?'

Two bass players are engaged for a run of *Carmen*. After a couple of weeks, they agree to each take an afternoon off in turn to go and watch the matinee performance from the front of house.

Joe duly takes his break. Back in the pit that evening, Moe asks how it went.

'Great,' says Joe. 'You know that bit where the music goes "Boom Boom Boom Boom" – well there are some guys up top singing a terrific song about a toreador at the same time.'

A certain bartender is quite famous for being able to accurately guess people's IQs. One night a man walks in and talks to him briefly, and the bartender says, 'Wow! You must have an IQ of about 140! You should meet this guy over here.'

So the bartender introduces him to another smart guy at the bar and they talk for a while about nuclear physics and existential philosophy and have a great time.

A second man walks in and soon the bartender has guessed an IQ of about ninety for him. So he sits him down in front of the big-screen TV and he watches football with the other guys and has a hell of a time.

Then a third man stumbled in and talks to the bartender for a while. The bartender says to himself, 'Jeez! I think this guy's IQ must be about twenty-nine!' He takes him over to a man sitting at a little table back in the corner and says, 'You might enjoy talking with this guy for a while.'

After the bartender leaves, the man at the table says, 'So do you play French bow or German bow?'

W hy are harps like elderly parents?
Both are unforgiving and hard to get in and out of cars.

THE KEYBOARD SECTION

T he doorbell rings and the lady of the house discovers a workman, complete with tool chest, on her front porch.

'Madam,' he announces, 'I'm the piano tuner.'

The lady exclaims, 'Why, I didn't send for a piano tuner.'

The man replies, 'I know you didn't, but your neighbours did.'

What do you get when you drop a piano down a mine shaft?
A flat minor.

What do you get when you drop a piano on an army base?
A flat major.

Why is a 3m concert grand better than a studio upright?
Because it makes a much bigger *kaboom* when dropped over a cliff.

Why was the piano invented?
So musicians have somewhere to put their beers.

The audience at a piano recital are appalled when a telephone rings just off stage. Without missing a note the soloist glances toward the wings and calls, 'If that's my agent, tell him I'm working!'

THE WOODWIND SECTION

Two musicians are walking down the street, and one says to the other, 'Who was that piccolo I saw you with last night?'

The other replies, 'That was no piccolo, that was my fife.'

Why is a bassoon better than an oboe?
The bassoon burns longer.

What is a burning oboe good for?
Setting a bassoon on fire.

Why did the chicken cross the road?
To get away from the bassoon recital.

What is the difference between a clarinet and an onion?
Nobody cries when you chop a clarinet into little pieces.

What do you call a bass clarinettist with half a brain?
Gifted.

What's the difference between a saxophone and a lawn mower?
The neighbours are upset if you borrow a lawnmower and don't return it.

The soprano, not being smart enough to use birth control, says to her saxophonist lover, 'Honey, I think you better pull out now.'
　　He replies, 'Why? Am I sharp?'

A community orchestra is plagued by attendance problems. Several musicians are absent at each rehearsal. As a matter of fact, every player in the orchestra has missed several rehearsals, except for one very faithful oboe player. Finally, as the dress rehearsal draws to a close, the conductor takes a moment to thank the oboist for her faithful attendance.
　　She, of course, humbly responds, 'It's the least I could do, since I won't be at the performance.'

BRASS SECTION

A guy playing trombone in the opera gets a fantastic freelance gig on the day he has to play in the opera. He tries to find a replacement but without success. Finally he goes to his housekeeper and convinces him to be the replacement. 'I'll give you my other trombone. You just look at what the guy next to you is doing and it will be OK.'

Next morning he asks the housekeeper how it went.

'Catastrophe. Your colleague sent his housekeeper as well.'

H ow many trumpet players does it take to change a light bulb? Five. One to handle the bulb and four to tell him how much better they could have done it.

W hat's the difference between a trumpet player and the rear end of a horse?

I don't know either.

W hat's the difference between trumpet players and government bonds?

Government bonds eventually mature and earn money.

H ow do trumpet players traditionally greet each other? 'Hi. I'm better than you.'

H ow do you know when a trumpet player is at your door? The doorbell shrieks!

Why can't gorillas play the trumpet?
They're too sensitive.

What's the difference between a bass trombone and a chain saw?
It's easier to improvise on a chainsaw.

What do you call a trombonist with a beeper and a mobile telephone?
An optimist.

What is the difference between a dead trombone player lying in the road, and a dead squirrel lying in the road?
The squirrel might have been on his way to a gig.

How many trombonists does it take to change a light bulb?
Just one, but he'll do it too loudly.

How do you know when there's a trombonist at your door?
His hat says, 'Domino's Pizza.'

How do you improve the aerodynamics of a trombonist's car?
Take the Domino's Pizza sign off the roof.

What kind of calendar does a trombonist use for his gigs?
Year at a Glance.

How can you tell which kid on a playground is the child of a trombonist?

He doesn't know how to use the slide, and he can't swing.

What is the dynamic range of the bass trombone?
On or off.

How do you get your viola section to sound like the horn section?

Have them miss every other note.

What is the difference between a French horn section and a '57 Chevy?

You can tune a '57 Chevy.

What do you get when you cross a French horn player and a goalpost?

A goalpost that can't march.

How many French horn players does it take to change a light bulb?

Just one, but he'll spend two hours checking the bulb for alignment and leaks.

Why is the French horn a divine instrument?
Because a man blows in it, but God knows what comes out of it.

What's the range of a tuba?
Twenty yards if you've got a good arm!

How many tuba players does it take to change a light bulb?
Three! One to hold the bulb and two to drink 'till the room spins.

How do you fix a broken tuba?
With a tuba glue.

These two tuba players walk past a bar . . .
Well, it could happen!

PERCUSSION SECTION

Why are orchestra intermissions limited to twenty minutes?
So you don't have to retrain the drummers.

What did the drummer get on his IQ test?
Drool.

How do you know when a drummer is knocking at your door?
The knock slows down.

Why do bands have bass players?
To translate for the drummer.

Did you hear about the time the bass player locked his keys in the car?

It took two hours to get the drummer out.

How many drummers does it take to change a light bulb?

None. They have a machine to do that.

What do you do with a horn player that can't play?

Give him two sticks, put him in the back, and call him a percussionist.

Why is it good that drummers have a teaspoon more brains than horses?

So they don't disgrace themselves in parades.

What's the difference between a drummer and a drum machine?

With a drum machine you only have to punch the information in once.

Heard backstage, 'Will the musicians and the drummer please come to the stage!'

A drummer, sick of all the drummer jokes, decides to change his instrument. After some thought, he decides on the accordion. So he goes to the music store and says to the owner, 'I'd like to look at the accordions, please.'

The owner gestures to a shelf in the corner and says, 'All our accordions are over there.'

After browsing, the drummer says, 'I think I'd like the big red one in the corner.'

The store owner looks at him and says, 'You're a drummer, aren't you?'

The drummer, crestfallen, says, 'How did you know?'

The store owner says, 'That "big red accordion" is the radiator.'

A researcher arrives in Indonesia to gather data for his thesis. Accompanied by his trusty guide, he seeks out a very remote locale for researching the mating behaviour of the giant rat of Sumatra. Around dusk of the first day, he's sitting by the campfire with his guide when in the distance, he hears tribal drums. They get louder. The guide announces, 'I don't like the sound of those drums.'

The dusk turns to evening. The drums get louder. The guide says, 'I really don't like the sound of those drums.'

Evening turns to dead of night. The drums get louder and louder, until it is obvious that the drummers must be quite close. The guide says again, 'I really don't like the sound of those drums.'

Suddenly the drums stop, and a voice from the darkness cries out, 'Hey man, he's not our regular drummer!'

Why do bands need roadies?
To translate what the drummer says.

A customer walks into a new store on the block that sells brains. There are three glass cases, each containing a nice, wet, quivering brain. The first one says 'Astrophysicist' and it costs $10. The second says, 'Avon salesman' and costs $1000. The third says, 'Drummer' and costs $10 000. The customer is confused, and questions the salesperson.

'I don't get it. Why would I want a drummer's brain for $10 000 when I can get an astrophysicists' for $10?'

The salesman replies, 'Because it's never been used.'

Two girls are walking along when they hear, 'Psst! Down here!' They both look down and see a frog sitting beside the road. The frog says to them, 'Hey, if you kiss me I'll turn into a world-famous drummer and make you both rich and famous!'

The two girls looked at each other, and one of them reaches down and grabs the frog and stuffs it in her pocket.

The other girl says, 'What did you do that for?'

The first replies, 'I'm not stupid. I know a talking frog is worth heaps more than a famous drummer.'

A guy walks into a shop.

'You got one of them Marshall Hiwatt AC30 amplification thingies and a Gobson StratoBlaster geetar with a Fried Rose tremulo?'

'You're a drummer, aren't you?'

'Duh, yeah. How'd you know?'

'This is a travel agency.'

'Hey buddy, how late does the band play?'

'Oh, about a half beat behind the drummer.'

Hey, did you hear about the drummer who finished high school?

Me either.

Why do guitarists put drumsticks on the dash of their car?
So they can park in the disabled spot.

One friend to another, 'Why do you hang around with that drummer'

'Beats me!'

How is a drum solo like a sneeze?
You can tell it's coming, but you can't do anything about it.

A man dies and goes to heaven. Contrary to what he expected, heaven is essentially a really long hallway
with doors on either side, each with a short IQ range listed on it. Inside, the rooms are perfectly tailored so that the conversation will match the intelligence of the people in them.

He opens the 170 door. 'Well,' comes the conversation inside, 'I've always found Fourier transforms to be a rather limited way of interconverting what are fundamentally –'

He slams the door. Too rich for him.

He heads down the hall a bit to the 115 zone and opens the door. 'I just read *Generation X*,' comes a voice, 'and though Coupland doesn't do too badly in identifying his generation's fundamental angst, I was a bit confused by –'

Slam! Not bad, but now the man is getting curious, and wants to see what is further down the scale. He tries 95. 'Hey, did you read the paper today? Says interest rates will go up again –'

Slam! How about 60? 'Huh. Thought *Married with Children* last night was pretty funny. Didn't get the bit about the hooters, though –'

Slam! It is getting pretty bad. He tries 35. The people inside are looking at one another and drooling.

Finally, he comes to the one marked with a 10. He hesitates, fearing what he will see when he opens it. But he does, seeing only two guys inside.

'So,' one says to the other, 'what size sticks do you use?'

VOCALIST SECTION

If you threw a violist and a soprano off a cliff, which one would hit the ground first?

Who cares?

What's the difference between a soprano and a terrorist?

You can negotiate with a terrorist.

What's the difference between a soprano and a piranha?

The lipstick.

What's the difference between a soprano and a pit bull?

The jewellery.

How can you tell that there's a vocalist at your front door?

She's forgotten the key and doesn't know when to come in.

How many sopranos does it take to change a light bulb?

One. She holds the bulb and the world revolves around her.

What's the difference between a Wagnerian soprano and the average All-Pro offensive lineman?
Stage makeup.

What's the difference between a Wagnerian soprano and a Wagnerian tenor?
About ten kilos.

How is a soprano different from a sewer rat?
Some people actually like sewer rats.

What is the difference between a soprano and a cobra?
One is deadly poisonous, and the other is a reptile.

How do you tell if a Wagnerian soprano is dead?
The horses seem very relieved.

What's the difference between a soprano and a Porsche?
Most musicians have never been in a Porsche.

A jazz musician dies and goes to heaven. He is told, 'Hey man, welcome! You have been elected to the Jazz All-Stars of Heaven – right up there with Satchmo, Miles, Django, all the greats. We have a gig tonight. Only one problem. God's girlfriend gets to sing.'

How many tenors does it take to change a light bulb?
Four. One to change the bulb and three to bitch that they could have done it if they had the high notes.

What do you see if you look up a soprano's skirt?
A tenor.

How do you tell if a tenor is dead?
The wine bottle is still full and the comics haven't been touched.

Where is a tenor's resonance?
Where his brain should be.

What's the definition of a male quartet?
Three men and a tenor.

How do you tell if a bass singer is actually dead?
Hold out a cheque.

How many bass singers does it take to change a light bulb?
None. They're so macho they prefer to walk in the dark and bang their shins.

An anthropologist decides to investigate the natives of a far-flung tropical island. He flies there and finds a guide with a canoe to take him up the river to the remote site where he will make his collections. About noon on the second day of travel up the river the anthropologist and the guide begin to hear drums. Being a city boy by nature, the anthropologist is disturbed by this.

He asks the guide, 'What are those drums?'

The guide turns to him and says 'Drums OK, but very bad when they stop.'

After some hours, the drums suddenly stop! This hits the anthropologist like a ton of bricks, and he yells at the guide, 'The drums have stopped, what happens now?'

The guide crouches down, covers his head with his hands and says, 'Bass solo.'

GUITARS AND BANJOS

What do you say to a banjo player in a three-piece suit?
Will the defendant please rise.

Why do some people take an instant aversion to banjo players?
It saves time in the long run.

How can you tell the difference between banjo songs?
By the names.

What's the least-used sentence in the English language?
'Isn't that the banjo player's Porsche?'

What does it mean when a guitar player is drooling out of both sides of his mouth?
The stage is level.

How do you get a guitar player to play softer?
Give him some sheet music.

How many lead guitarists does it take to change a light bulb?
None. They just steal somebody else's light.

What did the guitarist do when his teacher told him to turn his amplifier on?
  He caressed it softly and told it that he loved it.

How many bass guitarists does it take to change a light bulb?
Don't bother. Just leave it out. No-one will notice.

ACCORDION SECTION

What's the difference between an Uzi and an accordion?
The Uzi stops after twenty rounds.

What's an accordion good for?
Learning how to fold a map.

What do you call a group of topless female accordion players?
Ladies in Pain.

How can you tell that there's an accordionist at your front door?
He doesn't stop knocking even after you answer.

MINIMUM SAFE DISTANCES BETWEEN STREET MUSICIANS AND THE PUBLIC:

Violinist: 7m.

Bad violinist: 15m.

Tone-deaf guitar player who knows three chords: 75m.

Fifteen-year-old electric guitar player with a Nirvana fixation: 100m.

Accordionist: 60km.

CONDUCTING SECTION

A conductor and a violist are standing in the middle of the road. Which one do you run over first, and why?
The conductor. Business before pleasure.

What's the difference between a conductor and a sack of organic fertiliser?
The sack.

What do you have when a group of conductors are up to their necks in wet concrete?
Not enough concrete.

What's the difference between a symphony conductor and Dr Scholl's footpads?
Dr Scholl's footpads buck up the feet.

What's the difference between an opera conductor and a baby?
A baby sucks its fingers.

What's the difference between a pig and a symphony orchestra conductor?
There are some things a pig just isn't willing to do.

What is the ideal weight for a conductor?
About one kilogram, including the urn.

What's the definition of an assistant conductor?
A mouse trying to become a rat.

A musician calls the symphony office to talk to the conductor.
'I'm sorry, he's dead,' comes the reply.
The musician calls back twenty-five times, always getting the same reply from the receptionist. At last she asks him why he keeps calling.
'I just like to hear you say it.'

A musician arrives at the pearly gates.
'What did you do when you were alive?' asked St Peter.
'I was the principal trombone player of the London Symphony Orchestra.'
'Excellent! We have a vacancy in our celestial symphony orchestra for a trombonist. Why don't you turn up at the next rehearsal.'

So, when the time for the next rehearsal arrives our friend turns up with his heavenly trombone. As he takes his seat, God moves, in a mysterious way, to the podium and taps his baton to bring the players to attention. Our friend turns to the angelic second trombonist and whispers, 'So, what's God like as a conductor?'

'Oh, he's OK most of the time, but occasionally he thinks he's von Karajan.'

It is the night of the big symphony concert, and all the town notables show up to hear it. However, it is getting close to 8 p.m. and the conductor hasn't yet shown up. The theatre's manager is getting desperate, knowing that he'll have to refund everyone's money if he cancels the concert, so he goes backstage and asks the musicians if any of them can conduct.

None of them can, so he goes around and asks the staff if any of them can conduct. He has no luck there either, so he starts asking people in the lobby, in the hope that maybe one of them can conduct the night's concert.

He still hasn't found anyone, so he goes outside and starts asking people in the street if they can conduct. He has no luck whatsoever and by this time the concert is fifteen minutes late in starting. The assistant manager comes out to say that the crowd is getting restless and the people are ready to demand their money back. The desperate manager looks around and spies a cat, a dog, and a horse standing in the street.

'Oh, what the heck,' he exclaims, 'let's ask them. What do we have to lose?'

So the manager and assistant manager go up to the cat, and the manager asks, 'Mr Cat, do you know how to conduct?'

The cat meows 'I don't know, I'll try,' but though the cat tries really hard, it just can't stand upright on its hind legs. The manager sighs and thanks the cat, and then moves on to the dog.

'Mr Dog,' he asks, 'do you think you can conduct?'

The dog woofs, 'Let me see.'

But although it is able to stand up on its hind legs and wave its front paws around, it just can't keep upright long enough to last through an entire movement.

'Well, nice try,' the manager tells the dog and, with a sigh of resignation, he turns to the horse.

'Mr Horse,' he asks, 'how about you? Can you conduct?'

The horse looks at him for a second and then without a word turns around, presents its hind end, and starts swishing its tail in perfect four-four time.

'That's it!' the manager exclaims, 'the concert can go on.'

However, right then the horse drops a load of plop onto the street.

The assistant manager is horrified, and he tells the manager, 'We can't have this horse conduct! What will the orchestra think?'

The manager looks first at the horse's rear end and then at the plop lying in the street and replies, 'Trust me. From this angle, the orchestra won't even know they have a new conductor!'

A guy walks into a pet store wanting a parrot. The store clerk shows him two beautiful ones out on the floor.

'This one's $5000 and the other is $10 000,' the clerk says.

'Wow! What does the $5000 one do?'

'This parrot can sing every aria Mozart ever wrote.'

'And the other?' asks the customer.

'This one can sing Wagner's entire *Ring* cycle. There's another one in the back room for $30 000.'

'Holy moly! What does that one do?'

'Nothing that I can tell, but the other two parrots call him "Maestro".'

'**M**ummy,' says the little girl, 'can I get pregnant by anal intercourse?'

'Of course you can.' her mother replies. 'How do you think conductors are made?'

A new conductor is at his first rehearsal. It's not going well. He is as wary of the musicians as they are of him. As he leaves the rehearsal room, the timpanist sounds a rude little *bong*.

The angry conductor turns and says, 'All right! Who did that?'

A violinist is auditioning for the Halle orchestra in England. After his audition he is talking with the conductor.

'What do you think about Brahms?' asks the conductor.

'Ah . . .' the violinist replies, 'Brahms is a great guy. Real talented musician. In fact, he and I were just playing some duets together last week.'

The conductor is impressed. 'And what do you think of Mozart?' he asks him.

'Oh, he's just swell! I just had dinner with him last week,' replies the violinist.

Then the violinist looks at his watch and says he has to leave to catch the 1.30 p.m. train to London.

Afterwards, the conductor is discussing him with the board members. He says he feels very uneasy about hiring this violinist, because there seems to be a serious credibility issue. The conductor knows for certain that there is no 1.30 p.m. train to London.

A man and his son are walking through a cemetery. The boy asks, 'Look Daddy, they buried two people in the same grave.'

The father says, 'Two people? Let me see.'

So the father takes a look, and sure enough, the marker says, 'Here lies a symphony conductor and a humble man.'

A guy is so dumb his teacher gives him two sticks and he becomes a drummer. But he loses one, so he becomes a conductor.

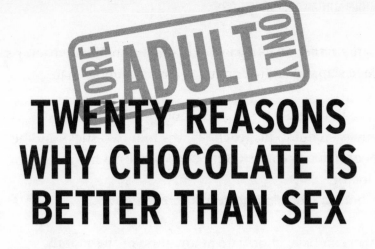

TWENTY REASONS WHY CHOCOLATE IS BETTER THAN SEX

1. You can *get* chocolate.

2. 'If you love me you'll swallow it' has real meaning with chocolate.

3. Chocolate satisfies even when it has gone soft.

4. You can safely have chocolate while you are driving.

5. You can make chocolate last as long as you want it to.

6. You can have chocolate in front of your mother.

7. If you bite the nuts too hard the chocolate won't mind.

8. Two people of the same sex can have chocolate without being called nasty names.

9. The word 'commitment' doesn't scare off chocolate.

10. You can have chocolate on top of your workbench or desk during working hours without upsetting your co-workers.

11. You can ask a stranger for chocolate without getting your face slapped.

12. You don't get hairs in your mouth with chocolate.

13. With chocolate there's no need to fake it.

14. Chocolate doesn't make you pregnant.

15. You can have chocolate at any time of the month.

16. Good chocolate is easy to find.

17. You can have as many kinds of chocolate as you can handle.

18. You are never too young or too old for chocolate.

19. When you have chocolate it does not keep your neighbours awake.

20. With chocolate, size doesn't matter.

ON THE FARM

*It must be the country air, or the silence, or the . . . Actually, it's
the people who live on farms that
make them such an ideal location for a joke.*

A ventriloquist goes for a walk in the country and sees a
farmer sitting on his porch with his dog. The ventriloquist
asks the farmer if he can talk to the dog.

'Dogs don't talk,' the farmer tells him.

'Well, can I try?'

'Sure, go ahead. Though you're wasting your time.'

'Hey dog, how's it goin'?' asks the ventriloquist.

'Doin' all right,' replies the dog.

The farmer is shocked, while the ventriloquist proceeds to
trick the farmer.

'Is this your owner?' the ventriloquist asks pointing at the
farmer.

'Yep,' the dog replies.

'How's he treat you?'

'Real good. He walks me twice a day, feeds me great food, and
takes me to the lake once a week to play.'

Next, the ventriloquist asks if he can speak to the farmer's
horse.

'Horses don't talk,' the farmer says.

Again, the ventriloquist insists until the farmer agrees.

'Hey horse, how's it goin'?' the ventriloquist asks.

'Cool,' the horse replies.

The farmer looks even more astonished than when the dog
spoke.

'Is this your owner?' the ventriloquist asks pointing at the farmer.

'Yep,' the horse replies.

'How's he treat you?'

'Pretty good, thanks for asking. He rides me regularly, brushes me down often, and keeps me in the barn to protect me from the elements.'

The ventriloquist then turns to the farmer again and asks, 'Mind if I talk to your sheep?'

The farmer gesticulates wildly and is hardly able to talk. Nevertheless, he manages to blurt out, 'Them sheep ain't nothin' but liars, every darned one of 'em!'

A chicken and an egg are lying in bed. The chicken is leaning against the headboard smoking a cigarette, with a satisfied smile on its face.

The egg, looking a bit pissed off, grabs the sheet, rolls over, and says, 'Well, I guess we finally answered *that* question!'

A salesman is talking to a farmer when he looks over and sees a rooster wearing pants, a shirt, and suspenders.

He says, 'What on earth is that all about?'

The farmer says, 'We had a fire in the chicken coop two months ago and all his feathers got singed off, so the wife made him some clothes to keep him warm.'

'OK, but that was two months ago. Why does he still wear them?'

The farmer replies, 'There ain't nothing funnier than watching him trying to hold down a hen with one foot and get his pants down with the other.'

A young lad from the city goes to visit his uncle, a farmer. For the first few days, the uncle shows him all the usual things, chickens, cows, crops, etc. After three days, however, it is obvious that the nephew is getting bored, and the uncle is running out of things to amuse him. Finally, the uncle has an idea.

'Why don't you grab a gun, take the dogs and go shooting?'

This seems to cheer the nephew up, and with enthusiasm, off he goes, dogs in tow. After a few hours, the nephew returns.

'How did you enjoy that?' asks the uncle.

'It was great!' exclaims the nephew. 'Got any more dogs?'

Ol' farmer John walks into the local watering hole and who should he see, but his old friend Chris the tractor salesman sitting up at the bar. Chris looks so down and dejected, that John just has to go up and say something to him.

'Say, Chris, how ya doing? How's the tractor selling business these days?'

If Chris looked sad before, at the mention of tractor sales, his face sinks even more, and a tear comes to his eye.

'John,' he says, shaking his head, 'I don't know what it is. I can't sell a tractor these days to save my life. I'll tell you, I just gotta sell one tractor, and soon, or I'll lose that dealership forever.'

'Well,' John says, taking the barstool next to him, 'If you think you got it bad, I got it worse. Now you listen to this: I went out to the barn the other morning to milk Bessie. That old cow gets more difficult as the years go by. Anyway, no sooner did I sit down on the milking stool and get to work, but ol' Bes started slappin' me with her tail. After a minute or so, I got fed up with it, so I threw a rope up over the rafters, and tied ol' Bessie's tail to the rafters. Then I got back to work. I didn't even get two squirts into the bucket, when Bes gives me a kick. Knocked me clean off the stool! Boy, if that didn't piss me off! So I get me another rope an' tie Bessie's right hind leg to the side of the milking stall, and get started trying to milk her again. Well by this time, Bessie's about livid, and she doesn't want any part of it, so she let's me have it with her other hind leg. I wasn't about to give in to this ol' cow, so I got me yet another piece of rope and tied Bessie's left leg to the side of the stall.'

Just then John pauses to take a sip of his beer. Chris, distracted for a moment from his own troubles, asks John, 'Well, did you finally get to milk her?'

'Well, yes and no, Chris. But I'll tell ya what . . . If you can convince my wife that I was out there to *milk* that cow, I'll buy a tractor from you!'

A farmer hires a uni student one summer to help around the farm.

At the end of the summer the farmer says, 'Son, since you have done such a fine job here this summer, I am going to throw a party for you.'

The uni student says, 'Great!'

So the farmer says, 'Well you better be able to handle a few beers because there will be lots of drinking.'

The student says, 'I can drink just as much as anyone else.'

And the farmer adds, 'There is also going to be a lot of fightin' so I hope you are ready.'

So the student responds, 'I have been working hard all summer and I think I'm in pretty good shape.'

'One more thing,' says the farmer. 'Did I mention that there· will be lots of sex?'

'You beauty!' shouts the student. 'I have been out here all summer and I have been dying for some action. What should I wear to this party?'

The farmer says, 'Nothing fancy. It's just going to be me and you.'

An extraordinarily handsome man decided he has the God-given responsibility to marry the perfect woman so they can produce children beyond comparison. With this as his mission he begins searching for the perfect woman. After a diligent, but fruitless, search up and down the east coast, he starts to head west. Shortly thereafter he meets a farmer who has three stunningly gorgeous daughters that positively take his breath away. So he explains his mission to the farmer, asking for permission to marry one of them.

The farmer simply replies, 'They're all lookin' to get married, so you came to the right place. Look them over and select the one you want.'

The man dates the first daughter. The next day the farmer asks for the man's opinion.

'Well,' says the man, 'she's just a weeeeee bit, not that you can hardly notice, but pigeon-toed.'

The farmer nods and suggests the man date one of the other girls; so the man goes out with the second daughter. The next day, the farmer again asks how things went.

'Well,' the man replies, 'She's just a weeeee bit, not that you can hardly tell, cross-eyed.'

The farmer nods and suggests he date the third girl to see if things are any better. So he does.

The next morning the man rushes in exclaiming, 'She's perfect, just perfect! She's the one I want to marry.'

So they are wed right away. Months later a baby is born. When the man visits the nursery he is horrified. The baby is the ugliest, most pathetic human you can imagine. He rushes to his father-in-law asking how such a thing could happen considering the parents.

'Well,' explains the farmer, 'she was just a weeeee bit, not that you could hardly tell, pregnant when you met her.'

Two stupid farmers have a mule that is a very hard worker. The only problem is that every time they go to put the mule back in his stall, his ears brush the top of the entrance and then the old mule goes nuts and kicks everything. One day, the farmers decide to cut an opening in the top of the entrance, to prevent this from happening. While they are working, a neighbour stops by and asks what they are doing, so they explain the problem. The neighbour suggests that they can save a lot of work and time if they simply take a shovel and dig the entrance down a little bit. The farmers thank their neighbour and he drives off.

Then one farmer says to the other, 'Some stupid neighbour we have, it's not his feet that are too long, it's his ears!'

Four farmers are seated at the bar in a tavern. At the table next to them sits a young woman.

The first man says, 'I think it's woomb.'

The second replies, 'No, it must be woooombh.'

The third says, 'You both have it wrong – it's woom.'

The fourth states, 'No, it has to be woommbbb.'

At this, the young woman can stand it no longer. She gets up, walks over to the farmers and says, 'Look, you hayseeds, it's womb. That's it, that's all there is to it.'

Then she leaves. Eventually, one of the farmers breaks the silence by saying, 'Well, I don't know. A slip of a girl like that, I don't see how she could know. I'll bet she's never even heard an elephant fart!'

A man is in love with a beautiful woman and he wants to marry her. The woman tells him that before they can get married he must ask her father, who is a farmer.

So the next day the man goes to the farmer and says, 'Sir I

love your daughter very much and I would like to ask for her hand in marriage.'

The farmer sits there and looks at him for a moment and then says, 'I will let you marry her, but first you must undertake a test.'

Willing to do anything to be able to marry the girl, the man agrees.

The farmer says, 'First you must jump the fence, swim the river and screw the cow in the barn.'

The man thinks that sounds easy enough, so he does it. When he is finished he asks the farmer, 'OK now can I marry your daughter?'

The farmer can't believe that the man has actually done those things and, thinking it is funny, he tells the man to go do it again. So the man jumps the fence, swims the river, and screws the cow, again.

When he is finished the man goes back to the farmer and asks 'Now may I marry your daughter?'

By this time the farmer is amazed that the man did all that a second time, and wonders if he will do it a third, so the farmer says, 'OK if you do all that one more time I will let you marry my daughter.'

So the man does it again. He jumps the fence, swims the river, and screws the cow. When he comes back to the farmer this time, the farmer says, 'OK now you can marry my daughter.'

The man says, 'To hell with you daughter. How much do you want for the cow?'

HUNTING AND FISHING

*There's something about people who go hunting
and fishing. I'm not saying they've got a screw
loose or anything but . . .*

In the middle of a forest, there is a hunter who is suddenly confronted by a huge, mean bear. In his fear, all his attempts to shoot the bear are unsuccessful. Finally, he turns and runs as fast as he can. The hunter runs and runs and runs, his lungs burn for lack of oxygen, his heart pounds so hard he feels like it will burst out of his chest. Then, suddenly, he ends up at the edge of a very steep cliff. His hopes are dim. Seeing no way out of his predicament, and with the bear closing in rather quickly, the hunter gets down on his knees, opened his arms, and exclaims, 'Dear Lord! Please give this bear some religion!'

The skies darken and lightning fills the air. Just a few metres short of the hunter, the bear comes to an abrupt stop, and glances around, somewhat confused.

Suddenly, the bear looks up into the sky, kneels and says, 'Thank you, Lord, for this food I'm about to receive . . .'

Two hunters are out looking for pheasant when they come upon the local farmer's daughter, sitting naked on a fence, sunning herself.

The first hunter asks, 'Are you game?'

She replies, 'I sure am, Honey!'

So the second hunter shoots her.

A guy is on his honeymoon near his favourite fishing lake. He fishes from dawn to dark with his favourite fishing guide. One day the guide mentions that the man seems to be spending his honeymoon fishing.

'Yes, but you know how I love to fish' the man replies.

'But aren't you newlyweds supposed to be into something else?' the guide asks.

'Yes, but she's got gonorrhoea; and you know how I love to fish.'

A few hours later the guide says, 'I understand, but that's not the only way to have sex.'

'I know, but she's got diarrhoea; and you know how I love to fish.'

The following day the guide says, 'Sure, but that's still not the only way to have sex.'

'Yeah, but she's got pyuria; and you know how I love to fish.'

Late that afternoon, thoroughly frustrated the guide comments, 'I guess I'm not sure why you'd marry someone with health problems like that.'

'It's 'cause she's also got worms; and you know I just love to fish.'

A man and his grandson, are fishing by a peaceful lake beneath some weeping willow trees. The man takes out a cigarette and lights it.

The grandson asks, 'Grandpa, can I try one of your cigarettes?'

'Can you touch your arsehole with your penis?' the grandfather asks.

'No,' says the grandson.

'Then you're not big enough,' says the grandfather.

A few minutes pass, and the man takes a beer out of his cooler and opens it.

Little Johnny says, 'Grandpa, can I have some of your beer?'

'Can you touch your arsehole with your penis?' he asks.

'No,' says the grandson.

'Then you're not old enough.'

Time passes and they continue to fish. The grandson gets hungry and he reaches into his lunch box, takes out a bag of cookies and eats one.

The grandfather looks at him and says, 'They look good, can I have one of your cookies?'

'Can you touch your arsehole with your penis?' asks Johnny.

'I most certainly can!' says the grandfather proudly.

'Then go screw yourself,' says Johnny, 'these are my cookies!'

Two hunters bump into each other every afternoon after a day's hunting. And every afternoon, one of the hunters has a bearskin, while the other has nothing. Eventually, the empty-handed hunter asks the other hunter how he manages to catch a bear each day.

'It's easy,' says the hunter.

'I go over to one of those holes in the mountain, stand in front of it and shout, "you stupid fat, ugly bear, get your stinking arse out off this hole!," then the bear comes out and I shoot it. Easy as.'

'I'll try that,' the other hunter says.

The next day, the first hunter comes out of the woods with a bear skin and bumps into the other hunter who is crawling around on his hands and knees, covered in blood and missing a leg.

'What happened to you man?'

'Aargh, I did what you told me to do. I went to a hole, started shouting and swearing at the bear and guess what happened?'

'What?'

'A bloody train came out.'

Two hunters go moose-hunting every winter without success. Finally, they come up with a foolproof plan. They get a very authentic female moose costume and learn the mating call of a female moose. The plan is to hide in the costume, lure the bull, then come out of the costume and shoot the bull. They set themselves up on the edge of a clearing, don their costume and begin to give the moose love-call. Before long, their call is answered as a bull comes crashing out of the forest and into the clearing.

When the bull is close enough, the guy in front says, 'OK, let's get out and get him.'

After a moment that seems like an eternity, the guy in the back shouts, 'The zipper is stuck! What are we going to do?'

The guy in the front says, 'Well, I'm going to start nibbling grass, but you'd better brace yourself.'

Two avid fishermen go on a fishing trip. They rent all the equipment: the reels, the rods, the wading suits, the rowboat, the car, and even a cabin in the woods. They spend a fortune.

The first day they go fishing, but they don't catch anything. The same thing happens on the second day, and on the third day. It goes on like this until finally, on the last day of their vacation, one of the men catches a fish.

As they're driving home they're really depressed. One guy turns to the other and says, 'Do you realise that this one lousy fish we caught cost us $1500?'

The other guy says, 'Wow! It's a good thing we didn't catch any more!'

On a cold winter day, an old man walks out onto a frozen lake, cuts a hole in the ice, drops in his fishing line and waits for a fish to bite. He is there for almost an hour without even a nibble when a young boy walks out onto the ice, cuts a hole in the ice not too far from the old man and drops in his fishing line. It only takes about a minute and *wham!* A largemouth bass takes his hook and the boy pulls in the fish.

The old man can't believe it but reckons it's just luck. But the boy drops in his line and within just a few minutes, pulls in another one.

This goes on and on until finally the old man can't take it any more since he hasn't caught a thing all this time.

He goes to the boy and says, 'Son, I've been here for over an hour without even a nibble. You have been here only a few minutes and have caught about half a dozen fish! How do you do it?'

The boy responds, 'Roo raf roo reep ra rums rrarm.'

'What was that?' the old man asks.

Again the boy responds, 'Roo raf roo reep ra rums rarrm.'

'Look,' says the old man, 'I can't understand a word you are saying.'

So, the boy spits into his hand and says, 'You have to keep the worms warm!'

Three guys go hunting and are sitting around the evening campfire exchanging their worst experiences.

The first guy says the worst thing that ever happened to him was being up on a scaffold seven storeys high, washing windows, when the scaffold collapsed and he fell, breaking every bone in his body. He was hospitalised for six months.

The second guy says the worst thing that ever happened to him was when he was hitch-hiking and a Greyhound bus ran over him, breaking his back and he wound up in the hospital for nearly a year.

The third guy is not saying anything, so one of the others asks him about his worst experience.

He says, 'Well, I'll tell you about the second-worst thing that ever happened to me. I was out hunting one time and I had to take a shit, so I stepped behind a tree, dropped my trousers, and crouched down into position.'

'Yeah? What happened next?' asks one of his friends.

'I got a little too close to the ground and *wham!* A bear trap snapped shut on my testicles.'

One of the other guys says, 'God! If that was the second worst, what in the world was the worst?'

He calmly replies, 'Oh, that would be when I reached the end of the chain . . .'

Two men go bear hunting. While one stays in the cabin, the other goes out looking for a bear. He soon finds a huge bear and shoot at it, but only wounds it. The enraged bear charges toward him, he drops his rifle and starts running for the cabin as fast as he can.

He runs pretty fast but the bear is just a little faster and gains on him with every step. Just as he reaches the open cabin door, he trips and falls flat. Too close behind to stop, the bear trips over him and goes rolling into the cabin.

The man jumps up, closes the cabin door and yells to his friend inside, 'You skin this one while I go and get another one!'

Two hunters are dragging their dead deer back to their car. Another hunter approaches pulling his along too.

'Hey, I don't want to tell you how to do something, but I can tell you that it's much easier if you drag the deer in the other direction. Then the antlers won't dig into the ground.'

After the third hunter leaves, the two decide to try it.

A little while later one hunter says to the other, 'You know, that guy was right. This is a lot easier!'

'Yeah, but we're getting farther from the truck,' the other adds.

A couple of young boys are fishing at their special pond off the beaten track. All of a sudden, the game warden jumps out of the bushes. Immediately, one of the boys throws his rod down and starts running through the woods like a bat out of hell. The game warden is hot on his heels. After about a half mile, the young man stops and stoops over with his hands on his thighs to catch his breath. The game warden finally catches up with him.

'Let's see yer fishin' licence, Boy!' the warden gasps.

With that, the boy pulls out his wallet and gives the game warden a valid fishing licence.

'Well, son,' says the game warden. 'You must be about as dumb as a box of rocks! You don't have to run from me if you have a valid licence!'

'Yes, Sir,' replies the young guy. 'But my friend back there, well, he don't have one.'

WHY FISHING IS BETTER THAN SEX

- When you go fishing and you catch something, that's good. If you're having sex and you catch something, that's bad.

- Fish don't compare you to other fishermen and don't want to know how many other fish you have caught.

- In fishing you lie about the one that got away. With sex you lie about the one you caught.

- You can catch and release a fish without having to lie and promise to still be friends after you've let it go.

- You don't have to change your line to keep catching fish.

- You can catch a fish on a twenty-cent night crawler. If you want to catch a woman you're talking at least dinner and a movie.

- Fish don't mind if you fall asleep while you're fishing.

WHAT THINGS ON YOUR RESUME REALLY MEAN

I know how to deal with stressful situations:
I'm usually on Prozac. When I'm not, I take lots of cigarette and coffee breaks.

I seek a job that will draw upon my strong communication and organisational skills:
I talk too much and like to tell other people what to do.

I'm extremely adept at all manner of office organisation:
I've used Microsoft Office.

I'm honest, hard-working and dependable:
I pilfer office supplies.

My pertinent work experience includes:
I hope you don't ask me about all the McJobs I've had.

I take pride in my work:
I blame others for my mistakes.

I'm balanced and centred:
I'll keep crystals at my desk and do Tai Chi in the lunch room.
I have a sense of humour:
I know a lot of corny, old jokes and I tell them badly.

I'm personable:
I give lots of unsolicited personal advice to co-workers.

I'm willing to relocate:
Anywhere's better that the prison I've just left.

My background and skills match your requirements:
You're probably looking for someone more
experienced.

I am adaptable:
I've changed jobs a lot.

I am on the go:
I'm never at my desk.

I'm highly motivated to succeed:
The minute I find a better job, I'm outta there.

I have formal training:
I'm a uni drop-out.

I interact well with co-workers:
I've been accused of sexual harassment.

Thank you for your time and consideration:
Wait! Don't throw me away!

I look forward to hearing from you soon:
Like, I'm gonna hold my breath waiting for your stupid form
letter thanking me for my interest and wishing me luck in my
future career.

UNIVERSITY LIFE

It's a wonder anyone ever gets through uni.

A father, passing through his son's uni town late one night on a business trip, thinks he will pay a surprise visit to his boy. Arriving at the college, he knocks on the door. After several minutes of knocking, a sleepy voice drifts down from a second floor window.

'Whattya want?'

'Does Billy Smith live here?' asks the father.

'Yeah!' replies the voice. 'Dump him on the front porch and we'll take care of him in the morning.'

An autopsy lecturer is giving an introductory lecture to a class of students. Standing over a corpse, he addresses the class.

'There are two things you need to make a career in medical forensics. First, you must have no fear.'

Having said that, he shoves his finger up the corpse's arsehole then licks it.

'Now you must do the same,' he tells the class.

After a couple of minutes of uneasy silence, the class do as instructed.

'Second,' the lecturer continues, 'you must have an acute sense of observation. For instance, how many of you noticed that I put my middle finger up this man's anus, but licked my index finger?'

A pre-med student takes an examination and the last question is: Give four advantages of breast milk.

The student begins to answer the question:

1. No need to sterilise bottles
2. Healthier for the child
3. Available whenever necessary

But the fourth point eludes him. When there are only a couple of minutes left to finish the exam he gets desperate and answers:

4. Available in attractive containers

O n the first day of uni, the Dean addresses the students, pointing out some of the rules. 'The female dormitory will be out-of-bounds for all male students, and the male dormitory for all female students. Anybody caught breaking this rule will be fined $20 the first time. Anybody caught breaking this rule the second time will be fined $60. Being caught a third time will cost you a fine of $180. Are there any questions?'

A male student in the crowd inquires, 'How much for a season pass?'

A girl goes into the doctor's office for a check-up. As she takes off her blouse, he notices a red 'H' on her chest.

'How did you get that mark on your chest?' asks the doctor.

'Oh, my boyfriend went to Harvard and he's so proud of it that he never takes off his Harvard sweatshirt, even when we make love,' she replies.

A couple of days later, another girl comes in for a check-up. As she takes off her blouse, he notices a blue 'Y' on her chest.

'How did you get that mark on your chest?' asks the doctor.

'Oh, my boyfriend went to Yale and he's so proud of it that he never takes off his Yale sweatshirt, even when we make love,' she replies.

A couple of days later, another girl comes in for a check-up. As she takes off her blouse, he notices a red 'M' on her chest.

'Do you have a boyfriend at Michigan?' asks the doctor.

'No, but I have a girlfriend at Wisconsin. Why do you ask?'

A visiting lecturer is giving a seminar on the supernatural. To get a feel for his audience, he asks, 'How many people here believe in ghosts?'

About ninety students raise their hands.

'Well that's a good start. Out of those of you who believe in ghosts, do any of you think you've ever seen a ghost?'

About forty students raise their hands.

'That's really good. I'm really glad you take this seriously. Has anyone here ever talked to a ghost?'

Fifteen students raise their hands.

'That's a great response. Has anyone here ever touched a ghost?'

Three students raise their hands.

'That's fantastic. But let me ask you one question further. Have any of you ever made love to a ghost?'

One student in the back raises his hand. The lecturer is astonished. He takes off his glasses, takes a step back, and says, 'Son, all the years I've been giving this lecture, no-one has ever claimed to have slept with a ghost. You've got to come up here and tell us about your experience.'

The student replies with a nod and a grin, and begins to make his way up to the podium.

The lecturer says, 'Well, tell us what it's like to have sex with a ghost.'

The student replies, 'Ghost? Damn. From back there I thought you said "goats"!'

DOCTORS AND NURSES

There's nothing at all funny about sickness and death. Unless it's happening to someone else.

A guy goes to see a doctor and after a series of tests the doctor comes in and says, 'I've got some good news and some bad news.'

'What's the bad news?' asks the patient.

'The bad news is that, unfortunately, you've only got three months to live.'

The patient is shocked, 'Oh my god! Well what's the good news then, doctor?'

The doctor points over to the secretary at the front desk, 'You see that blonde with the big tits, tight arse and legs that go all the way up to heaven?'

The patient says, 'Yes.'

The doctor smiles and replies, 'I'm banging her!'

M r Smith goes to the doctor's office to collect his wife's test results.

'I'm sorry, Sir,' says the receptionist, 'but there has been a bit of a mix-up and we have a problem. When we sent your wife's sample to the lab, the samples from another Mrs Smith were sent as well and we are now uncertain which one is your wife's. Frankly, that's either bad or terrible.'

'What do you mean?' asks Mr Smith.

'Well, one Mrs Smith has tested positive for Alzheimer disease and the other for AIDS. We can't tell which your wife's is.'

'That's terrible! Can we take the test over?'

'Normally, yes. But your medical insurance fund won't pay for these expensive tests more than once.'

'Well, what am I supposed to do now?' asks Mr Smith.

'The doctor recommends that you drop your wife off in the middle of town. If she finds her way home, don't sleep with her.'

A proctologist has grown tired of his career and decides to go back to study. After thinking about what he wants to do with the rest of his life, he decides to go to trade school to become a garage mechanic. After struggling through the first course, he takes the final exam. When he gets the results back he is amazed to find he got 200%.

'How in the world did I pass? I thought I was going to flunk this thing,' he says in wonder.

'Well,' replies the instructor, 'I gave you fifty points for getting the engine rebuilt, I gave you fifty points because it ran, and the other 100 points was from doing it all through the muffler.'

A man goes to an urologist and tells him that he is having a problem and that he is unable to get his penis erect. After a complete examination, the doctor tells the man that the muscles around the base of his penis are damaged from a prior viral infection and there is nothing he can do for him. However, he knows of an experimental treatment that might be applicable, if the man is willing to take the risk. The treatment consists of implanting muscle tissue from an elephant's trunk into the man's penis.

The man thinks about it for a while. The thought of going through life without ever experiencing sex again is just too much for him to bear. So, with the assurance that there will be no cruelty or adverse effect on the elephant, the man decides to go for it. A few weeks after the operation, he is given the green light to use his newly renovated equipment. As a result, he plans a romantic evening with his girlfriend and takes her to one of the best restaurants in the city. However, in the middle of dinner, he feels a stirring between his legs that continues to the point of being extremely painful. To release the pressure, he unzips his fly and immediately his penis springs from his pants, goes to the top of the table, grabs a potato, and then returns to his pants.

His girlfriend is stunned at first, but then with a sly smile on her face says, 'That was incredible. Can you do that again?'

With his eyes watering, he replies, 'I think I can, but I'm not sure if I can fit another potato up my arse.'

Narelle is probably the ugliest woman that the planet has ever sustained, but her friends are too embarrassed to tell her why she can't pull a bloke. She enquires of her doctor, who is equally reluctant, but who makes an appointment for her to see a Chinese doctor who is a specialist in personal relationships. She duly presents herself, and is somewhat taken aback at the first instruction from Dr Huong Kwack, which is

'Please take off all clothes.'

She complies.

The next instruction is, 'Please turn with back to me, bend forward and place head between legs.'

She does as requested, and is delighted to hear the instant diagnosis.

'I see problem. You have Zackery's disease.'

'What do you mean?'

'Your face Zackery the same as your arse.'

In a doctor's surgery, Merv sits waiting patiently to see Dr Strangeways. Suddenly, a nun rushes out of his surgery in tears. Somewhat taken aback, Merv goes in next.

'Morning doctor. That nun looked very upset.'

'Yeah, I told her she was pregnant.'

'A nun? Pregnant?'

'Oh, she isn't really. But it sure as hell cured her hiccups.'

A man visits his doctor for his regular check-up. The doctor is not too pleased with what he finds and asks the man to send his wife to see him. The wife goes to see the doctor who tells her that her husband has a very serious heart condition.

'Don't be too alarmed though,' the doctor reassures her. 'With the right treatment he can live a long and happy life. You will have to give him every attention. Treat him very gently. Don't ask him to do any work around the house. No lawn mowing or anything like that. In fact, you must pamper his every whim. Cook his favourite dishes. Never get cross with him when he gets difficult – and he will. Always do whatever it is he feels like doing. Spoil him totally and you will have your husband for a very long time.'

When she arrives home, the husband says, 'What did the doctor say?'

The wife replies, 'You're going to die.'

A woman comes home from the doctor.

'What did the doctor say?' her husband asks.

'He said I have the figure of an eighteen-year-old,' she replies.

'What did he say about your big fat arse,' quips the husband.

'Your name didn't come up.'

Nancy goes to the gynaecologist and he examines her.
He says, 'You have acute vaginitis.'

She says, 'Thank you.'

An old country doctor goes way out to the boondocks to
deliver a baby. It is so far out that there is no electricity.
When the doctor arrives, no-one is home except for the
labouring mother and her five-year-old child. The doctor
instructs the child to hold a lantern up high so he can see
while he helps the woman deliver the baby. The child does so,
the mother pushes, and after a little while, the doctor lifts the
newborn baby by the feet and spanks him on the bottom to get
him to take his first breath.

'Hit him again,' the child says. 'He shouldn't have crawled up
there in the first place.'

A tired doctor is awakened by a phone call in the middle of
the night.

'Please, you have to come right over,' pleads a distraught
young mother. 'My child has swallowed a contraceptive.'

The physician dresses quickly, but before he can get out the
door, the phone rings again.

'You don't have to come over after all,' the woman says with a
sigh of relief. 'My husband just found another one.'

A man's wife has been in a coma for several days following a
particularly nasty knock on the head. As usual, one of the
nurses in the hospital is giving her a wash in bed. As she
washes down the woman's body, she sponges her pubic hair.
Out of the corner of her eye the nurse thinks she has seen the
woman's eyebrows shudder. Not quite sure, she tries again.

This time, she actually did see some movement.

'Doctor, Doctor,' she calls, 'I saw some movement!'

The Doctor comes into the room and tries as well. Once more, they both see movement around the woman's eyes.

'Well this is good news,' says the doctor. 'I think we should call her husband and let him know.'

They call her husband and tell him that they have seen some movement. When he arrives, they explain that by touching the woman's pubic hair, they were seeing some sort of reaction in her facial muscles. The doctor suggests that the husband might like to try something a little more adventurous in order to provoke a stronger reaction.

'I suggest that we leave the room and that you try a little oral sex,' he says.

The husband agrees and is left alone in the room. Several moments later, all the emergency alarms and buzzers are activated. The doctor and a host of nurses run into the wife's room where they see the husband zipping up his jeans.

'Oops,' he says, 'I think I choked her.'

A woman goes to her doctor for a follow-up visit after the doctor has prescribed testosterone for her. She is a little worried about some of the side effects she is experiencing.

'Doctor, the hormones you've been giving me have really helped, but I'm afraid that you're giving me too much. I've started growing hair in places that I've never grown hair before.'

The doctor reassures her. 'A little hair growth is a perfectly normal side effect of testosterone. Just where has this hair appeared?'

'On my balls.'

When Ralph first notices that his penis is growing larger and staying erect longer, he is delighted, as is his wife. But after several weeks his penis has grown to nearly twenty inches. Ralph becomes quite concerned, so he and his wife go to see a prominent urologist. After an initial examination, the physician explains to the couple that, though rare, Ralph's condition can be cured through corrective surgery.

'How long will Ralph be on crutches?' the wife asks anxiously.

'Crutches? Why would he need crutches?' responds the surprised doctor.

'Well,' says the wife coldly, 'You *are* planning to lengthen Ralph's legs, aren't you?'

A man runs to the doctor and says, 'Doctor, you've got to help me. My wife thinks she's a chicken.'

The doctor says, 'How long has she had this condition?'

'Two years,' says the man.

'Then why did it take you so long to come and see me?'

The man shrugs his shoulders, 'We needed the eggs.'

The gynaecologist compliments the young woman on his examination table.

'Go home and tell your husband to prepare for a baby.'

'But I don't have a husband,' the girl replies.

'Then, go home and tell your lover.'

'But I don't have a lover. I've never had a lover.'

'In that case,' the doctor sighs, 'go home and tell your mother to prepare for the second coming of Christ.'

A concerned patient asks the doctor if masturbation is harmful. 'Not usually,' answers the doctor. 'Not unless you do it too often.'

'How about three times a day?' the patient asks.

'That seems a little excessive. Why don't you get a girlfriend?'

'Oh, I already have a girlfriend,' the patient replies.

'I mean a girl you can live with and have sex with,' says the doctor.

The patient says, 'I've got one just like that.'

So the doctor asks, 'Then why do you masturbate three times a day?'

'Because she won't have sex during mealtimes.'

One afternoon, a man goes to his doctor and tells him that he hasn't been feeling well lately. The doctor examines the man, leaves the room, and comes back with three different bottles of pills.

The doctor says, 'Take the green pill with a big glass of water when you wake up. Take the blue pill with a big glass of water after you eat lunch. Then just before going to bed, take the red pill with another big glass of water.'

Startled to be put on so much medicine, the man stammers, 'Jeez Doc, exactly what is my problem?'

The doctor replies, 'You're not drinking enough water.'

A man walks into the doctor's surgery and flips his penis onto the desk and says, 'I'd like you to have a look at this Doc.'

The doctor looks and says, 'I can see nothing wrong with it.'

'I know, but it's a bloody beauty isn't it?'

A middle aged woman has a heart attack and is taken to the hospital. While on the operating table she has a near-death experience. During that experience she sees God and asks if this is it. God says no and explains that she has another thirty years to live. Upon her recovery she decides to stay in the hospital and have a face-lift, liposuction, a breast augmentation, a tummy tuck, etc. She even has someone come in and change her hair colour. She reckons since she's got another thirty years she might as well make the most of it. She walks out of the hospital after the last operation and is killed by an ambulance speeding up to the hospital.

She arrives in front of God and complains, 'I thought you said I had another thirty years.'

God replies, 'I didn't recognise you.'

Two doctors are in a hospital hallway one day complaining about Nurse Molly.

'She's incredibly mixed up,' says one doctor. 'She does everything absolutely backwards. Just last week, I told her to give a patient 2mg of morphine every ten hours, she gave him 10mg every two hours. He damn near died on us.'

The second doctor says, 'That's nothing. Earlier this week, I told her to give a patient an enema every twenty-four hours. She tried to give him twenty-four enemas in one hour. The guy damn near exploded.'

Suddenly they hear a bloodcurdling scream from down the hall.

'Oh my God!' says the first doctor, 'I just realised I told Nurse Molly to prick Mr Smith's boil.'

A man walks into a crowded doctor's office.
As he approaches the desk the receptionist asks, 'Yes Sir, may we help you?'

'There's something wrong with my dick,' he replies.

The receptionist is shocked and says, 'You shouldn't come into a crowded office and say things like that.'

'Why not? You asked me what was wrong and I told you,' he says.

'We do not use language like that here,' she says. 'Please go outside and come back in and say that there's something wrong with your ear or whatever.'

The man walks out, waits several minutes and re-enters. The receptionist smiles smugly and asks, 'Yes?'

There's something wrong with my ear,' he states.

The receptionist nods approvingly.

'And what is wrong with your ear, Sir?'

'I can't bloody piss out of it,' the man replies.

An old man goes to the doctor for his yearly physical, his wife tagging along.

When the doctor enters the examination room, he tells the old man, 'I need a urine sample, a stool sample and a sperm sample.'

The old man, being hard of hearing, looks at his wife and yells, 'What?' What did he say? What's he want?'

His wife yells back, 'He needs your underwear.'

A woman goes to her doctor complaining that she is exhausted all the time. After the diagnostic tests show nothing, the doctor gets around to asking her how often she has intercourse.

'Every Monday, Wednesday and Saturday,' she says.

The doctor advises her to cut out Wednesday.

'I can't,' says the woman. 'That's the only night I'm home with my husband!'

A man with a bad stomach complaint goes to his doctor and asks him what he can do.

The doctor replies that the illness is quite serious, but can be cured by inserting a suppository up his anal passage. The man agrees and so the doctor warns him of the pain, tells him to bend over and shoves the thing way up his behind. The doctor then hands him a second dose and tells him to do the same thing in six hours. So, the man goes home and later that evening tries to get the second suppository inserted, but he finds that he cannot reach himself properly to obtain the required depth. He calls his wife over and tells her what to do. The wife nods, puts one hand on his shoulder to steady him and with the other shoves the medicine home.

Suddenly the man screams, 'Arrgghhhh!'

'What's the matter?' asks the wife, 'Did I hurt you?'

'No,' replies the man, 'but I just realised that when the doctor did that, he had *both* hands on my shoulder.'

A n elderly married couple go to the doctor for their annual medical check-ups.

After the examination, the doctor says to the elderly man, 'You appear to be in good health. Do you have any medical concerns that you would like to discuss with me?'

'In fact, I do,' says the man. 'After I have sex with my wife for the first time, I am usually hot and sweaty. And then, after I have sex with my wife the second time, I am usually cold and chilly.'

'This is very interesting,' replies the doctor. 'Let me do some research and get back to you.'

After examining the elderly woman, the doctor says, 'Everything appears to be fine. Do you have any medical concerns that you would like to discuss with me?'

The woman replies that she has no questions or concerns.

The doctor then asks, 'Your husband had an unusual concern.

He claims that he is usually hot and sweaty after having sex with you the first time and then cold and chilly after the second time. Do you know why?'

'Oh that old buzzard!' she replies. 'That's because the first time is usually in summer and the second time is usually in winter.'

An eighty-year-old man is having an annual physical. When it is over, the doctor says, 'I'm afraid you have a serious heart murmur. Do you smoke?'

'No,' replies the man.

'Do you drink in excess?'

'No,' replies the man.

'Do you have a sex life?'

'Yes, I do!'

'Well,' says the doc, 'I'm afraid with this heart murmur, you'll have to give up half your sex life.'

Looking perplexed, the old man says, 'Which half? The looking or the thinking?'

The seven-year-old tells her mum, that a little boy in her class asked her to play doctor.

'Oh, dear,' the mother sighs nervously. 'What happened, honey?'

'Nothing, he made me wait forty-five minutes and then double-billed the insurance company.'

One day a young married couple are in their bedroom making love. All of a sudden a bumble bee enters the bedroom window. As the young woman parts her legs the bee enters her vagina.

The woman starts screaming, 'Oh my god, help me, there's a bee in my vagina.'

The husband immediately takes her to the local doctor and explains the situation.

The doctor thinks for a moment and says, 'Hmm, tricky situation. But I have a solution to the problem if young Sir will permit.'

The husband is very concerned and agrees that the doctor can use whatever method he likes to get the bee out of his wife's vagina.

The doctor says, 'OK, what I'm gonna do is rub some honey over the top of my penis and insert it into your wife's vagina. When I feel the bee getting closer to the tip of my dick I shall withdraw it and the bee should hopefully follow my penis out of your wife's vagina.'

The husband nods and gives his approval.

The young woman says, 'Yes, yes, whatever, just get on with it.'

So the doctor, after covering the tip of his penis with honey, inserts it into the young woman's vagina.

After a few gentle strokes, the doctor says, 'I don't think the bee has noticed the honey yet. Perhaps I should go a bit deeper.'

So the doctor goes deeper. After a while the doctor begins shafting the young woman very hard indeed. The young woman begins to quiver with excitement, she begins to moan and groan aloud.

'Oh doctor, doctor!' she shouts.

The doctor, concentrating very hard, looks like he is enjoying himself. He then put his hands on the young woman's breasts and starts making loud noises.

The husband, at this point, suddenly becomes very annoyed and shouts, 'Now wait a minute, what the hell do you think you're doing?'

The doctor, still concentrating, replies, 'Change of plan, I'm gonna drown the bastard.'

Queen Elizabeth II is visiting one of New York's finest hospitals and during her tour of the wards she passes a room where one of the male patients is masturbating.

'Oh God,' says the Queen. 'That's disgraceful, what is the meaning of this?'

The doctor leading the tour explains, 'I am sorry your Royal Highness, but this man has a very serious condition where his testicles fill up rapidly with semen. If he doesn't do what he is doing at least five times per day, he could swell up and he might die'

'Oh, I am sorry,' says the Queen. 'I was unaware that such a medical condition existed.'

On the same floor they soon pass another room where a young, blonde nurse is performing oral sex on another patient.

'Oh my God,' says the Queen. 'What's happening here?'

The doctor replies, 'Same problem, better health plan.'

Three elderly men are at the doctor's office for a memory test.

The doctor asks the first man, 'What is three times three?'

'Two hundred and seventy four,' he replies.

The doctor rolls his eyes and looks up at the ceiling, and says to the second man, 'It's your turn. What is three times three?'

'Tuesday,' replies the second man.

The doctor shakes his head sadly, then asks the third man, 'OK, your turn. What's three times three?'

'Nine,' says the third man.

'That's great!' says the doctor. 'How did you get that?'

'Simple,' he says, 'just subtract 274 from Tuesday.'

A very frustrated man visits his doctor.
'Doc, you've gotta help me! My wife just isn't interested in

sex anymore. Haven't you got a pill or something I can give her?'

'Look, I can't prescribe anything –'

'Doc, we've been friends for years. Have you ever seen me this upset? I'm desperate! I can't think, I can't concentrate, my life is going utterly to hell! You've got to help me.'

The doctor opens his desk drawer and removes a small bottle of pills.

'Ordinarily, I wouldn't do this. These are experimental, the tests so far indicate that they're *very* powerful. Don't give her more than *one*, understand? Just *one*.'

'I don't know, doc. She's awfully cold.'

'One. No more. In her coffee. OK?'

'Um . . . OK.'

He thanks the doc and heads for home where his wife has dinner waiting. When dinner is finished, she goes to the kitchen to bring dessert. In fumbling haste, he pulls the pills from his pocket and drops one into his wife's coffee. He thinks for a moment, hesitates, then drops in a second pill. And then he begins to worry. The doctor did say they were powerful. Then an inspiration strikes . . . he drops one pill into his own coffee. His wife returns and they enjoy their dessert and coffee. Sure enough, a few minutes after they finish, his wife shudders a little, sighs deeply and heavily, and a strange look enters her eyes. In a near-whisper and in a tone of voice he has never heard her use before, she says, 'I need a man.'

His eyes glitter and his hands tremble as he replies, 'Me too.'

Two elderly couples are enjoying a friendly conversation when one of the men asks the other, 'Fred, how was the memory clinic you went to last month?'

'Outstanding,' Fred replies. 'They taught us all the latest psychological techniques – visualization, association. It made a huge difference for me.'

'That's great! What was the name of the clinic?'

Fred goes blank. He thinks and thinks, but can't remember. Then a smile breaks across his face and he asks, 'What do you call that red flower with the long stem and thorns?'

'You mean a rose?'

'Yes, that's it!' He turns to his wife. 'Rose, what was the name of that clinic?'

Doctor: Nurse, how is that little boy doing, the one who swallowed ten twenty-cent coins?

Nurse: No change yet.

What's the difference between a nurse and a nun?
A nun only serves one God.

A nurse is showing some student nurses through a hospital. 'This will be the most hazardous section in the hospital for you. The men on this floor are almost well.'

The nurse who can smile when things go wrong is probably going off duty.

Did you hear about the nurse who died and went straight to hell?

It took her two weeks to realise that she wasn't at work anymore!

Doctor: Did you take the patient's temperature?
DNurse: No. Is it missing?

TOP TEN REASONS TO BECOME A NURSE

1. The pay is better than selling fast food, though the hours aren't as good.

2. The fashionable shoes and sexy white uniforms.

3. Needles: It's better to give than to receive.

4. Reassuring your patients that all bleeding stops . . . eventually.

5. Exposing yourself to rare, exotic and exciting new diseases.

6. Interesting aromas.

7. Doing enough charting to navigate around the world.

8. Celebrating the holidays with all your friends . . . at work.

9. Taking comfort that most of your patients survive no matter what you do to them.

10. Courteous and infallible doctors who always leave clear orders in perfectly legible handwriting.

YOU MIGHT BE A NURSE IF . . .

. . . when using a public toilet, you wash your hands with soap for a full minute and turn off the faucets with your elbows.

. . . your favourite dream is the one where you leave a mess at a patient's bedside and tell a doctor to clean it up.

. . . men assume you must be great in bed because of the nine billion porn movies about nurses.

. . . everyone, including complete strangers, tells you about each and every ache and pain they have.

. . . you want to put your foot through the TV screen every time you see a nurse on a soap opera doing nothing but talking on the phone and flirting with doctors.

. . . you can almost *see* the germs on doorknobs and telephones.

. . . you can watch the goriest movie and eat anything afterwards, even spaghetti with lots of tomato sauce.

. . . you use a plastic 30cc medicine cup for a shot glass.

How many nurses does it take to change a light bulb? As many as the doctor orders.

How many triage nurses does it take to change a light bulb? One, but the bulb will have to spend four hours in the waiting room.

How many doctors does it take to change a light bulb? Only one, but he has to have a nurse to tell him which end to screw in.

'**D**octor, please hurry. My son swallowed a razor-blade.'
'Don't panic, I'm coming immediately. Have you done anything yet?'

'Yeah, I shaved with the electric razor.'

'**D**octor, Doctor, you've got to help me – I just can't stop my hands shaking!'
'Do you drink a lot?'
'Not really – I spill most of it!'

'**D**octor, doctor, will I be able to play the violin after the operation?'
'Yes, of course . . .'
'Great! I never could before!'

One day a farmer catches a travelling salesman making love to his youngest daughter. Yelling 'You son of a bitch!' he shoots the amorous salesman in the groin with a .12-gauge shotgun.

The screaming salesman quickly takes off for town to find a doctor. He finds one, but the physician takes one look at the man's perforated pecker and tells him that nothing can be done for him.

'Oh, please do something,' begs the salesman. 'I'm a rich man. I can pay you anything.'

'Sorry, son,' says the doctor. 'There's nothing I can do. However, there's a man across the street that might be able to help you.'

'Oh really? Is he a specialist?' asks the salesman.

'No,' says the doctor, 'he's a piccolo player. He'll teach you how to hold it without pissing in your face!'

A patient wakes up after an operation and the surgeon tells him, 'I'm afraid we're going to have to operate on you again. I left my rubber gloves inside you.'

'Well, if that's all it is, I'd rather pay for them and be done with it.'

A doctor and his wife are having a big argument at breakfast. 'You aren't so good in bed either,' he shouts and storms off to work.

By midmorning, he decides he'd better make amends and phones home. After many rings, his wife picks up the phone.

'What took you so long to answer?'

'I was in bed.'

'What were you doing in bed this late?'

'Getting a second opinion.'

Doctor: I have some bad news and some very bad news.

Patient: Well, might as well give me the bad news first.

Doctor: The lab called with your test results. They said you have twenty-four hours to live.

Patient: Twenty-four hours! That's terrible! *What* could be *worse*? What's the very bad news?

Doctor: I've been trying to reach you since yesterday.

Doctor: I've got very bad news – you've got cancer and Alzheimer's.

Patient: Well, at least I don't have cancer.

A man walks into a doctor's office. He has a cucumber up his nose, a carrot in his left ear and a banana in his right ear.

'What's the matter with me?' he asks the doctor.

The doctor replies, 'You're not eating properly.'

A young woman goes to her doctor complaining of pain.

'Where are you hurting?' asks the doctor.

'I hurt all over,' says the woman.

'What do you mean, all over?' asks the doctor, 'be a little more specific.'

The woman touches her right knee with her index finger and yells, 'Ow, that hurts.'

Then she touches her left cheek and again yells, 'Ouch! That hurts, too.'

Then she touches her right earlobe.

'Ow, even *that* hurts,' she cried.

The doctor checks her thoughtfully for a moment and tells her his diagnosis, 'You have a broken finger.'

'Doctor, are you sure I'm suffering from pneumonia? I heard about a doctor treating someone for pneumonia but he finally died of typhus.'

'Don't worry, it won't happen to me. If I treat someone for pneumonia, he will die of pneumonia.'

A man goes to see his doctor because he is suffering from a miserable cold. His doctor prescribes some pills, but they don't help. On his next visit the doctor gives him a shot, but that doesn't do any good either.

On his third visit the doctor tells the man, 'Go home and take a hot bath. As soon as you finish bathing throw open all the windows and stand in the draft.'

'But doc,' protests the patient, 'if I do that, I'll get pneumonia.'

'I know,' says the doctor, 'I can cure pneumonia.'

A SHORT HISTORY OF MEDICINE

'Doctor, I have an ear ache.'

2000 B.C.:	'Here, eat this root.'
1000 B.C.:	'That root is heathen, say this prayer.'
1850 A.D.:	'That prayer is superstition, drink this potion.'
1940 A.D.:	'That potion is snake oil, swallow this pill.'
1985 A.D.:	'That pill is ineffective, take this antibiotic.'
2000 A.D.:	'That antibiotic is artificial. Here, eat this root!'

A pipe bursts in a doctor's house and he calls a plumber. The plumber arrives, unpacks his tools, does mysterious plumber-type things for a while, and hands the doctor a bill for $600.

The doctor exclaims, 'This is ridiculous! I don't even make that much as a doctor.'

The plumber quietly answers, 'Neither did I when I was a doctor.'

A doctor says to his car mechanic, 'Your fee is several times more per hour then we get paid for medical care.'

'Yeah, but you see, doc, you always have the same model, it hasn't changed since Adam. We have to keep up to date with new models coming out every year.'

'The doctor said he would have me on my feet in two weeks.'
'And did he?'
'Yes, I had to sell the car to pay the bill.'

A fellow walks into a doctor's office and the receptionist asks him what he has.

He says, 'Shingles.'

So she takes down his name, address and medical insurance number, and tells him to take a seat.

A few minutes later a nurse's aid comes out and asks him what he has.

He says, 'Shingles.'

So she takes down his height, weight and a complete medical history. Then she tells him to wait in the examining room.

Ten minutes later a nurse comes in asks him what he has.

He says, 'Shingles.'

So she gives him a blood test, a blood pressure test and an electrocardiogram, and tells him to take off all his clothes and wait for the doctor.

Fifteen minutes later the doctor comes in and asks him what he has.

He says, 'Shingles.'

The doctor asks, 'Where?'

He says, 'Outside in the truck. Where do you want them?'

A woman, calling Mount Sinai Hospital, says, 'Hello, I want to know if a patient is getting better.'

The voice on the other end of the line says, 'What is the patient's name and room number?'

She says, 'Yes, darling! She's Sarah Finkel, in Room 302.'

The man on the phone says, 'Oh, yes. Mrs Finkel is doing very well. In fact, she's had two full meals, her blood pressure is fine, she's going to be taken off the heart monitor in a couple of hours and if she continues this improvement, Dr Cohen is going to send her home Tuesday.'

The woman says, 'Thank God! That's wonderful! Oh! That's fantastic! That's wonderful news!'

'From your enthusiasm, I take it you must be a close family member or a very close friend!'

She says, 'I'm Sarah Finkel in 302. Cohen, my doctor, doesn't tell me a word!'

An old fellow comes into the hospital, truly on death's door due to an infected gallbladder. The surgeon who removed the gallbladder is adamant that his patients be up and walking in the hall the day after surgery, to help prevent blood clots forming in the leg veins. The nurses walk the patient in the hall as ordered, and after the third day the nurse tells the doctor how he complains bitterly each time they do. The surgeon tells them to keep walking him.

After a week, the patient is ready to go. His children come to pick him up and thank the surgeon profusely for what he has done for their father. The surgeon is pleased and appreciates the thanks, but tells them that it was really a simple operation and he was lucky to get him in time.

'But doctor, you don't understand,' they say, 'Dad hasn't walked in over a year!'

If it is dry, add moisture; if it is moist, add dryness. Congratulations, now you are a dermatologist.

A man goes to the eye doctor. The receptionist asks him why he is there.

The man complains, 'I keep seeing spots in front of my eyes.'
The receptionist asks, 'Have you ever seen a doctor?'
'No, just spots.'

Patient: I always see spots before my eyes.
Doctor: Didn't the new glasses help?
Patient: Sure, now I see the spots much clearer.

A veterinarian is feeling ill and goes to see her doctor. The doctor asks her all the usual questions about symptoms, how long they have been occurring, etc.

She interrupts him, 'Hey look, I'm a vet. I don't need to ask my patients these kinds of questions: I can tell what's wrong just by looking. Why can't you?'

The doctor nods, looks her up and down, writes out a prescription, and hands it to her.

'There you are. Of course, if that doesn't work, we'll have to have you put down.'

'Are you an organ donor?'
'No, but I once gave an old piano to the Salvation Army.'

A man needing a heart transplant is told by his doctor that the only heart available is that of a sheep. The man finally agrees and the doctor transplants the sheep heart into the man. A few days after the operation, the man comes in for a check-up.

The doctor asks him, 'How are you feeling?'
The man replies, 'Not baaaaad!'

Whats the difference between a general practitioner and a specialist?

One treats what you have, the other thinks you have what he treats.

THINGS YOU DON'T WANT TO HEAR DURING SURGERY:

• Oops!

• Has anyone seen my watch?

• That was some party last night. I can't remember when I've been that drunk.

• Damn! Page 47 of the manual is missing!

• Well this book doesn't say that . . . What edition is your manual?

• OK, now take a picture from this angle. This is truly a freak of nature.

• Better save that. We'll need it for the autopsy.

• Come back here with that! Bad dog!

• Wait a minute, if this is his spleen, then what's that?

• Hand me that . . . uh . . . that uh . . . that thingy.

• If I can just remember how they did this on ER last week.

• Hey, has anyone ever survived 500ml of this stuff before?

- Damn, there go the lights again.

- Ya know, there's big money in kidneys. Hell, the guy's got two of 'em.

- Everybody stand back! I lost my contact lens!

- Could you stop that thing from beating; it's throwing my concentration off.

- I wish I hadn't forgotten my glasses.

- Well folks, this will be an experiment for all of us.

- Sterile, shcmerile. The floor's clean, right?

- What do you mean he wasn't in for a sex change!

- What do you mean he's not insured?

- This patient has already had some kids, am I correct?

- Nurse, did this patient sign the organ donation card?

- Don't worry. I think it's sharp enough.

- What do you mean 'You want a divorce?'!

- I don't know what it is, but hurry up and pack it in ice.

- Let's hurry, I don't want to miss *Bay Watch*.

- That laughing gas stuff is pretty cool. Can I have some more of that?

- Hey Charlie, unzip the bag on that one, he's still moving.

- Did the doctor know he would look like that afterwards?

- Of course I've performed this operation before, nurse!

- Fire! Fire! Everyone get out!

At a medical convention, a male doctor and a female doctor start eyeing each other. The male doctor asks the female doctor to dinner and she accepts. As they sit down at the restaurant, she excuses herself to go and wash her hands.

After dinner, one thing leads to another and they end up in her hotel bedroom. Just as things get hot, the female doctor interrupts and says she has to go and wash her hands. When she comes back they go for it. After the sex session, she gets up and says she is going to wash her hands.

As she comes back the male doctor says, 'I bet you are a surgeon.'

She confirms and asks how he knew.

'Easy, you're always washing your hands.'

She then says, 'I bet you're an anaesthesiologist.'

'Wow, how did you guess?' asks the male doctor.

'I didn't feel a thing.'

Three doctors are in a duck hide and a bird flies overhead. The general practitioner looks at it and says, 'Looks like a duck, flies like a duck . . . it's probably a duck.'

He shoots at it but misses and the bird flies away.

The next bird flies overhead, and the pathologist looks at it, then looks through the pages of a bird manual, and says, 'Hmmmm . . . green wings, yellow bill, quacking sound. Might be a duck.'

He raises his gun to shoot it, but the bird is long gone. A third bird flies over.

The surgeon raises his gun and shoots almost without looking, brings the bird down, and turns to the pathologist.

'Go see if that was a duck.'

A guy has been suffering from severe headaches for years with no relief. After trying all the usual cures he's referred to a headache specialist by his family doctor. The doctor asks him what his symptoms are.

'I get these blinding headaches; kind of like a knife across my scalp and –'

He is interrupted by the doctor, 'And a heavy throbbing right behind the left ear.'

'Yes! Exactly! How did you know?'

'Well I am the world's greatest headache specialist, you know. But I myself suffered from that same type of headache for many years. It is caused by a tension in the scalp muscles. This is how I cured it: Every day I would give my wife oral sex. When she came she would squeeze her legs together with all her strength and the pressure would relieve the tension in my head. Try that every day for two weeks and come back and let me know how it goes.'

Two weeks go by and the man comes back.

'Well, how do you feel?' asks the doctor.

'Doc, I'm a new man! I feel great! I haven't had a headache since I started this treatment! I can't thank you enough. And, by the way, you have a lovely home.'

WHY DID THE CHICKEN CROSS THE ROAD?

Dr Seuss:
Did the chicken cross the road?
Did he cross it with a toad?
Yes!
The chicken crossed the road,
But why it crossed,
I've not been told!

Ernest Hemingway:
To die. In the rain.

Martin Luther King Jr:
I envision a world where all chickens will be free to cross roads without having their motives called into question.

Grandpa:
In my day, we didn't ask why the chicken crossed the road. Someone told us that the chicken crossed the road, and that was good enough for us.

Jerry Falwell:
Because the chicken was gay! Isn't it obvious? Can't you people

see the plain truth in front of your face? The chicken was going to the 'other side'. That's what *they* call it: the 'other side'. Yes, my friends, that chicken is gay. And, if you eat that chicken, you will become gay too. I say we boycott all chickens until we sort out this abomination that the liberal media whitewashes with seemingly harmless phrases like 'the other side'. That chicken should not be free to cross the road. It's as plain and simple as that.

Ken Starr:
I intend to prove that the chicken crossed the road at the behest of the president of the United States of America in an effort to distract law enforcement officials and the American public from the criminal wrongdoing our highest elected official has been trying to cover up. As a result, the chicken is just another pawn in the president's ongoing and elaborate scheme to obstruct justice and undermine the rule of law. For that reason, my staff intends to offer the chicken unconditional immunity provided he cooperates fully with our investigation. Furthermore, the chicken will not be permitted to reach the other side of the road until our investigation and any Congressional follow-up investigations have been completed. (We are also investigating whether Sid Blumenthal has leaked information to the Rev Jerry Falwell, alleging the chicken to be homosexual in an effort to discredit any useful testimony the bird may have to offer, or at least to ruffle his feathers.)

Pat Buchanan:
To steal a job from a decent, hardworking American.

Aristotle:
It is in the nature of chickens to cross the road.

Karl Marx:
It was a historical inevitability.

Saddam Hussein:
This was an unprovoked act of rebellion and we were quite justified in dropping fifty tons of nerve gas on it.

Ronald Reagan:
What chicken?

Captain James T Kirk:
To boldly go where no chicken has gone before.

Fox Mulder:
You saw it cross the road with your own eyes.
How many more chickens have to cross before you believe it?

Freud:
The fact that you are at all concerned that the chicken crossed the road reveals your underlying sexual insecurity.

Bill Gates:
I have just released eChicken 98, which will not only cross roads, but will lay eggs, file your important documents, and balance your cheque-book – and Internet Explorer is an inextricable part of eChicken.

Einstein:
Did the chicken really cross the road or did the road move beneath the chicken?

Bill Clinton:
I did not cross the road with *that* chicken. What do you mean by chicken? Could you define chicken please?

Louis Farrakhan:
The road, you will see, represents the black man. The chicken crossed the 'black man' in order to trample him and keep him down.

The bible:
And God came down from the heavens, and He said unto the chicken, 'Thou shalt cross the road.' And the chicken crossed the road, and there was much rejoicing.

Colonel Sanders:
What? I missed one?

EATING OUT

Jokes about food go back a very long way.
I'm sure the first joke ever told was something
along the lines of 'Eve, there's a worm in this apple'
'Well don't yell it out or they'll all want one.'

A woman is feeling a bit down in the dumps and decides to treat herself to a meal at a very expensive restaurant. She manages to get a table, even though the place is very busy, and she enjoys a delicious meal on her own. Aware of her financial limitations, she doesn't go overboard but does make sure she enjoys herself. When the head waiter brings the bill, she's horrified to see the total – $250! She didn't expect this at all. Realising there's no point complaining, she hands over her credit card.

When the waiter returns with the slip for her to sign, she asks him, 'Would you mind holding my breasts while I sign my name please?'

The waiter is taken aback. In all his years in the job he's never been asked that before. But he is always eager to please the customer and he obliges. When the woman gets up to leave, the waiter's curiosity gets the better of him. He catches up with her at the door.

'I'm sorry to bother you Miss but I'd like to know why you asked me to do that just now.'

'Oh it's quite simple really,' she replies, 'I love to have my breasts held when I'm being screwed!'

An overweight businessman decides it is time to lose some weight. He takes his new diet seriously, even changing his driving route to avoid his favourite bakery. One morning, however, he arrives at work carrying a gigantic coffee-cake. His colleagues tell him off but he just smiles.

'This is a very special coffee-cake,' he explains. 'I accidentally drove by the bakery this morning and there in the window were a host of goodies. I felt this was no accident, so I prayed, "Lord, if you want me to have one of those delicious coffee-cakes, let me have a parking place directly in front of the bakery." And sure enough, the eighth time around the block, there it was.'

A man and a woman are having dinner in a fine restaurant. Their waitress, taking another order at a table a few paces away, notices that the man is slowly sliding down his chair and under the table, with the woman acting unconcerned. The waitress watches as the man slides all the way down his chair and out of sight under the table. Still, the woman dining across from him appears calm and unruffled, apparently unaware that her dining companion has disappeared.

After the waitress finishes taking the order, she comes over to the table and says to the woman, 'Pardon me, Ma'am, but I think your husband just slid under the table.'

The woman calmly looks up at her and replies firmly, 'No he didn't. He just walked in the door.'

Three couples are dining together.
The American husband says to his wife, 'Pass me the honey, Honey.'

The English husband says to his wife, 'Pass me the sugar, Sugar.'

The Australian husband says to his wife, 'Pass me the steak, Dumb cow.'

Two men are in a restaurant and order fish. The waiter brings a dish with two fish, one larger than the other.

One of the men says to the other, 'Please help yourself.'

The other one says, 'OK,' and helps himself to the larger fish.

After a tense silence, the first one says, 'Really, now, if you had offered me the first choice, I would have taken the smaller fish!'

The other one replies, 'What are you complaining for. You have it, don't you?'

'What flavours of ice cream do you have?' inquires the customer.

'Vanilla, strawberry and chocolate,' answers the new waitress in a hoarse whisper.

Trying to be sympathetic, the customer asks, 'Do you have laryngitis?'

'No,' replies the new waitress with some effort, 'just . . . erm . . . vanilla, strawberry and chocolate.'

A traveller becomes lost in the Sahara desert. Realising his only chance for survival is to find civilization, he begins walking. Time passes, and he becomes thirsty. More time passes, and he begins feeling faint.

He is on the verge of passing out when he spies a tent about 500m in front of him. Barely conscious, he reaches the tent and calls out, 'Water!'

A Bedouin appears in the tent door and replies sympathetically, 'I am sorry, Sir, but I have no water. However, would you like to buy a tie?'

With this, he brandishes a collection of exquisite silken neckwear.

'You fool,' gasps the man. 'I'm dying! I need water!'

'Well, Sir,' replies the Bedouin, 'if you really need water, there is a tent about 2km south of here where you can get some.'

Without knowing how, the man summons sufficient strength to drag his parched body the distance to the second tent. With his last bit of strength he tugs at the door of the tent and collapses.

Another Bedouin, dressed in a costly tuxedo, appears at the door and enquires, 'May I help you Sir?'

'Water!' is the feeble reply.

'Oh, Sir,' replies the Bedouin, 'I'm sorry, but you can't come in here without a tie!'

Did you hear about the new restaurant on the moon? Great food but no atmosphere.

Waiter, what's this fly doing in my soup?
Um, looks to me to be backstroke, Sir.

Waiter, there's a fly in my soup!
Don't worry Sir, the spider on the bread roll will get 'im.

Waiter, there's a fly in my soup!
No Sir, that's a cockroach, the fly is on your steak.

Waiter, there's a fly in my soup!
Keep it down Sir, or they'll all want one.

Waiter, there's a fly in my soup!
It's OK, Sir, there's no extra charge!

Waiter, there's a fly in my soup!
Force of habit, Sir. Our chef used to be a tailor.

Waiter, there's a fly in my soup!
Couldn't be, Sir. The cook used them all in the raisin bread.

Waiter, there is a fly in my soup!
I know, but unfortunately we are out of turtle.

Waiter, there is a fly in my soup!
Sorry Sir, maybe I missed it when I removed the other three.

Waiter, there's a fly in my soup!
Surely not, Sir. It must be one of those vitamin bees you hear so much about.

Waiter, there's a fly swimming in my soup!
Then we've served you too much soup, the fly should be wading.

Waiter, there's a dead fly in my soup!
Yes Sir, it's the hot water that kills them.

Waiter, there's a dead fly in my soup!
What do you expect for $5 – a live one?

Waiter, waiter, there's a bee in my soup.
Yes Sir, it's the fly's day off.

Waiter, I'd like a cup of coffee, please, with no cream.
I'm sorry, Sir, but we're out of cream. How about with no milk?

Waiter, this coffee tastes like dirt!
Yes Sir, that's because it was only ground this morning.

Waiter, what is this stuff?
That's bean salad Sir.
I know what it's been, but what is it now?

Waiter, I can't seem to find any oysters in this oyster soup.
Would you expect to find angels in angel cake?

Waiter, your tie is in my soup!
That's all right, Sir, it's not shrinkable.

Waiter! Your thumb's in my soup!
Don't worry, Sir, it's not that hot!

A waiter brings a customer the steak he ordered, with his thumb over the meat.

'Are you crazy?' yells the customer, 'What are you doing with your hand on my steak?'

'What?' asks the waiter, 'You want it to fall on the floor again?'

'Tea or coffee, gentlemen?' asks the waiter.

'I'll have tea,' says the first customer.

'Me, too – and be sure the cup is clean!' says the second customer.

Soon the waiter returns with two cups of tea.

'Two teas,' he says. 'Which of you gentlemen asked for the clean cup?'

Waiter, waiter, do you have frog's legs?

Certainly, Sir!

Well hop over here and get me a sandwich!

And how did you find your steak Sir?

Well, quite accidentally. I moved this slice of tomato and there it was.

Waiter, get me a hot dog.

With pleasure, Sir.

No, with mustard.

Waiter: These are the best eggs we've had for years.

Diner: Well, bring me some fresh ones then.

How many waiters does it take to change a light bulb?
None, a burned out bulb can't catch a waiter's eye.

How many waitresses does it take to change a light bulb?
Three. Two to stand around bitching about it and one to go get the manager.

How many cafeteria staff does it take to change a light bulb?
'Sorry, we closed eighteen seconds ago, and I've just cashed up.'

How many McDonald's counter girls does it take to change a light bulb?
Two. One to change it and one to put some fries with it.

GROWING OLD GRACEFULLY

It's great fun making fun of the elderly.
They're too frail to fight back.

An eighty-five-year-old man marries a beautiful twenty-five-year-old woman. Because her new husband is so old the woman decides that on their wedding night they should have separate suites. She is concerned that the old fellow could over exert himself. After the festivities she prepares herself for bed and for the knock on the door she is expecting. Sure enough the knock comes and there is her groom ready for action. They start making love and all goes well. He then leaves her room and she prepares to go to sleep for the night. After a few minutes there's a knock on the door and there is the old man again, ready for more action. Somewhat surprised she consents to further sex which is again successful. When it is over, the octogenarian bids her a fond goodnight and leaves. She is very tired now and is close to sleep when, again, there is a knock at the door. There he is, fresh as a twenty-five-year-old and ready for more action. Once again they make love.

As they're lying alongside each other afterwards, the young bride says to him, 'I am really impressed that a guy your age has enough juice to go for it three times. I've been with guys less than half your age that were only good for one . . . you're great.'

The man looks confused, and turns to her and says, 'Have I been in here before?'

A couple who have been married for over fifty years are sitting on the sofa.

The wife says, 'Dear, do you remember how you used to sit close to me?'

He moves over and sits close to her.

'Dear,' she continues, 'do you remember how you used to hold me tight?'

He reaches over and holds her tight.

'And,' she goes on, 'do you remember how you used to hug me and kiss me and nibble on my ear?'

With that, her husband gets up and starts to walk out of the room.

'Where are you going?' she asks.

'Well,' answers the husband, 'I have to go and get my teeth.'

A fter forty years of marriage, Frankenstein and the Bride of Frankenstein come to a stand-still in their love life. Each night Frankenstein 'comes' home from work, eats his dinner, and sits in front of the television until he falls asleep. Dissatisfied with this arrangement, the Bride decides to see a therapist.

'He's never in the mood,' complains the Bride.

'Try a romantic candlelit dinner,' suggests the therapist.

The next day, the Bride returns to the therapist with a frown on her face.

'He's still not in the mood,' she complains.

'This time,' the therapist recommends, 'try something more seductive. Put on some sexy lingerie and lure him into the bedroom.'

But the Bride returns to the therapist the following day complaining that her monster of a husband is still not in the mood.

As a final piece of advice, the therapist says, 'You should try to recreate the moment that first sparked your romance.'

The next day the Bride returns with a huge grin on her face.

'Thank you so much,' she says to the therapist. 'Last night, I forced Frankenstein to come outside in the middle of the lightening storm. And right there, in our backyard, he made love to me like it was our very first time.'

'Making love in a lightening storm put him in the mood?' asks the therapist.

'Well,' says the Bride of Frankenstein, 'I tied a kite to his penis.'

Two old ladies are walking through a museum and get separated. When they run into each other later the first old lady says, 'My! Did you see that statue of the naked man back there?'

The second old lady replies, 'Yes! I was absolutely shocked! How can they display such a thing! My gosh the penis on it was so large!'

And the first old lady blurts out, 'And cold, too!'

A woman is in the bar of a cruise ship and she asks the bartender for a scotch and two drops of water.

As the bartender gives her the drink, she says, 'It's my eightieth birthday today and I'm on this cruise to celebrate.'

The bartender says, 'Well, since it's your birthday I'll buy you a drink. In fact, I'll take care of this one for you.'

As she finishes her drink, the woman to her right says, 'I guess I should buy you a drink, too.'

The old woman says, 'All right. Bartender I want a scotch and two drops of water.'

'Coming up,' says the bartender.

As she finishes her drink, the man to her right says, 'Since I'm the only one around you that hasn't bought you a drink I guess I better buy you one as well.'

The old woman says, 'Great. Bartender I want a scotch and two drops of water.'

'Coming right up,' the bartender says.

As he gives her the drink he says, 'Ma'am I'm dying of curiosity. Why only two drops of water?'

The old woman replies, 'Sunny you learn that when you are my age, you can hold your liquor but you sure can't hold your water.'

A couple have been married for fifty years. They are sitting at the breakfast table one morning when the old gentleman says to his wife, 'Just think, honey, we've been married for fifty years.'

'Yeah,' she replies, 'just think, fifty years ago we were sitting here at this breakfast table together.'

'I know,' the old man says, 'we were probably sitting here naked as jaybirds fifty years ago.'

'Well,' Granny snickers, 'what do you say . . . should we get naked?'

So the two strip to the buff and sit down at the table.

'You know, honey,' the little old lady whispers, 'my nipples are as hot for you today as they were fifty years ago.'

'I'm not surprised,' replies Gramps. 'One's in your coffee and the other is in your oatmeal.'

An old woman is riding in an elevator in a very lavish New York City building, when a young and beautiful woman gets into the elevator, smelling of expensive perfume.

She turns to the old woman and says arrogantly, 'Romance' by Ralph Lauren, $150 for 300ml!'

Then another young and beautiful woman gets on the elevator. She also very arrogantly turns to the old woman saying, 'Chanel No. 5, $200 for 300ml!'

About three floors later, the old woman has reached her destination and is about to get off the elevator. Before she leaves, she looks both beautiful women in the eye, then bends over and farts and says, 'Broccoli. Two dollars a kilo.'

A ninety-year-old man lives in a rest home and gets a weekend pass. He stops in his favourite bar and sits at the end and orders a drink. He notices a seventy-year-old woman at the other end of the bar and he tells the bartender to buy the lovely young lady a drink. As the evening progresses, the old man joins the lady and they go to her apartment, where they get it on.

Four days later, the old man notices that he is developing a drip, and he heads for the rest home doctor. After careful examination the doctor asks the old man if he has engaged in sex recently.

The old man says, 'Sure.'

The doctor asks if he can remember who the woman is and where she lives.

'Sure, why?'

'Well you'd better get over there, you're about to come.'

A police car pulls up in front of grandma's house and grandpa gets out. The polite policeman explains to grandma that the poor gentleman was lost in the park and couldn't find his way home.

'Oh dear,' says grandma, 'You've been going to that park for over thirty years. How could you get lost?'

Leaning close to grandma, so that the policeman can't hear, grandpa whispers, 'I wasn't lost. I was just too tired to walk home.'

The little boy greets his grandmother with a hug and says, 'I'm so happy to see you grandma. Now maybe daddy will do the trick he has been promising us.'

His grandmother is curious.

'What trick is that my dear?' she asks.

The little boy replies, 'I heard daddy tell mummy that he would climb the bloody walls if you came to visit us again.'

An old lady and an old man are sitting in their retirement home. The man turns to the woman and says, 'I bet you can't tell how old I am.'

She says, 'OK.'

She then unzips his fly, feels around for a while and finally says, 'You're seventy-three.'

'That's amazing!' the man exclaims. 'How did you know?'

She replies, 'You told me yesterday.'

An elderly couple have been dating for some time and decide it is finally time to marry. Before the wedding they embark on a long conversation regarding how their marriage will work. They discuss finances, living arrangements and so on. Finally the old man decides it is time to broach the subject of their connubial relationship.

'How do you feel about sex?' he asks, rather hopefully.

'Well, I'd have to say I like it infrequently,' she responds.

The old guy pauses, then he asks, 'Was that one word or two?'

A guy goes to his grandmother's house and takes one of his friends with him. While he's talking to his grandmother, his friend starts eating the peanuts on the coffee table and finishes them off.

As they are leaving, the friend says, 'Thanks for the peanuts.'

She says, 'Yeah, since I lost my dentures I can only suck the chocolate off 'em.'

An old lady is visiting a famous museum and knocks over a large vase which smashes on the ground. An attendant rushes over, aghast.

'That vase,' the attendant cries, 'was over five hundred years old!'

'Oh, thank God!' says the old lady. 'I thought it was a new one.'

An eighty-five-year-old man visits his doctor to get a sperm count. The man is given a jar and told to bring back a sample. The next day he returns to the doctor with an empty jar.

'What happened?' asks the doctor.

'Well,' the old man starts, 'I asked my wife for help. She tried with her right hand, then she tried with her left – nothing. Then she tried with her mouth, first with her teeth in, then with her teeth out, still nothing. We even called Evelyn, the lady next door, but still nothing.'

The doctor bursts out, 'You asked your neighbour?'

'Yep, no matter what we tried we couldn't get that damn jar open.'

Sitting with her cat, an old woman is polishing a lamp she's found in the attic. Suddenly a genie appears and offers her three wishes. She wishes to be rich, to be young again, and for her cat to be turned into a handsome prince. There is a puff of smoke and the woman finds herself twenty years old again and surrounded by riches. The cat has become a gorgeous prince.

As she melts into his embrace, he whispers to her, 'Bet you're sorry now that you had me neutered.'

Mavis and Lizzie, two elderly widows in a retirement village are curious about the latest arrival in their building, a quiet, nice-looking gentleman who keeps to himself.

Lizzie says, 'Mavis, you know I'm shy. Why don't you go over to him at the pool and find out a little about him. He looks so lonely.'

Mavis agrees, and later that day at the pool, she walks up to him and says, 'Excuse me, mister. I hope I'm not prying, but my friend and I were wondering why you look so lonely.'

'Of course I'm lonely,' he says, 'I've spent the past twenty years in prison.'

'You're kidding! What for?'

'For killing my third wife. I strangled her.'

'What happened to your second wife?'

'I shot her.'

'And, if I may ask, your first wife?'

'We had a fight and she fell off a building.'

'Oh my,' says Mavis. Then turning to her friend on the other side of the pool, she yells, 'Yoo-hoo, Lizzie. He's single.'

An old lady in a nursing home is wheeling up and down the halls in her wheelchair making sounds like she's driving a car.

As she's going down the hall, an old man jumps out of a room and says, 'Excuse me Ma'am but you were speeding. Can I see your drivers licence?'

She digs around in her purse a little, pulls out a candy wrapper, and hands it to him. He looks it over, gives her a warning and sends her on her way. Up and down the halls she goes again.

Again, the same old man jumps out of a room and says, 'Excuse me Ma'am but I saw you cross over the centre line back there. Can I see your registration please?'

She digs around in her purse, pulls out a store receipt and hands it to him. He looks it over, gives her another warning and sends her on her way. She zooms off again up and down the halls weaving all over. As she comes to the old man's room again, he jumps out. He's stark naked and has an erection.

The old lady in the wheelchair looks up and says, 'Oh, no, not the breathalyser again!'

An older lady is lonely, and decides that she needs a pet to keep her company. So off to the pet shop she goes. Forlornly, she searches but nothing seems to catch her interest, except one ugly frog. As she walks by the barrel he is in, he looks up and winks at her.

He whispers, 'I'm lonely too, buy me and you won't be sorry.'

The old lady thinks, why not? She hasn't found anything else. So, she buys the frog and takes it to her car.

Driving down the road the frog whispers to her, 'Kiss me, you won't be sorry.'

So, the old lady thinks what the hell, and kisses the frog.

Immediately the frog turns into an absolutely gorgeous, sexy, handsome, young prince. Then the prince kisses her back, and you know what the old lady turns into?

The first motel she can find.

YO MOMMA

Yo momma's so ugly, a fly wouldn't sit on her.

Yo momma's so ugly, even Rice Bubbles won't talk to her.

Yo momma's so ugly, her dentist treats her by mail.

Yo momma's so ugly, her doctor is a veterinarian.

Yo momma's so ugly, her face is closed on weekends.

Yo momma's so ugly, her face is like a melted willy.

Yo momma's so ugly, her mum had to be drunk to breastfeed her.

Yo momma's so ugly, her mum had to tie a steak around her neck to get the dog to play with her.

Yo momma's so ugly, her nickname is Damn!

Yo momma's so ugly, her vibrator turned limp.

Yo momma's so ugly, I heard that your dad first met her at the pound.

Yo momma's so ugly, I wouldn't screw her with a stolen dick.

Yo momma's so ugly, if ugly were bricks she'd have her own house.

Yo momma's so ugly, instead of putting the bungee cord around her ankle, they put it around her neck.

Yo momma's so ugly, it looks like she sleeps on a bed of nails face down.

Yo momma's so ugly, I've seen cow pies I'd rather do it with.

Yo momma's so ugly, just after she was born, her mother said 'What a treasure!' and her father said 'Yes, let's go bury it.'

Yo momma's so ugly, on Halloween the kids trick or treat her by phone.

Yo momma's so ugly, people dress up as her for Halloween.

Yo momma's so ugly, she could curdle urine.

Yo momma's so ugly, she could make a freight train take a gravel road.

Yo momma's so ugly, she could scare a dog off a meat truck.

Yo momma's so ugly, she could scare the chrome off a bumper.

Yo momma's so ugly, she could scare the moss off a rock.

Yo momma's so ugly, she's ready for Halloween 365 days a year.

Yo momma's so ugly, she gives Freddy Krueger nightmares.

Yo momma's so ugly, she has a face that would sink a thousand ships.

Yo momma's so ugly, she has to get her vibrator drunk first.

Yo momma's so ugly, she has to sneak up on a glass of water.

Yo momma's so ugly, she has to sneak up on a hurricane to catch a breeze.

Yo momma's so ugly, she has to sneak up on her mirror.

Yo momma's so ugly, she is very successful at her job: Being a scarecrow.

Yo momma's so ugly, she just got a job at the airport sniffing for drugs.

Yo momma's so ugly, she looked out the window and got arrested for mooning.

Yo momma's so ugly, she looks like a bulldog licking piss off a thistle.

Yo momma's so ugly, she looks like she's been bobbing for French fries.

Yo momma's so ugly, she looks like the elephant-man chewing on a wasp.

Yo momma's so ugly, she makes onions cry.

Yo momma's so ugly, she makes my arse pucker.

Yo momma's so ugly, she practices birth-control by leaving the lights on.

Yo momma's so ugly, she puts on her makeup in the dark.

Yo momma's so ugly, she scares the roaches away.

Yo momma's so ugly, she tried to take a bath and the water jumped out.

Yo momma's so ugly, she turned Medusa to stone.

Yo momma's so ugly, she walked past a mirror and it exploded.

Yo momma's so ugly, she won't even play with herself.

Yo momma's so ugly, she wore a pork chop to get the dog to play.

Yo momma's so ugly, she'd scare a buzzard off a gut wagon.

Yo momma's so ugly, she's the cover girl for iodine.

Yo momma's so ugly, Ted Dansen wouldn't date her.

Yo momma's so ugly, when she looks at a glass of milk it turns to cheese.

Yo momma's so ugly, your father takes her to work with him so that he doesn't have to kiss her goodbye.

Yo momma's so ugly, the American government moved Halloween to her birthday.

Yo momma's so ugly, her psychiatrist makes her lie face down.

Yo momma's so ugly, the tide won't even take her out.

Yo momma's so ugly, they didn't give her a costume when she auditioned for *Star Wars*.

Yo momma's so ugly, they filmed *Gorillas in the Mist* in her shower.

Yo momma's so ugly, they only wanted her feet for the freak show.

Yo momma's so ugly, they pay her to put her clothes on in strip joints.

Yo momma's so ugly, they put her in dough and make monster cookies.

Yo momma's so ugly, they threw her away and kept the afterbirth.

Yo momma's so ugly, they turn off the cameras when she walks into a bank.

Yo momma's so ugly, they use her in prisons to cure sex offenders.

Yo momma's so ugly, when she was a child, she was fed with a slingshot!

Yo momma's so ugly, when I first saw her, my momma was nauseous.

Yo momma's so ugly, when she cries the tears run up her face.

Yo momma's so ugly, when she goes to the beach the tide won't come in.

Yo momma's so ugly, when she joined an ugly contest, they said 'Sorry, no professionals.'

Yo momma's so ugly, when she sits in the sand the cat tries to bury her.

Yo momma's so ugly, when she walks by the bathroom the toilet flushes.

Yo momma's so ugly, when she was born her incubator windows were tinted.

Yo momma's so ugly, when she was born the doctor slapped her momma.

Yo momma's so ugly, when she went to jump in the lake the lake jumped out.

Yo momma's so ugly, when she went to the beautician it took twelve hours . . . for a quote.

Yo momma's so ugly, when you look up ugly in the dictionary it has her picture.

Yo momma's so ugly, yo daddy rather kiss her arse than look in her face.

Yo momma's so ugly, you can only tell which bit's her face by the ears.

Yo momma's so ugly, the zookeepers said thanks for bringin' the bitch back.

Yo momma's so stupid, her brain cells are on the endangered species list.

Yo momma's so stupid, her brain cells die alone.

Yo momma's so stupid, I saw her standing on an empty bus.

Yo momma's so stupid, it takes her a day to cook a three-minute egg.

Yo momma's so stupid, it takes her half an hour to make two-minutes noodles.

Yo momma's so stupid, it takes her a month to get rid of the seven-day itch.

Yo momma's so stupid, it takes her a week to get rid of a twenty-four-hour virus.

Yo momma's so stupid, it take her two hours to watch *60 Minutes*.

Yo momma's so stupid, she asks for a price check at the $2 shop.

Yo momma's so stupid, she bought a solar-powered torch.

Yo momma's so stupid, she bought a video camera to record cable TV shows at home.

Yo momma's so stupid, she called Dan Quayle for a spell check.

Yo momma's so stupid, she called the 7-11 to see when they closed.

Yo momma's so stupid, she called the cocaine hot line to order some.

Yo momma's so stupid, she cooked her own complimentary breakfast.

Yo momma's so stupid, she could trip over a cordless phone.

Yo momma's so stupid, she tried to read an audio book.

Yo momma's so stupid, she gets lost in thought.

Yo momma's so stupid, she got fired from a blow-job.

Yo momma's so stupid, she got fired from the M&M's factory for throwing away all the Ws.

Yo momma's so stupid, she got hit by a cup and told the cops she got mugged.

Yo momma's so stupid, she got hit by a parked car.

Yo momma's so stupid, she got stuck on the escalator for three hours.

Yo momma's so stupid, she hears it's chilly outside so she gets a bowl.

Yo momma's so stupid, she jumped out the window and went up.

Yo momma's so stupid, she ordered a cheeseburger from McDonald's and said 'Hold the cheese.'

Yo momma's so stupid, she ordered her sushi well done.

Yo momma's so stupid, she put a quarter in a parking meter and waited for a gumball to come out.

Yo momma's so stupid, she returned a puzzle complaining it was broken.

Yo momma's so stupid, she sat on a window ledge thinking she'd get framed.

Yo momma's so stupid, she saw a sign that said Wet Floor so she did.

Yo momma's so stupid, she sits on the TV and watches the couch.

Yo momma's so stupid, she stepped on a crack and broke her own back.

Yo momma's so stupid, she stole free bread.

Yo momma's so stupid, she thinks Christmas wrap is Snoop Doggy Dogg's holiday album.

Yo momma's so stupid, she thinks a hot meal is stolen food.

Yo momma's so stupid, she thinks a quarterback is a refund.

Yo momma's so stupid, she thinks asphalt is a skin disease.

Yo momma's so stupid, she thinks Delta Airlines is a sorority.

Yo momma's so stupid, she thinks Fleetwood Mac is a new hamburger at McDonalds!

Yo momma's so stupid, she thinks gangrene is a golf course.

Yo momma's so stupid, she thinks innuendo is an Italian suppository.

Yo momma's so stupid, she thinks Johnny Cash is a pay toilet.

Yo momma's so stupid, she thinks manual labour is a Mexican worker.

Yo momma's so stupid, she thinks menopause is a button on the stereo.

Yo momma's so stupid, she thinks O.J. Simpson is some kind of fruit juice.

Yo momma's so stupid, she thinks she needs a token to get on the soul train.

Yo momma's so stupid, she thinks Sherlock Holmes is a housing project.

Yo momma's so stupid, she thinks socialism means partying.

Yo momma's so stupid, she thinks softball is a venereal disease.

Yo momma's so stupid, she tells everyone that she is illegitimate because she can't read.

Yo momma's so stupid, she took a job cutting grass offshore.

Yo momma's so stupid, she takes a ruler to bed to see how long she sleeps.

Yo momma's so stupid, she took a shower and got brain-washed.

Yo momma's so stupid, she took a spoon to the Super Bowl.

Yo momma's so stupid, she took an umbrella to see *Purple Rain*.

Yo momma's so stupid, she took the Pepsi challenge and chose Jif.

Yo momma's so stupid, she tried to commit suicide by jumping off the curb.

Yo momma's so stupid, she tried to drop acid but the car battery fell on her foot.

Yo momma's so stupid, she tried to hang herself with a cordless phone.

Yo momma's so stupid, she watches *The Three Stooges* and takes notes.

Yo momma's so stupid, she took her bathers to the car pool.

Yo momma's so stupid, she went to a footy game and drowned in the waves.

Yo momma's so stupid, she wrote 'M, F, sometimes Wed' under 'SEX?'

Yo momma's so fat, a picture of her fell off the wall.

Yo momma's so fat, after sex she smokes a turkey.

Yo momma's so fat, all the restaurants in town have signs that say, 'Maximum Occupancy: 240 Patrons or Yo Momma.'

Yo momma's so fat, they give her the menu at restaurants and she replies, 'Yes please.'

Yo momma's so fat, at the zoo the elephants started throwing her peanuts.

Yo momma's so fat, Dr Marten had to kill three cows just to make her a pair of shoes.

Yo momma's so fat, even Bill Gates couldn't pay for her liposuction.

Yo momma's so fat, every time she walks in high heels she strikes oil.

Yo momma's so fat, her belly jiggle is the first ever perpetual motion machine.

Yo momma's so fat, her big toe got stuck in the cat flap.

Yo momma's so fat, her bum cheeks have different area codes.

Yo momma's so fat, her cereal bowl came with a lifeguard.

Yo momma's so fat, her doctor is a grounds keeper.

Yo momma's so fat, her high school picture was an aerial photograph.

Yo momma's so fat, her legs are like spoiled milk – white and chunky!

Yo momma's so fat, her picture takes two frames.

Yo momma's so fat, her toes bleed when she walks.

Yo momma's so fat, I had to roll her in flour and look for the wet spot.

Yo momma's so fat, I had to slap her thigh and ride the wave in.

Yo momma's so fat, I had to take a train and two busses just to get on her good side.

Yo momma's so fat, I got lost when I tried to walk around her.

Yo momma's so fat, I took her to a dance and the band skipped.

Yo momma's so fat, I tried to drive around her and I ran out of gas.

Yo momma's so fat, if she weighed two more kilos she'd get group insurance.

Yo momma's so fat, if she died you'd have to take her out in two trips.

Yo momma's so fat, instead of wide leg jeans, she wears wide load.

Yo momma's so fat, it says Picture Continued on Back on her drivers licence.

Yo momma's so fat, it takes a forklift to help her stand up.

Yo momma's so fat, light gets stuck near her.

Yo momma's so fat, mosquitoes see her and scream buffet.

Yo momma's so fat, NASA has a satellite orbiting around her.

Yo momma's so fat, people jog around her for exercise.

Yo momma's so fat, people use her dandruff as quilts.

Yo momma's so fat, she sets off car alarms when she runs.

Yo momma's so fat, she broke her leg, and gravy poured out.

Yo momma's so fat, she can lie down or stand up and her height doesn't change.

Yo momma's so fat, she can smell bacon frying in Canada.

Yo momma's so fat, she can use Mt Everest for a dildo.

Yo momma's so fat, she can't reach her back pocket.

Yo momma's so fat, she can't stay on a basketball court for three seconds without getting called for a key violation.

Yo momma's so fat, she doesn't have cellulite she's got cellu-heavy.

Yo momma's so fat, she eats Wheat Thicks.

Yo momma's so fat, she fell and made the Grand Canyon.

Yo momma's so fat, she fell in love and broke it.

Yo momma's so fat, she gets stuck in her dreams.

Yo momma's so fat, she got a run in her blue jeans.

Yo momma's so fat, she had her baby pictures taken by satellite.

Yo momma's so fat, she got hit by a truck and asked 'Who threw that rock?'

Yo momma's so fat, she has to pull down her pants to get into her pockets.

Yo momma's so fat, she had her ears pierced by harpoon.

Yo momma's so fat, she had stretch marks when she was
a virgin.

Yo momma's so fat, she has to get out of bed to roll over.

Yo momma's so fat, she had to go to Sea World to get baptised.

Yo momma's so fat, she has a part-time job as a trampoline!

Yo momma's so fat, she has been declared a natural habitat for
condors.

Yo momma's so fat, she has her own area code!

Yo momma's so fat, she has her own brand of jeans: FA – FatArse
Jeans.

Yo momma's so fat, she has her own gravity.

Yo momma's so fat, she has more rolls than a baker's truck.

Yo momma's so fat, she has shocks on her toilet seat.

Yo momma's so fat, she has to buy two airline tickets.

Yo momma's so fat, she has to go outside to put on deodorant.

Yo momma's so fat, she has to go outside to sit around the
house.

Yo momma's so fat, she has to lie down to tie her shoe.

Yo momma's so fat, she has to use hoola-hoops to hold her
socks up.

Yo momma's so fat, she influences the tides.

Yo momma's so fat, she irons her clothes in the driveway.

Yo momma's so fat, she jumped for joy and got stuck.

Yo momma's so fat, she keeps her diaphragm in a pizza box.

Yo momma's so fat, she looks like she's smuggling a Volkswagen.

Yo momma's so fat, she makes Big Bird look like a rubber duck.

Yo momma's so fat, she makes Free Willy look like a Tic Tac.

Yo momma's so fat, she makes sumo wrestlers look anorexic.

Yo momma's so fat, she puts on her lipstick with a paint-roller.

Yo momma's so fat, she rocks herself to sleep trying to
get up.

Yo momma's so fat, she shaves her legs with a lawn mower.

Yo momma's so fat, she shows up on radar.

Yo momma's so fat, she stepped on a rainbow and made skid marks.

Yo momma's so fat, she takes baths in swimming pools.

Yo momma's so fat, she thinks a balanced meal is a ham in each hand.

Yo momma's so fat, she thinks gravy is a beverage.

Yo momma's so fat, she uses a mattress as a maxi-pad.

Yo momma's so fat, she uses a pillowcase as a sock.

Yo momma's so fat, she uses a satellite dish as a diaphragm.

Yo momma's so fat, she uses a VCR as a beeper.

Yo momma's so fat, she uses trees to pick her teeth.

Yo momma's so fat, she uses the freeway as a water slide.

Yo momma's so fat, she wakes up in sections.

Yo momma's so fat, she was born with a silver shovel in her mouth.

Yo momma's so fat, she was Miss Arizona – class Battleship.

Yo momma's so fat, she was zoned for commercial development.

Yo momma's so fat, she went to the beach and sold shade.

Yo momma's so fat, she went to the movies and sat next to everyone.

Yo momma's so fat, she went to the salad bar and pulled up a chair.

Yo momma's so fat, she's 36-24-36 . . . but that's her forearm, neck, and thigh.

Yo momma's so fat, she's got more chins than a Hong Kong phone book.

Yo momma's so fat, she's got smaller fat women orbiting around her.

Yo momma's so fat, she's on both sides of the family.

Yo momma's so fat, she's sits on coal and farts out a diamond.

Yo momma's so fat, she's works in the movies – as the screen.

Yo momma's so fat, she climbed Mt Fuji with one step.

Yo momma's so fat, the AIDS quilt wouldn't cover her.

Yo momma's so fat, the airline charges her a round-trip ticket for each flight.

Yo momma's so fat, the highway patrol made her wear 'Caution! Wide Load' signs.

Yo momma's so fat, the horse on her Polo shirt is real.

Yo momma's so fat, the last time she saw 90210 was on the scales.

Yo momma's so fat, they had to grease a door frame and hold a chocolate bar on the other side to get her through.

Yo momma's so fat, they have to grease the bath tub to get her out.

Yo momma's so fat, they invented super extra strength ultra SlimFast.

Yo momma's so fat, they mistake her for a country.

Yo momma's so fat, to her, light food means under four tonnes.

Yo momma's so fat, to lose a few kilos she takes off her girdle.

Yo momma's so fat, when a cop saw her he told her, 'Hey you two break it up!'

Yo momma's so fat, when her beeper goes off people think she's backing up.

Yo momma's so fat, when I got on top of her my ears popped.

Yo momma's so fat, when I said I wanted 'Pigs in a blanket' she got back in bed.

Yo momma's so fat, when she bungee jumps she brings down the bridge too.

Yo momma's so fat, when she falls it measures on the Richter scale.

Yo momma's so fat, when she gets in an elevator, it has to go down.

Yo momma's so fat, when she goes to a restaurant she gets a quote.

Yo momma's so fat, when she goes to an all you can eat buffet, they have to install speed bumps.

Yo momma's so fat, when she has sex she has to give directions.

Yo momma's so fat, when she moves her arse, she has to make two trips.

Yo momma's so fat, when she lies on the beach no-one else gets any sun.

Yo momma's so fat, when she moons people they turn into werewolves.

Yo momma's so fat, when she puts her foot down she clears rainforests.

Yo momma's so fat, when she runs she makes the CD player skip . . . at the radio station.

Yo momma's so fat, when she sings, it's over!

Yo momma's so fat, when she sits on my face I can't hear the stereo.

Yo momma's so fat, when she steps on the scale it says, 'One at a time please.'

Yo momma's so fat, when she steps on the scale it says, 'Sorry we don't do livestock.'

Yo momma's so fat, when she steps on the scale it says. 'To be continued.'

Yo momma's so fat, when she sweats everyone around her wears raincoats.

Yo momma's so fat, when she tiptoes, everyone yells, 'Stampede!'

Yo momma's so fat, when she tripped over on 4th Ave she landed on 12th.

Yo momma's so fat, when she turns around they throw her a welcome-back party.

Yo momma's so fat, when she walked in front of the TV I missed three commercials.

Yo momma's so fat, when she walks she leaves snail tracks.

Yo momma's so fat, when she was diagnosed with a flesh-eating disease, the doctor gave her five years to live.

Yo momma's so fat, when she wears a yellow raincoat people yell out, 'Taxi!'

Yo momma's so fat, when she wears her X jacket helicopters try to land.

Yo momma's so fat, when she went to get a water bed, they put a blanket across Lake Michigan.

Yo momma's so fat, when she went to the beach Greenpeace tried to drag her back in the water.

Yo momma's so fat, when she wore a shirt with an AA on it, people thought it was American Airlines biggest jet.

Yo momma's so fat, you can't tell if she is coming or going.

Yo momma's so fat, you couldn't tell where her boobs end and her arms begin.

Yo momma's so fat, you have to roll over twice to get off her.

DEATH AND DYING

*This section is for those people who, like me, find funerals
to be far more enjoyable and jolly than weddings.*

A fine funeral is ordered for a woman who has henpecked her husband, driven her kids half nuts, scrapped with the neighbours at the slightest opportunity, and even made neurotics of the cat and dog with her explosive temper. As the casket is lowered into the grave, a violent thunderstorm breaks, and the pastor's benediction is drowned out by a blinding flash of lightning, followed by terrific thunder.

'Well, at least we know she got there all right,' comments her husband.

A ninety-year-old woman decides that she's seen and done everything, and the time has come to depart from this world. After considering various methods of doing away with herself, she comes to the conclusion that the quickest and surest method is to shoot herself through the heart. The trouble is, she isn't certain about exactly where her heart is, so she phones her doctor and asks him. He tells her that her heart is located two inches above her left nipple. So she shoots herself in the left kneecap.

A funeral is held for the man who wrote the song *Hokey Pokey*. Unfortunately, the undertakers have problems putting the body in the casket. They put his left leg in but it came back out. Then they put his right leg in . . .

An old maid lives in a tiny village. In spite of her old age, she is still a virgin and she is very proud of it. She knows her last days are getting closer, so she tells the local undertaker that she wants the following inscription on her tombstone: 'Born as a virgin, lived as a virgin, died as a virgin.'

Not long after, the old maid dies peacefully, and the undertaker tells his men what the lady has said. The men go to carve it in, but as the lazy no-goods they are, they think the inscription is unnecessarily long.

They simply write: 'Returned unopened'.

Becky is on her deathbed with her husband, John, maintaining a steady vigil by her side. As he holds her fragile hand, his warm tears run silently down his face, splashing onto her face, and rousing her from her slumber. She looked up and her pale lips began to move slightly.

'My darling John,' she whispers.

'Hush, my love,' he says. 'Go back to sleep. Shhh. Don't talk.'

But she is insistent. 'John,' she says in her tired voice. 'I have to talk. I have something I must confess to you.'

'There's nothing to confess,' replies the weeping John. 'It's all right. Everything's all right, go to sleep now.'

'No, no. I must die in peace, John,' she says. 'I slept with your brother, your best friend and your father.'

John musters a pained smile and strokes her hand.

'Hush now Becky, don't torment yourself. I know all about it,' he says. 'Why do you think I poisoned you?'

One of the workers at the brewery falls in a huge vat of beer and drowns. At the funeral, his wife is crying, 'Oh, Ben, Ben, you never had a chance.'

His foreman says, 'What do you mean, 'never had a chance'? He got out twice to take a piss.'

A funeral service is being held in a synagogue for a woman who has just passed away. At the end of the service the pallbearers are carrying the casket out, when they accidentally bump into a wall, jarring the casket.

They hear a faint moan. They open the casket and find that the woman is still alive.

She lives for ten more years and then dies. A ceremony is again held at the same synagogue and at the end of the ceremony the same pallbearers are again carrying the casket.

As they are walking out, the husband cries, 'Watch out for that wall!'

THE GARDEN OF EDEN

And in the Beginning, there was . . . a joke.

Adam is walking around the Garden of Eden feeling very lonely, so God asks him, 'What is wrong with you?'

Adam tells God he doesn't have anyone to talk to.

God says, 'And that's a problem? OK, I'll find you some company. This company will cook for you day and night, wash your clothes and keep the garden in order; will bear your children and never ask you to get up in the middle of the night to take care of them; will not nag you, will always be the first to admit being wrong when you've had a disagreement and will always agree with every decision you make. The company will never have a headache, and will freely give you sex, love and compassion whenever needed. But it's going to be expensive Adam. It's going to cost you an arm and a leg.'

'An arm and a leg?' says Adam. 'Wow.'

He thinks for a few seconds, then asks, 'Well, what can I get for just a rib?'

After a few days, the Lord calls Adam to him, and says, 'It is time for you and Eve to begin the process of populating the earth, so I want you to start by kissing Eve.'

Adam answers, 'Yes Lord, but what's a "kiss"?'

So the Lord gives Adam a brief description and Adam takes Eve by the hand, behind a nearby bush.

A few minutes later, Adam emerges and says, 'Lord, that was enjoyable.'

And the Lord replies, 'Yes, Adam, I thought you'd enjoy that, and now I'd like you to caress Eve.'

And Adam says, 'Lord, what's a "caress"?'

So the Lord gives Adam a brief description and Adam again goes behind the bush with Eve.

Quite a few minutes later, Adam returns smiling and says, 'Lord, that was even better than the kiss.'

And the Lord says, 'You've done well, Adam, and now I want you to make love to Eve.'

And Adam says, 'Lord, what's "making love"?'

So the Lord again gives Adam directions, and Adam goes behind the bush with Eve.

But this time he reappears in two seconds. Adam says, 'Lord, what's a "headache"?'

God is just about done creating the universe. He has a couple of left-over things in his bag of creations, so he stops by to visit Adam and Eve in the Garden of Eden. He tells the couple that one of the things he has to give away is the ability to stand up and pee.

'It's a very handy thing,' God tells the couple, who he finds hanging around under an apple tree. 'I was wondering if either one of you wanted that ability?'

Adam pops a cork. He jumps up and begs, 'Oh, give that to me! I'd love to be able to do that! It seems the sort of thing a man should do. Oh please, oh please, oh please, let me have that ability. I'd be so great! When I'm working in the garden or naming the animals, I could just let it rip, I'd be so cool. Oh please, God, let it be me who you give that gift to, let me stand and pee, oh please!'

On and on he goes like an excited little boy. Eve just smiles and shakes her head at the display. She tells God that if Adam really wants it so badly, and it sure seems to be the sort of thing that will make him happy, she really doesn't mind if Adam is the one given the ability to stand up and pee. And so God gives Adam this gift. And it is . . . well, good.

'Fine,' God says, looking back into his bag of left-over gifts. 'What's left here for you Eve? Oh yes, multiple orgasms.'

One day in the Garden of Eden, Eve calls out to God, 'Lord, I have a problem!'

'What's the problem, Eve?'

'Lord, I know you've created me and have provided this beautiful garden and all of these wonderful animals, and that hilarious comedic snake, but I'm just not happy.'

'Why is that, Eve?' comes the reply from above.

'Lord, I am lonely. And I'm sick to death of apples.'

'Well, Eve, in that case, I have a solution. I shall create a man for you.'

'What's a "man", Lord?'

'This man will be a flawed creature, with aggressive tendencies, an enormous ego and an inability to empathise or listen to you properly. All in all, he'll give you a hard time. But, he'll be bigger, faster and more muscular than you. He'll also need your advice to think properly. He'll be really good at fighting and kicking a ball about, hunting fleet-footed ruminants, and not altogether bad in the sack.'

'Sounds great,' says Eve, with an ironically raised eyebrow. 'What's the catch, Lord?'

'Well, you can have him on one condition.'

'What's that, Lord?'

'You'll have to let him believe that I made him first.'

YOU KNOW YOU'RE HAVING A BAD DAY WHEN . . .

- Your horn sticks on the freeway behind thirty-two Hell's Angels.

- The worst player on the golf course wants to play you for money.

- You call suicide prevention and they put you on hold.

- You get to work and find a *60 Minutes* news team waiting in your office.

- Your birthday cake collapses from the weight of the candles.

- You find your son's GI Joe doll dressed in drag.

- You turn on the evening news and they are showing emergency routes out of the city.

- Your twin sister forgets your birthday.

- Your four-year-old tells you that it's almost impossible to flush a grapefruit down the toilet.

- You realise that you just sprayed spot remover under your arms instead of deodorant.

- You have to sit down to brush your teeth in the morning.

- You start to pick up the clothes you wore home from the party last night . . . and there aren't any.

- It costs more to fill up your car than it did to buy it.

- You wake up to the soothing sound of running water . . . and remember that you just bought a waterbed.

- Your car payment, house payment, and girlfriend are three months overdue.

- Everyone avoids you the morning after the company office party.

- The bird singing outside your window is a vulture.

- You wake up and your braces are stuck together.

- You call your answering service and they tell you it's none of your business.

- Your blind date turns out to be your ex-wife.

- Your income tax refund cheque bounces.

- You put both contact lenses in the same eye.

- You compliment the boss' wife on her unusual perfume and she isn't wearing any.

- You need one bathroom scale for each foot.

- You call your wife and tell her that you would like to eat out tonight and when you get home there is a sandwich on the front porch.

- The restaurant bill has been on the table for ten minutes . . . and no-one has touched it.

- Nothing you own is actually paid for.

- You go on your honeymoon to a remote little hotel and the desk clerk, bell hop, and manager have a 'Welcome Back' party for your new spouse.

- You receive a 150-page instruction booklet on how to save money . . . from the electric company.

- Airline food starts to taste good.

- Your mother approves of the person you are dating.

- Your doctor tells you that you are allergic to chocolate chip cookies.

- You have to borrow from your VISA card to pay off your MasterCard.

- You realise that you have memorised the back of your cereal box.

- You take longer to get over sex than you did to have it.

- Your cat abandons the nice box you prepared for her and has her kittens in your dresser drawer.

- Everyone loves your drivers licence picture.

- You realise that the phone number on the bathroom wall of the bar is yours.

- Your kids start treating you the same way you treated your parents.

- Your Aunt Maddie, who has two poodles and a chihuahua, tells you that her doctor just recommended plenty of rest in a warm, dry climate . . . and you live in Alice Springs.

- The health inspector condemns your office coffeemaker.

- You look out the window of the aeroplane and the Goodyear Blimp is gaining on you.

- The gypsy fortune teller offers to refund your money.

- People think you are forty . . . and you really are.

- Your new lover calls to tell you 'Last night was terrific.' And you remember that you were home by yourself.

- Everyone is laughing but you.

PEARLY GATES AND DOWN BELOW

Death is no laughing matter. Or is it?

A minister dies and is waiting in line at the pearly gates. Ahead of him is a guy who's dressed in sunglasses, a loud shirt, leather jacket and jeans.

St Peter addresses this guy, 'Who are you, so that I may know whether or not to admit you to the kingdom of heaven?'

The guy replies, 'I'm Joe Cohen, taxi-driver.'

St Peter consults his list. He smiles and says to the taxi-driver, 'Take this silken robe and golden staff and enter the kingdom of heaven.'

The taxi-driver goes into heaven with his robe and staff, and it's the minister's turn.

He stands erect and booms out, 'I am Joseph Snow, pastor of Saint Mary's for the last forty-three years.'

St Peter consults his list. He says to the minister, 'Take this cotton robe and wooden staff and enter the kingdom of heaven.'

'Just a minute,' says the minister. 'That man was a taxi-driver and he gets a silken robe and golden staff. How can this be?'

'Up here, we work by results,' says St Peter. 'While you preached, people slept; while he drove, people prayed.'

A new arrival in hell is brought before the devil. The devil tells his demon to put the man to work on a rock pile with a huge sledgehammer in forty-degree heat with 95% humidity. At the end of the day, the devil goes to see how the man is doing, only to find him smiling and singing as he pounds rocks. The man explains that the heat and hard labour are very similar to those on his beloved farm back in Pennsylvania. The devil tells his demon to turn up the heat to forty-five degrees, with 100% humidity. At the end of the next day, the devil again checks on the new man, and finds him still happy to be sweating and straining. The man explains that it feels like the old days, when he had to clean out his silo in the middle of August on his beloved farm back in Pennsylvania. At this, the devil tells his demon to lower the temperature to zero with a 20kph wind. At the end of the next day, the devil is confident that he will find the man miserable. But, instead the man is singing louder than ever, twirling the sledgehammer like a baton.

When the devil asks him why he is so happy, the man answers, 'Cold day in hell – the Eagles must have won the Super Bowl.'

B ill Gates dies and is up at the pearly gates.
St Peter says to him, 'Well, you've got a choice. Have a look around here. Pop down to hell and see what Satan has to offer. Check us out, and then let me know your decision.'

Bill has a look around heaven. There are lots of people singing hymns and praising the Lord. He goes down to hell. There are beautiful beaches, lots of sun, sand and attractive women. He loves it.

He goes back to St Peter and says, 'Look, I know you're really doing good things here, but hell seems more with it. More my kind of scene, you know what I mean? No hard feelings, but I pick hell.'

'No worries. You've got it.'

Bill finds himself back in hell, neck deep in fire and brimstone, suffering eternal torment. He can't work it out.

'Hey! St Peter!' he yells. 'Where have all the beautiful girls and long beaches gone?'

'Sorry if you got confused,' says St Peter. 'That was just the demo version.'

A guy dies and reports immediately at the gates of heaven and St Peter says, 'In checking our records, I find that you have never done anything outstanding enough to get you into heaven.'

'What do you mean?' the guy asks. 'What about when I came to the aid of the little old man who was being pushed around by those motorcycle thugs?'

Obviously impressed, St Peter looks though the record books again. Finding nothing, he says, 'You did that?'

The guy says, 'Yes, I kicked over a couple of bikes and told them to pick on someone their own size.'

St Peter is puzzled. He says, 'There is absolutely no record of it. When did it happen?'

'Oh, about ten minutes ago.'

An attractive young woman with raven-black hair and wide eyes approaches the gates of heaven.

Looking her over, St Peter says, 'And may I ask, young lady, if you are a virgin?'

'I am,' is her demure reply.

Not wanting to appear distrustful but having to be cautious, St Peter calls over an angel to examine her. Several minutes later the angel returns.

'She's a virgin,' the angel states, 'though I'm obliged to inform you that she does have seven small dents in her maidenhead.'

Thanking the angel, St Peter takes his place behind the ledger and faces the girl.

'Well, miss, we're going to admit you. What is your name?'

She replies sweetly, 'Snow White.'

St Peter is manning the pearly gates when forty people from New York City show up. Never having seen anyone from the Big Apple at heaven's door, St Peter says he will have to check with God. After hearing the news, God instructs him to admit the ten most virtuous people from the group.

A few minutes later, St Peter returns to God breathless and says, 'They're gone!'

'What? All of the New Yorkers are gone?' asks God.

'No!' replies St Peter. 'The pearly gates.'

Henry Ford dies and is brought before the pearly gates. There, St Peter asks him why he should get to enter into the gates, and Ford says, 'because my creation, the automobile, is the single most popular thing ever invented.'

'Really,' says St Peter, 'what about the creation called 'woman?''

'Well,' says Ford, 'there is too much protrusion on the front end, the rear end wobbles too much, and it chatters at high speeds!'

St Peter checks his records and says, 'that may be, but according to our records a lot more men are riding our invention than yours.'

Four nuns all die together. They are lined up at the pearly gates being asked a series of questions by St Peter.

The last question asked is, 'Have you ever touched a penis?'

The first nun replies, 'Once, with the tip of my finger.'

St Peter tells her to dip her finger in holy water, then she can pass into heaven.

The second nun replies, 'Once, I held one in my hand.'

St Peter tells her to place her hand into holy water, then she can pass into heaven.

Suddenly, the nun that's standing fourth in line pushes ahead of the nun who had been third in line. St Peter asks her why she has done such a thing.

She replies, 'St Peter, if you think I'm going to gargle that holy water after she sits her arse in it, you're crazy.'

A lawyer dies in a car accident on his fortieth birthday and finds himself greeted at the pearly gates by a brass band.

St Peter runs over to him, shakes his hand and says, 'Congratulations!'

The lawyer asks, 'What for?'

St Peter replies, 'What for? We're celebrating the fact that you lived to be 160 years old!'

The lawyer is puzzled. 'That's not true. I only lived to be forty.'

St Peter scratches his head, 'That's impossible. We've added up your time sheets.'

Two men waiting at the pearly gates strike up a conversation. 'How'd you die?' the first man asks the second.

'I froze to death,' says the second.

'That's awful,' says the first man. 'How does it feel to freeze to death?'

'It's very uncomfortable at first,' says the second man. 'You get the shakes, and you get pains in all your fingers and toes. But eventually, it's a very calm way to go. You get numb and you kind of drift off, as if you're sleeping. How about you, how did you die?'

'I had a heart attack,' says the first man. 'You see, I knew my wife was cheating on me, so one day I showed up at home unexpectedly. I ran up to the bedroom, and found her alone, knitting. I ran down to the cellar, but no-one was hiding there. I ran up to the second floor, but no-one was hiding there either. I ran as fast as I could to the attic, and just as I got there, I had a massive heart attack and died.'

The second man shakes his head. 'That's so ironic,' he says.

'What do you mean?' asks the first man.

'If you had only stopped to look in the freezer, we'd both still be alive.'

An elderly couple are killed in an accident and find themselves being given a tour of heaven by St Peter.

'Here is your ocean-side condo,' he says. 'And over there are the tennis courts, swimming pool, and two golf courses. If you need any refreshments, just stop by any of the many bars located throughout the area.'

'Heck, Gloria,' the old man hisses when St Peter walks off. 'We could have been here ten years ago if you hadn't heard about all that stupid oat bran, wheat germ and low-fat food.'

Three men die in a car accident and meet Jesus himself at the pearly gates.

The Lord speaks unto them saying, 'I will ask you each a simple question. If you tell the truth I will allow you into heaven, but if you lie, hell is waiting for you.'

To the first man the Lord asks, 'How many times did you cheat on your wife?'

The first man replies, 'Lord, I was a good husband. I never cheated on my wife.'

The Lord replies, 'Very good! Not only will I allow you in, but for being faithful to your wife I will give you a huge mansion and a limo for your transportation.'

To the second man the Lord asks, 'How many times did you cheat on your wife?'

The second man replies, 'Lord, I cheated on my wife twice.'

The Lord replies, 'I will allow you to come in, but for your unfaithfulness, you will get a four-bedroom house and a BMW.'

To the third man the Lord asks, 'So, how many times did you cheat on your wife?'

The third man replies, 'Lord, I cheated on my wife about eight times.'

The Lord says, 'I will allow you to come in, but for your unfaithfulness, you will get a one-room apartment, and a Volkswagon for your transportation.'

A couple of hours later the second and third men see the first man crying his eyes out.

'Why are you crying?' the two men ask. 'You got the mansion and limo!'

'I'm crying because I saw my wife a little while ago, and she was riding a skateboard!'

Jesus is strolling through heaven when he sees an old man sitting on a cloud, staring disconsolately into the distance.

'Old man,' says Jesus, 'this is heaven! Why are you so sad?'

The old man doesn't bother to turn as he says, 'I've been looking for my son and haven't been able to find him.'

Jesus says, 'Tell me about it.'

'Well,' says the old man, still gazing at the sunlit horizon, 'on earth I was a carpenter, and one day my son went away. I never heard from him again, and I was hoping I'd find him here, in heaven.'

His heart pounding suddenly in his chest, Jesus bends over the old man and says, 'Father?'

The old man turns and cries, 'Pinocchio?'

A guy goes to hell and is met by the devil who explains that the punishments of the inmates are changed every thousand years and he is to select his first punishment. The first room has a young guy on the wall being whipped. The new guy is not keen on this and asks to see the next room.

The next room has a middle-aged guy being tortured with fire.

The new guy immediately asks to see the third room. It has a really old guy chained to the wall getting a blow job from a gorgeous blonde. The guy jumps at the chance and selects that room.

The devil walks into the room taps the blonde on the shoulder and says, 'OK, you can stop now. You've been relieved.'

A cowboy dies and, as he was a bad fellow, he goes straight down to hell. When he gets down there the devil is waiting.

The devil says, 'You have three choices for ways to spend your eternity. Do you pick door number one, two or three?'

The cowboy says, 'Let me check what's behind door number one.'

The door opens and he sees hundreds of people standing on their heads on a wood floor.

'I don't want this,' he says, 'let's try door number two'

The door opens and he sees hundreds of people standing on their heads on a hard cement floor.

'Woah! I don't want to spend the rest of my life like that! What's behind door number three?'

The door opens and he sees hundreds of people drinking coffee, and having a good time, but they are all up to their knees in horse poo.

'I'm a cowboy, I'm used to horse dung. I'll go with door number three,' he says.

The devil hands him a cup of coffee and introduces him to the crowd and leaves him to it.

After ten minutes, the devil comes back in and says, 'Coffee break's over. Everybody back on their heads.'

In heaven:
The cooks are French;
The policemen are English;
The mechanics are German;
The lovers are Italian;
The bankers are Swiss.

In hell:
The cooks are English;
The policemen are German;
The mechanics are French;
The lovers are Swiss;
The bankers are Italian.

PLAYING WITH BALLS (AND OTHER SPORTS)

Sport is about the challenge, teamwork and fair play.
The hell it is! It's about making fun of those who
support teams that your team always beats.

In the year 2020, Romeo Beckham, the son of English soccer star, David Beckham, is selected to play for England. He is delighted with his selection but is aware of the pressure that is on him. As David Beckham's son, Romeo's soccer career has been played out in front of the media since he decided to become a professional soccer player. Romeo wonders whether he should add to the pressure by wearing the number seven shirt made famous by his father or reduce the pressure by choosing another number. He seeks advice from his father.

After considering the matter in silence for a few minutes, David finally responds by saying, 'Romeo, Romeo, wear the four out there, Romeo.'

A man walks into a Melbourne bar with a dachshund under his arm. The dog is wearing a St Kilda football team jersey and socks, and is festooned with Saints pom-poms.

The bartender says, 'Hey! No pets are allowed in here! You'll have to leave!'

The guy begs him, 'Look, I'm desperate. We're both big fans, the TV is broken, and this is the only place around where we can see today's game!'

After securing a promise that the dog will behave, and warning him that he and the dog will be thrown out if there's any trouble, the bartender relents and allows them to stay in the bar and watch the game. The game begins with the bounce-down and the Saints immediately get the ball and kick a goal. With that the dog jumps up on the bar, and begins walking up and down the bar giving high-fives to everyone.

The bartender says, 'Wow, that is the most amazing thing I've ever seen! What does the dog do when the Saints win a game?'

The owner replies, 'I don't know, I've only had him for four years.'

Mama and Papa Bear are accused of child abuse. Baby Bear is put on the stand to testify and is asked by the judge, 'Do you want to live with Papa Bear?'

'No,' Baby Bear replies, 'he beats me.'

Then the judge asks, 'Do you want to live with Mama Bear?'

'No,' Baby Bear replies, 'she beats me too.'

So the Judge says, 'Who do you want to live with then?'

Baby Bear replies, 'I want to live with the Chicago Bears, they don't beat anybody.'

An Aussie is holidaying in the USA. He finds himself in a mid-west bar. Sitting all alone in the corner is an old Native American man looking very old and decrepit.

'Who's that old bloke,' the Aussie asks the barman.

'He,' says the barman 'is an old Indian medicine man, a font of all knowledge, he knows the answer to all questions.'

The Aussie wanders over to the old guy and says, 'They tell me you know everything. If that's so, who did St Kilda play in the 1966 Australian Rules Grand Final.'

'Collingwood,' replies the old man.

THE MORE ADULT ONLY JOKE BOOK

'What was the result?'

'St Kilda won by a point.'

'Amazing' says the Aussie. 'Now who scored the winning point?'

'Barry Breen,' replies the old man.

Now this has impressed the hell out of the Aussie who can't wait to get back home and tell everybody about this old medicine-man who knows everything. Several years pass and the Aussie finds himself back in the same part of the USA. Remembering the old Indian he goes back to the bar just on the off chance he's still alive. And there he is, still sitting in the same old corner sipping root beer. The Aussie wanders over.

'How!' he says, thinking that was the proper way to greet an Indian.

'A wobbly kick from the right forward pocket,' replies the old man.

A man has the best seat in the stadium for the Grand Final. As he sits down, another man comes down and asks if anyone is sitting in the seat next to him.

'No,' he says, 'The seat is empty.'

'That's incredible,' says the man. 'Who in their right mind would have a seat like this for the Grand Final, the biggest sporting event in the world, and not use it?'

The man says, 'Well, actually, the seat belongs to me. I was supposed to come with my wife, but she passed away. This is the first Grand Final we haven't been to together since we got married in 1985.'

'Oh . . . I'm sorry to hear that. That's terrible. But couldn't you find someone else – a friend or relative, or even a neighbour to take the seat?'

The man shakes his head. 'No. They're all at the funeral.'

420 • THE MORE ADULT ONLY JOKE BOOK

A champion jockey is about to enter a major steeplechase race on a new horse.

The horse's trainer meets him before the race and says, 'All you have to remember with this horse is that every time you approach a jump, you have to shout, "Alllleee Ooop!" really loudly in the horse's ear. Providing you do that, you'll be fine.'

The jockey thinks the trainer is mad but promises to shout the command. The race begins and they approach the first hurdle. The jockey ignores the trainer's ridiculous advice and the horse crashes straight through the centre of the jump but somehow manages to stay on its feet. They carry on and approach the second hurdle. The jockey, somewhat embarrassed, whispers 'aleeee ooop' in the horse's ear. The same thing happens – the horse crashes straight through the centre of the jump but again just stays on its feet. At the third hurdle, the jockey thinks, 'It's no good, I'll have to do it,' and yells, 'Alllleee Ooop!' really loudly.

Sure enough, the horse sails over the jump with no problems. This continues for the rest of the race, but due to the earlier problems the horse only finishes third. The trainer is fuming and asks the jockey what went wrong.

The jockey tries to protect himself and replies, 'Nothing is wrong with me, it's this bloody horse. What is he, deaf or something?'

The trainer replies, 'Deaf? Deaf? He's not deaf, he's blind.'

C oming home from his Little League game, Billy swings open the front door very excited. Unable to attend the game, his father immediately wants to know what happened.

'So, how did you do, son?' he asks.

'You'll never believe it!' Billy says. 'I was responsible for the winning run!'

'Really? How'd you do that?'

'I dropped the ball.'

During the Super Bowl, there is another football game of note between the big animals and the little animals. The big animals are crushing little animals and at half-time, the coach makes a passionate speech to rally the little animals.

At the start of the second half, the big animals have the ball. The first play, the elephant gets stopped for no gain. The second play, the rhino is stopped for no gain. On third down, the hippo is thrown for a five-yard loss.

The defence huddles around the coach and he asks excitedly, 'Who stopped the elephant?'

'I did,' says the centipede.

'Who stopped the rhino?'

'Uh, that was me too,' says the centipede.

'And how about the hippo? Who hit him for a five-yard loss?'

'Well, that was me as well,' says the centipede.

'So where were you during the first half?' demands the coach.

'Well,' says the centipede, 'I was having my ankles taped.'

Before the final match, the American wrestler's trainer comes to him and says, 'Now don't forget all the research we've done on this Russian. He's never lost a match because of this "pretzel" hold he has. Whatever you do, don't let him get you in this hold. If he does, you're finished.'

The wrestler nods in agreement.

Now, to the match: The American and the Russian circle each other several times looking for an opening. All of a sudden the Russian lunges forward, grabbing the American and wrapping him up in the dreaded pretzel hold. A sigh of disappointment goes up from the crowd, and the trainer buries his face in his hands for he knows all is lost. He can't bring himself to watch the ending.

Suddenly there is a scream, a cheer from the crowd, and the trainer raises his eye just in time to see the Russian flying up in the air. The Russian's back hits the mat with a thud, and the American weakly collapses on top of him, getting the pin and winning the match.

The trainer is astounded. When he finally gets the American wrestler alone, he asks, 'How did you ever get out of that hold? No-one has ever done it before!'

The wrestler answers, 'Well, I was ready to give up when he got me in that hold, but at the last moment, I opened my eyes and saw this pair of balls right in front of my face. I thought I had nothing to lose, so with my last bit of strength I stretched out my neck and bit those babies just as hard as I could. You'd be amazed how strong you get when you bite your own balls.'

A baseball manager who has an ulcer is in his physician's office for a check-up.

'Remember,' the doctor says, 'don't get excited, don't get mad, and forget about baseball when you're off the field.' Then he adds, 'By the way, how come you let the pitcher bat yesterday with the tying run on second and two men out in the ninth?'

GOLF

Someone once told me that there were more jokes about golf than any other sport – but that none of them were funny. You be the judge!

A young woman has been taking golf lessons. She has just started playing her first round of golf when she suffers a bee sting. The pain is so intense that she decides to return to the clubhouse.

Her golf pro sees her come into the clubhouse and asks, 'Why are you back in so early? What's wrong?'

'I was stung by a bee.'

'Where?' he asks.

'Between the first and second hole,' she replies.

He nods knowingly and says, 'Apparently your stance is too wide.'

A guy stands over his tee shot for what seems an eternity, looking up, looking down, measuring the distance, figuring the wind direction and speed, driving his partner nuts.

Finally his exasperated partner says, 'What's taking so long? Hit the blasted ball!'

The guy answers, 'My wife is up there watching me from the clubhouse. I want to make this a perfect shot.'

'Forget it man. You don't stand a snowball's chance in hell of hitting her from here.'

A very attractive couple are playing golf and the wife hits a beautiful, long shot – right through the window of a house. Horrified, the couple go to the house to apologise and offer to pay for the damage. A tall, handsome man answers the door.

'Come in! Come in!' he cries.

The couple, embarrassed by the smiling welcome, confess to breaking the window.

'I know, I know,' says the man. 'And I'm pleased you did.'

The couple exchange confused glances.

'You see that urn?' the man continues, pointing to what had been an antique masterpiece but is now lying in pieces on the floor.

'Oh no!' the wife cries. 'Don't tell me I've broken that too!'

'Don't be worried,' says the man. 'You see I've been in that urn for years and years. I'm a genie and you have set me free.'

The couple just stare at him in amazement.

'Now,' says the genie. 'I have the power to grant three wishes. Why don't we share them. One each.'

Turning to the wife he says, 'What is your greatest wish?'

'Well,' she says hesitantly, 'I would like to think I could have peace of mind and a quiet, calm life forever.'

'Done!' says the genie. 'And what about you Sir?'

The husband doesn't waste a minute to reply. 'I would like to have enough money to live a life of total luxury, to be able to afford expensive cars, take super cruises and live in the best stateroom on the ship, and have a grand house – with servants.'

'Done!'

The husband looks extremely pleased and asks the genie his wish.

The genie looks slightly embarrassed. 'That's rather delicate actually.' He turns to the wife and says, 'Do you mind if I speak to your husband alone for a moment?'

'Not at all,' she says.

The genie takes the husband aside. 'You have a very beautiful wife. I know I shouldn't ask this but my wish would be to spend just one night alone with her. What do you think?'

'Well I'm not sure,' says the husband. 'I'd have to discuss it with her and see how she feels about it.'

'Naturally,' says the genie.

The couple gave the proposition some thought and then the wife says that the genie is, after all, giving them a lifetime of peace, security and luxury. Maybe it isn't really too big an ask – just one night.

'If you're OK with it, I am,' says the husband.

'Actually,' says the wife with a smile, 'he's not unattractive you know. I'm really quite happy to oblige.'

The genie and the wife have a wonderful night together and the next morning the genie says, 'I really want to thank you. I've had a marvellous time with you and I think you quite enjoyed it too.'

'Oh I did,' says the wife.

Please, the genie says, 'Do you mind if I ask you just one question? How old is your husband?'

'Forty-three.'

At this the genie raises his eyebrows. 'And he still believes in genies?'

Three men are playing in a golf tournament: one is an eye surgeon, one is a priest and the other is an engineer. The club captain comes through checking the field and asks if everything is going alright.

'No,' they say. 'Those men ahead are dreadfully slow and holding up the field.'

'Oh, be patient with them,' says the captain. 'They're blind.'

'That's terrible,' says the eye surgeon. 'Send them to me and I'll see if there's anything I can do for them.'

The priest says, 'I'll pray for them.'

The engineer says, 'Why can't they play at night?'

A golfer is in a competitive match with a friend, who is ahead by a couple of strokes. The golfer says to himself, 'I'd give anything to sink this next putt.'

A stranger walks up to him and whispers, 'Would you give up a quarter of your sex life?'

The golfer thinks the man is crazy and that his answer will be meaningless, but also that perhaps this is a good omen, so he says, 'OK,' and sinks the putt.

Two holes later he mumbles to himself, 'Boy, if I could only get an eagle on this hole.'

The same stranger moves to his side and says, 'Would it be worth another quarter of your sex life?'

The golfer shrugs and says, 'Sure.'

He makes an eagle. On the final hole, the golfer needs yet another eagle to win. Though he says nothing, the stranger moves to his side and says, 'Would you be willing to give up the rest of your sex life to win this match?'

The golfer says, 'Certainly!'

He makes the eagle. As the golfer walks to the club house, the stranger walks alongside and says, 'You know, I've really not been fair with you because you don't know who I am. I'm the devil, and from now on you will have no sex life.'

'Nice to meet you,' says the golfer. 'My name's Father O'Malley.'

The antenatal class is in full swing with pregnant women and their partners learning how to breathe properly and how to provide support at birth.

At one point, the teacher announces, 'Ladies, exercise is good for you. Walking is especially beneficial. And, gentlemen, it wouldn't hurt you to take the time to go walking with your partner!'

One man raises his arm to ask a question.

'Yes?' asks the teacher.

'Is it all right if she carries a golf bag while we walk?'

'**F**orgive me father, for I have sinned.'

'What is your sin, my child?' the priest asks.

'Well,' the man says, 'I used some horrible language this week and I feel absolutely terrible.'

'When did you use this awful language?' asks the priest.

'I was playing golf and hit an incredible drive that looked like it was going to go over 300m, but it struck a phone line that was hanging over the fairway and fell straight down to the ground after going only about 100m.'

'Is that when you swore?'

'No, Father,' says the man. 'After that, a squirrel ran out of the bushes and grabbed my ball in his mouth and began to run away.'

'Is that when you swore?' asks the Father again.

'Well, no,' says the man. 'You see, as the squirrel was running, an eagle came down out of the sky, grabbed the squirrel in his talons and began to fly away.'

'Is that when you swore?' asks the amazed priest.

'No, not yet,' the man replies. 'As the eagle carried the squirrel away in his claws, it flew towards the green. And as it passed over a bit of forest near the green, the squirrel dropped my ball.'

'Did you swear then?' asks the now impatient priest.

'No, because as the ball fell it struck a tree, bounced through some bushes, careened off a big rock, and rolled through a sand trap onto the green and stopped within six inches of the hole.'

'You missed the bloody putt, didn't you?' sighs the priest.

A man and his friend meet at the clubhouse and decide to play a round of golf together. The man has a little dog with him and on the first green, when the man holes out a 10m putt, the little dog starts to yip and stands up on its hind legs.

The friend is quite amazed at this clever trick and says, 'That dog is really talented. What does he do if you miss a putt?'

'Somersaults,' says the man.

'Somersaults?' says the friend, 'That's incredible. How many does he do?'

'Hmmm,' says the man. 'That depends on how hard I kick him in the arse.'

A couple of women are playing golf one sunny afternoon. The first of the twosome tees off and watches in horror as the ball heads directly toward a foursome of men playing the next hole. Sure enough, the ball hits one of the guys, and he immediately clasps his hands together at his crotch, falls to the ground, and rolls around in agony. The woman rushes over and immediately begins to apologise. She then explains that she is a physical therapist and offers to help ease his pain.

'Ummph, ooh, nooo, I'll be alright . . . I'll be fine in a few minutes,' he replies as he remains in the foetal position, still clasping his hands together at his crotch. But she persists and he finally allows her to help him. She gently takes his hands away and lays them to the side, loosens his pants and puts her hands inside, beginning to massage him.

'Does that feel better?' she asks.

'Ohhh, Yeah. It feels really great,' he replies. 'But my thumb still hurts like hell!'

A golfer who is well into his golden years has a lifelong ambition to play a particular hole at Pebble Beach, California, the way the pros do it. The pros drive the ball out over the water onto the green that is on a spit of land that juts out off the coast. It is something he has tried hundreds of times without success. His ball always falls short, into the water. Because of this he never uses a new ball on this particular hole. He always picks out one that has a cut or a nick. One year he goes out to Pebble Beach to try again. When he comes to the fateful hole, he tees up an old cut ball and says a silent prayer. Before he hits it, however, a powerful voice from above says: 'Wait, replace that old ball with a brand-new ball.'

He complies, with some slight misgiving, despite the fact that the Lord seems to be implying that He is going to let him finally achieve his lifelong ambition. As he steps up to the tee once more, the voice booms down again, 'Wait. Step back. Take a practice swing.'

So he steps back and takes a practice swing. The voice booms out again, 'Take another practice swing.'

He does. Silence follows.

Then the voice speaks out again, 'Put back the old ball.'

God, Jesus and John the Baptist are playing golf up in heaven. On the first tee, John the Baptist leads off and hits a big blast right down the middle; it rolls to a stop about 270m out, a perfect lie. Jesus steps up next and kills the ball, sending it about 300m straight, perfect lie. God steps up and waggles and wiggles and then badly hooks his ball into the trees. As it flies in, a huge oak is struck by lightning and splits, one half falling into the path of the oncoming ball and knocking it into the fairway. As it comes to a rest, a bare 50m out, a squirrel darts out of the woods on the other side and grabs the ball and takes off towards the left-side woods. Before he gets in, an eagle swoops down and grabs the squirrel, carrying it aloft down the fairway. Just as it passes over the green, the eagle is pelted by hailstones, whereupon it drops the squirrel (still clutching the ball) onto the green about 1m from the hole. Dazed, the squirrel spits the ball out where it rolls up and stops on the lip of the cup. Suddenly there is an earthquake! The ball drops in . . . a hole in one!

Jesus stares at John the Baptist with a pissed-off look, then turns to God and says, 'Dad? We gonna play golf, or are you just gonna screw around?'

Two friends decide to have a round of golf. Their tee shots are horrible. One guy hits the ball way left, the other hits it way right. They decide that the shots are so bad they will just meet up at the hole. So the first guy looks and looks and finds his ball sitting down deep in a field of beautiful buttercups. He promptly pulls out his seven-iron and starts whacking away. Buttercups are flying everywhere but the ball won't come out. Finally Mother Nature gets mad.

She comes up from the ground and says to the man, 'I've created this beautiful field of buttercups and you have no respect for them at all, now they are ruined. I have to punish you. Since these are buttercups your punishment is that you cannot have butter for a year.'

The man starts to laugh and goes back to whacking at the buttercups.

Mother Nature says, 'Hey, this is no laughing matter. What do you find so funny?'

The man smiles and says, 'My mate is over on the other side in the pussy willows.'

Two guys go for a game of golf and one says, 'I'm getting some balls, do you need some?'

The other man says he has one.

'What do you mean you have one? How can you play a whole round of golf with only one ball? What if you lose it?' he asks.

'It's a special ball, you can't lose it.'

'What if it falls in the water?' asks the first man.

The second man says, 'It floats.'

'What if it's in the bushes and you can't see it?'

'It beeps.'

'What if it's dark?'

'It glows it the dark. You just can't lose it,' the second man says.

'Wow, where did you get it?' the first man asks.

'I found it.'

Three women are out playing golf one day and one of them hits her ball into the woods. She goes into the woods to looks for it and finds a frog in a trap.

The frog says to her, 'If you release me from this trap, I will grant you three wishes.'

The woman frees the frog and the frog says, 'Thank you, but I failed to mention that there is a condition to your wishes – that whatever you wish for, your husband will get ten times more or better.'

The woman says, 'That's OK,' and for her first wish she wants to be the most beautiful woman in the world.

The frog warns her, 'You do realise this wish will also make your husband the most handsome man in the world, an Adonis, and that women will flock to him.'

The woman replies, 'That's OK, because I will be the most beautiful woman and he will only have eyes for me.'

So, *poof!* She's the most beautiful woman in the world.

For her second wish, she wants to be the richest woman in the world.

The frog says, 'That will make your husband the richest man in the world and he will be ten times richer than you.'

The woman says, 'That's OK because what is mine is his, and what is his is mine.'

So, *poof!* She's the richest woman in the world.

The frog then inquires after her third wish and she answers, 'I'd like a mild heart attack.'

A lovely afternoon finds a fellow and his wife out playing golf. They have had a wonderful time and the man has had a near perfect game. The final hole, by far the most difficult, wraps around an old barn. With a terrible slice the man puts the barn between his ball and the green. Knowing that the strokes that it will take to get around the barn will destroy his score, he begins to rant and rave. His wife, hating to see him ruin such a great afternoon, makes a suggestion.

'What if I were to hold open the barn doors? That way you could send it right through the barn onto the green.'

He thinks this over and decides that it will work. With his wife holding open the barn door he lines up with the hole and gives the ball a terrific *whack!* The ball shoots through the air and right into his wife's head, killing her instantly. Months go by, and the man mourns all the while. His friends, hating to see him in such a state, convince him to get back onto the golf course with them. They end up at the same course and on the final hole, oddly enough, another terrible slice puts the old barn between his ball and the green. Again he begins to rant and rave at what this dilemma will do to his score. He friend, wanting to please him, makes a suggestion.

'What if I were to hold open the barn doors? That way you could send it right through the barn onto the green.'

'No,' the man replies, 'last time I did that I got two over par.'

Robert goes golfing every Saturday. One Saturday, he comes home three hours late. His wife asks him, 'What took you so long?'

Robert says, 'That was the worst game of golf I've ever played. We got up to the first tee, and Charlie hit a hole-in-one and immediately dropped dead of a heart attack.'

His wife says, 'That's terrible!'

Robert says, 'I know. Then, for the rest of the game, it was hit the ball, drag Charlie, hit the ball, drag Charlie, hit the ball, drag Charlie . . .'

A foursome is on the last hole when the last golfer drives off the tee and hooks into a cow pasture. He advises his friends to play through and he will meet them at the clubhouse. They follow the plan and wait for their friend. After a considerable time he appears dishevelled, bloody, and badly beaten up. They all want to know what happened.

He explains 'I went over to the cow pasture but I couldn't find my ball. I noticed a cow wringing her tail in obvious pain. I went over and lifted her tail and saw a golf ball solidly embedded. It was a yellow ball so I knew it wasn't mine. Then a woman came out of the bushes, apparently searching for her lost golf ball. I lifted the cow's tail and asked, "Does this look like yours?" And that's the last thing I can remember.'

A man is about to tee off on the golf course when he feels a tap on his shoulder and a man hands him a card that reads, 'I am a deaf-mute. May I play through, please?'

The first man angrily gives the card back, and communicates that no, he may *not* play through, and that his disability did not give him such a right.

The first man whacks the ball onto the green and leaves to finish the hole.

Just as he is about to sink the ball into the hole he is hit in the head with a golf ball, laying him out cold.

When he comes to a few minutes later, he looks around and sees the deaf-mute sternly looking at him, one hand on his hip, the other holding up four fingers.

THE LAWS OF GOLFING

L aw 1: No matter how bad your last shot was, the worst is yet to come. This law does not expire on the 18th hole, since it has the supernatural tendency to extend over the course of a tournament, a summer and, eventually, a lifetime.

Law 2: Your best round of golf will be followed almost immediately by your worst round ever. The probability of the latter increases with the number of people you tell about the former.

Law 3: Brand new golf balls are water-magnetic. Though this cannot be proven in the lab, it is a known fact that the more expensive the golf ball, the greater its attraction to water.

Law 4: Golf balls never bounce off trees back into play. If one does, the tree is breaking a law of the universe and should be cut down.

Law 5: No matter what causes a golfer to stuff up a shot, all his playing partners must solemnly chant 'You looked up,' or invoke the wrath of the universe.

Law 6: The higher a golfer's handicap, the more qualified he deems himself as an instructor.

Law 7: Every par-three hole in the world has a secret desire to humiliate golfers. The shorter the hole, the greater its desire.

Law 8: Topping a three-iron is the most painful torture known to man.

Law 9: Palm trees eat golf balls.

Law 10: Sand is alive. If it isn't, how do you explain the way it works against you?

Law 11: Golf carts always run out of juice at the farthest point from the clubhouse.

Law 12: A golfer hitting into your group will always be bigger than anyone in your group. Likewise, a group you accidentally hit into will consist of a football player, a professional wrestler, a convicted murderer and a tax auditor – or some similar combination.

Law 13: All three-woods are demon-possessed.

Law 14: Golf balls from the same 'sleeve' tend to follow one another, particularly out of bounds or into the water (see Law 3).

Law 15: A severe slice is a thing of awesome power and beauty.

Law 16: 'Nice lag' can usually be translated to 'lousy putt'. Similarly, 'tough break' can usually be translated 'way to miss an easy one, sucker'.

Law 17: The person you would most hate to lose to will always be the one who beats you.

Law 18: The last three holes of a round will automatically adjust your score to what it really should be.

Law 19: Golf should be given up at least twice per month.

Law 20: All vows taken on a golf course shall be valid only until the sunset of the same day.

101 THINGS *NOT* TO SAY DURING SEX

1. But everybody looks funny naked!
2. You woke me up for that?
3. Did I mention the video camera?
4. Do you smell something rotten?
5. *(In a janitor's closet)* And they say romance is dead . . .
6. Try breathing through your nose.
7. A little rug burn never hurt anyone!
8. Is that a Medic-Alert pendant?
9. Sweetheart, did you lock the back door?
10. But whipped cream makes me break out.
11. Person 1: This is your first time . . . right?
    Person 2: Yeah . . . today
12. *(In the No Tell Motel)* Hurry up! This room rents by the hour!
13. Can you please pass me the remote control?
14. Do you accept Visa?
15. Zzzzzzzzzzzzzzzzzzzzzzzzzzzzzzzz
16. On second thoughts, let's turn off the lights.
17. And to think I was really trying to pick up your friend!
18. So much for mouth-to-mouth.
19. *(Using body paint)* Try not to leave any stains, OK?
20. Hope you're as good looking when I'm sober.
21. *(Holding a banana)* It's just a little trick I learned at the zoo!
22. Do you get any premium movie channels?
23. Try not to smear my make-up, will ya!
24. *(Preparing to use peanut butter)* But I just steam-cleaned this couch!
25. Got any penicillin?

26. But I just brushed my teeth.
27. Smile, you're on *Candid Camera*!
28. I thought *you* had the keys to the handcuffs!
29. I want a baby!
30. So much for the fulfilment of sexual fantasies!
31. *(In a ménage à trois)* Why am I doing all the work?
32. Maybe we should call Dr Ruth.
33. Did you know the ceiling needs painting?
34. I think you have it on backwards.
35. When is this supposed to feel good?
36. Put that blender back in the kitchen where it belongs!
37. You're good enough to do this for a living!
38. Is that blood on the headboard?
39. Did I remember to take my pill?
40. Are you sure I don't know you from somewhere?
41. I wish we got the *Playboy* channel.
42. That leak better be from the waterbed!
43. I told you it wouldn't work without batteries!
44. But my cat always sleeps on that pillow.
45. Did I tell you my Aunt Martha died in this bed?
46. If you quit smoking you might have more endurance.
47. No, really . . . I do this part better myself!
48. It's nice being in bed with a woman I don't have to inflate!
49. This would be more fun with a few more people.
50. You're almost as good as my ex!
51. Do you know the definition of statutory rape?
52. Is that you I smell or is your mattress stuffed with rotten potatoes?
53. You look younger than you feel.
54. Perhaps you're just out of practice.
55. You sweat more than a galloping stallion.
56. They're not cracker crumbs, it's just a rash.
57. Now I know why she dumped you.
58. Does your husband own a sawn-off shotgun?

59. You give me reason to conclude that foreplay is overrated.
60. What tampon?
61. Have you ever considered liposuction?
62. And to think, I didn't even have to buy you dinner!
63. What are you planning to make for breakfast?
64. I have a confession to make . . .
65. I was so horny tonight I would have taken a duck home!
66. Are those real or am I just behind the times?
67. Were you by any chance repressed as a child?
68. Is that a hanging sculpture?
69. You'll still vote for me, won't you?
70. Did I mention my sex-change operation?
71. I really hate women who actually think sex means something!
72. Did you come yet, dear?
73. I'll tell you who I'm fantasising about if you tell me who you're fantasising about.
74. A good plastic surgeon can take care of that in no time!
75. Does this count as a date?
76. Oprah Winfrey had a show about men like you!
77. Hic! I need another beer for this please.
78. I think biting is romantic – don't you?
79. You can cook, too right?
80. When would you like to meet my parents?
81. Maybe it would help if I thought about someone I really like.
82. Have you seen *Fatal Attraction*?
83. Sorry about the name tags, I'm not very good with names.
84. Don't mind me . . . I always file my nails in bed.
85. *(In a phone booth)* Do you mind if I make a few phone calls?
86. I hope I didn't forget to turn the gas oven off. Do you have a light?
87. Don't worry, my dog's really friendly for a Doberman.

88. Sorry but I don't do toes!
89. You could at least *act* like you're enjoying it!
90. Petroleum jelly or no petroleum jelly, I said NO!
91. Keep it down, my mother is a light sleeper.
92. I'll bet you didn't know I work for *The Enquirer*.
93. So that's why they call you Mr Flash!
94. My old girlfriend used to do it a *lot* longer!
95. Is this a sin too?
96. I've slept with more women than Wilt Chamberlain!
97. Hey, when is it going to be my friend's turn?
98. Long kisses clog my sinuses.
99. Please understand that I'm only doing this for a raise.
100. How long do you plan to be 'almost there'?
101. You mean you're *not* my blind date?

LAUGHING AT DISABILITIES

MORE ADULT ONLY

Making fun of people with disabilities is the bottom of the barrel. But that's what we're about, scraping the very bottom of the bad taste joke barrel.

Three guys enter a disabled swimming contest. The first has no arms. The second no legs and the third has no body, he's just a head. They all line up, the whistle blows and *splash!* They're all in the pool.

The guy with no arms takes the lead instantly but the guy with no legs is closing fast. The head of course sinks straight to the bottom.

Ten lengths later and the guy with no legs finishes first. He can still see bubbles coming from the bottom of the pool, so he decides he had better dive down to rescue the head.

He picks up the head, swims back up to the surface and places the head at the side of the pool, where upon the head starts coughing and spluttering.

Eventually the head catches his breath and shouts, 'Three years I've spent learning to swim with my bloody ears, then two minutes before the whistle, some arsehole puts a swimming cap on me!'

A blind man is seen waiting at a street corner with his guide dog. After a short wait the dog starts leading the blind man across the street against the red light. First a car comes screeching to a halt mere centimetres away from him, but still the dog leads on, then a bicyclist almost wipes him out and curses as he goes by. Finally in the last lane a truck swerves and barely misses him. After they reach the far corner the blind man reaches in his pocket and pulls out a cookie and offers it to the guide dog. At this point another man who has watched the entire episode interrupts.

'Why are you rewarding that dog after he endangered your life and almost got you run over by a car, bicycle and truck?' asks the man.

The blind man responds, 'I'm not rewarding him, I'm just trying to find out which end is his head so I can kick him in the arse.'

A blind man is describing his favourite sport, parachuting. When asked how he is able to parachute, he says that just about everything is done for him.

'I am placed in the door with my guide dog and told when to jump. My hand is placed on my release ring for me and out I go with the dog.'

'But how do you know when you are going to land?' he is asked.

'I have a very keen sense of smell, and I can smell the trees and grass when I am 100m from the ground,' he answers.

'But how do you know when to lift your legs for the final arrival on the ground?' he is again asked.

He quickly answers, 'Oh, the dog's leash goes slack.'

A blind man walks into a store with his guide dog. All of a sudden, he picks up the leash and begins swinging the dog over his head.

The manager runs up to the man and asks, 'What are you doing?'

The blind man replies, 'Just looking around.'

A deaf-mute walks into a pharmacy to buy condoms. He has difficulty communicating with the pharmacist, and cannot see condoms on the shelf. Frustrated, the deaf-mute finally unzips his pants, places his dick on the counter, and puts down a $5 note next to it.

The pharmacist unzips his pants, does the same as the deaf-mute, and then picks up both bills and stuffs them in his pocket. Exasperated, the deaf-mute begins to curse the pharmacist wildly in sign language.

'Look,' the pharmacist says, 'if you can't afford to lose, you shouldn't bet.'

Two dwarfs decide to treat themselves to a vacation in Las Vegas. At the hotel bar, they're dazzled by two women, and wind up taking them to their separate rooms. The first dwarf is disappointed, however, as he's unable to reach a certain physical state that would enable him to join with his date. His depression is enhanced by the fact that, from the next room, he hears cries of 'One, two, three . . . Huh!' all night long.

In the morning, the second dwarf asks the first, 'How did it go?'

The first whispers back, 'It was so embarrassing. I simply couldn't get an erection.'

The second dwarf shakes his head.

'You think that's embarrassing? I couldn't even get on the bed!'

A guy stops in to visit his friend who is paralysed from the waist down. His friend says, 'My feet are cold. Would you get me my sneakers for me?'

The guy goes upstairs, and there are his friend's two gorgeous daughters.

He says, 'Hi, girls. Your dad sent me up here to screw you.'

The first daughter says, 'That's not true.'

He says, 'I'll prove it.'

He yells down the stairs, 'Both of them?'

His friend yells back, 'Of course, both of them!'

Two guys meet after not having seen each other for many, many years.

The first guy asks the second guy, 'How have things been going?'

The second guy, speaking very slowly tells the first guy, 'I w..a..s.. a..l..m..o..s..t m..a..r..r..i..e..d.'

The first guy says in amazement 'Hey! you don't stutter any more.'

'Y..e..s I w..e..n..t t..o a d..o..c..t..o..r a..n..d h..e t..o..l..d m..e t..h..a..t i..f I s..p..e..a..k s..l..o..w..l..y I w..i..l..l n..o..t s..t..u..t..t..e..r.'

The first friend congratulates him on not stuttering anymore and asks why he is no longer engaged to his girlfriend.'

'W..e..l..l m..y f..i..a..n..c..e..e a..n..d I w..e..r..e s..i..t..t..i..n..g o..n h..e..r p..o..r..c..h a..n..d t..h..e d..o..g w..a..s s..c..r..a..t..c..h..i..n..g h..i..s b..a..c..k a..n..d I t..o..l..d h..e..r t..h..a..t w..h..e..n w..e a..r..e m..a..r..r..i..e..d s..h..e c..a..n d..o t..h..a..t f..o..r m..e a..n..d s..h..e t..h..r..e..w t..h..e r..i..n..g i..n m..y f..a..c..e.'

'Why should she throw the ring in your face for that?' asks the first friend.

'W..e..l..l I s..p..e..a..k s..o s..l..o..w..l..y t..h..a..t b..y t..h..e t..i..m..e s..h..e l..o..o..k..e..d a..t t..h..e d..o..g. h..e w..a..s l..i..c..k..i..n..g h..i..s b..a..l..l..s.'

A guy is standing at a urinal when he notices that he is being watched by a midget. Although the little fellow is staring at him intently, the guy doesn't get uncomfortable until the midget drags a small stepladder up next to him, climbs it, and proceeds to admire his privates at close range.

'Wow,' comments the midget, 'Those are the nicest balls I have ever seen!'

Surprised and flattered, the man thanks the midget and starts to move away.

'Listen, I know this is a rather strange request,' says the little fellow, 'but I wonder if you would mind if I touched them?'

Again the man is rather startled, but seeing no real harm in it, he obliges the request.

The midget reaches out, gets a tight grip on the man's balls, and says, 'OK, hand me your wallet or I'll jump off the ladder!'

PETS AND OTHER ANIMALS

I wonder if animals tell jokes about humans.

One night a man breaks into a house and is in the middle of stealing the home entertainment centre, when out of nowhere he hears, 'Jesus is watching.'

This totally spooks him so he searches around with his torch. Up in the corner he finds a birdcage with a parrot inside.

Relieved, he says, 'pretty Polly,' to which the parrot replies, 'Jesus is watching.'

The thief asks the bird what his name is and the bird says 'Moses.'

The thief says, 'What a silly name for a bird.'

The bird replies, 'You think that's funny, the Rottweiler's name is Jesus.'

A local business is looking for office help. They put a sign in the window saying: 'Help Wanted. Must be able to type, must be good with a computer and must be bilingual. We are an Equal Opportunity Employer.'

A short time afterwards, a dog trots up to the window, sees the sign and goes inside. He looks at the receptionist and wags his tail, then walks over to the sign, looks at it and whines. Getting the idea, the receptionist gets the office manager. The office manager looks at the dog and is surprised, to say the least. However, the dog looks determined, so he leads him into the office. Inside, the dog jumps up on the chair and stares at the manager.

The manager says, 'I can't hire you. The sign says you have to be able to type.'

The dog jumps down, goes to the typewriter and types out a perfect letter. He takes out the page and trots over to the manager, gives it to him, then jumps back on the chair.

The manager is stunned, but then tells the dog, 'The sign says you have to be good with a computer.'

The dog jumps down again and goes to the computer. He demonstrates his expertise with various programs, produces a sample spreadsheet and database and presents them to the manager.

By this time the manager is totally dumbfounded! He looks at the dog and says, 'I realise that you are a very intelligent dog and have some interesting abilities. However, I still can't give you the job.'

The dog jumps down and goes to the sign and puts his paw on the part about being an Equal Opportunity Employer.

The manager says, 'Yes, but the sign also says that you have to be bilingual.'

The dog looks him straight in the face and says, 'Meow.'

Two female mice are talking one day. The first mouse is telling her friend about her new boyfriend.

'He is really very nice, kind, considerate, smart. And good looking? Wow! He is really good looking. Would you like to see a picture?'

Her friend says, 'Sure.'

So the first mouse pulls out a picture and shows it to her friend who says, 'Wait a minute. This isn't a mouse. This is a bat!'

'What?' says the first mouse. She takes the picture back, looks at it again and says, 'You're right. He is a bat. And what a liar. He told me he was a pilot.'

A man brings a very limp dog into the veterinary clinic. As he lays the dog on the table, the doctor pulls out his stethoscope and places the receptor on the dog's chest.

After a moment or two, the vet shakes his head sadly and says, 'I'm sorry, but your dog has passed away.'

'What?' screams the man. 'How can you tell? You haven't done any testing on him or anything. I want another opinion.'

With that, the vet turns and leaves the room. In a few moments, he returns with a Labrador Retriever. The Retriever goes right to work, checking the poor dead dog out thoroughly with his nose. After a considerable amount of sniffing, the Retriever sadly shakes his head and says, 'Bark'.

The veterinarian then takes the Labrador out and returns in a few moments with a cat, who also carefully sniffs out the poor dog on the table. As had his predecessors, the cat sadly shakes his head and says, 'Meow'.

He then jumps off the table and runs out of the room. The veterinarian hands the man a bill for $600. The dog's owner goes berserk.

'What, $600! Just to tell me my dog is dead? This is outrageous!'

The vet shakes his head sadly and says, 'If you had taken my word for it, the charge would have been $50, but with the lab work and the cat scan . . .'

D own in San Diego, Joe is sitting on the deck of his condo and spots a gorilla in one of his palm trees. Not knowing what else to do, he calls the San Diego Zoo. They are happy to hear from him because one of their gorillas has escaped and they say they will send someone out right away to capture it. Very shortly a truck pulls up to Joe's condo and the driver asks Joe to help him. This zoo attendant has a ladder, handcuffs, a Doberman and a rifle. He tells Joe he will climb up the tree and shake the gorilla out of the tree. When the gorilla hits the ground he will be stunned and the Doberman will bite him in the balls and then Joe can put the handcuffs on the gorilla.

Joe says, 'That sounds reasonable, but what's the rifle for?'

'Well,' the zoo attendant says, 'once in a great while, the gorilla shakes me out of the tree, and if that happens, shoot the damned dog.'

A man walking through the jungle is brutally attacked by a lion. Luckily a witch doctor sees the whole thing and fixes him up using ancient methods. In place of his own eye he gets an eagle's eye, in place of his own arm he gets a gorilla's arm and in place of his penis he gets an elephant's trunk.

'Come back in six months to show me how it's going,' says the witch doctor.

Six months later the man comes back and is profuse in his thanks.

'I can see for miles with this eagle's eye, I'm the world's best arm wrestler with this gorilla's arm but there's a problem with the elephant's trunk.'

'What's that?' asks the witch doctor.

'It keeps on picking up grass and shoving it up my arse!'

There are three dogs all in the pound. The first dog turns to the second dog and asks, 'What are you in for?'

The dog replies, 'Well my master said that if I keep chewing up his newspapers he will put me to sleep. I kept chewing them and today I'm getting put to sleep.'

The other dogs start to comfort him. The second dog turns to the third dog and asks him the same question.

The dog replies, 'Well my master said that if I kept drinking out of the toilet I would get put to sleep. And here I am about to get put to sleep.'

The other dogs start to comfort him too. Then the second and third dog turn to the first dog and ask him the same question.

The dog says, 'When my mistress got out of the shower her towel fell off of her, and when she bent over I just couldn't help myself and started to screw her up the arse.'

The dogs say, 'Oh, we understand why you're getting put to sleep.'

The first dog turns around and says, 'I'm not here to get put to sleep, I'm here to get my nails trimmed.'

A man owns a horny parrot. Every time the man reaches into the cage, the bird humps his arm. He invites his mother to tea and the bird keeps using foul language. Finally he takes the parrot to a vet.

The vet examines the bird extensively and says, 'Well, you have a horny male parrot. I have a sweet young female bird, and for $15 your bird can go in the cage with mine.'

The guy's parrot is listening and says, 'Come on! Come on! What are you waiting for?'

Finally the guy says, 'All right.'

He hands over the $15. The vet takes the parrot, puts him in the cage with the female bird and closes the curtain.

Suddenly, 'Kwah! Kwah! Kwah!' The cage starts shaking and feathers come flying out.

The vet says, 'Holy gee,' and runs across the room and opens the curtain.

The male bird has the female bird down on the bottom of the

cage with one claw. With the other claw he's pulling out all her feathers.

He's saying, 'For fifteen bucks, I want you naked, bitch. Naked!'

A guy owns a parrot which does nothing but swear. The parrot has embarrassed its owner on many occasions when visitors have called. Time and again the man has told the parrot to use better language but the parrot just continues swearing. In fact, he uses worse language, just to piss his owner off even more.

On one occasion, the man locks the bird in a kitchen cabinet. But this only aggravates the bird and he claws and scratches and screeches. When the guy finally lets him out, the bird cuts loose with a stream of vulgarities that would make a veteran sailor blush. At that point, the guy is so mad that he throws the bird into the freezer. For the first few seconds there is a terrible din. The bird kicks and claws and thrashes about. Then suddenly, it gets very quiet. At first the guy just waits, but then he starts to think that the bird might be hurt or deeply chilled. After a couple of minutes of silence, he's so worried that he opens the freezer door.

The bird calmly climbs onto the man's outstretched arm and says, 'I'm very sorry about the trouble I gave you. I'll do my best to improve my vocabulary from now on.'

The man is astonished. He can't understand the transformation that has taken place.

Then the parrot says, 'By the way, what did the chicken do?'

A duck walks into a convenience store and asks the clerk, 'Do you have any grapes?'

The clerk says no, and the duck leaves. The next day, the duck returns and asks, 'Do you have any grapes?'

The clerk again says no, and the duck leaves. The day after that, the duck walks in the store again and asks, 'Do you have any grapes?'

The clerk screams at the duck, 'You've come in here twice before and asked if we had any grapes. I tell you no every time! I swear if you come back in here again, and ask for grapes, I'll nail your webbed feet to the floor.'

The duck leaves, and returns the next day.

This time he asks, 'Do you have any nails?'

The clerk replies, 'No.'

The duck says, 'Good! Got any grapes?'

A man takes his Rottweiler to the vet and says to him, 'My dog's cross-eyed. Is there anything you can do for it?'

'Well,' says the vet, 'let's have a look at him.'

So he picks the dog up by the ears and has a good look at its eyes.

'I'm going to have to put him down,' says the vet.

'Just because he's cross-eyed?' says the man.

'No, because he's heavy,' says the vet.

A vampire bat comes flapping in from the night, covered in fresh blood, and parks himself on the roof of the cave to get some sleep. Pretty soon all the other bats smell the blood and begin hassling him about where he got it. He tells them to go away and let him get some sleep, but they persist until finally he gives in.

'OK, follow me,' he says.

He flies out of the cave with hundreds of bats behind him. Down through a valley they go, across a river and into a forest full of trees. Finally he slows down and all the other bats excitedly mill around him.

'Now, do you see that tree over there?' he asks.

'Yes, yes, yes!' the bats all scream in a frenzy.

'Good,' says the first bat, 'because I didn't!'

A male whale and a female whale are swimming off the coast of Japan, when they notice a whaling ship. The male whale recognises it as the same ship that had harpooned his father many years earlier.

He says to the female whale, 'Let's both swim under the ship and blow out of our air holes at the same time and it should cause the ship to turn over and sink.'

They try it and sure enough, the ship turns over and quickly sinks.

Soon however, the whales realise that the sailors have jumped overboard and are swimming to the safety of the shore. The male is enraged that they are going to get away and says to the female, 'Let's swim after them and gobble them up before they reach the shore.'

But the female is reluctant to follow him.

'Look,' she says, 'I went along with the blow job, but I absolutely refuse to swallow the seamen.'

A lion wakes up one morning feeling really rowdy and mean. He goes out and corners a small monkey and roars, 'Who is the mightiest of all jungle animals?'

The trembling monkey says, 'You are, mighty lion!'

Later, the lion confronts a wildebeest and fiercely bellows, 'Who is the mightiest of all jungle animals?'

The terrified wildebeest stammers, 'Oh great lion, you are by far the mightiest animal in the jungle!'

On a roll now, the lion swaggers up to an elephant and roars, 'Who is the mightiest of all jungle animals?'

Fast as lightning, the elephant snatches up the lion with his trunk and slams him against a tree half a dozen times, making the lion feel like it's been run over by a safari wagon. The elephant then stomps on the lion until he looks like a corn tortilla and then ambles away.

The lion lets out a moan of pain, lifts his head weakly and hollers after the elephant, 'Jeez, just because you don't know the answer, you don't have to get so pissed off!'

Upon entering the little country store, a stranger notices a sign saying: 'Danger! Beware of Dog!' posted on the glass door. Inside, he notices a harmless old hound dog asleep on the floor beside the cash register.

He asks the store manager, 'Is that the dog folks are supposed to beware of?'

'Yep, that's him,' the manager replies.

The stranger can't help but be amused.

'That certainly doesn't look like a dangerous dog to me. Why in the world would you post that sign?'

'Because,' the owner replies, 'before I posted that sign, people kept tripping over him.'

Deep within a forest a little turtle begins to climb a tree. After hours of effort he reaches the top, jumps into the air waving his front legs and crashes to the ground. After recovering, he slowly climbs the tree again, jumps, and falls to the ground.

The turtle tries again and again while a couple of birds sitting on a branch watch his sad efforts. Finally, the female bird turns to her mate.

'Dear,' she chirps, 'I think it's time to tell him he's adopted.'

A certain zoo has acquired a female of a very rare species of gorilla. Within a few weeks, the gorilla becomes very difficult to handle. Upon examination, the zoo veterinarian determines the problem. The gorilla is on heat. To make matters worse, there are no male gorillas available. While reflecting on their problem, the zoo administrators notice Paul, an employee responsible for cleaning the animals' cages. Paul, it is rumoured, possesses ample ability to satisfy any female, but he isn't very bright. So, the zoo administrators think they might have a solution. Paul is approached with a proposition. Would he be willing to screw the gorilla for $500? Paul shows some interest, but says he will have to think the matter over carefully. The following day, Paul announces that he will accept their offer, but only on three conditions.

'First,' he says, 'I don't want to kiss her. Secondly, I want nothing to do with any offspring that may result from this union.'

The zoo administration quickly agrees to these conditions, so they ask for his third condition.

'Well,' says Paul, 'you've gotta give me another week to come up with the $500.'

S idney is a fourteen-year-old boy with an interest in the sciences. One summer day he conducts his own experiment. With his twelve-year-old sister Sophie in tow, he catches a large bullfrog in a local pond. Sidney tells Sophie her job is to write down the results of the experiment.

He draws a line in the sand, places the frog on the line, prods the frog with a small twig from the rear and shouts, 'Jump, frog!'

The frog jumps and Sidney measures the distance.

'Three metres . . . write that down, Sophie,' he says.

Next, he brings the frog back to the starting point and removes the frog's right front leg.

Again he prods it and shouts, 'Jump, frog!'

The frog jumps 2m, and on Sidney's instruction, Sophie writes it down. Again the frog is brought back. This time, the left front leg is removed.

Again 'Jump, frog!' Sidney reports, 'One metre . . . write it down.'

The next time, Sidney removes the large right back leg. Then, he prods the frog and shouts, 'Jump, frog!'

The frog jumps 50cm. 'Write it down, Sophie.'

Finally, Sidney removes the frog's remaining back left leg, puts it down and prods the frog with the twig shouting, 'Jump, frog! Jump, frog!'

The frog doesn't jump.

Sophie looks at Sidney and asks, 'So what should I write down?'

Sidney thinks a moment, then tells Sophie to write, 'When you remove all the legs from a frog, it turns deaf.'

Two storks are sitting in their nest – a father stork and a baby stork. The baby stork is crying and crying and the father stork is trying to calm him.

'Don't worry, son. Your mother will come back. She's only bringing people babies and making them happy.'

The next night, it's father's turn to do the job. Mother and son are sitting in the nest and the baby stork is crying.

The mother says, 'Son, your father will be back as soon as possible, but now he's bringing joy to new mummies and daddies.'

A few days later, the stork's parents are desperate. Their son is absent from the nest all night. Shortly before dawn, he returns and the parents ask him where he's been all night.

The baby stork says, 'Just scaring the shit out of uni students!'

A guy sees a sign in front of a house: 'Talking Dog for Sale.' He rings the bell and the owner tells him the dog is in the backyard. The guy goes into the backyard and sees a mutt sitting there.

'You talk?' he asks.

'Yep,' the mutt replies.

'So, what's your story?'

The mutt looks up and says, 'Well, I discovered this gift pretty young and I wanted to help the government, so I told the CIA about my gift, and in no time they had me jetting from country to country, sitting in rooms with spies and world leaders, 'cause no-one thought a dog would be eavesdropping. I was one of their most valuable spies for eight years running. The jetting around really tired me out, and I knew I wasn't getting any younger and I wanted to settle down. So I signed up for a job at the airport to do some undercover security work, mostly wandering near suspicious characters and listening in. I uncovered some incredible dealings there and was awarded a batch of medals. I had a wife, a mess of puppies, and now I'm retired.'

The guy is amazed. He goes back in and asks the owner what he wants for the dog. The owner says, 'Ten dollars.'

The guy says he'll buy him but asks the owner, 'This dog is amazing. Why on earth are you selling him?'

The owner replies, 'He's such a bloody liar.'

A very lonely woman buys a parrot from a pet store, complete with cage. Before purchasing it she gets a guarantee that the parrot will talk and then she takes the parrot home. In a week and a half she returns to the store very disappointed.

'The parrot doesn't talk.'

'Did you buy a mirror?'

'No.'

'Every parrot needs a mirror.'

So she buys a mirror and installs it in the parrot's cage. Another week and a half goes by and she returns.

'The parrot still doesn't talk.'

'Did you buy a ladder?'

'No.'

'Every parrot needs a ladder.'

So she buys a ladder and installs it in the cage. Another week and a half pass and she returns.

'The parrot still doesn't talk.'

'Did you buy a swing?'

'No.'

'Every parrot needs a swing.'

So she buys a swing and installs it in the cage. A week and a half later she returns. She is furious.

The store owner asks, 'Did the parrot talk?'

'No. He died.'

'Oh, that's terrible. Did he say anything before he died?'

'Yes.'

'What?'

'He gasped "Don't they have any food down at that store?"'

HARD DRIVES AND FLOPPIES

Why are there so many jokes about computer geeks? I guess it's because they're a sitting target.

A helicopter is flying above Seattle when an electrical malfunction disables all of the aircraft's navigational and communications equipment. Due to the cloud and haze, the pilot can't determine his location, or the course to the nearest airport. Finally, he sees a tall building and flies towards it. He circles, makes a handwritten sign that says 'Where Am I?' and holds it up in the helicopter's window.

The people in the building respond quickly. They write their own sign and hold it up in the window. It says 'You Are in a Helicopter.'

The pilot smiles, waves, turns the aircraft around and heads directly for Seattle airport.

After they land on the ground, the co-pilot asks the pilot how the 'You Are in a Helicopter' sign had helped him determine their position.

'Easy,' says the pilot. 'The information they gave me was technically correct, but totally useless, so I knew that had to be the Microsoft building.'

One day Bill complains to his friend, 'My elbow really hurts, I guess I should see a doctor.'

His friend offers, 'Don't do that. There's a computer at the chemist that can diagnose anything quicker and cheaper than a doctor. Simply put in a sample of your urine and the computer will diagnose your problem and tell you what you can do about it. It only costs $10.'

Bill reckons he has nothing to lose, so he fills a jar with a urine sample and goes to the chemist. Finding the computer, he pours in the sample and deposits the $10. The computer starts making some noise and various lights start flashing. After a brief pause out pops a small slip of paper on which is printed: 'You have tennis elbow. Soak your arm in warm water. Avoid heavy lifting. It will be better in two weeks.'

Late that evening, while thinking how amazing this new technology is and how it will change medical science forever, Bill begins to wonder if this machine can be fooled. He decides to give it a try. He mixes together some tap water, a stool sample from his dog and urine samples from his wife and daughter. To top it off, he masturbates into the concoction.

He goes back to the chemist, locates the machine, pours in the sample and deposits the $10. The computer again makes the noise and prints out the following message: 'Your tap water is too hard. Get a water softener. Your dog has worms. Get him vitamins. Your daughter is using cocaine. Put her in a rehabilitation clinic. Your wife is pregnant with twin girls. They aren't yours. Get a lawyer. And if you don't stop jerking off, your tennis elbow will never get better.'

An artist, a lawyer, and a computer scientist are discussing the merits of a mistress. The artist tells of the passion and the thrill which comes with the risk of being discovered. The lawyer warns of the difficulties. It can lead to guilt, divorce and bankruptcy. Not worth it. Too many problems.

The computer scientist says, 'It's the best thing that's ever happened to me. My wife thinks I'm with my mistress.

My mistress thinks I'm home with my wife, and I can spend all night on the computer.'

Three women are sitting around talking about their husbands' performances as lovers.

The first woman says, 'My husband works as a marriage counsellor. He always buys me flowers and candy before we make love. I like that.'

The second woman says, 'My husband is a motorcycle mechanic. He likes to play rough and spank me sometimes. I kind of like that.'

The third woman just shakes her head and says, 'My husband works for Microsoft. He just sits on the edge of the bed and tells me how great it's going to be when I get it.'

There are three engineers in a car: an electrical engineer, a chemical engineer and a Microsoft engineer. Suddenly the car just stops by the side of the road, and the three engineers look at each other wondering what can be wrong.

The electrical engineer suggests stripping down the electronics of the car and trying to trace where a fault might have occurred.

The chemical engineer, not knowing much about cars, suggests that the fuel might be becoming emulsified and getting blocked somewhere.

Then, the Microsoft engineer, not knowing much about anything, comes up with a suggestion, 'Why don't we close all the windows, get out, get back in, open the windows again, and maybe it'll work!'

An engineer, a manager and a programmer are driving down a steep mountain road. The brakes fail and the car careens down the road out of control. Halfway down, the driver manages to stop the car by running it against the embankment, narrowly avoiding a cliff. They all get out, shaken by their close escape from death, but otherwise unharmed.

The manager says, 'To fix this problem we need to organise a committee, have meetings, and through a process of continuous improvement, develop a solution.'

The engineer says, 'No that would take too long, and besides that method has never worked before. I have my trusty pen-knife here and I will take apart the brake system, isolate the problem and correct it.'

The programmer says, 'I think you're both wrong. I think we should all push the car back up the hill and see if it happens again.'

A man walks into a Silicon Valley pet store looking for a monkey. The storeowner points towards three identical-looking monkeys in politically correct, animal-friendly natural mini-habitats.

'The one to the left costs $500,' says the storeowner.

'Why so much?' asks the customer.

'Because it can program in C,' answers the storeowner.

The customer inquires about the next monkey and is told, 'That one costs $1500, because it knows Visual C++ and object-relational technology.'

The startled man then asks about the third monkey.

'That one costs $3000,' answers the storeowner.

'$3000!' exclaims the man. 'What can that one do?'

The owner replies, 'To be honest, I've never seen it do a single thing, but it calls itself a consultant.'

Reaching the end of a job interview, the human resources person asks the young programmer, 'And what starting salary were you looking for?'

The programmer says, 'In the neighbourhood of $75 000 a year, depending on the benefits package.'

The HR person says, 'Well, what would you say to a package of five weeks vacation, fourteen paid holidays, full medical and dental, company-matching superannuation funding to 50% of salary, and a company car leased every two years, say, a red Corvette?'

The programmer sits up straight and says, 'Wow! Are you kidding?'

The HR Person says, 'Certainly, but you started it.'

Young Susie is having trouble with her computer so she calls Wes, the computer guy, over to her desk. Wes clicks a couple of buttons and solves the problem.

As he is walking away Susie calls after him, 'So, what was wrong?'

He replies, 'It was an "ID ten T" error.'

A puzzled expression runs over Susie's face.

'An "ID ten T" error? What's that, in case I need to fix it again?'

He gives her a grin. 'Haven't you ever seen an "ID ten T" error before?'

Susie replies, 'No.'

'Write it down,' he says, 'and I think you'll work it out.'

I D 1 0 T

Jesus and Satan have a discussion as to who is the better programmer. This goes on for a few hours until they come to an agreement to hold a contest, with God as the judge.

They sit themselves at their computers and begin. They both

type furiously, lines of code streaming up the screen, for several hours straight. Seconds before the end of the competition, a bolt of lightning strikes, taking out the electricity. Moments later, the power is restored, and God announces that the contest is over.

He asks Satan to show what he has come up with. Satan is visibly upset, and cries, 'I have nothing. I lost it all when the power went out.'

'Very well, then,' says God, 'let us see if Jesus fared any better.'

Jesus enters a command, and the screen comes to life in a vivid display, the voices of an angelic choir pour forth from the speakers. Satan is astonished.

He stutters, 'B-b-but how? I lost everything, yet Jesus' program is intact. How did he do it?'

God smiles all-knowingly, 'Jesus saves.'

A computer programmer happens across a frog in the road. The frog pipes up, 'I'm really a beautiful princess and if you kiss me, I'll stay with you for a week.'

The programmer shrugs his shoulders and puts the frog in his pocket.

A few minutes later, the frog says, 'OK, OK, if you kiss me, I'll give you great sex for a week.'

The programmer nods and puts the frog back in his pocket.

A few minutes later, 'Turn me back into a princess and I'll give you great sex for a whole year!'

The programmer smiles and walks on.

Finally, the frog says, 'What's wrong with you? I've promised you great sex for a year from a beautiful princess and you won't even kiss a frog?'

'I'm a programmer,' he replies. 'I don't have time for sex. But a talking frog is pretty neat.'

How many internet mail list subscribers does it take to change a light bulb?

1331:

- One to change the light bulb and post to the mail list that the light bulb has been changed.
- Fourteen to share similar experiences of changing light bulbs and how the light bulb could have been changed differently.
- Seven to caution about the dangers of changing light bulbs.
- Twenty seven to point out spelling and grammar errors in posts about changing light bulbs.
- Fifty three to flame the spell checkers.
- One hundred and fifty six to write to the list administrator complaining about the light bulb discussion and its inappropriateness to this mail list.
- Forty one to correct spelling in the spelling and grammar flames.
- One hundred and nine to post that this list is not about light bulbs and to please take this email exchange to alt.lite.bulb.
- Two hundred and three to demand that cross-posting to alt.grammar, alt.spelling and alt.punctuation about changing light bulbs be stopped.
- One hundred and eleven to defend the posting to this list, saying that we are all use light bulbs and therefore the posts *are* relevant to this mail list.
- Three hundred and six to debate which method of changing light bulbs is superior, where to buy the best light bulbs, what brand of light bulbs work best for this technique, and what brands are faulty.
- Twenty seven to post URLs where one can see examples of different light bulbs.
- Fourteen to post that the URLs were posted incorrectly, and to post corrected URLs.
- Three to post links they found from the URLs that are relevant to this list which makes light bulbs relevant to this list.

- Thirty three to concatenate all posts to date, then quote them including all headers and footers, and then add 'Me too.'
- Twelve to post to the list that they are unsubscribing because they cannot handle the light bulb controversy.
- Nineteen to quote the 'Me toos' to say, 'Me three.'
- Four to suggest that posters request the light bulb FAQ.
- One to propose a new alt.change.lite.bulb newsgroup.
- Forty seven to say this is just what alt.physic.cold_fusion was meant for, leave it there.

DR SEUSS EXPLAINS COMPUTERS

If a packet hits a pocket on a socket on a port
and the bus is interrupted as a very last resort
and the address of the memory makes your floppy disk abort
then the socket packet pocket has an error to report.

If your cursor finds a menu item followed by a dash and
the double-clicking icon puts your window in the trash
and your data is corrupted 'cause the index doesn't hash
then the situation's hopeless and your systems gonna crash!

If the label on the cable on the table at your house says the
network is connected to the button on your mouse
but your packets want to tunnel on another protocol
that's repeatedly rejected by the printer down the hall
and your screen is all distorted by the side effects of gauss
so your icons in the window are as wavy as a souse
then you may as well reboot and get the hell out with a bang
'cause as sure as I'm a poet, the sucker's gonna hang!

When the copy of your floppy's getting sloppy on the disk
and the microcode instructions cause unnecessary risk

then you have to flash your memory and you'll want to RAM
   your ROM
quickly turn off the computer and be sure to tell your mum.

TWELVE STEP PROGRAM OF RECOVERY FOR WEB ADDICTS

1. I will have a cup of coffee in the morning and read my
   paper newspaper like I used to, before the Web.

2. I will eat breakfast with a knife and fork and not with one
   hand typing.

3. I will get dressed before noon.

4. I will make an attempt to clean the house, wash clothes, and
   plan dinner before even thinking of the Web.

5. I will sit down and write a longhand letter to those
   unfortunate few friends and family that are
   Web-deprived.

6. I will call someone on the phone who I cannot contact via
   the Web.

7. I will read a book . . . if I still remember how.

8. I will listen to those around me talk about their needs and
   stop telling them to turn the TV down so I can hear the
   music on the Web.

9. I will not be tempted during TV commercials to check for
   email.

10. I will try and get out of the house at least once a week, if it is necessary or not.

11. I will remember that my bank is not forgiving if I forget to balance my cheque-book because I was too busy on the Web.

12. Last, but not least, I will remember that I must go to bed sometime . . . and the Web will always be there tomorrow!

At a computer expo, Bill Gates compares the computer industry with the auto industry and states, 'If GM had kept up with technology like the computer industry has, we would all be driving $25 cars that got 100km to the litre.'

General Motors addresses this comment by releasing the statement, 'Yes, but would you want your car to crash twice a day?'

Furthermore:
- Every time they repainted the lines on the road you would have to buy a new car.
- Occasionally your car would die on the freeway for no reason, and you would just accept this, restart and drive on.
- Occasionally, executing a manoeuvre would cause your car to stop and fail and you would have to re-install the engine. For some strange reason, you would accept this too.
- You could only have one person in the car at a time, unless you bought 'Car95' or 'CarNT'. But, then you would have to buy more seats.
- Macintosh would make a car that was powered by the sun, was reliable, five times as fast, twice as easy to drive, but would only run on five percent of the roads.
- The Macintosh car-owners would get expensive Microsoft upgrades for their cars, which would make their cars run much slower.

- The oil, gas and alternator warning lights would be replaced by a single General Car Default warning light.
- New seats would force everyone to have the same size arse.
- The airbag system would say, 'Are you sure?' before going off.

IF RESTAURANTS FUNCTIONED LIKE MICROSOFT

Patron: Waiter!

Waiter: Hi, my name is Bill, and I'll be your Support. What seems to be the problem?

Patron: There's a fly in my soup!

Waiter: Try again, maybe the fly won't be there this time.

Patron: No, it's still there.

Waiter: Maybe it's the way you're using the soup; try eating it with a fork instead.

Patron: Even when I use the fork, the fly is still there.

Waiter: Maybe the soup is incompatible with the bowl; what kind of bowl are you using?

Patron: A *soup* bowl!

Waiter: Hmmm, that should work. Maybe it's a configuration problem; how was the bowl set up?

Patron: You brought it to me on a saucer; what has that to do with the fly in my soup?

Waiter: Can you remember everything you did before you noticed the fly in your soup?

Patron: I sat down and ordered the Soup of the Day!

Waiter: Have you considered upgrading to the latest Soup of the Day?

Patron: You have more than one Soup of the Day each day?

Waiter: Yes, the Soup of the Day is changed every hour.

Patron: Well, what is the Soup of the Day now?

Waiter: The current Soup of the Day is tomato.

Patron: Fine. Bring me the tomato soup, and the bill. I'm running late now.

Waiter leaves and returns with another bowl of soup and the bill.

Waiter: Here you are, Sir. The soup and your bill.

Patron: This is potato soup.

Waiter: Yes, the tomato soup wasn't ready yet.

Patron: Well, I'm so hungry now, I'll eat anything.

Waiter leaves.

Patron: Waiter! There's a gnat in my soup!

The bill:

Soup of the Day – $5.00

Upgrade to newer Soup of the Day – $2.50

Access to support – $1.00

IS YOUR COMPUTER MALE OR FEMALE? YOU DECIDE!

The top five reasons computers must be female:

1. No-one but their creator understands their logic.
2. Even your smallest mistakes are immediately committed to memory for future reference.
3. The native language used to communicate with other computers is incomprehensible to everyone else.
4. The message, 'bad command or filename', is about as informative as 'If you don't know why I'm mad at you, then I'm certainly not going to tell you.'
5. As soon as you make a commitment to one, you find yourself spending half your pay cheque on accessories for it.

The top five reasons computers must be male:

1. They have a lot of data, but are still clueless.
2. They are supposed to help you solve problems, but half the time they *are* the problem.
3. As soon as you commit to one you realise that, if you had waited a little longer, you could have obtained a better model.
4. In order to get their attention, they have to be turned on.
5. Big power surges knock them out for the rest of the night.

WHAT IF PEOPLE BOUGHT CARS LIKE THEY BOUGHT COMPUTERS?

Helpline: General Motors Helpline, how can I help you?
Customer: I got in my car and closed the door, and nothing happened!
Helpline: Did you put the key in the ignition slot and turn it?
Customer: What's an ignition?
Helpline: It's a starter motor that draws current from your battery and turns over the engine.
Customer: Ignition? Motor? Battery? Engine? How come I have to know all of these technical terms just to use my car?

Helpline: General Motors Helpline, how can I help you?
Customer: My car ran fine for a week, and now it won't go anywhere!
Helpline: Is the petrol tank empty?
Customer: Huh? How do I know?
Helpline: There's a little gauge on the front panel, with a needle, and markings from 'E' to 'F'. Where is the needle pointing?

Customer:	It's pointing to 'E.' What does that mean?
Helpline:	It means that you have to visit a petrol station, and buy some more petrol.
Customer:	What!? I paid $12 000 for this car! Now you tell me that I have to keep buying more components? I want a car that comes with everything built in!

Helpline:	General Motors Helpline, how can I help you?
Customer:	Your car sucks!
Helpline:	What's wrong?
Customer:	It crashed, that's what went wrong!
Helpline:	What were you doing?
Customer:	I wanted it to run faster, so I pushed the accelerator pedal all the way to the floor. It worked for a while, and then it crashed – and now it won't start!
Helpline:	It's your responsibility if you misuse the product. What do you expect us to do about it?
Customer:	I want you to send me one of the latest versions that doesn't crash anymore!

Helpline:	General Motors Helpline, how can I help you?
Customer:	Hi! I just bought my first car, and I chose your car because it has automatic transmission, cruise control, power steering, power brakes, and power door-locks.
Helpline:	Thanks for buying our car. How can I help you?
Customer:	How do I work it?
Helpline:	Do you know how to drive?
Customer:	Do I know how to what?
Helpline:	Do you know how to drive?
Customer:	I'm not a technical person! I just want to go places in my car!

ACCOUNTANTS AND THEIR ILK

Finding humour in accountants is like drawing water from a stone. Only harder. Here are a few attempts.

Two accountants are in a bank, when armed robbers burst in. While several of the robbers take the money from the tellers, others line up the customers, including the accountants, against a wall, and proceed to take their wallets, watches, etc. While this is going on, one of the accountants stuffs something into the other accountant's hand.

Without looking down, the accountant whispers, 'What's this?'

The other accountant replies, 'It's that $50 I owe you.'

An accountant is having a hard time sleeping and goes to see his doctor. 'Doctor, I just can't get to sleep at night.'

'Have you tried counting sheep?'

'That's the problem. I make a mistake and then spend three hours trying to find it.'

A patient is at her doctor's office after undergoing a complete physical exam. The doctor says, 'I have some very grave news for you. You only have six months to live.'

The patient asks, 'Oh doctor, what should I do?'

The doctor replies, 'Marry an accountant.'

'Will that make me live longer?' asks the patient.

'No,' says the doctor, 'but it will *seem* longer.'

Why do accountants make good lovers?
They're great with figures.

Why don't accountants read novels?
Because the only numbers in them are page numbers.

If an accountant's wife cannot sleep, what does she say?
'Darling, could you tell me about your work?'

A fifty-four-year-old accountant leaves a letter for his wife one evening which reads: 'Dear Wife, I am fifty-four years old, and by the time you get this letter I will be at the Grand Hotel with my beautiful and sexy, eighteen-year-old secretary.'

When he arrives at the hotel, there's a letter waiting for him that reads as follows: 'Dear Husband, I too am fifty-four years old, and by the time you receive this letter I will be at the Savoy Hotel with my eighteen-year-old toy boy. Because you are an accountant, you will surely appreciate that eighteen goes into fifty-four many more times than fifty-four goes into eighteen.'

A business owner tells her friend that she is desperately searching for an accountant.

Her friend asks, 'Didn't your company hire an accountant a short while ago?'

The business owner replies, 'That's the accountant I've been searching for.'

A business owner is interviewing people for a management position. He decides to select the individual that can answer the question, 'How much is two plus two?'

The engineer pulls out his slide rule and shuffles it back and forth, and finally announces, 'It lies between 3.98 and 4.02.'

The mathematician says, 'In two hours I can demonstrate it equals four with the following short proof.'

The physicist declares, 'It's in the magnitude of 1×101.'

The logician pauses for a long while and then says, 'This problem is solvable.'

The social worker says, 'I don't know the answer, but I'm glad that we discussed this important question.

The attorney states, 'In the case of Svenson vs the State, two plus two was declared to be four.'

The trader asks, 'Are you buying or selling?'

The accountant looks at the business owner, then gets out of his chair, goes to see if anyone is listening at the door, and pulls the drapes. Then he returns to the business owner, leans across the desk and says in a low voice, 'What would you like it to be?'

A young accountant spends a week at his new office with the retiring accountant he is replacing. Each and every morning, as the more experienced accountant begins the day, he opens his desk drawer, takes out a worn envelope, removes a yellowing sheet of paper, reads it, nods his head, looks around the room with renewed vigour, returns the envelope to the drawer, then begins his day's work.

After the old accountant has retired, the new accountant can hardly wait to read for himself the message contained in the envelope in the drawer, particularly since he feels unworthy to be replacing such a wise, highly esteemed accountant.

'Surely,' he thinks to himself, 'it must contain the great secret to his success, a wondrous treasure of inspiration and motivation.'

His fingers tremble anxiously as he removes the mysterious envelope from the drawer and reads the following message:

'Debits in the column toward the file cabinet.

Credits in the column toward the window.'

Three engineers and three accountants are travelling by train to a conference. At the station, the three accountants each buy a ticket and watch as the three engineers only buy one ticket.

'How are three people going to travel on only one ticket?' asks an accountant.

'Watch and you'll see,' answers an engineer.

They all board the train. The accountants take their respective seats but all three engineers cram into a rest room and close the door behind them. Shortly after the train has departed, the conductor comes around collecting tickets.

He knocks on the toilet door and says, 'Tickets, please!'

The door opens just a crack and a single arm emerges with a ticket in hand. The conductor takes it and moves on. The accountants see this and agree it is a clever idea.

So after the conference, the accountants decide to copy the engineers on the return trip and save some money. When they get to the station, they buy one ticket for the return trip. To their astonishment, the engineers don't buy a ticket at all.

'How are you going to travel without a ticket?' asks one perplexed accountant.

'Watch and you'll see,' answers an engineer.

When they board the train all three accountants cram into a toilet and the three engineers cram into another one nearby. The train departs. Shortly afterward, one of the engineers leaves his toilet and walks over to the toilet where the accountants are hiding.

He knocks on the door and says, 'Tickets, please!'

FUNNY NEWSPAPER HEADLINES

SOMETHING WENT WRONG IN JET CRASH, EXPERT SAYS

POLICE BEGIN CAMPAIGN TO RUN DOWN JAYWALKERS

DRUNK GETS NINE MONTHS IN VIOLIN CASE

IRAQI HEAD SEEKS ARMS

IS THERE A RING OF DEBRIS AROUND URANUS?

PROSTITUTES APPEAL TO POPE

PANDA MATING FAILS; VETERINARIAN TAKES OVER

INCLUDE YOUR CHILDREN WHEN BAKING COOKIES

CLINTON WINS ON BUDGET, BUT MORE LIES AHEAD

PLANE TOO CLOSE TO GROUND, CRASH PROBE TOLD

MINERS REFUSE TO WORK AFTER DEATH

JUVENILE COURT TO TRY SHOOTING DEFENDANT

STOLEN PAINTING FOUND BY TREE

TWO SISTERS REUNITED AFTER 18 YEARS AT CHECK-OUT COUNTER

WAR DIMS HOPE FOR PEACE

IF STRIKE ISN'T SETTLED QUICKLY, IT MAY LAST A WHILE

COLD WAVE LINKED TO TEMPERATURES

ENFIELDS COUPLE SLAIN; POLICE SUSPECT HOMICIDE

RED TAPE HOLDS UP NEW BRIDGES

TYPHOON RIPS THROUGH CEMETERY; HUNDREDS DEAD

KIDS MAKE NUTRITIOUS SNACKS

NEW VACCINE MAY CONTAIN RABIES

MAN STRUCK BY LIGHTNING FACES BATTERY CHARGE

NEWSPAPER HEADLINES WITH DOUBLE MEANINGS

MARCH PLANNED FOR NEXT AUGUST

LA VOTERS APPROVE URBAN RENEWAL BY LANDSLIDE

PATIENT AT DEATH'S DOOR – DOCTORS PULL HIM THROUGH

QUEEN MARY HAVING BOTTOM SCRAPED

KILLER SENTENCED TO DIE FOR SECOND TIME IN 10 YEARS

NEVER WITHHOLD HERPES INFECTION FROM LOVED ONE

IT'S ALL IN THE MIND

*I've never fully understood the difference between a
psychologist, a psychiatrist and a therapist. All I know
is that they're all obsessed by sex. Hey! Who ain't?*

A man goes to a psychologist and says, 'I got a real problem,
I can't stop thinking about sex.'

The psychologist says, 'Well let's see what we can find out.'

He pulls out his ink blots. 'What is this a picture of?' he asks.

The man turns the picture upside down then turns it around
and states, 'That's a man and a woman on a bed making love.'

The psychologist says, 'Very interesting,' and shows him the
next picture. 'And what is this a picture of?'

The man looks and turns it in different directions and says,
'That's a man and a woman on a bed making love.'

The psychologist tries again with a third ink blot, and asks
the same question, 'What is this a picture of?'

The patient again turns it in all directions and replies, 'That's
a man and a woman on a bed making love.'

The psychologist states, 'Well, yes, you do seem to be
obsessed with sex.'

'Me?' demands the patient. 'You're the one who keeps
showing me the dirty pictures.'

A young woman takes her troubles to a psychiatrist.
'Doctor, you must help me,' she pleads. 'It's gotten so that
every time I date a nice guy, I end up in bed with him. And then
afterwards, I feel guilty and depressed for a week.'

'I see,' nods the psychiatrist. 'And you, no doubt, want me to strengthen your will power and resolve in this matter.'

'For God's sake, no!' exclaims the woman. 'I want you to fix it so I won't feel guilty and depressed afterwards.'

When the new patient is settled comfortably on the couch, the psychiatrist begins his therapy session.

'I'm not aware of your problem,' the doctor says. 'So perhaps, you should start at the very beginning.'

'Of course,' replies the patient. 'In the beginning, I created the heavens and the earth . . .'

In a psychiatrist's waiting room two patients are having a conversation.

One says to the other, 'Why are you here?'

The second answers, 'I'm Napoleon, so the doctor told me to come here.'

The first is curious and asks, 'How do you know that you're Napoleon?'

The second responds, 'God told me I was.'

At this point, a patient on the other side of the room shouts, 'No I didn't!'

Joe has been seeing a psychoanalyst for four years to treat his fear of monsters under his bed. It has been years since he has had a good night's sleep. Furthermore, his progress is very poor, and he knows it. So, one day he stops seeing the psychoanalyst and decides to try something different.

A few weeks later, Joe's former psychoanalyst meets his old client in the supermarket, and is surprised to find him looking well-rested, energetic, and cheerful.

'Doc!' Joe says, 'It's amazing! I'm cured!'

'That's great news!' the psychoanalyst says. 'You seem to be doing much better. How?'

'I went to see another doctor,' Joe says enthusiastically, 'and he cured me in just *one* session.'

'One?' the psychoanalyst asks incredulously.

'Yeah,' continues Joe, 'my new doctor is a behaviourist.'

'A behaviourist?' the psychoanalyst asks. 'How did he cure you in one session?'

'Oh, easy,' says Joe. 'He told me to cut the legs off of my bed.'

A distraught man goes to see a psychologist.

'How may I help you?' the therapist asks.

'Every night I have the same dream. I'm lying in bed and a dozen women walk in and try to rip my clothes off and have wild sex with me.'

'And then what do you do?' the psychologist asks.

'I push them away,' the man says.

'Then what do you want me to do?' the psychologist asks.

'Break my arms!'

A psychiatrist is conducting a group therapy session with three young mothers and their small children.

'You all have obsessions,' he observes.

To the first mother he says, 'You are obsessed with eating. You've even named your daughter Candy.'

He turns to the second mum. 'Your obsession is money. Again, it manifests itself in your child's name, Penny.'

At this point, the third mother gets up, takes her little boy by the hand and whispers, 'Come on, Dick, let's go.'

Jim has suffered from bedwetting for most of his life. Even now, as a married man, he still wets his bed. Finally his wife has all she can take and orders him out of the house until he is cured. Jim goes to the doctor, who advises him to see a psychiatrist since his chronic bed-wetting is probably due to a mental or emotional disorder. About three weeks later, he returns home wearing a cheerful face.

His wife meets him at the door and cries, 'Honey, you look so happy, are you cured?'

'Nope,' replies Jim, 'but now when I wet the bed, I'm proud.'

A psychiatrist visits a California mental institution and asks a patient, 'How did you get here? What was the nature of your illness?'

The patient replies, 'Well, it all started when I got married and I guess I should never have done that. I married a widow with a grown daughter who then became my stepdaughter. My dad came to visit us, fell in love with my lovely stepdaughter, then married her. And so my stepdaughter was now my stepmother. Soon, my wife had a son who was, of course, my daddy's brother-in-law since he is the half-brother of my stepdaughter, who is now, of course, my daddy's wife. So, as I told you, when my stepdaughter married my daddy, she was at once my stepmother. Now, since my new son is brother to my stepmother, he also became my uncle. As you know, my wife is my step-grandmother since she is my stepmother's mother. Don't forget that my stepmother is my stepdaughter. Remember, too, that I am my wife's grandson. But hold on just a few minutes more. You see, since I'm married to my step-grandmother, I am not only the wife's grandson and her hubby, but I am also my own grandfather. Now can you understand how I got put in this place?'

After staring blankly with a dizzy look on his face, the psychiatrist replies, 'Move over!'

A wife goes to see a therapist and says, 'I've got a big problem, doctor. Every time we're in bed and my husband climaxes, he lets out an ear-splitting yell.'

'My dear,' the doctor says, 'that's completely natural. I don't see what the problem is.'

'The problem is,' she complains, 'It wakes me up!'

THE BANKING SECTOR

I only just found out that the word 'banker' is a real term. I always thought it was rhyming slang.

A little old lady goes into a bank one day, carrying a bag of money. She asks to speak with the bank manager to open an account. The staff usher her into the manager's office and the manager asks how much she wants to deposit.

She replies, '$165 000!' and dumps the cash on his desk.

The manager is curious as to how she came by all this cash, so he asks her, 'Ma'am, where did you get this money?'

The old lady replies, 'I make bets.'

The manager then asks, 'Bets? What kind of bets?'

The old woman says, 'Well, for example, I'll bet you $25 000 that your balls are square.'

'Ha!' laughs the manager, 'That's a stupid bet. You can never win that kind of bet!'

The old lady challenges, 'So, would you like to take my bet?'

'Sure,' says the manager, 'I'll bet $25 000 that my balls are not square!'

The old lady says, 'OK, but since there is a lot of money involved, may I bring my lawyer with me tomorrow at 10 a.m. as a witness?'

'Sure!' replies the confident manager.

That night, he is very nervous about the bet and often checks his balls in the mirror. The next morning, at precisely 10 a.m., the little old lady appears with her lawyer at the manager's office. She introduces the lawyer to the manager and repeats the bet, '$25 000 says the manager's balls are square.'

The manager agrees with the bet again and the old lady asks him to drop his pants so they can all see. The manager complies. The little old lady peers closely at his balls and then asks if she can feel them.

'Well, OK,' says the manager, 'I suppose $25 000 is a lot of money, so you should be absolutely sure.'

Just then, he notices that the lawyer is quietly banging his head against the wall. The manager says, 'What's wrong with your lawyer?'

She replies, 'Nothing, except I bet him $100 000 that at 10 a.m. today, I'd have the bank manager's balls in my hand!'

A guy walks into a bank and says to the teller at the window, 'I want to open a bloody cheque account.'

The teller replies, 'I beg your pardon, what did you say?'

'Listen up dammit, I said I want to open a bloody cheque account right now.'

'Sir, I'm sorry but we do not tolerate that kind of language in this bank.'

The teller leaves the window and goes over to the bank manager and tells him about her situation. They both return and the manager asks, 'What seems to be the problem here?'

'There's no damn problem,' the man says, 'I just won $50 million in the lottery and I want to open a bloody cheque account in this damn bank!'

'I see Sir,' the manager says, 'and this bitch is giving you a hard time?'

J ohn Paul Getty once said 'If you owe the bank $100, that's your problem. If you owe the bank $100 million, that's the bank's problem.'

Einstein dies and goes to heaven only to be informed that his room is not yet ready.

'I hope you will not mind waiting in a dormitory. We are very sorry, but it's the best we can do and you will have to share the room with others.'

Einstein says that this is no problem at all and that there is no need to make such a great fuss. So the doorman leads him to the dorm. They enter and Albert is introduced to all of the present inhabitants.

'See, here is your first room mate. He has an IQ of 180.'

'That's wonderful!' says Albert. 'We can discuss mathematics.'

'And here is your second room mate. His IQ is 150.'

'That's wonderful!' says Albert. 'We can discuss physics.'

'And here is your third room mate. His IQ is 100.'

'That's wonderful! We can discuss the latest plays at the theatre.'

Just then another man moves out to capture Albert's hand and shake it.

'I'm your last room mate and I'm sorry, but my IQ is only 80.'

Albert smiles back at him and says, 'So, where do you think interest rates are headed?'

At a country-club party a young man is introduced to an attractive girl. Immediately he begins paying her court and flattering her outrageously. The girl likes the young man, but she is taken aback by his fast and ardent pitch. She is amazed when after thirty minutes he seriously proposes marriage.

'Look,' she says. 'We only met half an hour ago. How can you be so sure? We know nothing about each other.'

'You're wrong,' the young man declares. 'For the past five years I've been working in the bank where your father has his account.'

A young banker decides to get his first tailor-made suit. So he goes to the finest tailor in town and gets measured. A week later he goes in for his first fitting. He puts on the suit and he looks stunning, he feels that in this suit he can really do business.

As he is preening himself in front of the mirror, he reaches down to put his hands in the pockets and to his surprise he finds that there are no pockets. He mentions this to the tailor.

'Didn't you tell me you were a banker?' the tailor asks.

The young man answers, 'Yes, I did.'

The tailor says, 'Who ever heard of a banker with his hands in his own pockets?'

A man walks into a New York City bank and says he wants to borrow $2000 for three weeks. The loan officer asks him what kind of collateral he has. The man says, 'I've got a Rolls Royce – keep it until the loan is paid off. Here are the keys.'

The loan officer promptly has the car driven into the bank's underground parking for safe keeping, and gives the man $2000.

Three weeks later the man comes into the bank, pays back the $2000 loan, plus $10 interest, and regains possession of the Rolls Royce.

The loan officer asks him, 'Sir, if I may ask, why would a man who drives a Rolls Royce need to borrow $2000?'

The man answers, 'I had to go to Europe for three weeks, and where else could I store a Rolls Royce for that long for $10?'

Jones applies to a finance agency for a job, but he has no experience. He is so intense that the manager gives him a tough account with the promise that if he collects all the money owing on it, he'll get the job.

Two hours later, Jones comes back with the entire amount.

'Amazing,' the manager says. 'How did you do it?'

'Easy,' Jones replies. 'I told him if he didn't pay up, I'd tell all his other creditors that he paid us.'

HIS AND HERS ATM MACHINES

HIS:
1. Pull up to ATM
2. Insert card
3. Enter PIN and account
4. Take cash, card and receipt
5. Drive away

HERS:
1. Pull up to ATM
2. Back up and pull forward to get closer
3. Shut off engine
4. Put keys in purse
5. Get out of car because you're too far from machine
6. Hunt for card in purse
7. Insert card
8. Hunt in purse for grocery receipt with PIN written on it
9. Enter PIN
10. Study instructions
11. Hit cancel
12. Re-enter correct PIN
13. Check balance
14. Look for envelope
15. Look in purse for pen
16. Make out deposit slip
17. Endorse cheques
18. Make deposit
19. Study instructions

20. Make cash withdrawal
21. Get in car
22. Check make-up
23. Look for keys
24. Start car
25. Check make-up
26. Start pulling away
27. Stop
28. Back up to machine
29. Get out of car
30. Take card and receipt
31. Get back in car
32. Put card in wallet
33. Put receipt in cheque-book
34. Enter deposits and withdrawals in cheque-book
35. Clear area in purse for wallet and cheque-book
36. Check make-up
37. Put car in reverse
38. Put car in drive
39. Drive away from machine
40. Drive 3km
41. Release parking brake

THINGS YOU WOULD *NOT* WANT TO SEE HAPPEN AT THE ATM

- You go to get a balance inquiry, and instead of printing out a receipt the screen says, 'Not worth wasting paper' and ejects your card.

- You try to get a balance inquiry, and the screen says, 'Account not found' and keeps your card.

- You insert your card, and try to get some cash, and the ATM laughs and spits out your shredded card.

- You withdraw some money to pay some bills, count it, and the screen says, 'What, you thought there was some *extra* there? Ha!' and ejects your card clear across the room.

- You think you've got $100 in your account and go to take out $50, and the screen says, 'Not in this lifetime,' then laughs as you bang on the machine, trying desperately to get back the card that the machine has taken.

- You go to the ATM, and there's a 'Most Wanted'-type picture of you with a caption that reads, 'Wanted for trying to get water from a dry well.'

FUNNY SIGNS SEEN IN GREAT BRITAIN

IN A LAUNDROMAT: Automatic washing machines. Please remove all your clothes when the light goes out.

IN A LONDON DEPARTMENT STORE: Bargain Basement Upstairs.

IN AN OFFICE: Would the person who took the step ladder yesterday kindly bring it back or further steps will be taken.

IN ANOTHER OFFICE: After the tea break, staff should empty the teapot and stand upside down on the draining board.

ON A CHURCH DOOR: This is the gate of heaven. Enter ye all by this door. (This door is kept locked because of the draft. Please use side entrance.)

OUTSIDE A SECOND-HAND SHOP: We exchange anything – bicycles, washing machines etc. Why not bring your wife along and get a wonderful bargain?

QUICKSAND WARNING: Quicksand. Any person passing this point will be drowned. By order of the District Council.

NOTICE IN A DRY CLEANER'S WINDOW: Anyone leaving their garments here for more than thirty days will be disposed of.

IN A HEALTH FOOD SHOP WINDOW: Closed due to illness.

SPOTTED IN A SAFARI PARK: Elephants – please stay in your car.

SEEN DURING A CONFERENCE: For anyone who has children and doesn't know it, there is a day care on the first floor.

NOTICE IN A FIELD: The farmer allows walkers to cross the field for free, but the bull charges.

MESSAGE ON A LEAFLET: If you cannot read, this leaflet will tell you how to get lessons.

ON A REPAIR SHOP DOOR: We can repair anything (Please knock hard on the door – the bell doesn't work.)

SPOTTED IN A TOILET IN A LONDON OFFICE BLOCK: Toilet out of order. Please use floor below.

THE MILITARY

*We're a sick society! After all, we find humour in the
subtle art of killing, maiming and bombing (so long as we're
not the ones being killed, maimed and bombed).*

An American soldier, serving in World War II, returns
from several weeks of intense action on the German
frontlines. He is granted R&R and finds himself on a train bound
for London. The train is very crowded, so the soldier walks the
length of the train, looking for an empty seat. The only
unoccupied seat is next to a well-dressed, middle-aged woman.
Actually, the seat is not technically unoccupied. It is being used
by her little dog.

The war-weary soldier asks, 'Please, Ma'am, may I sit in that
seat?'

The English woman looks down her nose at the soldier, sniffs
and says, 'You Americans. You are such a rude class of people.
Can't you see my little Fifi is using that seat?'

The soldier walks away, determined to find a place to rest, but
after another trip down to the end of the train, finds himself
again facing the woman with the dog.

Again he asks, 'Please, lady. May I sit there? I'm very tired.'

The English woman wrinkles her nose and snorts, 'You
Americans! Not only are you rude, you are also arrogant.
Imagine!'

The soldier doesn't say anything else. He just leans over, picks
up the little dog, tosses it out the window of the train and sits
down in the empty seat. The woman shrieks and demands that
someone defends her and chastises the soldier.

An English gentleman sitting across the aisle speaks up, 'You know, Sir, you Americans do seem to have a penchant for doing the wrong thing. You eat holding the fork in the wrong hand. You drive your cars on the wrong side of the road. You boil your tea to make it hot and put ice in to make it cold, a dash of lemon to make it sour and then sugar to make it sweet. And now, Sir, you've thrown the wrong bitch out of the window.'

It's the end of the Vietnam War and some Einstein in the Pentagon decides that every decorated US Marine will be presented with a specially struck medal on the tarmac of Edwards Air Force Base. But they are three short, and to cover their embarrassment, they pretend that the final three have been singled out for a special honour. Each of them is marched into the Medical Unit and advised that Uncle Sam will give them $1000 for every centimetre which lies between any two parts of their body they choose.

The first is a hulking Indiana farmer who earns enough for a new farm from the distance between the top of his head and the soles of his feet. The second, an Iowa basketball player, buys his entire team for the stretch between his armpit and the tip of his index finger.

The third is a scrawny Arkansas cotton worker who insists 'Ah wanna be measured from mah foreskin to mah balls, man.'

'Come on, soldier,' advises the supervising medic sympathetically, 'You gotta do better than that.'

But the Marine insisted, 'Ah wanna be measured from mah foreskin to the base of mah balls.'

Not wishing to upset him, they agree, and he drops his pants with a grin. The medic looks at him in amazement.

'Where are your balls, soldier?'

'Back in Vietnam.'

I suppose,' snarls the leathery sergeant to the private, 'that when you're discharged from the army, you'll wait for me to die, just so you can spit on my grave.'

'Not me,' observes the private. 'When I get out of the army, I never want to stand in line again.'

D uring camouflage training in Louisiana, a private, disguised as a tree trunk, makes a sudden move and is spotted by a visiting general.

'You simpleton!' the officer barks. 'Don't you know that by jumping and yelling the way you did, you could have endangered the lives of the entire company?'

'Yes Sir,' the solder answers apologetically. 'But, if I may say so, Sir, I did stand still when a flock of pigeons used me for target practice and I never moved a muscle when a large dog peed on my lower branches but when two squirrels ran up my pants leg and I heard the bigger one say, "Let's eat one now and save the other until winter," well that did it.'

T hree generals, one from the army, another from the marines, and a third from the air force, are having a debate with a navy admiral about whose soldiers are the bravest.

To prove his point, the air force general calls over an airman, 'Airman! Climb that flagpole, and once you are at the top, sing *Wild Blue Yonder*, and then jump off!'

'Yes Sir!' replies the airman.

He takes off for the flagpole like a shot, scales it, sings the anthem, salutes and jumps off, hitting the ground at attention. The general dismisses him.

'Now that's bravery!' exclaims the general.

'Ah, that's nothing,' says the admiral, 'Seaman!'

A seaman appears, 'Yes, Sir!'

'Take this weapon,' as he offers him an M14, 'scale that flagpole, balance yourself on top, stand at attention, present arms, and sing *Anchors Aweigh*, salute each of us, and jump off.'

'Yes Sir!' replies the seaman.

He sprints for the flagpole with the weapon high over his head, and completes the task perfectly.

'Now that's courage!' says the admiral.

'Courage, nothin',' snorts the army general. 'Get over here, private!'

'Yes Sir!' replies a private.

'Put on full combat gear, load your rucksack with these rocks, scale that flagpole, come to attention, present arms, sing the national anthem, salute each of us, and then climb back down, head first.'

'Yes Sir!' replies the private, and completes the task.

'Now that is a brave man! Beat that!'

They all look to the marine.

'Private,' he says.

'Yes Sir!'

'Put on full combat gear. Put these two dogs in your pack. Using only one hand, climb that flagpole. At the top, sing *The Halls of Montezuma* put your knife in your teeth, and dive off, headfirst.'

The private snaps to attention, looks at the general and says, 'Screw you Sir!'

The general turns to the others and says, 'Now *that's* bravery!'

It is World War III. The US has succeeded in building a computer able to solve any strategic or tactical problem. Military leaders are assembled in front of the new machine and instructed to feed difficult tactical problem into it. They describe a hypothetical situation to the computer and then ask the pivotal question: attack or retreat? The computer hums away for an hour and then comes up with the answer.

'Yes.'

The generals look at each other, somewhat stupefied. Finally one of them submits a second request to the computer.

'Yes what?'

Instantly the computer responds, 'Yes Sir!

It's 5 a.m. in the morning at the US marine boot camp, well below freezing, and the soldiers are asleep in their barracks.

The drill sergeant walks in and bellows, 'This is a birthday suit inspection! I wanna see you all formed up outside butt-naked now!'

So, the soldiers quickly jump out of bed, naked and shivering, and run outside to form up in their three ranks. The sarge walks out and yells, 'Close up the ranks, conserve your body heat!'

So they close in slightly. The captain comes along with his swagger stick. He goes to the first soldier and whacks him right across the chest with it.

'Did that hurt?' he yells.

'No, Sir!' comes the reply.

'Why not?'

'Because I'm a US marine, Sir!'

The captain is impressed, and walks on to the next man. He takes the stick and whacks the soldier right across the rear.

'Did *that* hurt?'

'No, Sir!'

'Why not?'

'Because I'm a US marine, Sir!'

Still extremely impressed, the captain walks to the third guy, and sees he has an enormous erection. Naturally, he gives his target a huge whack with the swagger stick.

'Did *that* hurt?'

'No, Sir!'

'Why not?'

'Because it belongs to the guy behind me, Sir!'

THE MORAL OF THE STORY IS . . .

Forget Satre, forget Plato, and forget Confucius. It's stories like these that teach you the real meaning of life.

A horse is stumbling home from the pub after a solid night of drinking when he falls into a huge hole by the side of the road. No matter how hard he tries, he cannot climb out. He starts to panic, knowing that Farmer Brown will be furious if he is not at work on time. Along comes a chicken.

'Hey chicken!' cries the horse. 'You have to help me. I'm pissed and I gotta get home for work or the farmer will drag me to the glue factory.'

The chick looks at the horse, then at the hole, and finally tells the horse that he is far too small to haul the horse up. He has no other choice but to leave him there. The horse suddenly has an idea.

'I've got it! Go home and get the farmer's Porsche, drive over here and tie a rope to the bumper and drag me out of this hole and home.'

The chicken agrees and sure enough, it works. A few days later, the horse is walking by the same bar and past the same hole when he finds the chicken pissed out of his head and clucking around aimlessly at the bottom of the hole.

'Hey, horse!' the chicken shouts. 'You gotta help me! I can't make it out and the farmer will chop my neck if I'm not home in the morning to give him eggs.'

The horse looks at the chicken and at the hole and admits

that although he owes him a huge favour, he couldn't possibly get down to pick him up. So the chicken tells the horse to go home and get the farmer's Porsche and come back and get him. But the horse tells the chicken that while it sounds like a great idea, he's far too big to fit in the car. The chicken starts to cry and the horse feels so badly that he begins to rack his brains to find a solution to help out the chicken, who, after all, had saved his arse. Finally, he has an idea. He stands over the hole and lets down his huge horse cock. He tells the chicken to grab on and proceeds to pull him out of the hole. The chicken gets home on time and all is well.

The moral of this story is: If you're hung like a horse; you don't need a Porsche to pick up chicks.

It's a beautiful day on the stream. A fish sees a fly hovering over the water and the fish says to himself, 'If that fly comes just five centimetres closer, I'm going to jump up, swallow it and have a great lunch.'

At the same time, a bear is hiding in the woods, watching the fish. He says to himself, 'When that fish grabs the fly I'm going to grab the fish and have a good lunch.'

Meanwhile, a hunter is watching the fly, the fish, and the bear and he says to himself, 'When that fish jumps up and the bear comes out from hiding to catch it I'm going to shoot that bear and have a nice trophy for myself.'

At the same time, a rat is watching the hunter closely. 'When he bends over to shoot the bear, I'm going to grab the sandwich out of the hunter's back pocket.'

Nearby there's a cat. The cat thinks, 'As soon the hunter bends over to shoot the bear and the rat goes for the sandwich, I'm going to jump for the rat and have myself and good lunch.'

So anyway, the fly goes five centimetres closer, the fish jumps up and catches it, the bear grabs the fish, the hunter bends over and shoots the bear, the rat grabs the sandwich from the hunter's back pocket and the cat jumps for the rat, misses it and lands in the water.

The moral of the story is: It takes a hell of a lot just to get a pussy wet.

Two bored casino dealers are waiting at a craps table. A very attractive blonde woman arrives and bets $20 000 on a single roll of the dice. She says, 'I hope you don't mind, but I feel much luckier when I'm nude.'

With that she strips from her neck down, rolls the dice and yells, 'Mama needs new clothes!'

Then she hollers, 'Yes! Yes! I won! I won!'

She jumps up and down and hugs each of the dealers. With that she picks up her winnings and her clothes and quickly departs.

The dealers just stare at each other dumbfounded. Finally, one of them asks, 'What did she roll?'

The other answers, 'I thought *you* were watching!'

Moral of the story: Not all blondes are dumb.

A non-conformist bird decides not to fly south for the winter.

He says, 'I've had enough of this flying south every winter, I'll just stay right here on this farm, what's the big deal, anyway?'

So he stays. Winter comes and is very cold. The non-conformist bird has never felt such cold weather and is afraid that he might freeze to death. Realising he has made a big mistake by staying, he heads to a nearby barn for shelter. On his way to the barn, it begins to snow. The poor bird is cold, tired and hungry.

'Why did I stay?' he asks himself as he collapses on the ground.

As he lies there covered by the snow, a cow comes by. The cow, feeling the need to relieve himself, craps right on the bird.

At first the bird is angry and says, 'Who did this horrible thing to me? How dare someone crap on me! I'll get him for this.'

The crap is too heavy for him to free himself. But, after a while the crap begins to warm him and he forgets all about his anger. In fact he is so warm that he begins to sing. A buzzard passing by overhears the singing and goes down to investigate. As he clears away the crap he finds the bird. The bird is so happy to be free from the crap that he thanks the buzzard, who then decides to eat the little bird.

The moral of this story: Just because someone craps on you, it does not make them your enemy, and just because someone gets you out of the crap, it does not make them your friend.

In a classroom of third graders, the teacher says to the kids, 'Today, class, we will be telling stories that have a moral to them.'

She explains what a moral to a story is and asks for volunteers. Little Suzie raises her hand.

'I live on a farm and we have a chicken that laid twelve eggs, we were excited to have twelve more chickens but only six of them hatched,' she says.

'That's a good story, now what is the moral?' asks the teacher.

'Don't count your chickens before they hatch.'

'Very good Suzie, anyone else?'

'Yes teacher,' says Ralphie. 'I was carrying some eggs I bought for my mum in my bicycle basket one day and I crashed my bike and all the eggs broke.'

'That's a nice story, what is the moral?'

'Don't put all your eggs in one basket.'

'Very good Ralphie, anyone else?'

'Yes teacher,' says little Johnny. 'My Aunt Karen is in the army and when she was in the Gulf War, she parachuted down with only a gun, twenty bullets, a knife, and a six-pack of beer. On her way down, she drank the six pack. When she landed, she shot twenty Iraqis and killed ten of them with her knife.'

'Very interesting, Johnny, what is the moral to your story?'

'Don't screw with Aunt Karen when she's drunk.'

A little girl is out with her grandmother when they come across a couple of dogs mating on the sidewalk.

'What are they doing, Grandma?' asks the little girl.

The grandmother is embarrassed, so she says, 'The dog on top has hurt his paw, and the one underneath is carrying him to the doctor.'

'They're just like people, aren't they Grandma?'

'How do you mean?' asks the grandmother.

'Offer someone a helping hand,' says the little girl, 'and they screw you every time!'

HOW MANY ... DOES IT TAKE TO CHANGE A LIGHT BULB?

How many Californians does it take to screw in a light bulb?
None. They screw in a hot tub.

How many psychiatrists does it take to change a light bulb?
Only one, but the light bulb has to want to change.

How many surrealist painters does it take to change a light bulb?
A fish.

How many male chauvinist pigs does it take to change a light bulb?
None. Let the bitch cook in the dark.

How many men does it take to change a light bulb?
Four. One to actually change it, and three friends to brag to about how he screwed it.

How many paranoid people do you need to change a light-bulb?
And who's asking?

How many women with PMS does it take to change a light bulb?
Six
Why?
It just does OK!

How many psychoanalysts does it take to screw in a light bulb?
How many do you think it takes?

How many Microsoft hardware engineers does it take to change a light bulb?
None, they redefine darkness as an industry standard.

How many law lecturers does it take to change a light bulb?
Hell, you need 250 just to lobby for the research grant.

How many Pentium designers does it take to screw in a light bulb?
1.99904274017, but that's close enough for non-technical people.

How many electrical engineers does it take to change a light bulb?
We don't know yet. They're still waiting on a part.

How many hardware engineers does it take to change a light bulb?
None. They'll fix it in software.

How many software engineers does it take to change a light bulb?
It's a hardware problem.

How many tech writers does it take to change a light bulb?
None. The user can work it out.

How many software developers does it take to change a light bulb?
The light bulb works fine on the system in my office.

How many Apple employees does it take to screw in a light bulb?
Seven. One to screw it in and six to design the T-shirts.

How many perverts does it take to screw in a light bulb?
One, but it takes the entire staff of the emergency room to remove it.

How many actors does it take to change a light bulb?
One hundred. One to screw it in and the other ninety-nine to say 'I could've done that!'

How many Zen masters does it take to change a light bulb?
A tree in the golden forest.

How many Los Angeles policemen does it take to break a light bulb?
We did not break it. It fell down the stairs.

How many lawyers does it take to change a light bulb? Whereas the party of the first part, also known as 'Lawyer', and the party of the second part, also known as 'Light Bulb', do hereby and forthwith agree to a transaction wherein the party of the second part (Light Bulb) shall be removed from the current position as a result of failure to perform previously agreed upon duties, i. e., the lighting, elucidation, and otherwise illumination of the area ranging from the front (north) door, through the entryway, terminating at an area just inside the primary living area, demarcated by the beginning of the carpet, any spillover illumination being at the option of the party of the second part (Light Bulb) and not required by the aforementioned agreement between the parties. The aforementioned removal transaction shall include, but not be limited to, the following steps:

1. The party of the first part (Lawyer) shall, with or without elevation at his option, by means of a chair, step stool, ladder or any other means of elevation, grasp the party of the second part (Light Bulb) and rotate the party of the second part (Light Bulb) in a counter-clockwise direction, this point being non-negotiable.
2. Upon reaching a point where the party of the second part (Light Bulb) becomes separated from the party of the third part ('Receptacle'), the party of the first part (Lawyer) shall have the option of disposing of the party of the second part (Light Bulb) in a manner consistent with all applicable state, local and federal statutes.
3. Once separation and disposal have been achieved, the party of the first part (Lawyer) shall have the option of beginning installation of the party of the fourth part ('New Light Bulb').

This installation shall occur in a manner consistent with the reverse of the procedures described in step one of this self-same document, being careful to note that the rotation should occur in a clockwise direction, this point also being non-negotiable.

Note: The above described steps may be performed, at the option of the party of the first part (Lawyer), by any or all persons authorised by him, the objective being to produce the most possible revenue for the party of the fifth part, also known as the 'Partnership'.

WE WISH YOU A MERRY CHRISTMAS

*At any other time of year, the sight of a fat, hairy man
wearing red clothes and putting children on his knee
would involve the police and, probably, a long jail
sentence. For some reason, in mid-December each year,
we not only tolerate these people, we encourage them.*

A young man wants to purchase a Christmas present for his
new sweetheart. As they have not been dating very long,
after careful consideration, he decides a pair of gloves will strike
the right note: romantic but not too personal. Accompanied by
his sweetheart's younger sister, he goes to a department store
and buys a pair of white gloves. The sister purchases a pair of
panties for herself. During the wrapping, the clerk mixes up the
items and the sister gets the gloves and the sweetheart gets the
panties. Without checking the contents, the young man seals the
package and sends it to his sweetheart with the following note:

'I chose these because I noticed that you are not in the habit
of wearing any when we go out in the evening. If it had not been
for your sister, I would have chosen the long ones with the
buttons but she wears short ones that are easier to remove. These
are a delicate shade, but the lady I bought them from showed me
the pair she had been wearing for the past three weeks and they
are hardly soiled. I had her try yours on for me and she looked
really smart. I wish I was there to put them on for you the first
time as no doubt other hands will come in contact with them
before I have a chance to see you again. When you take them off,

remember to blow in them before putting them away as they will naturally be a little damp from wearing. Just think how many times I will kiss them during the coming year!

All my love.

P.S. The latest style is to wear them folded down with a little fur showing.'

A four-year-old boy is asked to give the meal blessing before Christmas dinner. The family members bow their heads in expectation. He begins his prayer, thanking God for all his friends, naming them one by one. Then he thanks God for Mummy, Daddy, brother, sister, Grandma, Grandpa, and all his aunts and uncles. Then he begins to thank God for the food. He gives thanks for the turkey, the dressing, the fruit salad, the cranberry sauce, the pies, the cakes, even the whipped cream. Then he pauses, and everyone waits and waits.

After a long silence, the young fellow looks up at his mother and asks, 'If I thank God for the broccoli, won't he know that I'm lying?'

Santa Claus needs a vacation. He decides to go to a town where the weather is warm and the people are friendly. He also wants a break from the celebrity buzz that usually surrounds him.

However, as soon as he arrives in town, people begin to point and say, 'Look! The big red guy! Isn't he someone famous?'

Santa thinks, 'Gee, I'll never get any rest if people start asking to sit on my lap and try to tell me all the things they want.'

So he decides to disguise himself. He buys a cowboy outfit complete with cowboy boots and cowboy hat.

'No-one will know me now. I look just like everyone else,' he thinks happily.

As soon as Santa starts walking down the street, people begin to point and say, 'Look! It's that famous Christmas personality.'

Santa rushes around a corner to hide. 'It's my beard,' he thinks. 'They recognise me because of my long white beard.'

So Santa goes to a barber and has his beard shaved off.

'I really look like everybody else now,' Santa thinks.

He walks down the street with a big smile on his face. Suddenly a man shouts 'It's him! It's him! Look everybody!'

Santa can't believe it. He was sure that no-one would recognise him. So he walks up to the man and says, 'How did you recognise me?'

The man looks at Santa and says, 'You? I don't know you. But isn't that four-legged guy with the big red nose behind you Rudolph?'

Two young boys are spending the night at their grandparents the week before Christmas. At bedtime, the two boys kneel beside their beds to say their prayers when the youngest one begins praying at the top of his lungs.

'I pray for a new bicycle! I pray for a new Nintendo! I pray for a new VCR!'

His older brother leans over and nudges him, 'Why are you shouting your prayers? God isn't deaf.'

The little brother replies, 'No, but Grandma is!'

The Crist family works at a zoo. Each year they predict the general luck and overall mood of the year by watching the gnu. If the gnu's ears are forward, that means a successful, joyous year is almost certain. But if his ears are laid back flat against his head, it means that an unlucky or very unhappy year is sure to come.

One year it is young Mary's turn to survey the animal and come up with the prediction. It is her first time solo and in her excitement, she forgets to take the key to the cage. She is late in coming to check on the gnu and she sees the wrong ear position. She predicts a bad year, when in fact it is quite good. To explain the error, the local newspaper runs the following headline a year later:

MARY CRIST MISSES A HAPPY GNU'S EAR!'

Santa Claus, like all pilots, gets regular visits from the Federal Aviation Administration. When the FAA examiner arrives for Santa's pre-Christmas flight check, Santa has already made the elves wash the sled and bathe the reindeer. He has also made sure that his log book and paperwork are in order. He knows that the FAA will examine all his equipment and then put Santa's flying skills to the test.

The examiner walks slowly around the sled. He checks the reindeer harnesses, the landing gear, and even Rudolph's nose. He painstakingly reviews Santa's weight and balance calculations for the sled's enormous payload. Finally, they are ready for the test ride. Santa gets in and fastens his seat belt and shoulder harness and checks the compass. Then the examiner hops in carrying, to Santa's surprise, a shotgun.

'What's that for?' asks Santa incredulously.

The examiner winks and says, 'I'm not supposed to tell you this ahead of time, but you're gonna lose an engine on takeoff.'

A beautiful innocent young woman wants to meet Santa Claus so she puts on a robe and stays up late on Christmas Eve. Santa arrives, climbs down the chimney, and begins filling the stockings.

He is about to leave when the woman says in a sexy voice, 'Oh Santa, please stay. Keep the chill away.'

Santa replies, 'Ho ho ho, Gotta go, gotta go. Gotta get the presents to the children, you know.'

The girl drops the robe to reveal a sexy bra and panties and says in an even sexier voice, 'Oh Santa, don't run a mile; just stay for a little while . . .'

Santa begins to sweat but replies, 'Ho ho ho, gotta go, gotta go. Gotta get the presents to the children, you know.'

The girl takes off her bra and says, 'Oh Santa. Please, stay.'

Santa wipes his brow but replies, 'Ho ho ho, gotta go, gotta go. Gotta get the presents to the children, you know.'

She loses the panties and says, 'Santa, why don't you stay?'

Santa, with sweat pouring off his brow, says, 'Hey hey hey, gotta stay, gotta stay! Can't get up the chimney with my pecker this way!'

What's red and white and gives presents to good little fish on Christmas?
Sandy Claws.

Why does Santa have three gardens?
So he can hoe hoe hoe.

What do you get when you cross a snowman with a vampire?
Frostbite.

Why was Santa's little helper depressed?
Because he had low elf esteem.

What do you get when you cross an archer with a gift-wrapper?
Ribbon hood.

What do you call people who are afraid of Santa Claus?
Claustrophobic.

What do snowmen eat for breakfast?
Snowflakes.

Why did the little girl change her mind about buying her grandmother a packet of handkerchiefs for Christmas?
Because she couldn't work out what size her grandmother's nose was.

What was so good about the neurotic doll the girl was given for Christmas?
It was wound up already.

What was wrong with the brand new electric train set that the boy received for Christmas?
Forty metres of track – all straight!

A BIT OF EVERYTHING

Some things just don't fit where they're supposed to. No, that
isn't a joke. It's a description of the jokes in this section.

An old man is eating in a truck stop when three Hells Angels
bikers walk in. The first walks up to the old man, pushes
his cigarette into the old man's pie and then takes a seat at the
counter. The second walks up to the old man, spits into his
milk and takes a seat at the counter. The third walks up to
the old man, turns over his plate, and then takes a seat at the
counter. Without a word of protest, the old man quietly leaves
the diner.

Shortly thereafter, one of the bikers says to the waitress,
'Humph, not much of a man, was he?'

The waitress replies, 'Not much of a truck driver either, he
just backed his big-rig over three motorcycles.'

Six guys are playing poker when Smith loses $500 on a single
hand, clutches his chest and drops dead at the table. Showing
respect for their fallen comrade, the other five complete their
playing time standing up.

Roberts looks around and asks, 'Now, who is going to tell the
wife?'

They draw straws. Rippington, who is always a loser, picks the
short one. They tell him to be discreet and gentle, and not to
make a bad situation any worse than it is.

'Gentlemen! Discreet? I'm the most discreet man you will ever
meet. Discretion is my middle name, leave it to me.'

Rippington walks over to the Smith house and knocks on the door. The wife answers and asks what he wants.

Rippington says, 'Your husband just lost $500 playing cards.'

She hollers, 'Tell him to drop dead!'

Rippington says, 'I'll tell him.'

Jim, Joe and Harry have been going to the same pub for as long as they can remember. And never have they won anything in the monthly raffle – until now. In the latest draw, all three of them have won a prize.

Jim is the first one of the three to get his name drawn. He wins 2kg of spaghetti sauce, four boxes of noodles, and 3kg of meatballs.

Joe has his name drawn next. He gets himself a holiday on the Gold Coast, four night's accommodation at the Mermaid Inn and a pair of tickets to see the *Wilson Triplets Bikinis on Ice Show*. Joe thinks that he has died and gone to heaven.

Harry is the last one to have his name drawn, he wins a toilet brush. A month later, they compare notes on their prizes.

Jim says, 'It was fantastic. I had spaghetti for three days. It was so good, and Marge didn't have to buy food for those three days. We saved so much money.'

Joe says 'Pat was so happy when I brought home those tickets. The Gold Coast was nice, the hotel was very luxurious and the Wilson Triplets, if I didn't know better, I would swear they were sisters.'

Then Jim turns to Harry, and asks him how his prize worked out.

Harry looks at them both and says, 'That toilet brush is nice, but I think I'll go back to using paper.'

It's the spring of 1957 and Bobby goes to pick up his date. He's a pretty hip guy with his own car. When he goes to the front door, the girl's father invites him in.

'Carrie's not ready yet. Why don't you have a seat?'

Carrie's father asks Bobby what they're planning to do. Bobby replies politely that they will probably just go to the soda shop or a movie.

'Why don't you two go out and screw? I hear all the kids are doing it!'

Naturally, this comes as quite a surprise to Bobby so he asks Carrie's dad to please repeat himself.

'Yeah,' says Carrie's father, 'Carrie really likes to screw; she'll screw all night if we let her!'

A few minutes later, Carrie comes downstairs in her little poodle skirt and announces that she's ready to go. Almost breathless with anticipation, Bobby escorts his date out the front door.

About twenty minutes later, Carrie rushes back into the house, slams the door behind her, and screams at her father, 'Dad, it's called the twist!'

One morning, Mr Toad wakes up to note with alarm that his penis has turned yellow. He rushes round to the tree in which Wise Old Owl is nesting, and shows him the affected part.

'No worries,' replies the owl. 'Down the track there, second burrow to the left, you'll find Dr Rabbit. He'll fix you up.'

No sooner has the toad departed than Millie Mouse arrives under Wise Old Owl's tree with a shining pair of pink tits, and seeks the owl's advice.

'Straight down the path,' replies Owl. 'Follow the yellow-dick toad.'

A Rolls Royce and a Mini Minor are stopped side by side at the traffic lights. The Mini driver, noticing the superior look on the face of the Rolls driver, begins baiting him.

'I suppose you have a cocktail cabinet in the back?'

'Yes,' replies the Rolls driver.

'A DVD player as well, I suppose.'

'Yes.'

'Quadraphonic speakers?'

'Of course.'

'Reclining seats?'

'Naturally.'

Just then the lights turn green and as a parting shot the Mini driver shouts, 'I'll bet you don't have a double bed in there.'

The Rolls driver is devastated. He drives immediately to the Rolls dealer and demands they arrange for a double bed to be fitted. As luck would have it, a few weeks later he is driving around town when he sees the Mini parked in a side street. He screams around the corner and parks behind the Mini. As he strides up to the Mini, he notices the windows are all fogged up. He knocks on the window. A hand inside wipes a circle in the foggy window and the Mini driver peers out.

'Do you remember me?' asks the Rolls driver.

'Yes, you're the Rolls driver I talked to the other day.'

'Well,' says the Rolls driver, 'I just wanted to let you know I've had a double bed installed.'

The Mini driver sighs, shakes his head slowly and says, 'You got me out of the shower to tell me that?'

M erv informs Kev, as they survey Merv's drought-stricken stock farm, 'I'm goin' to Canberra to collect a relief cheque.'

'What route are you taking?'

'Probably the wife. After all, she stuck by me in the '74 flood.'

A man is very rich indeed but despite having everything a man can have, he is still bored. To relieve his boredom, every year he holds an amazing party. Every year he throws a better party than the year before. But he is still bored. One year he has an idea. He fills the pool with crocodiles.

Halfway through the party, he announces, 'Anyone who can swim through my pool and get out the other side still alive can have my house.' There is silence. Then he adds, 'Anyone who can swim through my pool and get out the other side still alive can have my house and all my shares.' Still silence. Sweetening the offer he adds, 'Anyone who can swim through my pool and get out the other side still alive, can have my house, my shares and all my money.'

Suddenly, there's a loud splash. A man in the pool is fighting for his life with the crocodiles. It's a struggle, but he manages to swim across the pool. He just makes it to the other end and climbs out, half dead with one arm and one leg.

'Oh my god' says the rich man. 'That was incredible. When do you want the house?'

'I don't want the house' says the guy.

'When do you want my shares?'

'I don't want the shares.'

'When do you want all my money?'

'I don't want your money.'

So the rich guy says, 'Well what do you want then?'

'I want the bastard that pushed me in.'

Late at night, a drunk is on his knees underneath a street lamp. He is looking for something. A passer-by, being a good Samaritan, offers to help.

'What is it you have lost?' he asks.

'My watch,' replies the drunk. 'It fell off when I tripped over the pavement.'

The passer-by joins in the search but after a quarter of an hour, there is still no sign of the watch.

'Where exactly did you trip?' asks the passer-by.

'About half a block up the street,' replies the drunk.

'Then why are you looking for your watch here if you lost it half a block up the street?'

'Because the light's a lot better here.'

A man slips on some dog poo as he walks into a bar. Moments later, a Hell's Angel does the same thing.

'I just did that,' the first man says. So the Hell's Angel hits him.

If lawyers can be debarred and clergymen defrocked, it only seems fair that electricians can be delighted, musicians denoted, cowboys deranged, gardeners deflowered, models deposed, tree surgeons debarked, dry cleaners depressed and accountants left unaccounted for.

Two boys are playing football in Central Park when one is attacked by a rabid Rottweiler. Thinking quickly, the other boy rips off a board of the nearby fence, wedges it down the dog's collar and twists, breaking the dogs neck. A reporter who is strolling by sees the incident, and rushes over to interview the boy.

'Young Giants Fan Saves Friend From Vicious Animal,' he starts writing in his notebook.

'But I'm not a Giants fan,' the little hero replies.

'Sorry, since we are in New York, I just assumed you were,' says the reporter and starts again. 'Little Jets Fan Rescues Friend from Horrific Attack,' he writes.

'I'm not a Jets fan either,' the boy says.

'I assumed everyone in New York was either for the Giants or Jets. What team do you root for?' the reporter asks.

'I'm a Cowboys fan,' the child says.

The reporter starts a new sheet in his notebook and writes, 'Little Redneck Maniac Kills Beloved Family Pet.'

A white guy in a bar goes to the toilet. While he's standing there, a black guy comes in, stands beside him and whips out his massive dong. The white guy asks him how he got it.

The black guy tells him, 'Every night I tie a piece of cord round the end and pull it tight for five minutes.'

The white guy thanks him and leaves. The two meet up in the same toilets six months later.

'How are you doin' with the dick,' says the black guy.

'Excellent' says the white guy, 'look it's nearly all black.'

A married man thinks he will give his wife a birthday surprise by buying her a bra. He enters a lingerie shop, rather intimidated, but the salesgirls take charge and try to make him feel comfortable.

'What colour?' they ask. He settles for white.

'How much does it cost?' he asks.

'Twenty dollars.'

'Very good,' he thinks. All that remained is the size but he doesn't have the faintest idea. 'Now Sir, are they the size of a pair of melons? Coconuts? Grape fruits? Oranges?'

'No,' he says, 'nothing like that.'

'Come on, Sir, think. There must be something your wife's bust resembles.'

He thinks long and hard and then looks up and says, 'Have you ever seen a Cocker Spaniel's ears?'

A woman rushes home, bursting through the front door of her house and yelling to her husband, 'Pack your bags honey, I just won the lottery! All $10 million of it. Woooo hoooo!'

'That's great, sweetie!' he replies, 'but should I pack for the beach or for the mountains?'

'Who cares?' she replies, 'Just piss off!'

A man walks into a store to buy a Barbie doll for his daughter. 'How much is that Barbie in the window?' he asks the shop assistant.

In a condescending manner she responds, 'Which Barbie? We have Barbie Goes to the Gym for $19.95, Barbie Goes to the Ball for $19.95, Barbie Goes Shopping for $19.95, Barbie Goes to the Beach for $19.95, Barbie Goes Nightclubbing for $19.95, and Divorced Barbie for $265.'

The guy asks, 'Why is Divorced Barbie $265 when all the others are only $19.95?'

'That's obvious,' the assistant states, 'Divorced Barbie comes with Ken's house, Ken's car, Ken's boat and Ken's furniture.'

B ob always wanted a pair of authentic cowboy boots. Seeing some on sale one day, he buys them and wears them home, walking proudly. He walks into the bedroom and says to his wife, 'Notice anything different, Bessie?'

Bessie looks him over, 'Nope.'

Bob says excitedly 'Come on Bessie, take a good look. Notice anything different about me?'

Bessie looks again, 'Nope.'

Frustrated, Bob storms off into the bathroom, undresses, and walks back into the room completely naked except for his boots. Again he asks, a little louder this time, 'Notice anything different?'

Bessie looks up and says, 'Bob, what's different? It's hanging down today, it was hanging down yesterday, and it'll be hanging down again tomorrow.'

Furious, Bob yells, 'And do you know why it is hanging down, Bessie? It's hanging down because it's looking at my new boots!'

Bessie replies, 'Should'a bought a hat, Bob.'

Two women are having lunch together, discussing the merits of cosmetic surgery.

The first woman says, 'I need to be honest with you, I'm getting a boob job.'

The second woman says, 'Oh that's nothing, I'm thinking of having my arsehole bleached.'

The first replies, 'Funny, I just can't picture your husband as a blonde.'

The Hunchback of Notre Dame is up in the bell tower when he slips. Hitting his head on the bell, he rolls down the steps to the street below. Two men passing by run to his aid.

'I wonder who he is?' ponders one of them.

'Well I can't remember his name,' says the other, 'but his face rings a bell.'

A woman has a passion for baked beans. She loves them but unfortunately they have always had a very embarrassing and somewhat lively reaction to her. Then one day she meets a guy and falls in love. When it becomes apparent that they will marry she thinks to herself, 'He is such a sweet and gentle man, I would hate to lose him. I just have to give up beans.'

Some months later her car breaks down on the way home from work. Since she lives in the country, she calls her husband

and tells him that she will be late because she has to walk home. On her way she passes a small diner and the odour of the baked beans is more than she can stand. Since she still has miles to walk, she reckons that she will walk off any ill effects by the time she reaches home. So, she stops at the diner and before she knows it, she has consumed three large plates of baked beans. All the way home she farts. Upon arriving home, she feels reasonably sure she can control it.

Her husband seems excited to see her and exclaims delightedly, 'Darling, I have a surprise for dinner tonight.'

He then blindfolds her and leads her to her chair at the table. She seats herself and just as he is about to remove the blindfold from his wife, the telephone rings. He makes her promise not to touch the blindfold until he returns. He then goes to answer the phone. The baked beans she has consumed are still affecting her and the pressure is becoming almost unbearable, so while her husband is out of the room she seizes the opportunity, shifts her weight to one leg and lets it go. It is not only loud, but it smells like a fertiliser truck running over a skunk in front of a pulpwood mill. She takes her napkin and fans the air around her vigorously. Then, she shifts to the other cheek and rips three more, which remind her of cabbage cooking. Keeping her ears tuned to the conversation in the other room, she goes on like this for another ten minutes. When the phone farewells signal the end of her freedom, she fans the air a few more times with her napkin, places it on her lap and folds her hands upon it, smiling contentedly to herself. She is the picture of innocence when her husband returns. Apologizing for taking so long, he asks her if she peeked, and she assures him that she didn't. At this point, he removes the blindfold, and she is surprised.

There are twelve dinner guests seated around the table to wish her a happy birthday.

A wife and her husband are at their beach house. They are preparing a dinner party for some of their neighbours. Wanting to impress, the wife sends her husband out with a bucket to collect some fresh sea snails. Grudgingly he agrees. While he is collecting the snails, he notices a beautiful woman strolling alongside the water just a little further down the beach.

'Wouldn't it be great if she came over and talked to me,' he thinks.

A few minutes later, the woman is standing right over him. They start talking, she invites him back to her place and within moments of arriving they are in bed. It is so hot and heavy, that he is exhausted afterwards and passes out for a while. When he wakes up, it is almost time for the party. He gathers all his clothes, put them on as fast as he can, grabs his bucket of snails and runs home. He is in such a hurry that when he gets to the top of the stairs, he drops the bucket of snails. There are snails all down the stairs. The door opens just then, and his very angry wife is standing in the door wondering what's taken him so long. He looks at the snails, spread all down the steps, then he looks at her, then back at the snails.

He says, 'Come on guys, we're almost there.'

A guy gets in an elevator with a very large man. The large man starts talking.

'Hi! I'm 210cm tall, weigh 110kg, have a 40cm-long penis, a right ball that weighs 1kg and a left ball that weighs 1.5kg.' He then puts out a hand and adds, 'Turner Brown.'

All of a sudden the little guy faints. When he wakes he asks the big guy, 'What did you say?'

The guy repeats, 'Hi! I'm 210cm tall, weigh 110kg, have a 40cm-long penis, a right ball that weighs 1kg and a left ball that weighs 1.5kg.' Again, he puts out his hand and adds, 'Turner Brown.'

'Oh,' says the little guy, 'I thought you said turn around!'

A married couple are visited by an alien couple. The alien couple ask the human couple if they would like to swap partners for sex. They agree and the human woman and alien man are together.

She says, 'You have a small penis.'

The alien man replies, 'Pull my ears!'

So she pulls his ears and his penis becomes larger.

She is astonished and has the best sex of her life. When her husband and the female alien return, she asks him how was it.

He replies, 'It was great, but my ears hurt.'

A guy asks his friend, 'If you knew that they were about to drop an atomic bomb, what's the first thing you would do?'

Second guy says, 'I would screw the first thing that moved, what would you do?'

The first guy says, 'I would stand very still for half an hour.'

At school, Little Johnny is told by a classmate that most adults are hiding at least one dark secret, and that this makes it very easy to blackmail them by saying, 'I know the whole truth.'

Little Johnny decides to go home and try it out. He goes home, and is greeted by his mother.

He says, 'I know the whole truth.'

His mother quickly hands him $20 and says, 'Just don't tell your father.'

Quite pleased, the boy waits for his father to get home from work, and greets him with, 'I know the whole truth.'

The father promptly hands him $40 and says, 'Please don't say a word to your mother.'

Very pleased, the boy is on his way to school the next day when he sees the mailman at his front door. The boy greets him by saying, 'I know the whole truth.'

The mailman immediately drops the mail, opens his arms, and says, 'Then come give your daddy a great big hug.'

A man sees a picture of his wife in the nude hanging at an art show, and demands of her, 'Did you really pose for that?'

'Don't be ridiculous,' she replies, 'of course not. The artist painted it from memory.'

A woman rushes into the supermarket to pick up a few items. She heads for the express line where the clerk is talking on the phone with his back turned to her.

'Excuse me,' she says, 'I'm in a hurry. Could you check me out, please?'

The clerk turns, stares at her for a second, smiles and says, 'Not bad.'

A t an art exhibition, a couple is viewing a painting of three very naked, very black men sitting on a park bench. The unusual thing is that the men on the ends of the bench have black penises, but the man in the middle has a very pink penis. While the couple is scratching their heads trying to work this out, the artist walks by and notices the couple's confusion.

'Can I help you with this painting?' he asks.

'Well, yes,' says the gentleman. 'We were curious about this picture of the black men on the bench. Why is it that the man in the middle has a pink penis?'

'Oh,' says the artist. 'I'm afraid you've misinterpreted the painting. The three men are not Negroes, they're coal miners, and the fellow in the middle went home for lunch!'

'Look at me,' boasts the fit old man, pounding a very flat and firm stomach, having just finished 100 sit-ups before a group of young people.

'Fit as a fiddle! And you want to know why? I don't smoke, I don't drink, I don't stay up late, and I don't chase after loose women.' He smiles at them, teeth white, eyes aglitter, 'And tomorrow, I'm going to celebrate my ninetieth birthday.'

'Oh, really?' drawls one of the young onlookers, 'How?'

Two eggs have just been married and are on their honeymoon. While they are sitting on the bed making out, the female egg pushes the male egg away and says, 'I just have to go to the bathroom. I'll be back in a minute,' and off she goes.

Five minutes later the male egg sees his sexy wife walk out in a slinky egglige, wiping her hands up and down her smooth, oval body. Instantly, the male egg slaps his hands on the top of his head, covering it completely. The female egg looks at him and asks what he is doing.

He replies, 'The last time I was this hard, someone cracked me on the head with a spoon.'

Jim and Joe often go to the beach to pick up women. Unfortunately, Joe never has any luck, while Jim never fails. One day, Joe asks Jim the secret of his success. Jim promises to tell Joe, so long as Joe keeps it to himself.

After Joe agrees, Jim says, 'You see the fruit and vegetable shop over the road? Well, every time I come to the beach I buy a potato and put it in my swimming trunks. When the women see it they come running from miles around.'

Joe says, 'That's easy. I can do that.'

The next day, Joe goes over to the shop and picks out the

biggest, most perfectly shaped potato he can find. He then goes into the changing room and slips it into his swimming trunks. As he walks out onto the beach he immediately notices that women begin to take notice of him.

'Its working!' he thinks.

But soon he begins to realise that they are not looking interested but rather upset, almost disgusted, by the sight of him. He rushes over to Jim and asks, 'Jim, what's the problem? Why isn't it working?'

Jim takes one look and says, 'Because you're supposed to put the potato in the front!'

A guy is walking down the road looking very pleased with himself. He bumps into his friend who asks why he looks so happy.

'I just bought a great new hearing aid. It's fantastic.'

'Are you wearing it now?' the friend asks.

'Yup. It cost me $4000. It's top of the line.'

'Wow! What kind is it?' asks the friend.

'Twelve-thirty.'

What is a dyslexic agnostic insomniac?
Someone who lays awake at night wondering if there really is a dog.

One day a diver is exploring about 10m below sea level. He notices a guy at the same depth as him, but he has on no scuba gear whatsoever. The diver goes below another 10m and the other guy joins him a few minutes later. The diver goes below another 10m and minutes later the same guy joins him.

This confuses the diver, so he takes out a waterproof

chalk-and-board set, and writes, 'How the hell are you able to stay under this deep without equipment?'

The guy takes the board and chalk, erases what the diver has written, and writes, 'I'm drowning, you moron!'

A man lies spread out over three seats in the second row of a movie theatre. As he lies there moaning and breathing heavily, an usher comes over and says, 'That's very rude of you, Sir, taking up three seats. Don't you have any manners? Where did you come from?'

The man looks up, groaning, and says, 'The balcony.'

An unemployed guy goes door-to-door looking for work. One home-owner hands him a brush and a tin of paint and offers him $50 to paint his porch.

A few hours later the guy goes to the home-owner and says, 'I've finished. But I reckon you should know your car's a Ferrari not a Porsche.'

Prince Charles finds an ancient wine bottle in the cellar of Windsor Castle. When he opens it a genie flies out and grants him a wish. Charles is ecstatic, as just that morning he had reversed his Range Rover over the Queen's favourite corgi and squashed it flat. He asks the genie to bring the dog back to life before the Queen finds out.

The genie examines the dog which is splattered all over the drive and tells Charles that there is nothing at all he can do. The only way out is to chuck the dog in the dustbin and keep quiet. Charles then asks the genie if he can make his girlfriend, Camilla Parker-Bowles, beautiful and sexy, so that the media will stop making nasty comments about her.

The genie thinks for a moment, scratches his head and says, 'On second thoughts get that bloody dog out of the bin.'

A captain and his crew are in danger of being boarded by a pirate ship. As the crew become frantic, the captain bellows to his first mate, 'Bring me my red shirt!'

The first mate quickly retrieves the captain's red shirt, which the captain puts on and leads the crew into battle against the pirate boarding party. Although there are some casualties among the crew, the pirates are repelled.

Later that day, the lookout screams that there are now two pirate vessels sending boarding parties. The crew cowers in fear, but the captain, calm as ever, bellows, 'Bring me my red shirt!'

And once again the battle is on. Once again the captain and his crew repel both boarding parties, although this time there are more casualties.

Weary from the battles, the men sit around on deck that night recounting the day's occurrences when an ensign looks to the captain and asks, 'Sir, why did you call for your red shirt before the battles?'

The captain, giving the ensign a look that only a captain can give, exhorts, 'If I am wounded in battle, the red shirt does not show the wound and thus, you men will continue to fight unafraid.'

The men sit in silence marvelling at the courage of such a man. As dawn comes the next morning, the lookout screams that there are more pirate ships, ten of them, all with boarding parties on their way. The men become silent and look to the captain, their leader, for his usual command.

The captain, calm as ever, bellows, 'Bring me my brown pants!'

An explorer in the deepest Amazon suddenly finds himself surrounded by a bloodthirsty group of natives. Upon surveying the situation, he says quietly to himself, 'Oh God, I'm stuffed.'

There is a ray of light from heaven and a voice booms out, 'No you are not stuffed! Pick up that stone at your feet and bash in the head of the chief standing in front of you!'

So the explorer picks up the stone and proceeds to bash the hell out of the chief. As he stands above the lifeless body, breathing heavily and surrounded by 100 natives with a look of shock on their faces, God's voice booms out again, 'OK . . . now you're stuffed!'

A truck carrying copies of *Roget's Thesaurus* overturns on the highway. The local newspaper reports that the onlookers are 'stunned, overwhelmed, astonished, bewildered, and dumbfounded.'

Little Red Riding Hood is skipping down the road when she sees the Big Bad Wolf crouched down behind a log.

'My, what big eyes you have, Mr Wolf,' says Little Red Riding Hood.

The wolf jumps up and runs away. Further down the road Little Red Riding Hood sees the wolf again. This time he is crouched behind a tree stump.

'My, what big ears you have Mr Wolf,' says Little Red Riding Hood.

Again the wolf jumps up and runs away. Further down the track Little Red Riding Hood sees the wolf again, this time crouched down behind a road sign.

'My, what big teeth you have Mr Wolf,' taunts Little Red Riding Hood.

With that the Big Bad Wolf jumps up and screams, 'Will you piss off! I'm trying to take a shit.'

Three cowboys are sitting around a campfire, out on the lonesome trail, each with a tale of bravado for which cowboys are famous.

'I must be the meanest, toughest cowboy there is,' the first cowboy says with a sneer. 'Why, just the other day, a bull got loose in the corral and gored six grown men before I wrestled it to the ground, by the horns, with my bare hands.'

The second cowboy can't stand to be beaten.

'Why, that's nothing,' he says. 'I was walking down the trail yesterday when a 4m rattler made a move for me. I grabbed it with my bare hands, bit its head off and sucked down all of its poison! And I'm still here to tell the tale.'

All this time, the third cowboy remains silent and the first two turn to look at him as he slowly stokes the red-hot coals with his penis.

What do you get when you cross LSD with birth control? A trip without the kids.

Some tourists in the Museum of Natural History are marvelling at the dinosaur bones.

One of them asks the guard, 'Can you tell me how old the dinosaur bones are?'

The guard replies, 'They are three million, four years, and six months old.'

'That's an awfully exact number,' says the tourist. 'How do you know their age so precisely?'

The guard answers, 'Well, the dinosaur bones were three

million years old when I started working here, and that was four and a half years ago.'

A man decides to take off early from work and go drinking. He stays until the bar closes at 2 a.m., by which time he is extremely drunk. When he enters his house, he doesn't want to wake his wife, so he takes off his shoes and starts tip-toeing up the stairs. Half way up the stairs, he falls over backwards and lands flat on his rear end. That isn't so bad, except that he has a couple of empty beer bottles in his back pockets, and they break, and the broken glass carves up his buttocks. But, he is so drunk that he doesn't know he is hurt.

A few minutes later, as he is undressing, he notices blood, so he checks himself out in the mirror, and sure enough, his behind is badly ripped up. Well, he repairs the damage as best he can under the circumstances, and he goes to bed.

The next morning, his head is hurting, and his rear is hurting, and he is hunkering under the covers trying to think up some good story, when his wife comes into the bedroom.

'Well, you really tried one on last night,' she says. 'Where'd you go?'

'I worked late,' he says, 'and I stopped off for a couple of beers.'

'A couple of beers ? That's a laugh,' she replies. 'You got plastered last night. Where the heck did you go?'

'What makes you so sure I got drunk last night, anyway?'

'Well,' she replies, 'My first big clue was when I got up this morning and found a bunch of Band-Aids stuck to the mirror.'

A philosopher is doing a survey on a group of men, on the topic of happiness.

He tells them, 'I can prove to you that the amount of happiness has a relation to the amount of sex you have.'

He glances at his audience and sees a man in the right-hand corner, smiling.

'Sir, How often do you have sex?' the philosopher asks.

'Once a month.' the man answers.

Looking for another happy face, he spots a man in the middle, with a bigger smile.

He asks him, 'Sir, How often do you have sex?'

'Once a week,' the man shouts.

Trying to prove his theory further, he sees another man, laughing.

'You seem to be a very happy man. So how often do you have sex?'

'Well . . . every day,' the happy man answers.

'There, I am right. The amount of happiness is in relation to the amount of sex you have,' says the philosopher.

But far off at the end of the room, he sees a man with his hands in the air, laughing and jumping with so much happiness. So the philosopher says to him, 'You sure look like a very happy man?'

'Yes, yes, yes,' answers the very happy man.

'So how often do you get to have sex?' the philosopher asks.

The man answers, 'Once a year.'

The puzzled and embarrassed philosopher asks the man, 'What? Then why are you so happy?'

The man starts laughing and jumping and crying out, 'It's tonight, it's tonight!'

The Mafia is looking for a new man to be their bagman and collect money from all the businesses they are standing over. Feeling the heat from the police, they decide to use a deaf person for this job – if he ever gets caught, he won't be able to communicate to the police what he is doing.

On his first week, the deaf collector picks up over $50 000. But he gets greedy, decides to keep the money and stashes it in a safe place. The Mafia soon catch up with the deaf man and want to interrogate him. Unable to communicate with him, they take along a sign interpreter.

The Mafia boss says to the interpreter, 'Ask him where the money is?'

The interpreter signs, 'Where's the money?'

The deaf man replies, 'I don't know what you're talking about.'

The interpreter tells the boss, 'He says he doesn't know what you're talking about.'

The hood pulls out a .38 gun and places it in the ear of the deaf collector.

'Now ask him where the money is.'

The interpreter signs, 'Where is the money?'

The deaf man replies, 'The $50 000 is in Central Park, hidden in the third tree stump on the left from the West 78th Street gate.'

The interpreter turns to the boss, 'He says get stuffed!'

The Zen master steps up to the hot dog cart and says, 'Make me one with everything.'

The hot dog vendor fixes a hot dog and hands it to the Zen master, who pays with a $20 note. The hot dog vendor puts the bill in the cash drawer and closes the drawer.

'Where's my change?' asks the Zen master.

And the hot dog vendor responds, 'Change must come from within.'

A team of archaeologists is excavating in Israel when they come upon a cave. Written on the wall of the cave are the following symbols in order of appearance:

1. A dog
2. A donkey

3. A shovel
4. A fish
5. A Star of David

They decide it is a unique find and the writings are at least 3000 years old. They chop out the piece of stone and have it brought to the museum where archaeologists from all over the world come to study the ancient symbols. They hold a huge meeting after months of conferences to discuss the meaning of the markings.

The president of their society stands up and points at the first drawing and says, 'This looks like a dog. We can judge that this was a highly intelligent race as they had animals for companionship. To prove this statement you can see that the next symbol resembles a donkey, so, they were even smart enough to use animals to till the soil. The next drawing looks like a shovel of some sort, which means they had tools. Even further proof of their high intelligence is the fish which means that when a famine hit the earth and food didn't grow, they could take to the sea for food. The last symbol appears to be the Star of David which means they were evidently Hebrews.'

The audience applauds enthusiastically and the president smiles and says, 'I'm glad to see that you are all in full agreement with our interpretations.'

Suddenly a little old Jewish man stands up in the back of the room and says, 'I object to every word. The explanation of what the writings say is quite simple. First of all, everyone knows that Hebrew isn't read from left to right, but from right to left. Now, look at the markings. It says, "Holy mackerel, dig the ass on that bitch!"'

Two migrants arrive in the USA by boat and one says to the other, 'I hear that the occupants of this country actually eat dogs.'

'Odd,' the other one replies, 'but if we shall live in America, we might as well do as the Americans do.'

Nodding emphatically, the first migrant points to a hot-dog vendor and they both walk towards it.

'Two dogs, please,' says one of the migrants.

The vendor is only too pleased to oblige and he wraps both hot dogs in foil. Excited, the migrants hurry over to a bench and begin to unwrap their 'dogs'.

One migrant unwraps the wrapper, stares at it for a moment, leans over to the other and whispers cautiously, 'What part did you get?'

A high-court judge is at a bar in a high-class hotel where he is a regular visitor. He drinks into the small hours of the morning. On leaving the bar he vomits down the front of his suit then staggers to his parked car, which he manages to start and drives home in a most dangerous fashion. When he arrives at his mansion in a suburb, he falls out of the car, and staggers to the door, which his wife has opened. On seeing his state she asks what happened. Despite his condition, he thinks quickly.

'I had a few civil drinks in the Shelburne hotel, and when I came out a drunk got sick all over me. But the police caught him and he's up in front of me in the morning. I'll give the swine six months in jail,' he replies.

His wife then sends him to the shower and then bed, while she makes him some food and a hot drink. Having put his soiled clothes in the wash she returns to the bedroom with his food.

'How long did you say you would give the drunk in jail?' she asks.

'Six months,' he replies.

'Well you better make it twelve because he shat in your trousers as well.'

Why is a cemetery similar to a lavatory?
When you've got to go, you've got to go.

A man goes skydiving for the first time. After listening to the instructor for what seems like days, he is ready to go. Excited, he jumps out of the aeroplane. After a bit, he pulls the ripcord.

Nothing happens.

He tries again.

Still nothing.

He starts to panic, but remembers his back-up chute. He pulls that cord.

Nothing happens.

He frantically begins pulling both cords, but to no avail. Suddenly, he looks down and he can't believe his eyes. Another man is in the air with him, but this guy is going up!

Just as the other guy passes by, the skydiver – by this time scared out of his wits – yells, 'Hey, do you know anything about skydiving?'

The other guy yells back, 'No! Do you know anything about gas stoves?'

A woman who is rather old-fashioned, delicate, and elegant, especially in her language, is planning a week's vacation. So she writes to a campground and asks for a reservation.

She wants to make sure the campground is fully equipped, but doesn't quite know how to ask about the toilet facilities. She just can't bring herself to write the word 'toilet' in her letter. After much deliberation, she finally remembers the old-fashioned term 'bathroom commode'. But when she writes that down, she still thinks she is being too forward. So, she starts all over again, rewrites the letter and refers to the bathroom commode merely as the B.C.

'Does the campground have its own B.C.?' she writes.

Well, the campground owner isn't old-fashioned at all and when he gets the letter, he just can't work out what the woman is talking about. The B.C. business really stumps him.

After worrying about it for a while, he shows the letter to several campers, but they can't imagine what the lady means either. So the campground owner, finally coming to the conclusion that the lady must be asking about the location of the local Baptist Church, sits down and writes the following reply:

'Dear Madam: I'm sorry for the delay in answering your letter. I now take pleasure in informing you that a B.C. is located 15km north of the campground and is capable of seating 250 people at one time. I admit it is quite a distance away if you are in the habit of going regularly, but no doubt you will be pleased to know that a great number of people usually take their lunches along and make a day of it. They usually arrive early and stay late. The last time my wife and I went was six years ago and it was so crowded that we had to stand up the whole time we were there. It may interest you to know that right now, there is a supper being planned to raise money to buy more seats. They're going to hold it in the cellar of the B.C. I would like to say it pains me very much not to be able to go more regularly but it is through no lack of desire on my part. As we grow older, it seems to be more of an effort, particularly in cold weather. If you do decide to come down to our campground, perhaps I could go with you the first time you go, sit with you, and introduce you to all the other folks. Remember, this is a friendly community.'

God is looking down at earth and He sees all of the rascally behaviour that is going on. He decides to send an angel down to check it out.

When the angel returns, he tells God, 'Yes, it is bad on earth, 95% of the people are misbehaving and 5% are not.'

God thinks for a moment. 'Maybe I had better send down a second angel to get another opinion.'

So God sends another angel to earth. When the angel returns he goes to God and says, 'Yes, the earth is in decline, 95% are misbehaving and 5% are being good.'

God is not pleased. So He decides to email the 5% that are good because He wants to encourage them. Give them a little something to help them keep going.

Do you know what that email said? No? I didn't get one either.

Upon arriving home in eager anticipation of a leisurely evening, the husband is met at the door by his sobbing wife. Tearfully she explains, 'It's the pharmacist. He insulted me terribly this morning on the phone.'

Immediately, the husband drives into town to accost the pharmacist and demand an apology.

Before he can say more than a word or two, the pharmacist tells him, 'Now, just a minute – listen to my side of it. This morning the alarm failed to go off, so I was late getting up. I went without breakfast and hurried out to the car but I'll be damned if I didn't lock the house with both house and car keys inside. I had to break a window to get my keys. Driving a little too fast, I got a speeding ticket. Then, about three blocks from the store I got a flat tyre. When I finally got to the store there was a bunch of people waiting for me to open up. I got the store opened and started waiting on these people, and all the time the darn phone was ringing its head off. Then I had to break a roll of nickels against the cash register drawer to make change, and they spilled all over the floor. I got down on my hands and knees to pick up the nickels – the phone still ringing – when I came up I cracked my head on the open cash drawer, which made me stagger back against a showcase with a bunch of perfume bottles on it, and half of them hit the floor and broke. The phone was still ringing with no let up, and I finally got back to answer it.

It was your wife. She wanted to know how to use a rectal thermometer. Well, Mister, I told her!'

P olice arrest Malcolm Davidson, a twenty-seven-year-old, white, male resident of Wilmington, North Carolina, in a pumpkin patch at 11.38 p.m. Friday. Davidson is charged with lewd and lascivious behaviour, public indecency and public intoxication at the county courthouse on Monday. The suspect allegedly states that as he was passing a pumpkin patch, he decided to stop.

'You know, a pumpkin is soft and squishy inside, and there was no-one around here for miles. At least I thought there wasn't,' he states in a phone interview from the county courthouse jail.

Davidson goes on to state that he pulled over to the side of the road, picked out a pumpkin that he felt was appropriate to his purposes, cut a hole in it, and proceeded to satisfy his alleged 'need'.

'I guess I was just really into it, you know?' he comments with evident embarrassment.

In the process, Davidson apparently failed to notice the Wilmington municipal police car approaching and was unaware of his audience until Officer Brenda Taylor approached him.

'It was an unusual situation, that's for sure,' says Officer Taylor. 'I walked up to (Davidson) and he's . . . just working away at this pumpkin.' Taylor goes on to describe what happened when she approached Davidson.

'I just went up and said, 'Excuse me Sir, but do you realise that you are screwing a pumpkin?' He got real surprised as you'd expect and then looked me straight in the face and said, "A pumpkin? Damn . . . is it midnight already?"'

A man returns from the doctor and tells his wife that the doctor has told him he has only twenty-four hours to live. Given this prognosis, the man asks his wife for sex. Naturally, she agrees, and they make love.

About six hours later, the husband goes to his wife and says, 'Honey, you know I now have only eighteen hours to live. Could we please do it one more time?'

Of course, the wife agrees, and they do it again. Later, as the man gets into bed, he looks at his watch and realises that he now has only eight hours left.

He touches his wife shoulder, and asks, 'Honey, please . . . just one more time before I die.'

She says, 'Of course, Dear,' and they make love for the third time.

After this session, the wife rolls over and falls asleep. The man, however, worries about his impending death. He tosses and turns until he's down to four more hours. He taps his wife, who rouses.

'Honey, I only have four more hours. Do you think we could . . .'

At this point the wife sits up and says, 'Listen, I have to get up in the morning. You don't!'

O ver drinks one afternoon, two men are discussing former lovers. One man says that he once broke-up with a girl because she had a seemingly incurable speech impediment.

'I'm shocked,' says the other man. I didn't know you were prejudiced against disabled people. What was the girl's problem?'

Taking a sip, the first man pauses and reflects, 'She couldn't say "yes".'

A young couple bring their new baby home and the wife suggests that her husband should try his hand at changing nappies.

'I'm busy,' he says. 'I'll do the next one.'

The next time around she asks again. The husband narrows his eyes at his wife.

'I didn't mean the next nappy. I meant the next baby.'

There are several men sitting around in the locker room of a private gym after exercising. Suddenly a mobile phone on one of the benches rings. A man picks it up.

'Hello?'

'Honey, it's me. Are you at the gym?'

'Yes.'

'Great! I am at the mall two blocks from where you are. I just saw a beautiful mink coat. It's absolutely gorgeous! Can I buy it?'

'What's the price?'

'Only $1500.'

'Well, OK, go ahead and get it, if you like it that much.'

'Ahhh, and I also stopped by the Mercedes dealership and saw the 2003 models. I saw one I really liked. I spoke with the salesman, and he gave me a really good price . . . and since we need to exchange the BMW that we bought last year . . .'

'What price did he quote you?'

'Only $60 000'

'OK, but for that price I want it with all the options.'

'Great! But before we hang up, something else.'

'What?'

'It might look like a lot, but I was reconciling your bank account and I stopped by the real estate agent this morning and saw the house we had looked at last year. It's on sale! Remember? The one with a pool, an English garden, an acre of park area and a beachfront.'

'How much are they asking?'

'Only $450 000, a magnificent price, and I see that we have that much in the bank to cover it.'

'Well, then go ahead and buy it, but just bid $420 000. OK?'

'OK, sweetie, Thanks! I'll see you later! I love you!'

'Bye, I do too.'

The man hangs up, closes the phone's flap, and raises his hand and asks all those present, 'OK. Whose phone is this?'

A man enters a barber for a shave. While the barber is foaming him up, he mentions the problem he has getting a close shave around his cheeks.

'I have just the thing,' says the barber taking a small wooden ball from a nearby drawer. 'Just place this between your cheek and gum.'

The client places the ball in his mouth and begins to give the man the closest shave he has ever experienced.

After a few strokes, the client asks in garbled speech 'And what if I swallow it?'

'No problem,' says the barber. 'Just bring it back tomorrow like everyone else does!'

A circus owner advertises for a lion tamer and two young people show up. One is a good-looking lad in his mid-twenties and the other is a gorgeous blonde girl about the same age. The circus owner tells them, 'I'm not going to sugar coat it. This is one ferocious lion. He ate my last tamer so you guys better be good or you're history. Here's your equipment; chair, whip and a gun. Who wants to try out first?'

The girl says, 'I'll go first.'

She walks past the chair, the whip and the gun and steps right into the lion's cage. The lion starts to snarl and pant and begins to charge her. About half way there, she throws open her coat revealing her beautiful naked body.

The lion stops dead in his tracks, sheepishly crawls up to her and starts licking her ankles. He continues to lick her calves, kisses them and rests his head at her feet. The circus owner's mouth is on the floor.

He says, 'I've never seen a display like that in my life.'

He then turns to the young man and asks, 'Can you top that?'

The young man replies, 'No problem, just get that lion out of the way.'

A woman is picking through the frozen turkeys at the grocery store, but can't find one big enough for her family.

She asks a stock boy, 'Do these turkeys get any bigger?'

The stock boy replies, 'No Ma'am, they're dead.'

The little brother of an army radar operator asks, 'Jim, tell me how does radar work?'

'The radar transmitter emits brief impulses of electromagnetic waves which are reflected from the target and received by a special receiver. Since the speed at which electromagnetic waves propagate is exactly known and the time they take to travel to the target and back can be determined with a great degree of accuracy it is possible to determine the range to the target as well as the direction to it.'

His brother ponders a moment, then says, 'If you don't know, Jim, why don't you just say so?'

John invites his mother over for dinner. During the meal, his mother can't help noticing John's beautiful roommate. Over the course of the evening, while watching the two interact, she starts to wonder if there is more between John and his roommate than meets the eye.

Reading his mum's thoughts, John volunteers, 'I know what you must be thinking, but I assure you, Julie and I are just roommates.'

About a week later, Julie comes to John and says, 'Ever since your mother came to dinner, I've been unable to find the beautiful silver gravy ladle. You don't suppose she took it, do you?'

John says, 'Well, I doubt it, but I'll write her a letter just to be sure.'

So he sits down and writes:

'Dear Mum, I'm not saying you did take a gravy ladle from my house, and I'm not saying you did not take a gravy ladle. But the fact remains that one has been missing ever since you were here for dinner.'

Several days later, John receives a letter from his mother which reads:

'Dear Son, I'm not saying that you do sleep with Julie, and I'm not saying that you do not sleep with Julie. But the fact remains that if she was sleeping in her own bed, she would have found the gravy ladle by now. Love, Mum.'

A police officer, though scheduled for all-night duty at the station, is relieved of duty early and arrives home four hours ahead of schedule, at two in the morning. Not wanting to wake his wife, he undresses in the dark, creeps into the bedroom and starts to climb into bed.

Just then, his wife sits up and says, 'Mike, dearest, would you go down to the all-night chemist on the next block and get me some aspirin? I've got a splitting headache.'

'Certainly, honey,' he says, and feeling his way across the dark room, he gets dressed and walks over to the chemist.

As he arrives, the pharmacist looks up in surprise, 'Hey,' he says, 'I know you – aren't you a policeman? Officer Fenwick, right?'

'Yeah, so?' says the officer.

'Well what the heck are you doing all dressed up like the Fire Chief?'

An advertising team is working very late at night on a project due the next morning. Suddenly, a genie appears before them and offers each of them one wish.

The copywriter says, 'I've always dreamed of writing the great American novel and having my work studied in schools across the land. I'd like to go to a tropical island where I can concentrate, and write my masterpiece.'

The genie says, 'No problem!' and *poof!* The copywriter is gone.

The art director says, 'I want to create a painting so beautiful that it would hang in the Louvre Museum in Paris for all the world to admire. I want to go to the French countryside to work on my painting.'

The genie says, 'Your wish is granted!' and *poof!* The art director is gone.

The genie then turns to the account executive and says, 'And what is your wish?'

The account executive says, 'I want those two arseholes back here right now.'

Two employees for the gas company are on a house call. The younger man says to the older one, 'Jeez, you're old.'

'Yeah, that may be so, but I can still outrun you,' replies the older employee.

'How about a running race to see if you're right?' asks the younger employee.

With that they start running at full speed around that block. The older man keeps up with the younger man around the first corner, the second corner, the third corner. As they come up on the last corner, the younger man sees an elderly woman running as fast as her legs can carry her behind them. Puzzled by this, they both stop and ask her why she is running.

The old woman catches her breath and says, 'Well, you were

at my home checking my gas meter, and when I saw you running away, I thought I'd better run too!'

A man is hired by the circus to perform a necessary but rather unpleasant task. He is asked to walk behind the elephants in the centre ring, shovelling aside their droppings as they walk about. After a rather difficult evening at work, he goes to the circus cafeteria, sits with another worker, and starts complaining about his work.

'It's just terrible, walking behind those huge beasts and first dodging, then shovelling aside the dung they produce. My arms are tired, my shoes and pants are a mess, and I'll have to shower before I return home, because of the stink.'

His friend agrees, 'Why don't you just quit this miserable job and find something more rewarding to do? You have to have some skills and talents that you can put to use somewhere else.'

The man looks at him, stunned, 'You know, you're probably right, but I just can't give up the glamour of show business!'

A movie producer is lying by the pool at the Beverly Hilton. His partner arrives in a great state of excitement.

'How'd the meeting go?' asks the first guy.

'It went great,' says his buddy. 'Tarentino will write and direct for six million, Mel Gibson will star for eight, and we can bring in the whole picture for under fifty million.'

'Fabulous,' says the guy by the pool.

'There's just one catch,' his partner warns.

'What's the catch?'

'We have to put up ten thousand in cash.'

Stammerer: I h-h-heard tha-that you can hel-hel-help me.

Speech therapist: Yes, sure. Ease yourself into the chair, look straight into my eyes, and count slowly till ten.

Stammerer: O-one, t-two, th-th-three . . . eight, nine, ten. It's wonderful, I don't stammer anymore!

Speech therapist: My fee is $300.

Stammerer: H-h-how mu-mu-much?

Andy wants a job as a signalman on the railways. He is told to meet the inspector at the signal box.

The inspector asks him, 'What would you do if you realised that two trains were heading for each other on the same track?'

Andy says, 'I would switch the points for one of the trains.'

'What if the lever broke?' asks the inspector.

'Then I'd dash down out of the signal box,' says Andy, 'and I'd use the manual lever over there.'

'What if the manual lever had been struck by lightning?'

'Then,' Andy continues, 'I'd run back into the signal box and phone the next signal box.'

'What if the phone was engaged?'

'Well in that case,' perseveres Andy, 'I'd rush down out of the box and use the public emergency phone at the level crossing up there.'

'What if that was vandalised?'

'Oh well then I'd run into the village and get my uncle Silas.'

This puzzles the inspector, so he asks, 'Why would you do that?'

'Because he's never seen a train crash.'

An archaeologist is digging in the Negev Desert in Israel and comes upon a casket containing a mummy. After examining it, he calls the curator of a prestigious natural-history museum. 'I've just discovered a 3000-year-old mummy of a man who died of heart failure!' the excited scientist exclaims.

The curator replies, 'Bring him in. We'll check it out.'

A week later, the amazed curator calls the archaeologist.

'You were right about the mummy's age and cause of death. How in the world did you know?'

'Easy. There was a piece of paper in his hand that said, "10 000 shekels on Goliath".'

One day at a busy airport, the passengers on a commercial airliner are seated, waiting for the cockpit crew to show up so they can get underway. The pilot and co-pilot finally appear in the rear of the plane, and begin walking up to the cockpit through the centre aisle. Both appear to be blind. The pilot is using a white cane, bumping into passengers right and left as he stumbles down the aisle, and the co-pilot is using a guide dog. Both have their eyes covered with huge sunglasses. At first the passengers do not react; thinking that it must be some sort of practical joke. However, after a few minutes the engines start spooling up and the aeroplane starts moving down the runway. The passengers look at each other with some uneasiness, whispering among themselves and looking desperately to the stewardesses for reassurance. Then the aeroplane starts accelerating rapidly and people begin panicking. Some passengers are praying, and as the plane gets closer and closer to the end of the runway, the voices are becoming more and more hysterical. Finally, when the aeroplane has less than 5m of runway left, there is a sudden change in the pitch of the shouts as everyone screams at once, and at the very last moment the aeroplane lifts off and is airborne.

Up in the cockpit, the co-pilot breathes a sigh of relief and turns to the captain, 'You know, one of these days the passengers aren't going to scream and we're gonna get killed!'

WHY TRICK OR TREATING IS BETTER THAN SEX

- You are guaranteed to get at least a little something in the sack.
- If you get tired, you can wait ten minutes and go at it again.
- The uglier you look, the easier it is to get some.
- You don't have to compliment the person who gives you some.
- It's OK when the person you're with fantasises you're someone else, because you are.
- Forty years from now you'll still enjoy candy.
- If you don't like what you get, you can always go next door.
- It doesn't matter if the kids hear you moaning and groaning.
- Less guilt the morning after.
- You can do the whole neighbourhood.

JAIL VS WORK

IN PRISON . . . you spend the majority of your time in a 3m × 3m cell.
AT WORK . . . you spend the majority of your time in a 2m × 2m cubicle.

IN PRISON . . . you get three meals a day.
AT WORK . . . you only get a break for one meal and you pay for it.

IN PRISON . . . you get time off for good behaviour
AT WORK . . . you get more work for good behaviour

IN PRISON . . . the guard locks and unlocks all the doors for you.
AT WORK . . . you must carry around a security card and open all the doors for yourself.

IN PRISON . . . you can watch TV and play games.
AT WORK . . . you get fired for watching TV and playing games.

IN PRISON . . . you get your own toilet.
AT WORK . . . you have to share with some idiot who pees on the seat.

IN PRISON . . . they allow your family and friends to visit.
AT WORK . . . you can't even speak to your family.

IN PRISON . . . the taxpayers pay all expenses with no work required.

AT WORK . . . you get to pay all the expenses to go to work and then they deduct taxes from your salary to pay for prisoners.

IN PRISON . . . you spend most of your life inside bars wanting to get out.
AT WORK . . . you spend most of your time wanting to get out and go inside bars.

IN PRISON . . . you must deal with sadistic wardens.
AT WORK . . . they are called managers.

BEST JOKES IN
THE WORLD

*We've left the best until last. Two recent
world-wide competitions found that the following
two jokes were the funniest in the world.*

Sherlock Holmes and Dr Watson go camping, and pitch their
tent under the stars.

During the night, Holmes wakes his companion and says,
'Watson, look up at the stars, and tell me what you deduce.'

Watson says, 'I see millions of stars, and even if a few of those
have planets, it's quite likely there are some planets like earth,
and if there are a few planets like earth out there, there might
also be life.'

Holmes replies, 'Watson, you idiot. Somebody stole our tent.'

Two hunters are out in the woods when one of them
collapses. He doesn't seem to be breathing and his eyes are
glazed. The other guy whips out his mobile phone and calls the
emergency services.

He gasps, 'My friend is dead! What can I do?'

The operator says, 'Calm down, I can help. First, let's make
sure he's dead.'

There's a silence, then a shot is heard.

Back on the phone, the guy says, 'OK, now what?'